In the Realm of Nachan Kan

Mesoamerican Worlds: From the Olmecs to the Danzantes

In the Realm of Nachan Kan

POSTCLASSIC MAYA ARCHAEOLOGY AT LAGUNA DE ON, BELIZE

by Marilyn A. Masson

UNIVERSITY PRESS OF COLORADO

Published by the University Press of Colorado
5589 Arapahoe Avenue, Suite 206C
Boulder, Colorado 80303

The University Press of Colorado is a proud member of
the Association of American University Presses.

The University Press of Colorado is a cooperative publishing enterprise supported, in part, by Adams State University, Colorado State University, Fort Lewis College, Metropolitan State University of Denver, Regis University, University of Colorado, University of Northern Colorado, Utah State University, and Western State Colorado University.

Library of Congress Cataloging-in-Publication Data

Masson, Marilyn A.
   In the realm of Nachan Kan : Postclassic Maya archaeology at Laguna de On, Belize / by Marilyn A. Masson.
      p. cm. — (Mesoamerican worlds)
   Includes bibliographical references and index.
   ISBN 0-87081-567-9 (alk. paper) — ISBN 978-1-60732-356-3 (pbk : alk. paper)
   1. Laguna de On Site (Belize) 2. Mayas—Belize—Orange Walk District—Antiquities. 3. Maya pottery—Belize— Orange Walk District. 4. Mayas—Mexico—Chetumal (Province)—Kings and rulers. 5. Land settlement patterns—Belize—Orange Walk District. 6. Orange Walk District (Belize)—Antiquities. I. Title. II. Series.

F1435.1.L23 M37 2000
972.82'6—dc21

00-064828

For Linda Schele,
one of the greatest Mayanists of all time.
You raised the dawn of the next creation.

Contents

Figures

Tables

Preface

This book represents my current, and it seems ever evolving, thoughts and data pertaining to issues of the evolutionary processes of Postclassic Maya society. When my research began at Laguna de On in 1991, the name of which translates as the "Lake of the Alligator Pear," I saw this site as an opportunity to study the "collapse" of Maya civilization, and the end of southern lowlands culture as it had previously existed. The 1991 field project took place under the gracious tutelage of Fred Valdez Jr., who devoted his summer to teaching a University of Texas Archaeological Field School so that I could perform my dissertation research at this lagoon. I realized, halfway through writing my dissertation on this site in 1993, much to my chagrin, that the Maya that had occupied this lagoon before and after that temporal threshold of A.D. 900 were not so very different, archaeologically. They consumed similar diets based on maize staples, they procured similar lithic materials and fashioned similar agricultural and household implements out of them, built similar houses delineated with single rows of local stone, and similarly elevated their living platforms—probably in order to get more breeze, avoid more mosquitoes, and because they could. I realized, for myself, that Maya civilization had not collapsed, at least not at this rural aquatic location.

Right about this time, Linda Schele was undergoing one of her more substantial epiphanies at the University of Texas in deciphering the Milky Way clock, and her weekly graduate seminar lectures were packed with insights offered by ethnographers regarding modern Quichean, Zincantecan, Chamulan, and Yucatecan cosmology and ritual that closely paralleled aspects of religious mythology that she was cracking in the glyphic and calendric records of the Classic period Maya inscriptions. Needless to say, exposure to Linda's revelations drove the point home that the Classic period collapse had in fact led the way to a fascinating but poorly understood societal transformation. This volume represents my pursuit of tracking that interstice in space and time in the history of Maya culture and its implications for the anthropological study of civilizations.

This work owes a debt to many. This research has been supported by the Departments of Anthropology at the University at Albany–SUNY, Pacific Lutheran University, and the University of Texas–Austin, in addition to grants awarded by the Earthwatch Foundation, the Wenner-Gren Foundation, and the Foundation for the Advancement of Mesoamerican Studies. Continuing research at nearby lagoon sites has also been supported by these organizations and by the National Science Foundation. I am very grateful to these organizations for believing in this work. I hope that this and future works will realize the good faith that has been expressed in this project.

This book is dedicated to Linda Schele, who raised the curtain on an alternate way of studying and understanding Maya culture, past and present, to an extent that history has only begun to grasp. To have sat in her graduate seminars and watched Maya history and cosmology explode into view was, to understate dramatically, a priceless opportunity and magnificent honor. At the time, we knew it was special. Biweekly, a crowd of graduate students and faculty from several departments and resident Austinite Mayanist experts would gather in orbit around Linda, the eye of the hurricane, to share and learn of the latest developments and discoveries faxed to her from around the world, and her own daily revelations. Linda's uniquely synthetic work, first disseminated in those seminars, has changed the world, and touched many lives, including mine. The records I work with have now come alive with the history she and her colleagues have returned to them.

There are many other individuals who have contributed considerably to my development as an archaeologist and anthropologist. I will be forever grateful to Harry Shafer and Thomas Hester for allowing me to join the Colha Project in 1983, and for much encouragement, opportunities, and support ever since. Fred Valdez facilitated the first Laguna de On season in 1991, and I greatly appreciate the gentle but firm guidance and scholastic freedom that he provided me with as my dissertation advisor at the University of Texas. Patricia McAnany is another friend and mentor who has been there since the beginning, and her unique blend of humor and penetrating insight has added important dimensions to my perceptions of archaeology in many ways. This book benefited greatly from conversations with graduate students in my 1998 seminar at SUNY–Albany on the ethnohistory and archaeology of Yucatán, as well as contributions from John Justeson and Antje Gunsenheimer, who opted to attend these weekly meetings and share with us their expertise on Yucatec languages, archaeology, and ethnohistory. My interchanges over the phone and e-mail with Annabeth Headrick, a creative scholar and fastidious researcher, have also been very enlightening over the past couple of years.

Outside of the Maya realm, Michael Collins has put me through several revelatory "boot camp" exercises in hunter-gatherer archaeology, and he has helped me learn how to eke data out of the most silent of stone and bone assemblages. Opportunities to observe Mike's genius for reading the landscape profoundly affected the manner in which I viewed Laguna de On and its inconspicuous anthropogenic alterations. More recently, I would like to thank Michael E. Smith for provoking my thinking about Postclassic world systems, and for many helpful comments on this and other manuscripts.

I am also very grateful to the icons of Postclassic research, including Elizabeth Graham, David Pendergast, Diane Chase, Arlen Chase, Don Rice, Prudence Rice, Anthony Andrews, and David Freidel, who have been most tolerant, patient, and supportive of the fits and starts of my scholastic entrada into this realm, particularly my early attempts to disseminate and interpret the most preliminary of data from this island. Anthony Andrews and David Freidel shared their valuable literary references with me, and I deeply appreciate this favor.

Many colleagues have devoted portions of their summers to the Belize Postclassic Project. My husband, Robert Rosenswig, deserves particular mention for his role as collaborator in much of my field research. I am very grateful for his contagious interest in all matters archaeological, his rigorous methodologies, his irreverence, and his creativity. I would also very much like to acknowledge project staff members of past Laguna de On field and lab seasons, including students, staff, and consultants of the 1991–1997 seasons, especially Becky Adelman, Melissa Joy Shumake, Evon Moan, Ed Barnhart, Joy Becker, Annabeth Headrick, Shirley Mock, Norbert Stanchly, Jennifer Wharton, Georgia West, Alice Waid, Miguel Aguilera, Jason Barrett, Alex Mullen, Maxine Oland, Lisa Spillett, Margaret Briggs, Daniel Finamore, Thomas Stafford, George Bey, and my son, Alec Masson. Some talented artists have contributed to this project as well, and I would like to thank Pam Headrick, Anne Deane, Ben Karis, John Labadie, and James Masson for their fine illustrations.

I am deeply thankful for all of the Earthwatch volunteers and field school students who have chosen to join our summer research projects during the past four years, over many other possible options. The project was annually rejuvenated with the fresh energy and enthusiasm of those of you who came to Belize to learn and to contribute to this research. Your questions remind us of how interesting the past truly is.

The project's colleagues in Belize have also contributed tremendously to the success of this research. The archaeological commissioners of Belize— Allan Moore (1999–present), John Morris (1997–1998), and Brian Woodye

(1996)—have patiently endured this project's growing pains and have granted us permits to perform this research. In the village of San Estevan, Armando Castillo has been a great friend, facilitator in establishing our field camp, and member of the field staff team. I am also grateful to Amin Awe, Hermilo Morales, Raul Polanco, Lorenzo Morales, Paulino Cortez, and the San Estevan Town Council and Lyons Club, to Areli and Adrian Grajales and Armando Gomez of Laguna de On, and to Fabian and Deodoro Perez of Progresso Lagoon for much assistance. Victor Ayuso and Sonya Espat of Victor's Inn in Petville, Belize, have also become indispensable in the logistical aspects of research and provide an ever beckoning home away from home.

Finally, I would like to thank my family for all the support and cheerful neglect they have endured because of this research, and this book in particular. I would like to thank my parents, George and Hazel Andrews, my son, Alec Masson, and my husband, Robert Rosenswig, for everything.

In the Realm of Nachan Kan

1

Introduction: From the Eleventh Century Forward

This book offers a perspective on the social development of the Late Postclassic Lowland Maya world as observed from a small, rural, inland lagoon community in northern Belize. After three years of research at Laguna de On, with the collaboration of many colleagues, staff, students, and volunteers (see Masson and Rosenswig 1997, 1998a, 1998b, 1999), trends have been recognized in changing settlement patterns, economic systems, and ritual practice at this site that appear to be linked to broader regional processes of political and economic cultural development. The following pages represent an effort to examine patterns at Laguna de On within the wider context of Late Postclassic Maya society.

The Postclassic period, as defined herein, is an enduring one that extends from A.D. 1050 to A.D. 1500 without clear breaks in cultural organization as observed in material culture. Trends observed within this period are best described as points along a continuum. Processes of acceleration, amplification, and intensification of social, economic, and ideological institutions are indicated throughout this era. The lengthy duration of this period provides a first clue as to its prosperity and long-term stability (Chase and Chase 1985), a benefit, perhaps, of a deflated degree of political hierarchy in the Maya Lowlands. The Postclassic period, down to its very name, has suffered from its traditional definition primarily in terms of the era that preceded it (Pollock 1962; Proskouriakoff 1955; Willey 1986). While this book does not negate the significance of historical context by any means, it does represent an effort to assess the Postclassic period on its own terms. Although the precedents for research focusing primarily on the Postclassic are few in number compared to the Classic period (Pollock et al. 1962; Cowgill 1963; Bullard 1973; Rathje 1975; Pendergast 1981; Freidel and Sabloff 1984; Robles 1986a and 1986b; Andrews and Robles 1986; Sabloff and Andrews 1986; Chase and Rice 1985; Rice 1987; Fox 1987; Michaels 1987; Chase and Chase 1988; Walker 1990; Kepecs, Feinman, and Boucher 1994; and Kepecs

1998; among others), they are of substantial quality, and provide much pioneering data that has paved the way for the contextual analysis of Laguna de On.

Time begins in this book in the eleventh century. Specifically, this volume focuses on the processes of Postclassic secondary state formation in a strategically positioned, but poorly understood, region of the Maya Lowlands, northern Belize. The degree to which a small rural settlement can inform upon political dynamics is limited, however, as sites the size of Laguna de On were probably not the seats of government for the political elite. An effort is made in this volume to reach into the archives of the literature to find pertinent information about settlement and elite ideology that can provide some of the context for regional organization that cannot be understood from the sole examination of Laguna de On. Although small, Laguna de On was a prosperous and enduring community of industrious producers and consumers who conducted their lives in the "realm" of Nachan Kan and his predecessors.

Nachan Kan was a *halach uinic* (Roys 1957: 162), or regional lord, of the Chetumal province of northeastern Belize and southwestern Quintana Roo at the time of Spanish contact (Roys 1957; Jones 1989: Map 2). The use of the name of this historical personage in the title of this volume puts a face on Laguna de On's five-hundred-year occupation and emphasizes the fact that this community existed and thrived as part of a much larger whole. It is probable that Laguna de On was located on the southern boundary of Chetumal province, close to a territory to the south that has been identified as Dzuluinicob (Jones 1989: Map 2). Members of this community probably paid tribute to Nachan Kan and those halach uinics before him. According to ethnohistoric accounts of regional organization summarized by Roys (1957), Laguna de On citizens would have carried or canoed their products to regional markets that may have been organized by halach uinics and their factions, contributed warriors to such leaders when conflict was experienced with other provinces, brought censer offerings to calendrical festivals organized and hosted by lords like Nachan Kan and allied lineages, and perhaps exchanged marriage partners with communities under the domains of these leaders.

This volume examines the political, economic, and ideological relationships between Laguna de On and its neighbors in Chetumal province. It also reaches beyond the province boundaries, north to Yucatán and south to the Peten, and in its final conclusion realizes that the "realm" of Laguna de On is not limited to that of Chetumal province. This realm reached across zones of prosperity that extended throughout the parameters of the southern lowlands, particularly the Quintana Roo east coast of the Yucatán peninsula, the northern Yucatán sphere of Mayapan, riverine and coastal northern Belize, and the Peten Lakes region. The secondary state dynamics of northern Belize that affected community patterns at Laguna de On were in fact linked to a network of provinces that were engaged in a cycle of increasing regional integration and intensive interaction. Leaders of Chetumal province provided the infrastructure for political and economic mediation between communities such as Laguna de On and the outside world, as ethnohistorical models suggest (Roys 1957; Pina Chan 1978).

Although little attention is given to the Classic period and the Maya collapse in this volume, research at Laguna de On has its origins in this latter issue (Masson 1993, 1997). After preliminary surveys and collections at this lagoon by Meighan and Bennyhoff (Thomas Hester, personal communication 1993) and Thomas Kelly and John Masson (Kelly 1980), these investigations began under the direction of Fred Valdez (Valdez, Masson, and Santone 1992; Masson 1993) and have continued under the author and her colleagues (Masson and Rosenswig 1997, 1998a, 1998b, 1999). To the original research question posed at Laguna de On—Whatever became of the Maya after the ninth century southern lowlands collapse?—an answer has emerged. While not quite "business as usual," Maya civilization continued to develop in the mode of late stage secondary state formation (and reformation) in zones such as northern Belize, as Rathje and Sabloff (Rathje 1975; Sabloff and Rathje 1975) initially suggested twenty-five years ago.

After an adjustment period that is poorly understood and manifested in various ways at different sites (the Terminal Classic/Early Postclassic, A.D. 800–1050; see Sabloff and Andrews 1986, Masson and Mock n.d.), sites of the Late Postclassic are recognized in the vicinity of Laguna de On by well-developed ceramic complexes that appear by the turn of the eleventh century and link northern Belize to the Peten, with some Yucatecan influences (Ball 1977; Valdez 1987; Valdez and Mock 1985; Mock 1994; Masson and Mock n.d.). While some populations may have remained geographically stable after the Classic period demise (Pendergast 1985; Graham 1987; Don Rice 1988; Masson 1997), evidence summarized in this book suggests that migrations out of the Peten from south to north also contributed to the appearance of hallmark Late Postclassic ceramic styles and technologies and cultural reorganization or revitalization. Belize's intermediary position between the Peten and northern Yucatán is reflected in the emergence of ceramic traditions with strong southern roots that also incorporate certain technologies and styles of the northern Early Postclassic sphere and its long-distance trade connections to Mexico. Some scholars have also argued for migrations from the north into Belize at sites such as Nohmul and Colha (Chase and Chase 1982; Hester 1985; Michaels 1987; Mock 1994), but such evidence is not identified at Laguna de On (Masson 1997) or Lamanai (Pendergast 1985; Graham 1987). This variable evidence for Terminal Classic cultural changes suggests that this was an unstable, volatile period of adaptation and stress for some communities and a period of opportunity for others (Sabloff and Andrews 1986; Masson and Mock n.d.), which appears to have sorted itself out by the dawn of the eleventh century, when the history and processes charted in this volume truly begin.

Out of the milieu of the Terminal Classic/Early Postclassic emerge a number of northern Belize sites located in coastal, riverine, lacustrine, and other aquatic settings that appear affluent, prosperous, and integrated into an expanding, broad-ranging sphere of economic production and exchange. This volume provides a view of that emergent Postclassic Maya world, a view that represents an outward-looking perspective from the small settlement node of Laguna de On.

THEMES OF THIS BOOK

Community patterns at Laguna de On derive from the natural and cultural settings of this site's inland, rural, freshwater lagoon environment, as well as its intermediary position between the northern and southern lowlands zones. Chapter 2 describes the environmental context for the emergence of Postclassic society at Laguna de On. The formation of Late Postclassic settlements and polities in northern Belize appears to have been closely linked to topographic landform. Laguna de On is located in a lacustrine, riverine, and swamp ecotone, and its easy access to the Caribbean Sea would have provided distinct communication and economic advantage. The political geography of northern Belize and the greater Yucatán peninsula also provides an important context for understanding patterns at Laguna de On. The second half of Chapter 2 reviews models for Postclassic regional organization and evaluates aspects of these models that are reflected in settlement patterns of northern Belize as currently reported in the literature.

As much of the analysis of cultural systems from Laguna de On is based on diachronic trends observed in features and artifacts over time at this site, issues of chronology represent a critical hinge upon which interpretations of this material rest. Unfortunately, the chronology of the Postclassic period has been problematic, due to shallow deposits that make absolute and stratigraphic dating methods extremely difficult. A wealth of ethnohistoric sources has assisted in issues of Postclassic chronology, but they have overshadowed archaeological approaches at the important sites investigated earlier in this century in Yucatán such as Chichén Itzá (Lincoln 1986), Mayapan (Pollock et al. 1962) and Tulum (Lothrop 1924; Sanders 1960). Chapter 3 provides a review of the ceramic evidence for chronology in the Early and Late Postclassic periods, and represents an effort to synthesize some of the general patterns of utilitarian ceramic production trends over time. Ritual and restricted elite wares have been the focus of considerable study, and tend to exhibit idiosyncratic traits at individual sites that emphasize community differences. However, these distinctions mask an underlying utilitarian substrate of shared traditions from the Peten region, the Belize and east coast Quintana Roo regions, and areas of northern Yucatán during the Late Postclassic that are described in Chapter 3. This review of the origins of Late Postclassic ceramics is presented for the purpose of placing the ceramic assemblage and chronology of Laguna de On in a broader context. The ceramics from Laguna de On are highly eroded and fragmented (Mock 1998). No whole vessels have been recovered from this site. The study of this assemblage is ongoing, and the chronology from this site is partly based on the continuum of ceramic production observed throughout Laguna's sequence. The chronology is also based on the stratigraphic distribution of features and associated radiocarbon dates. The Laguna chronology is presented at the end of Chapter 3.

The features found in the Early and Late Facets of Laguna de On's occupation represent key aspects of diachronic community patterns observed at this site. Chapter 4 presents the results of the analysis of stratigraphy, features, architecture, and settlement at the site. Over time, an acceleration in ritual practice, household architectural differentiation, mortuary patterns, and public works construction at Laguna de On is observed. The materials recovered from these contexts provide additional information about Laguna de On's changing economy from A.D. 1050 to 1500. Artifacts of every category are analyzed in Chapter 5 in an assessment of subsistence and household maintenance activities at this community, local craft production industries, local exchange networks, and participation in long-distance exchange at this site. Spatial comparisons of artifact distributions also indicate the degree to which status differences are expressed within this community, and how these expressions change over time. Chapters 4 and 5 represent the best sort of contributions to understanding Postclassic society that can be made from a community such as Laguna de On. Detailed information on the economic organization of settlements of this nature are few, and communities such as Laguna de On represent an important substrate of producer settlements that provided the commodities that fueled Late Postclassic economic development and far-reaching international trade connections.

Further aspects of Postclassic social systems are reflected in ritual behavior. Chapter 6 explores the links between the political significance of kin-based power as manifested in lineage groups, or ch'ibal (Roys 1957: 4). Religious indicators are modest at Laguna de On compared to those found at Postclassic centers, but they are present in three discrete areas close to domestic zones at the center of Laguna de On Island and on the shore of the lagoon. These features and the behaviors associated with them represent small-scale versions of more substantial religious features found at political centers. The examination of the latter sheds light on the former, as political centers possess larger, more abundant, and better-preserved ritual features than those recovered at Laguna de On. The distribution and meaning of sculptures, murals, and architecture at Mayapan and Tulum are thus explored in Chapter 6, with some additional observations regarding murals at the site of Santa Rita. Patterns observed at these centers help to clarify the similarities and differences between household ritual and elite-focused ritual, links between lineages and political power, ways in which Postclassic religious practice finds its origins in traditions of earlier eras, and aspects of ritual that represent new innovations. Ritual patterns identified at these centers enhance the understanding of the censer shrines found at Laguna de On Island and the lagoon's shore.

The acceleration of ritual activity over time during the Late Postclassic has been a topic of scholarly interest since the recovery of numerous ceramic effigies in late lots at Mayapan (Tozzer 1941; Thompson 1957; Pollock et al. 1962; Smith 1971). This pan-regional religious intensification is discussed in Chapter 6 as it occurs in tandem with a general developmental upswing that is observed in all other realms of Postclassic society as well. It is probable that this religious revival served to integrate provinces with developing hierarchies, and it has been astutely suggested that religious events were closely tied to the facilitation of economic interaction (Freidel 1981; Miller 1982).

Chapter 7 of this volume discusses dynamic aspects of mature state formation as reflected in diachronic patterns of cultural development at the Laguna de On community and the Postclassic Maya world. By the eleventh century, regional Postclassic Maya cultures had taken root in the northern Belize region, as reflected by the establishment of affluent agrarian settlements such as Laguna de On and the emergence of new ceramic traditions of utilitarian redwares and unslipped forms that share common attributes of form and decoration with other Postclassic settlements across the southern lowlands (Valdez 1987; Masson and Mock n.d.). These ceramics reflect some attributes that are linked to earlier traditions (Ball 1977; Graham 1987; Walker 1990; Mock 1994), but they also incorporate attributes of northern Yucatán (Ball 1977; Chase and Chase 1982; Valdez and Mock 1985; Valdez 1987; Mock 1994). The material culture of Laguna de On indicates the participation of northern Belize sites in broader pan–Maya Lowlands and international Mesoamerican spheres. By this time, Laguna de On had established local producer-consumer relationships with nearby communities (Michaels 1987; Masson 1997), and its connection to long-distance networks is indicated by the presence of abundant quantities of obsidian at this site from the beginning of its occupation. Surplus industries at Laguna de On include ceramic manufacture, extraction of local chalcedony raw materials, and weaving. While these economic activities are well-reflected in the earliest stratigraphic levels and features at the island, there is little evidence for status differentiation, and few ritual indicators are observed at first. Members of the island settlement were of robust health and were relatively long-lived compared to those of the Terminal Classic shore occupation (Masson 1993, 1997; Rosenswig 1998). Environmental replenishment is observed in the abundant quantities of faunal bone at this site, and bone is largely absent at earlier Terminal Classic households at this lagoon.

These fundamental attributes of Laguna de On's eleventh-century economy do not appear to change substantially in the site's 450-year Postclassic occupation history. However, after the thirteenth century, growth trends are reflected at this site, including greater importation of long-distance commodities, evidence for moderate status distinctions in residential architecture and domestic artifact assemblages, and the presence of persuasive, integrative leadership reflected in public works projects and in the construction and use of ritual features. These trends are attributed to a cycle of economic florescence and accompanying rise of Postclassic elite culture along the east coast of the Yucatán peninsula and in Belize, in league with the northern capital of Mayapan and the maritime trade it fostered (Freidel and Sabloff 1984: 38; Robles and Andrews 1986; Sierra Sosa 1994).

The reproduction of Maya culture during the Postclassic period is thus observed in the material remains of several generations of families that occupied the Laguna de On community. The selective nature of this reproduction is clear, and institutions appear to have been replicated and transformed in a creative, innovative, recombinant manner from the ingredients of the past adjusted to the needs of the present. Acknowledging their historical traditions but not imprisoned by them, the occupants of Laguna de On joined their neighbors in Chetumal province and its allies in the definition of a new era in which institutions of political leadership, economic exchange, and religious ritual were geared toward integrating the multiple lineage factions that vied for leadership and the producer communities upon whose labor the stability of this society depended. This new era, termed by Western archaeologists as the "Postclassic" or "Decadent" period, is actually an important and underemphasized development in the evolution of civilizations. As Rathje and Sabloff have pointed out (Rathje 1975; Sabloff and Rathje 1975), maturing secondary states represent political formations that have overcome early statehood preoccupations with divine kings and big monuments in favor of economic affluence and more efficient investments of human labor and energy. This volume encapsulates a microcosm of this process of maturing secondary state development at the community level. Through this effort of contextualizing the archaeological record of Laguna de On, some important diachronic trends of Postclassic secondary state formation in the Maya area are revealed.

2

The Physical and Political Geography of Laguna de On

There seemed to brood over these sacred isles of the lagoon of On an air of silence and secretiveness, an air of something concealed, something held back from us of the mystery which hangs over the closing scenes of that wonderful Maya civilisation.

—THOMAS GANN 1928: 55

THE ENVIRONMENTAL SETTING OF LAGUNA DE ON

Laguna de On, or Honey Camp Lagoon, is a bright green, freshwater lagoon located about eleven kilometers east of Orange Walk Town, Belize (Figure 2.1). Its semisaline quality, which varies throughout the year with fluctuations in groundwater, prohibits the formation of typical algaes found in less saline neighboring lagoons. For this reason, the water is clear and the base of the lagoon is lined with white decomposed limestone, with quite beautiful effects. The maximum depth of the water is thirty feet. Laguna de On is situated on an ecotone, where karstic hardwood uplands meet a zone of swampy, sandy pine flats to the south (Figure 2.1; Masson 1993). To the northwest of the lagoon, two highly organic nonsaline freshwater lagoons are located, including Doubloon Bank Lagoon and Button Lagoon. The water of these lagoons is stained with tannic acids, and their shallow nature causes them to teem with the ecological food chain, including numerous species of fish, turtles, crocodiles, and waterfowl. Although these species are reported from Laguna de On, their density is much higher in the more organic lagoons, according to Belizeans who fish and hunt at these locations daily.

Laguna de On and its neighboring lagoons are part of a strip of wetlands referred to as Doubloon Bank Savanna, which extends from Doubloon Bank Lagoon in a southward crescent and nearly connects to the southwest shore of Laguna de On. Limnologist Mark Brenner (1987) suggests that the lagoon's

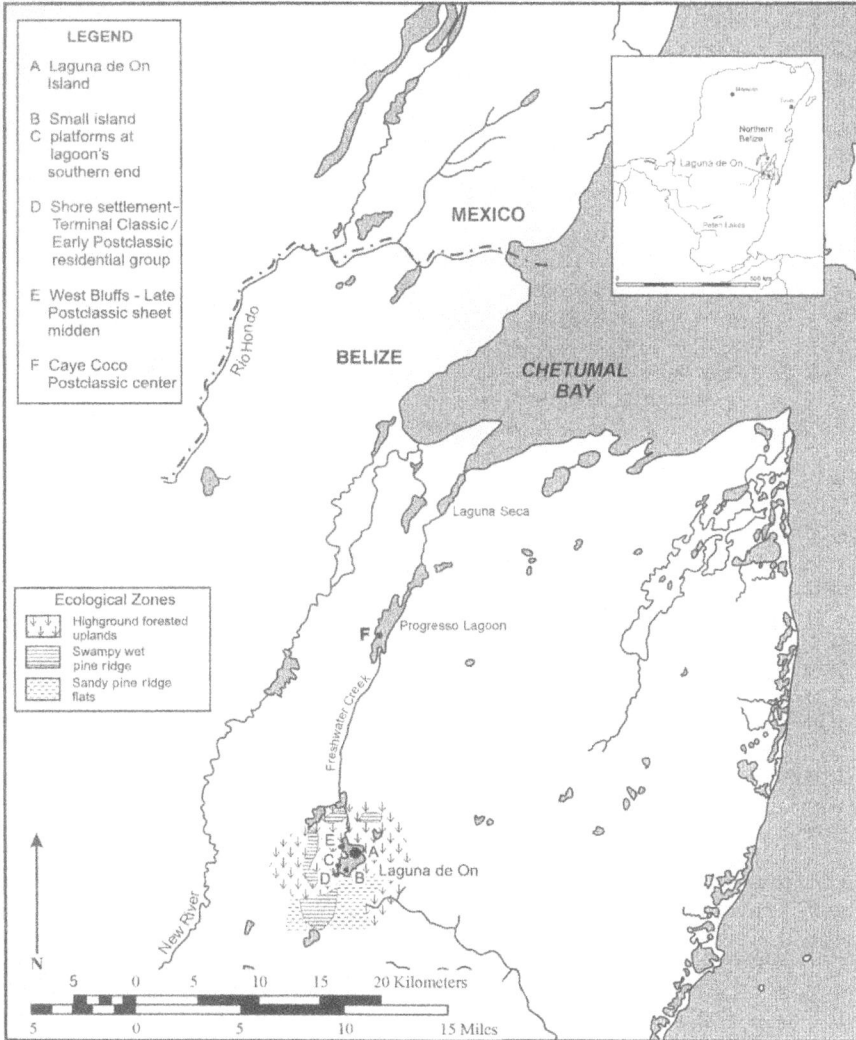

LEGEND

A Laguna de On Island

B Small island
C platforms at lagoon's southern end

D Shore settlement–Terminal Classic / Early Postclassic residential group

E West Bluffs - Late Postclassic sheet midden

F Caye Coco Postclassic center

Ecological Zones

- Highground forested uplands
- Swampy wet pine ridge
- Sandy pine ridge flats

2.1 The vicinity of Laguna de On in northern Belize.

salinity may also be related to soil characteristics of the lagoon itself or to precipitation. Brenner (1987) notes that the water chemistry consists of high percentages of sodium (19.7 percent), chloride (20.1 percent), calcium (15.9 percent), and magnesium (13.8 percent). Pollen cores taken from Laguna de On and analyzed by Barbara Leyden indicate poor preservation of pollen, yielding counts too low to permit reliable analysis. According to locals, it is possible to drink the water, although most people prefer to construct wells for drinking water a few meters back from the beach (Areli

Grajales, personal communication 1996). The limestone bedrock through which the wells on the shore are dug filters the water and makes it more potable and clean. Ancient wells have been located in archaeological surveys along Laguna de On Shore and in similar lagoon shore settings at Progresso Lagoon and Laguna Seca (Masson and Rosenswig 1998), where they are associated with Classic and Postclassic period surface scatters.

Geologically, the soils around the lagoon are diverse. Along the banks of the neighboring Doubloon Bank and Button Lagoons, deep organic clays are found that are richer than those found at Laguna de On. This site is located on the eastern extent of the "flinty soils" identified by Wright et al. (1959), also known as the "chert-bearing zone" documented by Hester and Shafer (Hester 1982; Shafer and Hester 1983; Hester and Shafer 1984). Although the Laguna de On flinty soils were formed under "intermittent lime enrichment" that are deemed suitable for agriculture, they are not the most highly rated soils for this purpose in this vicinity (Wright et al. 1959). Settlement at the lagoon is thus not explained by optimal ecological variables. However, there are advantages to cultivation opportunities in both wetland and upland locations. At Albion Island (Pohl, Bloom, and Pope 1990: 235; Miksicek 1990), Pulltrouser Swamp (Turner and Harrison 1983), and Colha (Shaw 1990; Hester et al. 1996), the strategy of cultivation of these two upland/wetland ecotones may have provided a form of insurance against climatic fluctuation.

The soils around Laguna de On bear low-grade chert and several types of high-quality chalcedonies. The chalcedony outcrops in cobble and tabular form (Oland 1998) and it represents an important resource used by pre-Columbian residents of the lagoon for production and exchange (McAnany et al. n.d.; Masson 1993; Oland 1998). Fine-quality white clay has also been identified at Laguna de On, found in pockets of limestone bedrock on the north island of the lagoon. Intrusive pits observed in these deposits suggest that ancient residents exploited this resource, probably for ceramic production (Rosenswig and Stafford 1998).

MODERN AND ANCIENT ENVIRONMENTAL IMPACTS AT LAGUNA DE ON

The Faunal Community

The karstic uplands, the low-lying pine flats, and the swamps around Laguna de On were home to a diverse biotic community that contributed to the subsistence of inhabitants of this vicinity. Faunal analyses in northern Belize from Postclassic components at Colha (Scott 1981, 1982; Shaw and Mangan 1994) and Laguna de On (Masson 1993, 1999a; Wharton and Stanchly 1998) have identified a range of animal species that were exploited during the Postclassic period (Table 2.1). Many other species are identified and hunted in the region today that are not often identified in the archaeological record, such as coatimundi, racoon, anteater, ocelot, and other small mammals (Victor Ayuso, personal communication). The presence of abundant tapir remains at Laguna de On indicates the existence of high-canopy jungle in this region during the Postclassic period after A.D. 1000. Tapir are semisolitary animals requiring large ranges of four to six square kilometers per individual (Matola 1995: 18). The fact that their remains are common at Laguna de On Island reflects a jungle ecology that was not duly affected by human predation. In contrast, tapir are absent in Classic period deposits at this lagoon. Further details of human ecology in the Postclassic are explored further in Chapter 5.

Wetland species also seem to have been abundant during the Postclassic period. Large pond turtles and crocodiles are recovered frequently in Postclassic faunal assemblages in this part of northern Belize. The size and frequency of these species also suggests that they were abundant throughout the Postclassic period at this site (Masson n.d.a).

Landscape Modification

Archaeological remains found at this lagoon extend from the Archaic period through the twentieth century. The Postclassic period shore settlement is detected in two vicinities: sheet middens and a shrine feature overlying bed-rock along north and northwest bluffs adjacent to the lagoon, and surface occupations overlying Terminal Classic period domestic groups at the south-west corner of the lagoon. These deposits are contemporary with island occupations in the lagoon, including the primary island settlement of

Table 2.1—Animal species in northern Belize forests during the Postclassic as identified in faunal analysis (compiled from Scott 1981, 1982; Shaw and Mangan 1994; Masson 1993, 1999a; Wharton and Stanchly 1998)

Perissodactyls
    Tapirus bairdii (tapir)

Artiodactyls
    Tayassu tajacu (collared peccary)
    Odocoileus virginianus (white-tailed deer)
    Mazama americana (brocket deer)

Carnivores
    Canis familiaris (dog)
    Bassariscus sumichrasti (ring-tailed cat)
    Felis onca (jaguar)

Continued on next page

Table 2.1—*continued*

Small mammals
    Dasypus novemcinctus (armadillo)
    Bassaricus sumichrasti (cacomistle)
    Coendou spp. (porcupine)
    Didelphis spp. (opossum)
Dasyproctidae family (large rodent)
    Cuniculus paca (paca)
    Dasyprocta agouti (agouti)
Birds
    Meleagris ocellata (ocellated turkey)
    Meleagris gallopavo (common wild turkey)
    Florida caerula (little blue heron)
    Butorides virenscens (green heron)
    Anhinga anhinga (American Anhinga)
Reptiles
    Iguanidae (iguanas)
    Serpentes (snakes)
    Crocodylus spp. (crocodile)
    Kinosternidae (mud turtles)
    Staurotypus triporcatus
    Geomyda pulcherrima (box turtle)
    Geomyda punctularia
    Geomyda areolata (brown belly)
    Emydidae (pond turtles)
    Chelydra serpentina (snapping turtles)
Amphibians
    Salientia (frogs and toads)
Osteichthyes (Bony fish)
    Galichthyes felis (estuarine catfish)
    Megalops spp. (tarpon)
    Carangidae (jacks)
    Archosargus probatocephalus (sheepshead)
    Lutjanidae (snapper)
    Albulidae (bonefish)
    Serranidae (grouper)
    Elopidae (ladyfish)
    Sphyraena barracuda (barracuda)
    Galeocerdo cuvieri (tiger shark)
    Pristidae (sawfish)
    Rajiformes (rays)
    Sciaenidae (drum)
Shellfish/Crustaceans
    Decapoda (crab)
    Pomacea spp. (pond apple)
    Pachychilus spp. (jute)
    Oliva spp. (olive)

Laguna de On Island, a large island at the lagoon's north end, and two additional smaller islands at the south end (Figure 2.1). On Laguna de On Island, midden deposits, soil and plaster house floors, rubble alignments and low platforms, terraces, walls, and cemeteries have been documented (Masson and Rosenswig 1997, 1998a). Modified island landscapes are common elsewhere in the Maya Lowlands, as documented for Isla Jaina and Isla Cerritos off the coasts of Campeche and Yucatán (Andrews et al. 1988).

The island deposits at Laguna de On Island are largely undisturbed, reaching depths of 50 centimeters to 1.5 meters, and structural remains are visible on the surface due to the tall canopy and light understory. In contrast, lagoon shore deposits are shallower (20–30 centimeters), more difficult to detect in thick secondary-growth vegetation, and they are quite vulnerable to destruction by development of lakeside properties. Much damage has been done to the archaeological resources of the shores of the lagoon due to construction of private weekend resorts. In this development, considerable earthmoving with heavy machinery has taken place, in some cases leaving quarries where mound groups were formerly located. Several structures that were observed and mapped during 1991 had disappeared by 1996. Even in 1991, there was evidence that several structures had been dismantled in the construction of the road that passes around the lagoon, as pre-Columbian construction fill materials were visible in the road itself adjacent to rubble concentrations (formerly mounds) by the side of the road. Such environmental impacts make it difficult to assess the magnitude and significance of the shoreside community. Unfortunately, this problem is common for many archaeological sites in Belize (Sidrys 1983: 74; Chase and Chase 1988: 7–8). The island site of Laguna de On is protected by a forestry reserve.

Landscape modification at this lagoon is an ancient practice that began in pre-Columbian times. Two small islands at the lagoon's south end have been identified as artificial platforms of lagoon sediment (Figure 2.1; Masson 1993, 1997). The relatively sterile fill of these island platforms was not immediately recognized as anthropogenic, as it lacked artifacts characteristically found in Classic period architecture. However, such small mounds of sandy lagoon clay do not naturally occur in this karstic geological setting, where bedrock is comprised of limestone marl. An unmodified island in the northeast corner of the lagoon showed little elevation by comparison to the two at the lagoon's south end. These small southern island platforms were looted extensively in the 1980s. The upper surfaces of these islands were tested in 1991 (Masson 1993), revealing shallow surface scatters and hearths of Late Postclassic date. One of these small island platforms has been connected to the lagoon shore in recent times by artificial sand fill brought in from the pine ridge within the past two decades (Figure 2.1; Wilfredo Coral, personal communication 1991). Its surface has also been partially destroyed and enhanced since 1991 with heavy equipment. The large north island of the lagoon (Laguna de On Island) was substantially modified during the Postclassic by terrace construction (described in Chapter 5).

AQUATIC SETTLEMENT SYSTEMS OF POSTCLASSIC NORTHERN BELIZE

Pre-Columbian landscape modification may have included canal building, although this possibility has not been verified. Locals state that Laguna de On was formerly connected to Button Lagoon by a canal (Areli Grajales, personal communication 1996), and some maps of northern Belize show this feature (Sidrys 1983: Figure 2; Jones 1989: Map 2). If this canal existed, it is grown over and not in use today. It is not known whether the canal was constructed by British loggers or in pre-Columbian times. Other British maps show Laguna de On connected directly by an east-west channel through another lagoon to the Caribbean Sea (Fancourt 1854, as redrawn in Diane Chase 1986: Figure 10), but perhaps this is more conceptual rather than geographically accurate. Access to the sea from Laguna de On was possible via Doubloon Bank and Button Lagoons, Freshwater Creek, Progresso Lagoon, John Piles Creek, and Laguna Seca. The Freshwater Creek drainage forms one of three south-north running waterways that follow tectonic rifts in northern Belize. The other two drainages are the New River and the Rio Hondo, both larger than Freshwater Creek. An elderly resident of Progresso Lagoon, Ernesto Villas (personal communication 1997) recalls that Freshwater Creek was formerly navigable in the early twentieth century, although it has now been silted in.

Considerable attention to the issue of Postclassic demography is found in the literature. The lack of Postclassic architectural remains at Classic period sites has been the basis for the interpretation of a decline in local populations (Fry 1990). Research at Belize sites such as Lamanai, Santa Rita, Tipu, and Laguna de On (Masson 1995; Chase and Chase 1988: 8–9; Diane Chase 1990; Jones, Rice, and Rice 1991; Pendergast, Jones, and Graham 1993) suggests that stratigraphic contexts for the recovery of Postclassic and Colonial period remains differ fundamentally from Classic period remains, and that Postclassic settlement zones are difficult to locate if architecture is used as a primary criteria for quantification. These problems are also characteristic of Postclassic period settlement in the Peten Lakes (Cowgill 1963; Rice and Rice 1985), and for Colonial period Maya settlement in Belize (Jones, Rice, and Rice 1991; Pendergast, Jones, and Graham 1993). Terminal Classic/Early Postclassic populations often ceased architectural construction and chose to inhabit and use dwellings and temples built in earlier times. Archaeological components of this period are thus confined to surface scatters in jungle topsoils at many sites (Graham 1985, 1987; Masson 1995). Cowgill (1963: 7) referred to the Early Postclassic period as the "postconstructional phase" at Tikal. This stratigraphic position can result in the increased erosion of Postclassic slips on temporally sensitive ceramics, making Postclassic period occupations harder to identify (Masson 1995). A lack of intact features in upper humic jungle layers also poses problems for radiocarbon dating of these later occupations. The intermingling of materials of earlier occupations with those of the Postclassic period can mask the latter (Graham 1985; Pendergast, Jones, and Graham 1993), particularly when continuities in artifact form or style occurred from Classic to Postclassic as is sometimes noted (Graham 1987).

A major settlement shift occurred in the tenth to eleventh centuries, when a large proportion of Postclassic populations were attracted to aquatic-oriented locations (Chase and Rice 1985: 6). Many sites in aquatic locations were newly founded, other settlements were founded upon the remains of earlier villages or towns, and some settlements grew from existing communities. Inland, upland Classic period Maya centers often report no evidence of Postclassic occupation (Demarest 1997; Fred Valdez, personal communication). Many inland locations were abandoned in the Postclassic period in favor of riverine, lacustrine, and coastal settings as observed in the Peten region (Cowgill 1963; Don Rice 1974; Rice and Rice 1985).

An example of continued occupation of a settlement from Classic to Postclassic is observed at the site of Barton Ramie in the Belize River Valley. At this site, sixty-two out of sixty-five structures built in earlier times were inhabited in the Postclassic period (Willey et al. 1965: 291; Thompson 1970: 81). Barton Ramie is an agrarian and primarily residential riverine settlement that was not abandoned at the end of the Classic period. The Postclassic period occupation of this site was not limited to surface dwelling, as 26 percent of the structures at this site (seventeen out of sixty-five mounds) were modified by construction activities during the Postclassic (Willey et al. 1965: Figure 172).

In northern Belize, the New River, the Rio Hondo, and Freshwater Creek, like Barton Ramie, are riverine locations where considerable Postclassic Maya settlement has been found (Lewenstein and Dahlin 1990; Ball 1985; Pendergast 1985, 1986; Daniel Finamore, personal communication) as indicated on Figures 2.2 and 2.3. Postclassic settlements along the New River include Lamanai (Pendergast 1981), San Estevan (Daniel Finamore, personal communication 1997), and NR5 (Daniel Finamore, personal communication 1997). Rio Hondo Postclassic sites include Albion Island (Lewenstein and Dahlin 1990) and others mapped by Sidrys (1983), as shown in Figures 2.2 and 2.3. Along the Freshwater Creek drainage, the sites of Laguna de On, Pucte, Caye Coco, Progresso, and the Last Resort site are located along the creek and its intermittent lagoons (Thompson 1939; Masson and Rosenswig 1998). Other sites of the Postclassic period are reported near various aquatic features by Sidrys (1983), as indicated in Figures 2.2 and 2.3. These aquatic features include relatively self-contained lagoons like Laguna de On, as well as coastal locations. Sites identified by Sidrys include Consejo, Sajomal, Libertad, Cerros, Chunox, Wilson's Beach, Carolina, Ramonal, Shipstern, Bandera, Cenote, Condemned Point, Laguna, Rocky Point, Sarteneja, Chan Chen, and Aventura and Patchakan (Sidrys 1983: Figure 2, Table 1). Coastal settlements also possess Postclassic occupations, including Cerros, Santa Rita, Ek Balam, Marco Gonzalez, Wild Cane Caye, and Ichpaatun and Tamalcab in Chetumal Bay of southern Quintana Roo (Escalona Ramos 1946; McKillop and Healy 1989; Andrews and Vail 1990; Guderjan and Garber 1995). Further to the west in Campeche, the site of Isla Civlituk represents yet another Postclassic island lagoon settlement in a pattern that resembles that of Laguna de On (E. Wyllys Andrews 1943; Alexander 1999).

According to Sidry's survey, deposits of smashed censers are found at some sites in northern Belize that lack Postclassic occupations. These include Aventura, Patchchacan, Saltillo, San Andres, Benque Viejo, Nohmul, Pozito, Betson Bank, and Guinea Grass (Sidrys 1983: 244). Site abandonment and subsequent pilgrimage is also reported at Colha (Valdez 1987: 231). These sites may have been the location of pilgrimage shrines around the northern Belize landscape as suggested for Cerros by Walker (1990), although further testing should be conducted to verify that Late Postclassic domestic occupations are not present at these sites, as some have only been briefly surveyed. If they were occupied, their significance as pilgrimage localities would not be diminished, as pilgrimage shrines are known to coexist with residential occupations during the Late Postclassic at Cozumel (Freidel and Sabloff 1984).

Ethnohistoric accounts confirm the location of Postclassic populations along the waterways of northern Belize. During colonial times, when the Spaniard D'Avila retreated from a failed attempt to establish a colony at Villa Real (near Bacalar, Mexico), he travelled down the coast of Belize. Searching for provisions, he voyaged inland up the Belize rivers and encountered villages along these waterways (Thompson 1970: 61; Jones 1989: 6–17).

Occasionally, Postclassic sites in northern Belize are found in locations that are not located directly on water avenues such as rivers, creeks, or coastlines, although they are still often near wetland locations. Examples of such inland sites that are close to wetlands include Colha, which is adjacent to Cobweb Swamp and Rancho Creek (Hester 1985; Michaels 1987, 1994; Michaels and Shafer 1994), and K'axob, adjacent to Pulltrouser Swamp (Fry 1991; McAnany 1995). These wetland sites represent very small Postclassic communities that are often found as veneer deposits on domestic structures built in earlier times or in the form of domestic middens (Taylor 1980; Hester 1985; Michaels 1987; Michaels and Shafer 1994). These sites have Postclassic surface scatters and middens as well as previous Formative and Classic period remains. Their open terrain encouraged the dispersal of Postclassic settlement in contrast to more concentrated patterns observed on islands, peninsulas, or shorelines. Lagoon-side and riverine settlements tend to follow a linear shoreside pattern (Pendergast 1985: 98; Chase and Chase 1988; Robles and Andrews 1986; Silva Rhoads and Hernandez 1991), not unlike riverine and coastal chiefdom settlements documented in the southeast region of North America. Ethnohistoric documents from the American Southeast suggest that such dispersed linear settlement groups maintained the option to nucleate in times of conflict through the maintenance of a fortified center (Steponaitis 1983: 172). Island settlements such as Laguna de On may have served such a purpose for its shore settlement, as has been proposed for Peten Lakes islands (Don Rice 1986: 339, 1988: 234).

Restructuring of Postclassic settlement systems reflects transformed political and economic organization of this period. The aquatic settlement focus of the Postclassic has been compared to similar patterns observed in the Formative period, in which riverine, swamp, and wetland focii were highly significant (Chase 1983: 1233; Chase and Rice 1985; Don Rice 1986: 302, 339). Classic period variability in settlement location, including inland and upland locations at a distance from natural watercourses, was probably a strategy supported by the increased centralization of political power and control observed for Classic period states, and perhaps it was encouraged by increased population levels (Rice and Culbert 1990). Classic period city-states possessed the capacity to control and organize upland hydraulic features such as reservoirs and canals (Scarborough, Connolly, and Ross 1994) and to exact subsistence tribute necessary to support political centers. The Postclassic shift back to aquatic-focused settlement has been previously recognized for the Peten Lakes/Tikal region (Chase and Rice 1985: 6–7), and the northern Belize data suggest that this strategy was significant across a broad geographic area of the lowlands. Proximity to perennial aquatic sources permitted the greater autonomy and relatively more decentralized organization of Postclassic period settlement.

POSTCLASSIC POLITICAL DYNAMICS

Four primary models found in the literature on Postclassic Maya political organization have affected the interpretation of political patterns at northern Belize archaeological sites. These models include the foreign invasion model, the mercantile society model, the segmentary lineage model, and the province model. These models of Postclassic society largely originate from the use of ethnohistoric data (Spanish and indigenous) in conjunction with the archaeological record. These models are briefly reviewed below, as they form critical points of reference for interpretations of settlement patterns of northern Belize and southern Quintana Roo. Aspects of each of these models have relevance for understanding the development and organization of the community of Laguna de On and its neighbors.

Foreign Invasion Model

The Lowland Maya region shares with other archaeological cultures around the world some serious methodological shortcomings with regard to identifying and equating ethnicity and style in the archaeological record (Schuyler 1980). Stylistic change can occur for a variety of reasons, and can be spread rapidly and broadly with or without an exchange of personnel. Numerous interpretations of "Mexican" stylistic-ethnic indicators have been proposed for Postclassic Maya sites in the lowlands (Thompson 1970; Tourtellot, Sabloff, and Carmean 1992; Chase and Chase 1982; Chase 1983: 1,277; Robles and Andrews 1986; Lincoln 1986; Don Rice 1986: 317–321) and the highlands (Carmack 1981; Fox 1987). The archaeological inquiry into the presence of foreigners is a legacy inherited from early investigations at Tulum (Lothrop 1924) and Mayapan (Pollock 1962; Roys 1962), where accounts of ethnic invasion in the mytho-historic *Books of Chilam Balam* were correlated with archaeological patterns of site formation and abandonment.

Investigators at Mayapan in particular (Pollock 1962: 4–8) superimposed ethnohistorically derived chronologies on the archaeological record, and verification of ethnohistoric accounts through separate lines of evidence was not a concern of this project. The historic links of documentary accounts to Mayapan are close in time and space, and they are abundant. These circumstances are ideal for the application of the direct historic method, and the incorporation of historic evidence by Carnegie investigators at Mayapan was inevitable. The *Chilam Balam* books and other accounts of Postclassic Maya ethnohistoric accounts, however, blend myth with history and prophecy to an extent that their historical accuracy is compromised (Roys 1962: 27, 30). These books are an incredible resource for Mayanists, but these chronicles were written by colonial Maya as late as the eighteenth century who were transcribing oral histories from memory after decades of colonial intervention (Roys 1933, 1962: 31). The *Chilam Balam* priests of various northern Yucatecan Maya towns were operating within agendas of their time. Nonetheless, accounts of significant events are found in several sources. These events were compiled originally in a chronology published by Barrera Vasquez and Morley (1949) from the *Chilam Balam* chronicles, Bishop Diego de Landa's *Relaciones de las Cosas de Yucatán* (1941), and the journeys of Fuensalida and Avendano to the Itzá kingdom (Villagutierre Soto-Mayor 1983/1701).

The literal adoption of the ethnic tales in these accounts is reflected in the Mayapan Postclassic chronology, which was classified into Early, Middle, and Late "Mexican" periods due to "Toltec" architecture (Pollock 1962: 5).

Current analysis of mythic histories from across Mesoamerica recognizes the political advantage of claiming "foreign" ties to legitimize power. The Mixtec codex account of Lord 8 deer, who receives foreign "sanction" from Lord 4 Jaguar (from a neighboring highland region) demonstrates the significance of exotic alliance (Pohl 1994: 93). Similar claims of foreign sanction are interpreted in monuments at Classic period Tikal and Monte Alban (Coggins 1983), which demonstrate the prevalence of this strategy. The *Books of Chilam Balam* relate the account of similar foreign affiliations of the Chichén Itzá polity, which are probably partly based in historical truth, and partly the product of political agendas.

It is probable that foreign migrations did take place during the Postclassic period (Carmack 1977, 1981; Don Rice 1986), although it is doubtful that they only began at this time (Schele 1995). The identification of foreign ethnic replacement in the Postclassic Maya archaeological record has traditionally begun with the origins of the Itzá and events surrounding the rise and fall of the center of Chichén Itzá (Lincoln 1986; Robles and Andrews 1986) and ends with a consideration of Aztec influences during the Late Postclassic (Miller 1982). Although it is not possible to review here the entire gamut of interpretations of Itzá "invasion" or "migration" to southern lowlands sites or the ethnicity (based on style) of Chichén Itzá itself, some representative arguments are discussed below.

Ethnic traits of northern Yucatán that have been identified as "Mexican" in locations such as Chichén Itzá, Dzibilchaltun, Seibal, Sayil, the Peten Lakes, and the Quiche Highlands include the following (Fox 1987; Tourtellot, Sabloff, and Carmean 1992; Diane Chase 1982: 103; Chase and Chase 1982): colonnaded rectangular buildings, long structures with single long benches, temples dedicated to the feathered serpent with stairways on three or four sides, flatbeam and mortar masonry, I-shaped enclosed ballcourts, small round structures, patio/quad/altar residential groups, façades coated with lime plaster, and Mixteca-Puebla–styled ceramics (not literally Cholula polychromes but the inclusion of "Mexican" motifs such as step frets). Many of these traits are indigenous to the Maya Lowlands, however. Precedents for long structures differ little from Classic period southern lowland "range" structures (with the addition of columns) and round structures are found from the Formative period onward in Belize (Sidrys 1983: 92–103). Schele notes that four-sided temples originate in the Maya area in the Formative period as seen at Uaxactun (1995).

These traits, according to the foreign invasion model, are thought to have spread to and from Chichén Itzá to other sites through hostile migrations (Fox 1987; Chase and Chase 1982; Michaels 1987). Sites such as Nohmul (Chase and Chase 1982) and Colha in Belize (Eaton 1980; Hester 1982, 1985) show evidence for violent incursions of groups from northern

Yucatán. Stylistic changes in lithic artifacts at Colha are also attributed to invasion of Itzá into northern Belize (Nash 1980; Hester 1982, 1985; Shafer 1979, 1982; Michaels 1987: 178; Michaels and Shafer 1994). Other studies suggest communities underwent a peaceful incorporation into the Chichén Itzá/Northern Yucatán emulation sphere (Pendergast 1981, 1986; Chase and Chase 1988: 83–85; Don Rice 1988). Arguments for either a hostile or peaceful transition are based on various types of evidence from different sites. At some sites such as Barton Ramie or Laguna de On, the occupation of domestic structures built in the Late Classic during the Terminal Classic/Early Postclassic period is strongly suggestive of a transition that did not affect some rural agrarian populations adversely (Willey et al. 1965; Masson 1993, 1995).

At Laguna de On, studies of local economic production and exchange show maintenance of specific intersite relationships from the Terminal Classic through Postclassic periods (Masson 1997). This pattern suggests that, at least for this site, some continuity is maintained among populations of producers familiar with ultralocal exchange relationships and procurement strategies. While ethnohistoric evidence for group migrations is extensive and no doubt reflects a legitimate process during the Postclassic centuries, it is probable that ethnic mixture of local and migrating groups resulted in many areas, as suggested for the Peten Lakes region (Don Rice 1986, 1988). Indeed, the Maya chronicles describe the nature of these migrations, which seem to be led by powerful elite males who are accompanied by affiliates of their lineages. For example, in describing the Itzá migration to Pole, the *Chilam Balam* of Chumayel notes that intermarrying with local populations occurred, "the remainder of the Itzá were increased in number, they took the women of Pole as their mothers" (Roys 1933: 70). The *Books of Chilam Balam* contain various references to the Itzá, who are portrayed at times as conquerors, and at times as refugees. As discussed in Chapters 3 and 6, the Itzá moved so often from north to south and back again, according to documentary sources, that tracking these events archaeologically could be very difficult.

Chichén Itzá's influence in northern Yucatán has been extensively documented (Ball 1982; Robles and Andrews 1986; Andrews et al. 1988; Bey, Hanson, and Ringle 1997; Suhler and Freidel 1998; Kepecs, Feinman, and Boucher 1994; Kepecs 1998). Some scholars suggest that Chichén's influence was stronger in the western half of the northern peninsula, and that eastern sites remained allied to Coba (Navarrete, Uribe, and Muriel 1979; Ball 1982: 110; Robles and Andrews 1986). Chichén-like wares are found beneath later remains at sites such as Cozumel (Robles 1986a, 1986b), and sites along the east coast possess trade wares that probably originate from Chichén (Ball 1982: 110). The degree of Chichén's influence at sites further to the south in Quintana Roo and Belize is not clear from ceramic studies.

Slatelike wares like those of Chichén are reported in low numbers at southern sites such as Becan (Ball 1977). Terminal Classic wares in Belize exhibit strong continuities with earlier traditions (Graham 1987). Some vessel forms and decorative attributes on Early Postclassic Belize assemblages are similar to those of Chichén (Mock 1994; Valdez and Mock 1985). Some aspects of slate paste technology are observed in Early Postclassic red-slipped vessels in northern Belize (Masson and Mock n.d.). Belize red-slipped vessels thus reflect an eclectic blend of redware vessel forms that originate earlier in the Peten Lakes region and Belize Valley (Pendergast 1981: 48–49; Ball 1982: 111), combined with Chichén-like attributes that are incorporated into local manufacture from interaction with Itzá traders. Over time, the north-south similarities in ceramic wares grow much closer, and the Belize zone was far more integrated with Mayapan than it was with Chichén Itzá—at least in terms of ceramic production.

The ceramics of Laguna de On (Mock 1997, 1998), Lamanai (Pendergast 1981: 6), and Colha (Mock 1994; Valdez and Mock 1985) bear the closest resemblance to the wares of Tulum, although they may be earlier in the Belize region. This pattern indicates close interprovincial relationships between Chetumal, Uaymil, Ecab, and Mani provinces, which were probably based on political alliance and economic trade. A full discussion of ceramic affinities of northern Belize is provided in Chapter 3.

The Postclassic Mercantile Model

During the Late Postclassic, the Mesoamerican world appears to have expanded its boundaries and cultivated an "international" interaction sphere that is reflected in evidence from shared artistic styles and accelerated interaction spheres (Robertson 1970; Miller 1982; Rathje 1975; Sabloff and Rathje 1975; Smith and Heath-Smith 1980). In fact, the promotion of international styles of shared religious iconography may have functioned in an important way to reconcile potential conflict among traders from diverse ethnic polities at important commercial sites such as Cozumel, Tulum, and Santa Rita, which served as ports of trade (Miller 1982; Chase and Chase 1988). A host of smaller sites on the Belizean coast performed a similar function on a smaller scale (McKillop and Healy 1989; Andrews and Vail 1990; Vail 1988).

Rathje and Sabloff (Rathje 1975; Sabloff and Rathje 1975) propose a mercantile model to explain the decline in investment in elaborate architecture and utilitarian crafts during the Postclassic period in northern Yucatán. They propose that labor investment formerly reserved for public works was transposed into commercial trade, and suggest that this economic-focused society was a logical outgrowth of the more internally focused, excessively hierarchical political structures of the Classic period. They portray the

Postclassic Maya as a more "efficient" society that had outgrown the need to invest labor into works that displayed the prestige of a small apical segment of society. This model provides a provocative and testable framework for interpreting long-term Maya cultural change. It represents an important effort to propose an evolutionary interpretation of the reduction in scale observed for Postclassic Maya expressions of power compared to the Classic period, rather than characterizing this period as the "death of a civilization" (Proskouriakoff 1955).

The efficient characteristics of Postclassic society identified by Sabloff and Rathje were centered on attributes of architecture and ceramic manufacture. The lack of investment in architecture reflected in low, eroding mound structures was interpreted as evidence for an "efficient" construction strategy that used less-permanent, perishable, or easily eroded materials such as wood and plaster. Public architectural features, furthermore, are claimed to be "dispersed" in residential zones rather than "concentrated" (Rathje 1975: 423). However, this generalization masks the fact that Mayapan does have a centralized, concentrated ceremonial precinct where the majority of the colonnaded halls and oratories are located and larger shrines and temples of this site are found. A critique of the characterizations of Postclassic ceramics as efficiently constructed is offered at the beginning of Chapter 5.

Despite problems with some of the evidence originally proposed for the mercantile model reviewed above, there is no doubt that Sabloff and Rathje (1975) correctly characterized a Late Postclassic society that was no longer focused on the expression of power in monumental works, which were greatly reduced in scale from the Classic. It is also clear that as economic production and trade burgeoned, a transformed society with a mercantile focus emerged during the Postclassic period, as these scholars observed. Their observation that a reduction in scale of political expression was correlated with a preference for the investment of social energies into trade has profoundly enhanced our understanding of this latest age of Maya history. The long-distance economic exchange facilitated by circum-Yucatecan canoe trade (Scholes and Roys 1948; Thompson 1970) is reflected in cosmopolitan artifact assemblages at even the smallest of settlements such as Laguna de On. Recent research has emphasized the participation of the Postclassic Maya communities contemporary with Chichén Itzá in a Mesoamerican world system that stimulated considerable growth in parts of northern Yucatán (Kepecs, Feinman, and Boucher 1994). Chapters 4, 5, and 6 of this book provide supporting evidence for the participation of Laguna de On and some of its contemporaries in a Postclassic international economy that was linked to the political activities of the centers of Chichén Itzá and Mayapan.

Segmentary State Model

The segmentary state model has been proposed to characterize both Classic period lowland networks of sites (Dunham 1990) as well as highland Postclassic sites (Carmack 1977, 1981; Dwight Wallace 1977; Fox 1987). In both the lowlands and the highlands, segmentary organization is inferred from patterns of site fissioning and fusion (Fox 1987: 23–35; Dunham 1990). In the highland Postclassic case, Maya political centers are thought to have been founded through local and long-distance "leap frog" migrations. How are segmentary lineages, the fundamental units of segmentary states, defined? Carmack (1981: 61–62), working in the Guatemalan highlands, notes that the "basic unit of such a system is the lineage with its brotherhood of men occupying the same territory, sharing obligations of wife-giving, collective labor, mutual defense, ritual and honor." Similarly, Fox (1987: 22) states that "segmentary lineages are estate-controlling, producing, and consuming descent groups who pool their military and political efforts with neighboring lineages according to genealogical and spatial proximity." These definitions certainly evoke principles that are familiar to ethnohistoric southern lowland descriptions of Maya social and economic organization (Quezada 1993).

Upon closer examination, it appears that both Classic and Postclassic Maya political systems express some key attributes of segmentary organization or segmenting tendencies within a more complex and centralized system (Houston 1993; De Montmollin 1989; Dunham 1990; Demarest 1992; Blanton et al.1996). Even as kin-based power is replaced by king-based power in the evolution of many archaic states, kin power remains important and articulates with higher political offices (McAnany 1995: 125, 131–136). As McAnany (1995) notes, the complementarity of kinship and kingship and the resolution of their contradictions is an important element of political systems that are dispersed across relatively unbounded geographic areas such as the Lowland Maya region. The vast extent of the Maya area and its numerous habitable local environments inhibited this society from centralizing in the manner of highland single-valley-based polities (Sanders and Price 1968).

Segmentary organization in the pre-Columbian Maya archaeological record has been tracked through the analysis of site development, the spatial organization of domestic groups and ritual architecture, the analysis of domestic and ritual features recovered in excavation, and ethnic divisions reflected in ceramic assemblages. Such analysis can be performed at the regional level (Fox 1987; De Montmollin 1989), or through the examination of a small number of sites (Dunham 1990) or individual communities (Blake 1985).

Hieroglyphic evidence provides some support for segmentary factions in the Classic period lowlands. Intraregional conflict, competition, and alliance formation are well documented in the Classic period hieroglyphs (Houston 1993; Martin and Grube 1995), and these conditions are characteristic of segmentary structures (Demarest 1992; Houston 1993; Fox 1987). Some Classic period states were more centralized and achieved stability beyond the capacity of segmentary states (Marcus 1976; Chase and Chase 1996; Mathews 1991, Martin and Grube 1995), which by their definition are small in scale and fragmented in nature.

Variability across space and time is observed in the degree of centraliza-tion embodied in "corporate" and "network" strategies recently identified for the Lowland Maya and other Mesoamerican cultures (Blanton et al. 1996; Blanton 1998). Network strategies are identified in the political organiza-tion of Classic period Maya kingdoms (Blanton et al. 1996: 12). According to these authors, the Classic Maya had a greater tendency to fragment into competing entities, were more focused on external prestige goods trade than home production, and placed greater political significance on kin-based power networks than societies that exhibited more centralized "corporate" forma-tions such as Teotihuacán (Blanton et al. 1996; Blanton 1998).

An important foundation of segmentary states is lineage power. Lin-eages have the capacity to aggregate into broader alliances as needed, but such bonds quickly deteriorate (Fox 1987: 15). Lineage autonomy, or the capacity for autonomy, is thus one criteria for the identification of segmen-tary structures in the archaeological record. Fox further suggests that lineages maintain autonomous landholdings and the means of production even when segmentary states become highly aggregated. Anthropological studies of political structure, however, suggest that kin-based power can only be carried so far before the numbers are too great and other cross-kin politi-cal structures such as kingship must evolve. As clarified by Sahlins (1961: 333), segmentary lineages were territorially based autonomous units that responded to opposition by centralizing.

Fox (1987: 112–138) has summarized evidence linking symbolic quadrupartite lineage divisions documented ethnohistorically in segmentary systems with architectural configurations that represent quadrupartite divi-sions. Quadrupartite divisions within communities can be observed in the form of barrios, groups of four temples, or four-sided temples that might reflect such organization of society (Coe 1965; Fox 1987: 112–138). The presence of four-sided temples at the sites of Chichén Itzá and Mayapan may be associated with founding or refounding of these sites, events that incor-porated aspects of quadupartite symbolism into their political geography. The refounding of Chichén Itzá in the Postclassic occurred when "the four divisions were called together" (Tozzer 1941: 21; Marcus 1993: 117).

Evidence suggests that Postclassic Maya communities were conceptually divided into quadrupartite sections (Coe 1965; Marcus 1993: 132). Due to the diachronic nature of archaeological sites, evidence for this conceptualization, which may have manifested itself through various spatial trends over three or four centuries of Postclassic occupation, is difficult to document. Maps of Postclassic communities at Mayapan (Pollock et al. 1962) or in the Peten Lakes (Johnson 1985; Rice and Rice 1985; Arlen Chase 1985) do not reflect clearly recognizable divisions of four. Barrios housing elites through various sectors of Postclassic sites have been identified (Diane Chase 1985, 1986; Chase and Chase 1988: 68–71; Diane Chase 1992; Silva Rhoads and Maria del Carmen Hernandez 1991: 77; Alexander 1999), although their correspondence to four divisions is not observed. At sites such as Laguna de On, where stone architecture is rare, the investigation of real or symbolic community partitioning is not possible.

At least twelve architectural complexes (temple/long structure/altar complex) identified at Mayapan may correspond to Landa's description of twelve families of priests and nobles residing there (Tozzer 1941: 40; Fox 1987: 24). Burials found beneath longhouse shrines at Mayapan and in the highlands (Fox 1987: 25) suggest the importance of lineage power at these communities. Different investigators tallying structural "groups" or "types" at Mayapan tend to come up with a range of numerical figures. For example, Diane Chase (1985: 113) tallies twenty-six colonnaded halls and ten temples in the site's center. Proskouriakoff described seventeen structural groups of civic/religious architecture in the site's center (1962a: 100–124). However, the diachronic nature of this site's formation could account for various numbers of structures that may not all have been in use at the same time. There are numerous references to quadrupartite and other denominations of community or regional partitioning in the accounts of the *Chilam Balam* and Landa (Coe 1965; Landa in Tozzer 1941: 21).

Ethnohistoric records also provide extensive evidence of lineage-based power at the time of Spanish contact. The rise and fall of Mayapan is attributable to the interplay of lineage-alliance factionalism. Tales of the unstable history of this polity attest to fissioning processes for which segmentary dynamics are infamous, though opposing factions were not necessarily those tied to divisions of the land as proposed in the segmentary model. The "League of Mayapan" referred to in the documents (Roys 1962; Landa 1941) suggests that communities allied with Mayapan originally organized themselves into a more centralized political confederation based at this site, also a capacity of segmentary polities. This alliance was a more permanent political arrangement lasting two hundred years (Barrera Vasquez and Morley 1949), however, and represents a more stable regional conglomerate than those that are characteristic of fully segmentary systems.

This latter point is significant. Although lineage structures were incorporated into Maya political organization of the Postclassic period (and

25

earlier), there existed crosscutting political institutions that transcended lineage factionalism and facilitated a greater degree of intergroup integration over longer periods of time. This capacity for maintaining a cooperating political sphere of semiautonomous subunits represents a fundamental difference between the political organization of Mayapan and more segmentary polities. Mayapan and smaller centers contemporary with it governed with the aid of an assembly institution, or *multepal* (Roys 1957). Multepal, or group rule, constituted a supralineage bureaucratic entity that provided important checks and balances and a forum for negotiating contradictions. Such assemblies enabled Mayapan and smaller centers to sustain political stability over the course of several generations.

In a recent publication, Blanton (1998) identifies the large-scale economic integration of semiautonomous local subunits (polities and communities) and the use of assembly rule in government as two aspects of "corporate" political strategies. The Postclassic Maya polity of Chichén Itzá is identified by Blanton et al. (1996) as an example of corporate political dogma. Polities that emphasize a "corporate" cognitive code may often do so in partial response to local historical tyranny, and institutions such as assembly rule and local semiautonomy can define themselves in opposition to highly centralized, hierarchical regimes that preceded them (Blanton et al. 1996: 14, Blanton 1998: 147). This may certainly have been the case for Postclassic Maya society, which rejected the institution of divine kingship (Schele and Freidel 1990). It is noteworthy, however, that all societies contain the contradictions that can culminate in their demise. Blanton et al. (1996) argue that corporate strategies only seek to suppress individual quests for monopolization of power and hierarchical development that are inherent in many human societies, and they succeed to varying degrees in space and time.

The divisiveness of Postclassic society, as recorded in the *Books of Chilam Balam*, was also balanced by ritual integration and economic interaction between communities and polities. It is plausible that the "doomsday" prophecies of the Maya chronicles were in part dispensed as a method of social control (Jones 1989; Antje Gunsenheimer, personal communication 1998). Yucatán, Quintana Roo, and Belize were part of a vast system of provinces that engaged in economic exchange (Roys 1957; Pina Chan 1978: 45). Macroregional affiliations are expressed in the Late Postclassic through utilitarian redware and unslipped ceramic traditions and censer rituals (discussed in Chapters 3 and 6). Calendrical ceremonies such as *katun* endings were celebrated throughout provinces and communities (Chapter 6). The lack of quadrupartite patterning visible in the settlement patterns of communities or regions of archaeological sites today does not mean this type of social division was not conceptually applied (Coe 1965).

The Province Model

The province model of Postclassic political organization has its origins in Roys's important work, *The Political Geography of the Yucatán Maya* (1957). Extracting information from various historical sources, he was able to approximate the boundaries of sixteen "provinces," or political territories, in existence at the time of Spanish contact. The province model is well founded in historical accounts, but the boundaries of provinces are in some cases vaguely defined and can be refined through continued historical research (Anthony Andrews 1984; Jones 1989). It is clear that each province was somewhat autonomous. Alliances among provinces formed an integral part of regional economic and political relationships (Andrews 1984) and their populations, political complexity, regional affiliations, and economic roles varied considerably (Quezada 1993; Marcus 1993). These provinces were also the home of communities that specialized in specific types of economic production that capitalized on local resources. Pina Chan (1978: 39–42) documents province-specific production specialization in combinations of items including cacao, honey, wax, fish, turkeys, corn, henequen, maguey, lumber, palms, feathers, copal, cochineal, dyes, flint, pottery, fur, obsidian textiles, and salt from colonial *encomienda* lists.

Evidence suggests that provinces were ranked into loose interprovincial hierarchies, at least for economic purposes. Jones (1989) discusses the subordinate position of the ruler of the Chetumal to the lord of the Acalan province to whom he had to pay tribute. Other than this arrangement, Chetumal was largely autonomous and seems to have been relatively influential and powerful compared to other provinces (Pina Chan 1978: 39). Chetumal is mentioned frequently in late pre-Columbian and protohistoric affairs of Yucatán, and travel to and from Chetumal is documented for merchant lords from Mayapan.

Variation is observed in the degree of hierarchy found within each province. Some territories had a hierarchy of offices beneath the *halach uinic* (or regional lords), including the *batabs* (town rulers), *ah cuch cabs* (councils beneath batabs but providing a balance of power), and other specialized officials such as *ah kulels* (deputies), *nacoms* (war chiefs), and *hol pops* (overseers). Other provinces were less centralized, less hierarchical, more peripheral, and less densely populated (Alexander 1999). In less centralized provinces, some communities were ruled by a batab without the integration of a halach uinic, and other territories may have been formed of loosely allied towns that lacked a batab (Roys 1957; Marcus 1993: Figure 3). The province model is currently undergoing critical reevaluation by scholars working in northern Yucatán (Alexander 1999). Ethnohistorical analyses by Okoshi (1992) and Quezada (1993) conclude that there is little evidence for province organization, and two forms of regional organization are identified (*kuchteel* and *batabil*) that represent affiliated territories of varied integration and hierarchy. The existence of some of the provinces is challenged, including Ecab (Okoshi 1992) and Uaymil (Anthony Andrews, personal communication 1999).

The province model is difficult to evaluate archaeologically through the interpretation of settlement patterns, as little comprehensive survey has been performed and common ceramic styles appear to crosscut province boundaries during the Late Postclassic period. Maps of northern Yucatán (such as Roys 1962: 24) tend to show estimated province boundaries and sites known during the Colonial period, rather than those of the Postclassic. Although the likelihood of Postclassic and colonial settlement overlap is great in this region, systematic 100 percent coverage archaeological survey has only been completed in one study area (Kepecs 1998). Detailed settlement information is patchy for the Late Postclassic southern lowlands. Most of the primary sites of the east coast of Quintana Roo and northern coastal Campeche have been reported by Andrews (1977) or Andrews and Vail (1990). A zone of Postclassic settlements in a lacustrine area of southern Quintana Roo has been located that comprised part of a vicinity referred to as the Uaymil province (Roys 1957; Harrison 1981). Several key historic sites of known and estimated locations have been published by Jones (1989: Map 2), but the remainder of the northern part of the Chetumal province has not been subjected to a full coverage survey. It is difficult to analyze the Chetumal province from the perspective of its southern, Belizean portion alone. A provisional summary of the settlement trends in this territory is offered below in spite of these limitations.

EARLY AND LATE POSTCLASSIC SITE HIERARCHIES IN THE CHETUMAL PROVINCE

The Postclassic period has been traditionally divided into two major subperiods in northern Yucatán, the Early (A.D. 1000–1200) and Late Postclassic (A.D. 1200–1517) (Andrews 1993). In Belize, some investigators have assigned a Middle Postclassic or intermediary phase to specific sites (Valdez 1987; Graham 1987), which overlaps temporally to the latter part of northern Yucatán's Early Postclassic and the early part of the Yucatán Late Postclassic (around A.D. 1100–1300, plus or minus 50 years). The root of this lack of correspondence between northern Yucatán and Belize chronologies is the fact that red-slipped ceramic traditions that differentiate the Terminal Classic/Early Postclassic from later Postclassic periods are recognized earlier in Belize than they are in the north, that is, before A.D. 1200.

Other investigators have dealt with this lack of perfect north-south temporal correspondence in a different manner, assigning an Early (A.D. 1150–1300) and Late Facet (A.D. 1300–1550) to the Late Postclassic of northern Belize (Chase and Chase 1988: Table 1; Walker 1990). In northern Yucatán, the Terminal Classic/Early Postclassic is now thought to be earlier than previously thought (Andrews 1993: 93; Bey, Hanson, and Ringle 1997). This observation implies that the ensuing Late Postclassic period was longer in the north than has been assumed (Robles and Andrews 1986: 90). For reasons that are fully described in Chapter 3, the use of two temporal facets is adopted in the chronological analyses of Laguna de On. The Postclassic period sites that were found on survey in northern Belize, however, have been temporally classified to either Early or Late Postclassic periods in the literature. The examination of settlement patterns over time, provided below, thus uses these temporal divisions, as the data were primarily reported in this way.

Ethnohistoric Evidence

Postclassic sites that have been identified in northern Belize and southern Quintana Roo are shown in Figures 2.2 and 2.3. This settlement data has been compiled from Thompson (1939), Diane Chase (1982), Sidrys (1983), and Walker (1990). Ethnohistoric sources claim that Yucatán was named *uluumil cuz etel ceh* or "the land of turkeys and deer" (Landa in Tozzer 1941: 4). Northern Belize is located in the southern part of the Yucatán peninsula (Figure 2.2). The capital of the Chetumal province at contact was a center of the same name (Chetumal), which is thought to be located at Santa Rita Corozal (Chase and Chase 1982; for alternate views see Lothrop 1924: 10; Jones 1989: Appendix 1). Chetumal was described as a town located two leagues from the sea, almost surrounded by water, with the sea on one side and a lagoon on the other (Oviedo y Valdez Lib. XXXII, cap. VI). Most of northern Belize and part of the Belize Valley area spoke Yucatec in Classic period times (Schele 1989: 7, Figure 5), as inscriptions transcribed from these areas spell out Yucatec words. This linguistic distribution provides important information about political alliance, social interaction spheres, and economic exchange that should be reflected in the archaeological record.

In the Late Classic and Terminal Classic/Early Postclassic periods, a vicinity around Laguna Bacalar was referred to as Siyancan-Bakhalal, which means "sky-born, surrounded by reeds" (Schele 1995). The name Siyancan was earlier used in the Maya Lowlands for the name of Yaxchilan (Schele 1995: 11), but no relationship has been proposed. According to the *Chilam Balam* of Mani chronicle, this location was "discovered" by the Itzá, who were travelling up from "the south" in Katun 2 Ahau before they discovered Chichén Itzá (as noted by Tozzer 1941:29). In Late Postclassic and colonial times, southern Quintana Roo and northern Belize comprised the Chetumal province (Roys 1957; Diane Chase 1982; Jones 1989). It is unclear what the relationship of the place name of Siyancan-Bakhalal is to the Chetumal province, but Laguna Bacalar (probably derived from Bakhalal) is on the boundary of the Uaymil and Chetumal provinces at Spanish contact according to Jones (1989: Map 2). It is not known if Siyancan-Bakhalal was a site or an earlier province name. Most other place names referring to migrations in the *Books of Chilam Balam* (such as Chakanputun, Pole, Motul, Tan Xuluc Mul, and Chichén Itzá) refer to specific settlements, so Siyancan-Bakhalal is most likely a community name also.

Laguna de On was located at the southern end of the protohistoric Chetumal province area, near the boundary of the Chetumal and Dzuluinicob territories (Jones 1989: Map 2). Based on the geographic (Freshwater Creek) and ceramic affiliations of Laguna de On with the north, however, it is probable that this site was most closely affiliated with Chetumal. The Chetumal province was affluent from the production of cacao and honey (Chase 1986). D'Avila's initial failed attempt at establishing the settlement of Villa Real was motivated by the desire to exploit the rich resources of this province (Jones 1989). D'Avila's defeat was followed by the atrocious retri-butions and conquest of this province by the Pacheco brothers of Bacalar. The Pacheco inquisition annihilated much of the population of this prov-ince on the Mexican side, and it stimulated refugee flight to the south and one of the first of many rebellions in the Belize frontier in 1547 (Jones 1989). This rebellion was led by a new indigenous capital of the province after the town of Chetumal had been abandoned, known as Chanlacan, probably located at Progresso Lagoon (Jones 1989: Map 2) on the island site of Caye Coco (Masson and Rosenswig 1998a, 1998b). This is the same water-way that connects Laguna de On to the Caribbean Sea, and Caye Coco was a significant political center in Late Postclassic times that would have prob-ably extracted tribute from Laguna de On and served as an intermediary for external trade contacts.

Prior to the Spanish Conquest, the Chetumal province was governed by a halach uinic, Nachan Kan. The existence of such an official suggests that this was one of the more hierarchical provinces of the Late Postclassic period. Settlement patterns also reflect this trend, as they exhibit a two- or three-tiered site hierarchy, with one paramount center, several smaller secondary centers, and a third tier of villages or hamlets (not unlike that observed for Mississippian chiefdoms, Smith 1978). The coexistence of mul-tiple centers during the Late Postclassic period in Belize suggests that such a three-tiered hierarchy must have existed. As Chetumal is documented his-torically to be the "capital" or paramount center of this province, other centers (such as Caye Coco) probably represent contemporary secondary centers or former seats of government that existed before the center of Chetumal came to power.

To the south and west of the Chetumal province, the Dzuluinicob prov-ince has been identified by Jones (1989: Map 2). This province includes the important Postclassic and colonial sites of Lamanai and Tipu, and connects two major riverine systems, the New River and the Belize River, via an important overland route. The area of this province is vast and numerous ecological zones and geographic boundaries are present within it. It is not known whether smaller provinces might have been defined within this region prior to protohistoric and colonial times. Little is known of the existence of secondary centers associated with Lamanai, which was clearly a paramount center for this region during part of the Postclassic period in Belize (Pendergast 1981, 1985).

Postclassic Archaeological Site Hierarchies

Political capitals in the Belize Postclassic are identified primarily at Lamanai and Santa Rita (Pendergast 1981, 1985; Diane Chase 1982; Chase and Chase 1988), based on the construction of architecture, the modification of or additions to Classic period architecture, and the recovery of burials with numerous grave goods (ceramic vessels, effigies, metal ornaments or bells) or elaborate caches. Both sites possess components that extend from the tenth to the sixteenth centuries (the seventeenth for Lamanai).

Lamanai's role as a Postclassic capital (Buk phase or Middle Postclassic) probably stemmed from its existing position as a Late Classic capital (Pendergast 1985). Unlike its neighbors, Lamanai is thought to have continued its existing role, embodying "stability through change" and even capitalizing on changing political dynamics associated with the collapse of many of its peers (Pendergast 1985). The modification of a Classic period monumental structure is thought to reflect the political importance of the site in the earlier centuries of the Postclassic period. The magnitude of Lamanai's role later in the Postclassic period (Cib phase) is less clear, though the types of deposits described from this period include important burials with effigy censers that suggest that some inhabitants of Lamanai continued to belong to the upper stratum of regional society at this time (Pendergast 1981).

Santa Rita is thought to have been a Late Postclassic capital based on the presence of numerous caches associated with residential groups. These caches are probably the remains of Uayeb calendrical ceremonies hosted by political leaders of the community as recorded in ethnohistoric documents (Diane Chase 1982, 1986, 1988). Santa Rita's political role is also based on the presence of murals discovered there by Gann (1918; Chase and Chase 1988) and the hypothesis that it was the location of the ethnohistorically recorded capital of Chetumal. Archaeological remains from the Early and Late Postclassic at Santa Rita do not reflect architectural grandeur, as most of the structures of this date represent line-of-stone buildings, or broad, flat basal platforms (Chase and Chase 1988). Some of these platforms were built during the Formative or Classic period (Sidrys 1983; Diane Chase 1982). The site is very dispersed and has been heavily impacted by the development of the town of Corozal (Chase and Chase 1988; Diane Chase 1990). It is no longer possible to assess its full extent. Descriptions of the deposits at Santa Rita suggest that the site was important in the Early and Late Postclassic periods, as many late deposits that were the focus of research at this site are underlain by earlier Postclassic components (Diane Chase 1982; Chase and Chase 1988).

A survey of northern Belize conducted by Sidrys (1983: Table 1, Figure 4) has identified several important Postclassic centers and supporting communities in the Corozal district. Some of Sidrys's sites that were important in the Early Postclassic remain significant in the Late Postclassic, following the Lamanai and Santa Rita pattern. An exception to this pattern may be Aventura, which was important in the Early Postclassic but appears to have converted to a pilgrimage center where only censers are found in the Late Postclassic (Sidrys 1983). The emergence of other new centers during the Late Postclassic suggests an organizational shift in this region after A.D. 1200. Sidrys's assessments are preliminary, as they are based on survey and limited excavations. As the Lamanai and Santa Rita projects have shown (Pendergast 1981; Chase and Chase 1988), many important Postclassic constructions are buried and are not detectable from the surface.

Nonetheless, Sidry's survey represents the most extensive documentation of Postclassic settlement on the regional level for Belize and it facilitates a preliminary view of diachronic patterns for this period. In Figures 2.2 and 2.3, his results are combined with those of others (Thompson 1939; Sanders 1960; Harrison 1981; Jones 1989; Lewenstein and Dahlin 1990; Andrews and Vail 1990; Guderjan and Garber 1995) to indicate the distribution of Early and Late Postclassic sites in the northern Belize/southern Quintana Roo region. For the purposes of this examination, "centers" are defined as either especially large sites (based on site area reported in Sidrys 1983: Table 1, Figure 4), sites with large Postclassic architecture or other conspicuous features attesting to wealth and power, or sites of high rank assigned by Sidrys (1983: Table 1). Supporting village or hamlet settlements are those that lack large size, conspicuous Postclassic period mounds or other features, or sites with low ranking assigned by Sidrys (1983: Table 1).

Early Postclassic (A.D. 1000–1200) sites in the Chetumal province vicinity include the following centers, in order of magnitude: Aventura, Sarteneja, Santa Rita/Wilson's Beach, and Shipstern (Figure 2.2). Supporting settlements of this period include Bandera, Cenote, Chan Chen, Consejo, Patchchakan, Nohmul, Albion Island (San Antonio), Colha, Kichpanha, Cerros, San Estevan, K'axob, Progresso Lagoon, Last Resort, and Laguna de On. In the Belize Valley, contemporary Early Postclassic settlements include Barton Ramie (Willey et al. 1965) and San Jose (Thompson 1939). Late Postclassic sites (defined as those occupied at any point in time between A.D.

1200 and 1500 in the Chetumal province vicinity) include the following five centers: Santa Rita/Wilson's Beach, Ichpaatun, Caye Coco, Sarteneja, and Bandera (Figure 2.3). Supporting settlements occupied within this time period include Albion Island (San Antonio), Kichpanha, Colha, Laguna de On, Aventura, Cerros, San Estevan, K'axob, Pucte, Cave, Cenote, Chan Chen, Condemned Point II, Consejo, Patchchakan, Ramonal, Sajomal, Shipstern, Xcanlum, Saltillo, Laguna, Carolina, Last Resort, Chunox, Tamalcab, and Bacalar. Known colonial sites in the southern Quintana Roo/ northern Belize vicinity include Santa Rita/Chetumal, Mazanahau/Mazanila, Xoca/Chable, Chequitaquil, Tamalcab/La Iglesia/Chinam, Rancho del Obispo, Bacalar, Uatibal/Last Resort, and Chanlacan/Caye Coco. Not all of these sites have been positively located (Jones 1989: Map 2).

For each period, four or five centers are identified in the region that extends north-south from Bacalar to Laguna de On and east-west from the Caribbean coast to the Rio Hondo. The presence of multiple contemporary centers in this province in each time period is compatible with a three-tier political model for this province, in which one center would have occupied a paramount position of political power, accompanied by lower-ranking supporting centers. Alternatively, this pattern may represent a set of relatively equivalently ranked local centers. During the Early Facet of the Postclassic, sixteen supporting villages (non-centers) are reported, compared to twenty-six such sites in the Late Postclassic. At first glance, these data may suggest an increase in the number of small communities during the Late Postclassic in the Chetumal vicinity. The ratio of centers to villages is thus approximately 1:4 in the Early Postclassic and 1:5.2 in the Late Postclassic. These comparable ratios suggest that the number of regional centers in the Chetumal province vicinity remained relatively stable over time, with a possible population increase. However, the use of the term "center" to describe large settlements during the Early Postclassic may be pushing the definition of this term as a node of political leadership. It is notable that with the exception of Lamanai and possibly Aventura, mound architecture or other conspicuous elite constructions is not observed at large Early Postclassic sites. This pattern contrasts with that of large Late Postclassic sites of this region, such as Ichpaatun, Caye Coco, and Santa Rita, which have clear expressions of elite power in the form of either architecture, murals, or stone monuments. This difference may signal a greater development of power hierarchies over time in this region.

The compilation of settlement data for the Early and Late Postclassic periods in the Chetumal vicinity (Figures 2.2 and 2.3) reflects one important pattern: population levels flourished in both periods. Systematic, full-coverage survey is likely to reveal many more sites in the Chetumal province vicinity than those listed above. A large number of sites are reported from northern Quintana Roo as well (Sanders 1960). Further work on chronological refinement at the regional level is needed before detailed settlement analysis is possible for this region.

A couple of problems may exist with the patterns identified above. First, sites dating to the Late Postclassic, defined for the purpose of this examination as those occupied from A.D. 1200 to 1500, cover three hundred years, compared to the two-hundred-year span of the Early Postclassic, A.D. 1000–1200. This pattern alone could result in more sites, but this is probably not the case. Most investigators from whom this data is extracted would include Terminal Classic/Early Postclassic sites in with classification of Early Postclassic (Diane Chase 1982; Sidrys 1983; Walker 1990). This inclusion could add at least one hundred years (A.D. 900–1000) of settlement and make comparisons more equitable. The second variable affecting increased numbers of Late Postclassic sites is the fact that they are later and occupy a stratigraphic position over Early Postclassic deposits. They are thus more easily spotted on the surface during survey. The assessment offered above is thus a preliminary attempt, which will hopefully be refined as more regional research is devoted to Postclassic settlement.

SUMMARY

Laguna de On is located in a fertile agrarian zone near the southern boundary of the Chetumal and Dzulunicob provinces (Jones 1989: Map 2). The relationship between these provinces in pre-Columbian times is not well known, but there is no record of conflict and shared ceramic utilitarian styles provide no indication of substantial differences in these subregions. This position may have put Laguna de On at an advantage for brokering the exchange of commodities between the provinces. However, the boundary location of Laguna de On may have made it vulnerable and in greater need of defense. The island core of this lagoon settlement would have provided a defensible location. It probably served as the civic center of the lagoon community and a location to which shore populations could retreat if threat of conflict was imminent. The site is located near the headwaters of Freshwater Creek, a waterway that linked it to trading networks along Belize's Caribbean coast. Between this site and the coast, however, a large island political center, Caye Coco, was situated. The role of Laguna de On in larger cultural networks of the Early and Late Postclassic periods was that of a rural settlement engaged in production of surplus crafts and consumables and the extraction of natural resources for exchange and tributary payments to centers such as Caye Coco that were probably modest. As Chapters 4 and 5 will describe, production of ceramics, textiles, probably cacao and honey, and the extraction of wild resources (fish, turtles, and terrestrial game) and chalcedonies were the prime foundations of this community's economy. It may also have moved commodities made by neighboring communities, such as Colha stone tools and other products from the Dzuluinicob province, northward to Caye Coco or coastal trading ports.

Investigations to date at Laguna de On and neighboring vicinities have revealed strip settlements along the shores of lagoons and creeks of the Freshwater Creek drainage, as well as on island sites such as Laguna de On, Caye Coco, and Caye Muerto (Masson and Rosenswig 1998). This chapter's preliminary tally of Postclassic settlements in the Chetumal province vicinity indicates a center-village ratio of 1:5.2 for the Late Postclassic. This ratio is increased, though not greatly, from a comparable 1:4 ratio during the preceding Early Postclassic periods. It is probably significant that the location of some political centers changed around A.D. 1200, suggesting that a realignment occurred in the power dynamics of this region. Preliminary as they are, these patterns support the hypothesis that a three-tiered political hierarchy existed in the Chetumal province vicinity prior to the arrival of the Spanish. The coexistence of multiple contemporaneous centers reflects a nested, complex hierarchy of polities that is analogous on a smaller scale to political structures documented for the southern lowlands during the Classic period (Matthews 1991; Marcus 1993). The relationship of these centers is not well understood. They may have formed an integrated, hierarchical regional polity, or they may reflect a group of coeval, equivalently ranked competitors. Further comparative research is needed to clarify the relationships of these centers to each other. The data reviewed in this chapter suggest that Laguna de On was operating within a moderately hierarchical regional landscape filled with a substantial number of settlements of different sizes and political significance.

Four models that characterize aspects of Postclassic period political development and settlement patterning were reviewed in this chapter. Attributes described in all of these models are observed to various degrees in the archaeological record of the Chetumal province. Evidence for foreign invasion is difficult to assess at the end of the Classic period, and this phenomenon has only been documented at a couple of sites. However, it is clear that foreign influence was felt in northern Belize by the Early Postclassic period. Ceramic attributes that resemble those of Chichén Itzá are combined with local southern red-slipped pottery traditions, and this incorporation is probably the result of the participation of northern Belize in the circum-Yucatán maritime trade network that formed the basis of Chichén Itzá's power. The process of migration of populations into northern Belize remains difficult to track archaeologically. It is most likely that migrations were common from south to north as well as the reverse, as suggested in documentary accounts. It is clear from the number of Postclassic settlements that if foreign invasion or migration were solely responsible for

35

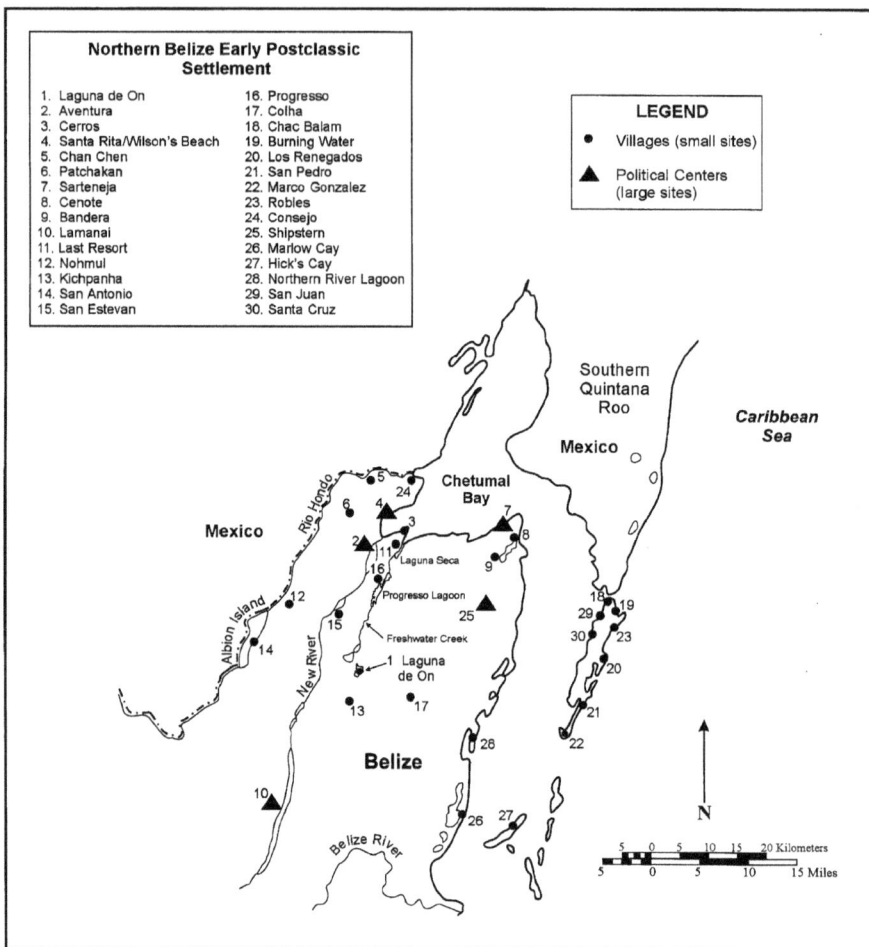

Northern Belize Early Postclassic Settlement

1. Laguna de On
2. Aventura
3. Cerros
4. Santa Rita/Wilson's Beach
5. Chan Chen
6. Patchakan
7. Sarteneja
8. Cenote
9. Bandera
10. Lamanai
11. Last Resort
12. Nohmul
13. Kichpanha
14. San Antonio
15. San Estevan
16. Progresso
17. Colha
18. Chac Balam
19. Burning Water
20. Los Renegados
21. San Pedro
22. Marco Gonzalez
23. Robles
24. Consejo
25. Shipstern
26. Marlow Cay
27. Hick's Cay
28. Northern River Lagoon
29. San Juan
30. Santa Cruz

LEGEND

● Villages (small sites)

▲ Political Centers (large sites)

2.2. Archaeological sites with reported Early Postclassic components in northern Belize (A.D. 900 or 1000 to A.D. 1200).

occupation of the Chetumal province in the Early Postclassic, these events would have involved thousands of people. More likely, migrations involved elite colonists and their lineage affiliates in more modest numbers. Such newcomers would have encountered a landscape settled with local populations, with whom they intermarried. The latter scenario is favored by this author, given the evidence for elite migrations and assimilations described in documents and suggested by architectural analysis (Don Rice 1988; Schele 1995). Later in the Postclassic period, long-distance (if not foreign) ties do link Belize to northern Quintana Roo and Mayapan, based on ceramic similarities discussed in Chapter 3.

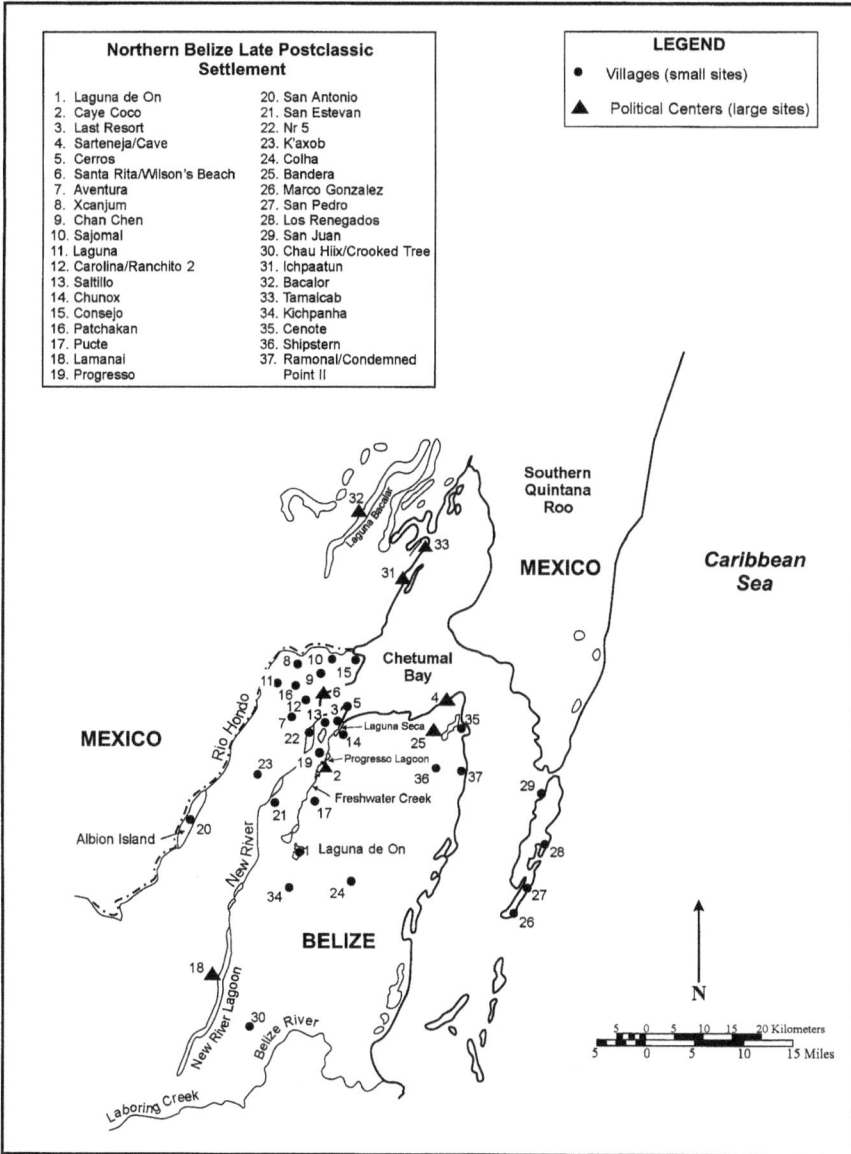

Northern Belize Late Postclassic Settlement

1. Laguna de On
2. Caye Coco
3. Last Resort
4. Sarteneja/Cave
5. Cerros
6. Santa Rita/Wilson's Beach
7. Aventura
8. Xcanjum
9. Chan Chen
10. Sajomal
11. Laguna
12. Carolina/Ranchito 2
13. Saltillo
14. Chunox
15. Consejo
16. Patchakan
17. Pucte
18. Lamanai
19. Progresso
20. San Antonio
21. San Estevan
22. Nr 5
23. K'axob
24. Colha
25. Bandera
26. Marco Gonzalez
27. San Pedro
28. Los Renegados
29. San Juan
30. Chau Hiix/Crooked Tree
31. Ichpaatun
32. Bacalor
33. Tamaicab
34. Kichpanha
35. Cenote
36. Shipstern
37. Ramonal/Condemned Point II

LEGEND

● Villages (small sites)

▲ Political Centers (large sites)

2.3. Archaeological sites with reported Late Postclassic components in northern Belize (A.D. 1200–1500).

Ceramic affinities suggest that Late Postclassic Belize was participating in a broad lowlands economic sphere of Yucatec speakers extending from the Peten Lakes through Belize, Quintana Roo, and Yucatán. Late Postclassic population growth was stimulated by accelerated economic production and trade along the east coast of the Yucatán peninsula (including Belize) during this time, as suggested by the mercantile model. The identification of multiple centers in northern Belize may indicate the presence of a number of competitors in this regions or a nested hierarchy as the documents imply (Roys 1957; Marcus 1993). Although the province model is currently under scrutiny, it remains a useful framework for the study of the Chetumal territory, which is well documented in ethnohistoric accounts as a cohesive political unit that was organized under the governance of a halach uinic at the time of Spanish contact. The integration of lineage factions in political assemblies is addressed more fully in Chapters 6 and 7. Although segmentary structures and processes do characterize elements of Late Postclassic Lowland Maya society, kin factions were transcended by important and effective supra-kin institutions. These themes of regional organization are further explored from the perspective of Laguna de On in subsequent chapters of this book.

3

Northern Belize Postclassic Ceramic Chronology

Problems in establishing the chronology in the Maya Postclassic period have impeded the analysis of cultural processes that occurred from the Classic southern lowland collapse to the arrival of the Spanish. There are four types of data that have been used to assess Postclassic chronology: ethnohistorical, iconographic, ceramic sequences, and absolute methods (radiocarbon or obsidian hydration). This chapter deals primarily with archaeological forms of chronological data for the Postclassic: ceramic typology and radiocarbon dates from Laguna de On. The uneven nature of historical and archaeological data sets has contributed to a number of conflicting accounts and interpretations of Postclassic Maya history and political evolution (Arlen Chase 1986; Ball 1985: 397; Lincoln 1986; Willey 1986: 37). Ethnohistoric information pertinent to the precontact period is primarily in the form of inexact mythic histories and prophecies recorded in Landa's *Relaciones de las Cosas de Yucatán* and the *Books of Chilam Balam* after the Spanish Conquest (Roys 1962). It is difficult to sort mythical events from historical facts in these chronicles, and the use of katun dates in these records makes it hard to know the century in which specific events may have taken place. Despite these limitations, these sources have contributed immeasurably to the analysis of Postclassic and Colonial period historical processes (Tozzer 1941; Barrera and Morley 1949; Roys 1957; Bricker 1981; Jones 1989; Marcus 1993; Schele, Grube, and Boot 1995). Some archaeological sequences, such as that of Mayapan, coincide closely with documentary evidence (Pollock 1962; Roys 1962). These are explored further at the conclusion of Chapter 6.

Cross-referencing of archaeological data with documentary accounts has been considerably hindered by the conditions of soil deposition at many Postclassic Maya sites (Sanders 1960; Graham 1985; Lincoln 1986; Prudence Rice 1986: 256; Pendergast, Jones, and Graham 1993). There are two major difficulties with Postclassic deposits that constrict sound chronological analysis: (1) their shallow surface position and eroded, disturbed condition, and (2) intermingling with earlier deposits. Postclassic populations commonly re-cycled edifices constructed in earlier times, without adding new construc-tion phases that would have clearly separated their occupational debris from that of the Classic period (Adams and Trik 1961; Cowgill 1963). Further compounding this problem is the fact that many Postclassic deposits are found in off-mound locations, often in areas in which soil formation is very poor (Sanders1960; Chase and Chase 1988; Diane Chase 1990; Pendergast 1981). These shallow deposits make ceramic seriation difficult, if not impos-sible at some sites (Brainerd 1958; Sanders 1960). In this chapter, issues of Postclassic ceramic chronology in Belize are discussed that provide the context for the chronological framework used in the analysis of materials from Laguna de On in subsequent chapters. Prior to the presentation of Laguna de On chronology, processes of cultural change and development are discussed that probably affected ceramic styles across the Maya Lowlands. These processes include migrations, the rise and fall of northern Yucatán political capitals, and the growth of international trade along the east coast of the peninsula.

The ongoing phenomenon of elite migrations during the Postclassic pe-riod is evident in documentary accounts. These multiple migrations repeat-edly occurred from south to north and the reverse (Roys 1933: 20, 77, 1957: 50; Barrera and Morley 1949; Schele, Grube, and Boot 1995). The docu-ments claim that lineage migrations came "from the east" at least once, involving a route that probably emerged out of the Peten, through Belize, up the east coast of the Yucatán peninsula to a northern destination (Barrera and Morley 1949: 29–30). Ceramic affinities linking these regions may reflect the movement of groups (Ball and Taschek 1989: 195). As much of Belize spoke Yucatec during the Classic period (Schele 1989: Figure 5), these migrations may reflect more of an intraregional phenomenon than an inter-regional, multi-ethnic one. Alternative hypotheses have proposed a foreign or Gulf Coast Maya identity for migrating Itzá peoples referenced in the *Books of Chilam Balam* (Thompson 1970; Robles and Andrews 1986; Fox 1987; Tourtellot, Sabloff, and Carmean 1992), a southern Peten origin for such groups (Schele, Grube, and Boot 1995), or the existence of two differ-ent groups, one from the Gulf Coast area and one from the Peten/Belize region (Ball and Taschek 1989). Ceramic evidence discussed in this chapter provides some indication of directions of influence in the Late Postclassic period. Processes of migration from south to north appear to have begun in the Classic period as early as the fifth century when the Itzá "discover" the site of Chichén Itzá in A.D. 455 (Barrera and Morley 1949: 29–31; Schele, Grube, and Boot 1995). Schele, Grube, and Boot (1995) proposed that these migrations and monuments associated with them reflect the maintenance of north-south alliances and affiliation long before the beginning of the Postclassic period.

Postclassic political events of northern Yucatán that are chronicled in the historical accounts, such as the establishment and destruction of the centers of Chichén Itzá and Mayapan, clearly had ripple effects in the southern lowlands. In addition to these major events, documentary sources refer repeatedly to political cycles associated with twenty-year katun periods (Barrera and Morley 1949; Bricker 1981; Jones 1989).

The analysis of Postclassic murals from the east coast Maya sites of Tulum and Santa Rita also provides important clues about Postclassic Maya interaction with the outside world (Robertson 1970; Smith and Heath-Smith 1980; Miller 1982; Quirarte 1982). They are important for a consideration of chronology because they have been used to assess historical contacts with foreign groups and for stylistic dating (Miller 1982). The ethnic issue is complex. While some mural stylistic conventions have been the basis for claims of Mexican ethnic intrusion (Robertson 1970: 88; Miller 1982: 74), many core aspects of these murals—including hieroglyphs, material culture (such as ceramic vessels), and deities (Taube 1992)—are clearly of Maya identity and resemble conventions found in the Dresden and Madrid Codices (Don Rice 1974: 111). Archaeological remains associated with the buildings that house the murals are also of local origin and foreign artifacts are not present (Chase and Chase 1988: 82–85).

Foreign elements in these murals are more likely the product of an "international style" of symbols shared across Late Postclassic Mesoamerica (Smith and Heath-Smith 1980; Ringle, Negron, and Bey 1998). The use of this style in ritual contexts may have eased tensions in multi-ethnic trading interactions thought to have occurred at such sites as Tulum (Miller 1982: 75–76) and Cozumel (Freidel and Sabloff 1984). Mural stylistic elements attest to an international realm of economic interaction in the Postclassic Mesoamerican world (Sabloff and Rathje 1975). Although Postclassic Maya murals have been stylistically dated to the fifteenth century (Miller 1982: 56–60; Quirarte 1982; Robertson 1970), associated ceramics could place them anytime during the thirteenth to fifteenth centuries (Sanders 1960; Ball 1982: 110–111). These centuries mark the economic florescence of other Late Postclassic centers including Mayapan (Smith 1971), Cozumel (Sabloff et al. 1974; Robles 1986a, 1986b; Freidel and Sabloff 1984: 179), and Santa Rita (Chase and Chase 1988). Tulum was clearly contemporary with this interaction sphere. Long (1919: 60) has proposed a tun ending date of A.D. 1355 for a sequence of calendrical glyphs on the Santa Rita murals, although others place them in the fifteenth century (Gann 1900; Sidrys 1983: 135).

CERAMIC CHRONOLOGY

The archaeological record of the southern lowlands is complex and variable across space and time. In northern Yucatán, the Early Postclassic is set at A.D. 1000–1200, followed by the Late Postclassic from A.D. 1200 to A.D. 1517 (Andrews 1993). In the southern area, the Late Postclassic period begins at least a century earlier (Chase and Chase 1985), and this has resulted in the assignment of at least two periods or facets to ceramic sequences that extend from A.D. 900 to A.D. 1500 or from A.D. 1000 to A.D. 1500 (Chase and Chase 1985: Figures 2 and 3). Some southern lowlands scholars identify a Middle and Late Postclassic period (Graham 1987: 81; Valdez 1994), while others split this period into early and late facets, which implies more continuity (Diane Chase 1982; Chase and Chase 1988; Prudence Rice 1987a: 95; Masson 1999a, 1999b). Recent revisions of northern Yucatán chronology suggest that Chichén Itzá may have declined as a center by A.D. 1000 (Bey, Hanson, and Ringle 1997; Ringle, Negron, and Bey 1998). New research also suggests that Late Postclassic ceramic traditions such as Mama Red may also originate earlier than A.D. 1200, perhaps around A.D. 1100 (Anthony Andrews, Fernando Robles, personal communication 1999). This date would place the northern wares in a closer temporal alignment to the northern Belize sequence proposed for Laguna de On, Lamanai, Santa Rita, and Cerros.

The ensuing discussion of the Postclassic sequence in terms of two primary Early and Late Postclassic periods reviews difficulties in reconciling various site-based chronologies. At Laguna de On, ceramics exhibit subtle changes throughout deposits that have been dated to radiocarbon ranges of A.D. 1050–1450 (Stafford 1998). A continuum of ceramic manufacture is represented at this site, although ongoing analysis is focusing on the identification of more diagnostic temporal attributes such as form and paste variations to help refine this chronology. The Laguna de On patterns most closely resemble ceramic sequences proposed for Santa Rita (Diane Chase 1982; Chase and Chase 1988: Table 1) and Cerros (Walker 1990), which recognize an Early and Late Facet of the Late Postclassic in a continuum of ceramic production that extends from A.D. 1150 to A.D. 1550 at these sites, and is observed from around A.D. 1050 to 1500 at Laguna de On. The Laguna de On ceramics also share characteristics with assemblages from Colha (Valdez and Mock 1985; Mock 1994, 1997, 1998) and Lamanai (Graham 1987).

The summary below of Postclassic Maya ceramic chronologies is presented in three sections. First, the development of attributes of Postclassic ceramics over time is reviewed from the Terminal Classic forward. Second, key issues pertaining to north-south chronological relationships are reviewed. Third, problems with the chronological phasing associated with Late Postclassic incense burners in northern Belize are addressed. This latter issue is potentially confusing, as it has complicated the identification of "Middle Postclassic" and "Late Postclassic" sequences. In an effort to resolve this confusion, an argument is made in this section for functional variation, which proposes that the Chen Mul censers are contemporary with slipped and unslipped utilitarian ceramics that have been assigned to earlier sequences at some sites. This interpretation is integral to the ceramic phasing at Laguna de On. The final section of this chapter presents the ceramic and radiocarbon chronology from this site, as it is currently understood.

DIACHRONIC DIAGNOSTIC CERAMIC ATTRIBUTES FROM THE EARLY TO LATE POSTCLASSIC PERIODS

The quantification of temporally diagnostic attributes over the 400- to 600-year Postclassic period in the southern lowlands is an elusive process as many ceramic types fall within a continuum of attribute development that does not exhibit clear breaks (Graham 1987). Forms of utilitarian slipped and unslipped ceramic vessels endure, while slip colors grade from an initial orange-red to deeper red slips toward the end of the sequence. The origins of southern lowlands redwares is thought by several scholars to be found in pottery manufactured during the Terminal Classic/Early Postclassic period from A.D. 800 or 1000/1100, based on developmental links in ceramic forms (Pendergast 1985; Graham 1987; Mock 1994). These similarities complicate Early Postclassic identifications, and continued links with these traditions make the dividing line between Early and Late Postclassic difficult to pinpoint. Despite these trends, the appearance of new utilitarian and ritual forms is useful in distinguishing the end of the Early Postclassic and onset of the subsequent Postclassic traditions, which occurred around the turn of the eleventh century in northern Belize (Graham 1987; Chase and Chase 1988; Walker 1990). The analysis of idiosyncratic ritual ceramic wares that are more limited in their distribution further assists in the assignment of chronological divisions (Chase and Chase 1988; Graham and Pendergast 1989).

Terminal Classic/Early Postclassic

The Early Postclassic of northern Belize has been either lumped or split with the Terminal Classic by various investigators. Generally, the Terminal Classic/Early Postclassic (TC/EP) in Belize corresponds to the early part of the Early Postclassic in northern Yucatán (Diane Chase 1982: 553–554). Throughout the TC/EP period (A.D. 800–1000/1100), lingering forms from the ninth century are observed, particularly in the form of TC striated wares and slipped rim ollas, basal break dishes, and tripod flat-based dishes with large hollow feet that may be the precursors of PC tripod sag-bottom dishes that are common at northern Belize Postclassic sites (Graham 1987: 76–78). Engraved cylindrical vessels of the ninth or tenth century at San Jose (Thompson 1939) and Lamanai (Graham 1987) anticipate the post-slip incising that is characteristic of Postclassic wares (Willey et al. 1965: Figures 242, 245; Valdez and Mock 1985).

The TC/EP period is often characterized by surface deposits that are domestic in nature. These deposits may be intermingled from two time periods or they may represent a genuine transitional period at various sites (Graham 1987: 73; Masson 1995; Masson and Mock n.d.). At the site of Colha, a clear hundred-year break after the Terminal Classic is observed prior to an Early Postclassic occupation at this site (Valdez 1987).

The fact that both TC and TC/EP components can be identified in Belize suggests that some deposits end in the tenth century and others endure longer, reflecting transitions in ceramic manufacture that hail the Postclassic period (Masson and Mock n.d.). These surface deposits are difficult to date by absolute means, due to their bioturbated nature (Graham 1987: 75; Masson 1995), which confounds analytical efforts and also causes them to be more highly eroded. The fact that the manufacture of Terminal Classic forms lingers into the Early Postclassic period can render the latter difficult to recognize. Settlement survey may attribute deposits to the Terminal Classic period rather than the TC/EP, based on the identification of forms associated with the former that linger into the latter. A similar problem has been noted for Copan, Honduras (Webster and Freter 1990).

The surface location of late deposits also contributes to a high erosion rate of ceramic sherds, which also obscures diagnostic surface treatment and typological classification based on such attributes. A high fragmentation rate of these assemblages makes even the identification of vessel form difficult. For example, of 12,491 sherds analyzed by Sanders from Tulum, less than 1 percent of this sample was diagnostic to vessel form (1960: Chart 1). Additional careful analysis of TC/EP surface deposits is needed to address issues of population dynamics during and immediately following the Classic period (Webster and Freter 1990).

The Early Postclassic period in Belize is generally hailed by the presence of index artifacts such as spindle whorls (Thompson 1939: 236; Willey et al. 1965: 402), net weights, abundant quantities of obsidian blades, and large amounts of faunal bone in domestic contexts of this period (Scott 1981, 1982; Diane Chase 1982: 481, 492, 493; Masson 1995). Side-notched bifacial projectile points provide an additional diagnostic hallmark (Shafer and Hester 1983; Michaels 1987; Graham 1987: 75). Pedestal base vessels also mark the TC/EP (Graham 1987: 78). These artifacts can help signal TC/EP or EP occupations in surface soils where ceramics may be highly eroded, or where populations are living in buildings built in earlier periods.

What types of ceramics comprise a TC/EP assemblage? A representative example is well reported from Structure 20 at Nohmul, Belize (Diane Chase 1982; Chase and Chase 1982). Ceramic types identified at this structure include Campbell's Red, Chembeku Modeled, Chambel Striated, Savinal Cream, Kik Red, Red Neck Mother Striated, Yantho Incised, Tzibana Gouged-

Incised, Metzabok Slate, Xixilic-Incised grater bowl with Mama Red–type nubbin feet. Had the first six ceramic types been found alone, this assemblage would be classified as TC. If the last four ceramic types have been found alone, then this assemblage would be more readily classified as EP. Found together, they represent a transition.

Ceramic forms of another typical TC/EP assemblage are described by Thompson (1939) for the San Jose V ceramic phase. This assemblage possesses unslipped and red-slipped storage jars with outcurving mouths, outcurved bowls with ring bases, redware jars with tapering mouths, incurving bowls with punctated shoulders, and tripod dishes with globular, elongated, or anthropomorphic legs (Thompson 1939: Figure 80). Trade wares of fine orange and slate ware are also among the San Jose V assemblage (Thompson 1939), as well as a locally made carved orangeware (1939: Figure 39). Thompson notes that "the line between San Jose IV and V is not definite" and that gradual transitions are noted (1939: 163). For example, he notes that a basal overlap dish from San Jose IV evolves into an outcurved bowl of San Jose V through the gradual lengthening and outcurving of the sides. Similarly, at Lamanai, the transition from the pedestal base of the TC/EP to the twelfth-century Buk phase chalice form is observed through the gradual elongation of the base and exaggeration of the lip (Graham 1987: 78). At Santa Rita, the TC/EP is defined by the appearance of Double Mouth water jars, Achote Black bowls, and Kik Red bowls, with some Yucatec influences indicated by the presence of Thin Slate and Puuc slatewares and tricklewares (Chase and Chase 1988: 61).

Where the Early Postclassic is separately defined, this period begins around A.D. 1000 at many sites when the TC/EP period ends (Thompson 1939: 236; Willey et al. 1965: Figure 3; Valdez 1987), suggesting that the transition is complete by this time. New ceramic forms that are classified as diagnostic to the Postclassic include red-slipped "sag-bottom" tripod dishes—which can exhibit a basal break, occasional flanges, exterior decorative incising, or "grater" dish interior incisions—small red-slipped ollas, and incurving rim bowls. Unslipped Postclassic wares include folded-rim ollas, a range of small jars and bowls, composite appliqué censerwares, and low numbers of comals (Valdez and Mock 1985; Mock 1994). These forms are not unique to the Early Postclassic, but are found through the Late Postclassic and into the Spanish colonial period. Their technological attributes appear to improve over time in the Peten Lakes region (Rice 1980: 72–75) and in northern Belize (Masson and Mock n.d.).

Ties of Postclassic Maya Ceramic Types with Earlier Traditions

What was the inspiration for the emergence of Postclassic redwares? Opinion is divided on this topic. Some emphasize the differences from the Classic period to the Postclassic (Valdez and Mock 1985; Mock 1994), while others point out the continuities with past traditions (Willey et al. 1965: 212; Pendergast 1981; Arlen Chase 1985: 198; Prudence Rice 1986: 282; Graham 1987; Ball and Taschek 1989: 195). At Barton Ramie, Willey and colleagues suggest that New Town phase Postclassic ceramics purposefully emulated decorative attributes of a range of earlier ceramic traditions from Middle Formative, Late Formative, Early Classic, and Late Classic periods (1965: 212). This pattern represents a cycling of stylistic conventions that is commonly observed in retrospective "fads" of contemporary societies.

Retrospective attributes of form or decoration noted by Willey and colleagues and others in Postclassic pottery are listed in Table 3.1. The application of a monochrome, waxy orange paste in the Early Postclassic Daylight Orange ceramics at Barton Ramie is similar to the slip of Late Formative Chicanel ceramics (Willey et al. 1965: 212; see also Cowgill 1963: 295). The propensity for the manufacture of waxy, red-slipped wares (Payil Red and Rita Red) of the Postclassic of northern Belize also is reminscent of Late Formative (Chicanel) Sierra Red wares, both in the numerical domination of the redwares among slipped ceramics of assemblages of each period and in the long duration of these redware traditions (Masson 1999c).

Shallow, outflaring tripod dishes are common in assemblages of the Late Classic and Postclassic periods, with the primary differences noted in the development of the sag-bottom base favored at Belize sites in the Postclassic versus the flat base of the Classic period. The flat-bottom tripod dish also continues at some Peten Early Postclassic sites (Cowgill 1963: Figure 5; Bullard 1973: 225, Figure 36; Prudence Rice 1986: Figure 8.2), but the sag-bottom form is also found (Bullard 1970: Figure 26; Prudence Rice 1986: Figure 8.2; Rice 1987a: Figure 40a–d).

Early Classic flanged dishes share much in common with this favored Postclassic bowl or dish form. One of the most distinctive features shared by Early Classic (Actuntan Orange and Dos Arroyos Polychrome) and Postclassic (Payil Red) dishes is the presence of a basal flange (Willey et al. 1965: 215f). Early Classic bowls and basal flanges also share decorative motifs with Postclassic basal flanges, including engraved or painted step-terrace motifs (Willey et al. 1965: Figures 208, 211; Smith 1971: Figure 41; Pendergast 1985: Figure 7.5; Robles 1986c: Foto 45). Cowgill (1963: 348) and Thompson (1939: Figure 59) publish further Late Classic precedents for this step-terrace element that is found on Postclassic ceramics.

Unslipped jars and ollas also represent a continuity with the past in attributes such as impressed fillets, punctation, and the placement of large lugs on jars, as observed as early as the Middle Formative Jenney Creek Mamom phase in Belize (Willey et al. 1965: Figures 189c,d,e, 190a) or San

Jose I (Thompson 1939: Figure 23). Triunfo striated and Red Neck Mother Striated Terminal Classic jar forms give way to functionally analogous large lug-handled jars of the Postclassic. Striated wares are associated with Early Postclassic levels at Tulum (Sanders 1960) and El Meco (Robles 1986c: Foto 33). This pattern is also true for the TC/EP in northern Belize. The Double Mouth Jar represents one form of Early Postclassic striated ware that is recognized in Belize (Sidrys 1983).There is some evidence that striated wares persist into late lots at Mayapan (Smith 1971: Table 4, Figures 28f, 29f, 29m) and never completely disappear throughout the Postclassic at Laguna de On and Caye Coco (Mock 1997, 1998).

Spiked incense vessels also date to at least the Late Formative (as shown on Kaminaljuyu Stela 1) and extend to the Terminal Classic at Uaxactun in Guatemala (Cowgill 1963: 352). They are also found in the Formative, Classic, and Early Postclassic periods of Belize and Quintana Roo (Thompson 1939: 125; Willey et al. 1965: Figures 195h, 209; Chase and Chase 1988: 84–85; Walker 1990; Ball 1977; Miller 1982: Plate 6).

Why would Postclassic forms recall those of a variety of earlier periods in Belize? Willey and colleagues suggest that Postclassic populations may have run out of new ideas, or that they became so decentralized that they lacked regional identity and standardization (1965: 384). Yet the recovery of these elements from the Peten, the Belize Valley, northern Belize, Quintana Roo, and Yucatán suggests that these forms were regionally standardized (Sabloff and Rathje 1975). Like many Postclassic cultures of Mesoamerica, conventions signifying ancestral places and origins were important tools for self-redefinition (Schele and Freidel 1990). There can be no doubt from the many recorded incidences of Postclassic modification of earlier structures (Fry 1985; Pendergast 1985) and movement of earlier deposits in new construction projects (Miller and Farriss 1979; Willey et al. 1965: 291; Chase and Chase 1988: 77–79) that these populations were aware of previous ceramic traditions. Emulation of earlier traditions may have been an innovative way of expressing affinities with the past. A renewed Postclassic interest in ancestral sites and ancestral places is argued elsewhere to have served an important integrative role during social transformations of this period (Walker 1990; Masson 1997).

Early Postclassic/Late Postclassic Transition

In trying to distinguish temporally sensitive attributes at Flores in the Peten Lakes, Cowgill (1963: 357) notes that effigy scroll feet occur earlier in red-slipped tripod dishes, in the Augustine ceramic complex. He further observes that plain (noneffigy) scroll feet occur in Augustine/Paxcaman transitional lots, and trumpet feet are most common in Paxcaman assemblages (1963: 358). Some evidence suggests that Augustine and Paxcaman at least

Table 3.1—Postclassic ceramic attributes found in earlier periods at selected sites: San Jose (Thompson 1939), Benque Viejo (Thompson 1942), Flores (Cowgill 1963), Barton Ramie (Willey et al. 1965: 384; Smith and Gifford 1965), and Lamanai (Graham (1987)

Attribute common in Postclassic assemblages	Middle Preclassic	Early Classic	Late Classic	Terminal Classic
Redware tripod dishes			Benque Viejo IIIa	Lamanai
basal-break dishes				Lamanai
shallow, out-flaring wall dishes			Barton Ramie	
sag-bottom dishes/bowls			Benque Viejo IIIa	
step-terrace feet			Benque Viejo IIIa	
step-terrace basal flange			Benque Viejo III, Barton Ramie	
miscellaneous basal flange		Dos Arroyos Polychrome, Acuntan Orange (Barton Ramie and many sites)		
painted step-fret decoration		many sites	Flores	
engraved step-fret decoration			Barton Ramie	
notched basal flange				Benque Viejo IV
oven-footed tripod				Benque Viejo IV
impressed filleted appliqué	Jenney Creek (Barton Ramie)		Benque Viejo IIIb	
large lugs on jars	Jenney Creek, San Jose I		San Jose	

continued on next page

Table 3.1—*continued*

Attribute common in Postclassic assemblages	Middle Preclassic	Early Classic	Late Classic	Terminal Classic
cone-shaped feet			Benque Viejo IIIb	
exterior punctate designs	Jenney Creek (Barton Ramie)	Viejo IIIa	Benque	
monochrome, waxy orange slip	Chicanel (many lowland sites)			
spiked censer vessels	Kaminaljuyu		Uaxactun	

partially overlap, or that they may represent contemporary traditions manufactured by neighboring geopolitical units (Prudence Rice 1986: 282–283).

In the Belize Valley, both Augustine- and Paxcaman-related ceramics are reported in the New Town Complex (Willey et al. 1965: 384). Ixpop Polychrome ceramics, resembling Topoxte ceramics, may have come from the Peten Lakes (Willey et al. 1965: 388). In this early report, Willey and colleagues do not consider that these complexes may be sequential rather than contemporary, as subsequent investigators have concluded. However, there is substantial overlap among Augustine and Paxcaman ceramics in the Peten (Arlen Chase 1986: 119), so the occurrence of Early and Late ceramic types at Barton Ramie most likely reflects this transition.

At Lamanai, it is noted that red slips are first common in the Terminal Classic, and a gradual preference for orange slips is seen over time (Graham 1987: 79), culminating in their full development during the Buk phase. The Buk phase begins by the twelfth century, and it has been radiocarbon dated from a series of burials associated with the ceramics (Pendergast 1981; Graham 1987: 81). These dates and the associated florescence of the Buk phase partly overlap with the time frame that has been associated with Augustine (A.D. 1000–1200) in the Peten, although Buk wares continue later in time. Buk phase orange redware ceramics were also recovered at Tipu, where they dated to the twelfth century and A.D. 1200 transition (Graham 1987: 86). The Buk phase may endure into the thirteenth century, according to Pendergast (1981), and transitions into Tulum-related Cib ceramics are reported in the fourteenth century (Graham 1987). The Buk phase, associated with well-developed orange redwares, is thus most securely dated to the twelfth century, and falls within the earlier portion of the Postclassic as generally defined for the southern and northern lowlands. Pendergast (1981, 1986) and Graham (1987: 82) rightfully caution, however, that ceramic complexes transform over time and are thus difficult to pinpoint in absolute sequences. Buk-phase diagnostics are well described and are quite useful for defining criteria of earlier Postclassic orange redwares in northern Belize. Attributes of these ceramics include orange lustrous slips, elaborate post-slip incision, bands around vessel exteriors, tripod hollow vented effigy feet, segmented flanges, collared rims on jars and bowls, basal-break pedestal-base bowls, chalices, ladle censers (with or without effigies), and censers and bowls with appliqué effigies (Graham 1987: 82). Effigy censers, bowls, and cups are said to anticipate later Chen Mul–like forms of the Late Postclassic (Graham 1987: 82, 86).

Ceramic attributes that have been attributed primarily to the Early Postclassic at Colha include the following: orange-slipped pottery, narrow rolled rims, vessel supports that are bulbous or rounded, incised designs that are deeply cut, mat designs, and other geometric motifs (Valdez and Mock 1985: 71). These attributes are thought to be affiliated with the Augustine complex of the Peten Lakes. Later, ceramics affiliated with the Paxcaman sphere of the Peten Lakes and the site of Tulum (Valdez and Mock 1985: 72) exhibit the following distinguishing characteristics: dark red slip, wide folded rims, cylindrical or effigy vessel supports, and free-flowing incised designs with interlocking scrolls. Valdez and Mock (1985: 73) believe this darker red-slipped complex emerged in the twelfth century.

At Mayapan, a mixture of Chichén Itzá–related slatewares is found to occur at early levels with Postclassic redwares (Pollock 1962: 6). The Sotuta complex at Chichén Itzá is primarily defined by Chichén Red ware, Chichén Unslipped, and Chichén Slate, with the presence of Plumbate and Fine Orange tradewares also noted (Smith 1971). Chichén Red ware includes the following forms: dishes, small-mouth high-neck jars, some incised decorations, wide-mouth jars, restricted direct-rim bowls, grater bowls, tripod dishes, cylindrical vases, flaring dishes, and vases. Designs include some incision of jars and dishes, and the scroll and step-fret design is common (Smith 1971: 170–181). Chichén Unslipped ceramics include striated and unstriated jars, hourglass censers, composite censers, appliqué-striated and tripod censers, ladle censers, flaring-sided bowls, globular bowls, and restricted-orifice bowls. According to Smith, Chichén Slate wares include dishes, restricted bowls, grater bowls, small- and wide-mouth jars, tripod dishes, ladle censers, Fine Orange vessels, jars, hemispherical bowls, tripod dishes, vases, and restricted-orifice bowls. Robert E. Smith (1971: 253) notes that the principal wares of red, unslipped, and slate ceramics at Chichén Itzá (Early Postclassic Sotuta phase) changed little from the preceding Cehpech phase (Terminal Classic), and that Chichén ceramics were made by Maya potters with little Toltec or

Mexican influence. These forms bear resemblances to those of the contemporary red-slipped and unslipped ceramics of northern Belize, although slips are less similar and the orange redware tradition is distinctive to southern lowlands EP sites. Northern Belize is located in an intermediate zone between northern Yucatán and the Peten, and EP assemblages of this region appear to incorporate selected elements of Chichén ceramic technology, such as imitation slate pastes and decorative incising, into local design (Valdez and Mock 1985; Masson and Mock n.d.).

The overlap of many ceramic attributes from Early to Late Postclassic complicates the assessment of chronological indicators of these periods (Rice and Rice 1985: 181), and a gradual transition is noted in the Peten (Arlen Chase 1986: 119), at Lamanai (Graham 1987), and at Santa Rita (Chase and Chase 1988). The Peten Paxcaman ceramic complex, extending from A.D. 1200 to contact, is one of the most long-lived ceramic traditions, especially if some of these wares were manufactured as late as the seventeenth century as suggested by Chase and Chase (1985: 15). The lengthy duration of this phase, considering its origins in even earlier Augustine Peten sphere ceramics, is an impressive indication of long-term societal stability.

Late Postclassic

Late Postclassic southern-lowland ceramics generally possess deeper red slips in contrast to earlier orange-red slips observed in this area. In northern Belize, the sites of Santa Rita and Lamanai serve as the primary indices for diagnostics ceramics of this period. The Cib phase ceramics at Lamanai are not as well understood in space and time as the preceding Buk phase (Graham 1987: 88). Shared attributes of Buk and Cib phase ceramics are observed alongside new attributes that resemble Tulum wares (Graham 1987: 88). The Late Postclassic Cib phase at Lamanai exhibits continuities with earlier Buk phase orangewares marked by post-slip incision, slipped and flanged pedestal base censers, hollow effigy feet, and collared strap-handle jars (Graham 1987: 88). Tulum (Payil Red) related traits that appear during this phase at Lamanai include sag-bottom dishes, hollow cylindrical vessel feet with pairs of circular vents, and a preference for a deeper red and less-lustrous slip (Graham 1987: 88). Chen Mul–like effigy censers are associated with these redwares, as well as small censers in the forms of pedestal base cups with effigies on the side (Graham 1987: 88–90). This assessement of the Cib phase does not include the unslipped utilitarian wares (Graham 1988: 88).

Chase and Chase (1988: 78–79) extend the Xabalxab complex at Santa Rita from A.D. 1150 to A.D. 1550 At Santa Rita, an earlier facet of this complex is thought to be related to Tulum Red wares, while the Late Facet seems more derivative of Mayapan-like ceramics as determined by censer subcomplexes at the site (Chase and Chase 1988: 61). Walker (1990: 80–115) provides a succinct description of Early and Late Facet Kanàn ceramic types from Cerros, which parallel the Early and Late Facet Xabalxab intervals defined for Santa Rita. Although they divide this complex into Early and Late Facets, distinguishing utilitarian slipped and unslipped characteristics of each facet is difficult (Chase and Chase 1988). Early Facet Xabalxab is described as possessing ceramics related to Payil Red and other Tulum wares, including the attributes listed above that are shared between Lamanai and Tulum (Chase and Chase 1988: 78). This Early Facet Xabalxab is thought to end around A.D. 1300, which implies that the Tulum sequence also ceases at this time (Chase and Chase 1988: 78–79). This interpretation conflicts with the majority of others sequences proposed for Tulum (Sanders 1960; Miller 1982; Barrera 1977; Ball 1982; Robles 1986c), which suggest this site was first occupied around A.D. 1200 and continued until around Spanish contact (or just before).

Late Xabalxab ceramics appear to include a number of ritual wares (Chase and Chase 1988: 78–79, Figure 11 [l–q]) as a series of cache deposits represent the later occupation of this site. The Late Xabalxab ceramics are compared to Lamanai Yglesias phase (A.D. 1450–1700) ceramics, also based primarily on ritual censer forms (Chase and Chase 1988: 79). Utilitarian forms associated with the Late Facet Xabalxab complex include Rita Red and Santa Unslipped ceramics (Diane Chase 1982, 1984). Differences in paste suggest a local evolution of technology from earlier Payil-related ceramics. While some forms are shared between Rita Red and Payil, the addition of new forms, such as lug-handled long-necked "parenthesis-rim" jars and flat-bottomed tripod bowls, are noted among Rita varieties that resemble those at Mayapan (Diane Chase 1982, 1984; Walker 1990: 80–115). The addition of new forms to existing assemblages in the latter half of the Late Postclassic period is an important marker for the influence of Mayapan at Belize sites.

At Mayapan, most ceramic types of the Hocaba and Tases phases defined for the Late Postclassic are shared (see Appendix, this volume, compiled from Smith 1971). Shared wares include the following types: Mama Red, Papacal Incised, Yacman Striated, Peto Cream wares, and Xcanchakan Black-on-Cream wares. A few types are added to this list in the Tases phase (Appendix). Most of the exclusively Tases-affiliated wares are either present in low numbers at the site, or they represent specialty vessels of a ritual nature (like Chen Mul effigies). For example, Mama Red jars represent 83 percent of the Hocaba red-slipped wares at the site and 63 percent of the Tases red-slipped wares (Appendix). Most of the remaining red-slipped wares are represented by shallow tripod dishes in both phases (9 percent Hocaba, 17 percent Tases; Appendix). Unslipped wares (other than Chen Mul) are primarily represented by Yacman Striated utilitarian jars and bowls (74 percent Hocaba, 64 percent Tases; Appendix). The Appendix illustrates the overlap of types found in these phases in the fastidiously analyzed assemblage of Mayapan, and the difficulty in distinguishing Early and Late Facet utilitarian ceramics within the Late Postclassic in the northern or southern lowlands. As a result, the Hocaba and Tases phases are combined by scholars currently working in the northern lowlands today (Robles 1986c). Ritual ceramics, however, appear to be far more sensitive to change.

Links Between Southern and Northern Lowland Ceramic Assemblages

In general, Augustine- and Tulum-related (Payil Red, Smith 1971) redware ceramics originate earlier at southern lowlands sites compared to those in the north, as summarized in Figure 3.1. This trend partly accounts for the insertion of a Middle Postclassic phase into Belize sequences or the placement of starting dates for the Late Postclassic at earlier points in time at southern sites of Belize and the Peten. Redware ceramics in the Peten Lakes regions are reported from the early part of the tenth century (Diane Chase 1982; Chase and Chase 1986: Figure 4; Prudence Rice 1987a: 40–42). Related wares appear in the Belize Valley at Barton Ramie by A.D. 950, as part of the New Town phase (Willey et al. 1965; Diane Chase 1982, Chase and Chase 1985: Figure 3). These redwares are documented in northern Belize at Colha (Hester 1985: 38; Valdez and Mock 1985) in the Buk phase at Lamanai (Graham 1987) by the mid-eleventh century, and a few few years later at Santa Rita in the Xabalxab complex A.D. 1150 (Chase and Chase 1988: Table 1). Tulum Red at Tulum (Sanders 1960; Ball 1982) or related wares at Cozumel (Connor 1983) and El Meco (Robles 1986c) appear further to the north by A.D. 1200. The Mama Red ceramic complex at Mayapan appears by A.D. 1200 (Smith 1971), although scholars working at the site today believe it may be at least a hundred years earlier (Robles and Andrews 1986: 90; Anthony Andrews, Fernando Robles, personal communication 1999). If this new revision is correct and Mayapan Mama Red and Tulum Red wares appear around the turn of the twelfth century, then this will make them more fully contemporary with the Payil Red wares found in northern Belize. The implications for the northern Late Postclassic chronology are not yet fully understood, although this is one reason why scholars now suggest that the Late Postclassic redwares appeared by A.D. 1100 at northern sites. An earlier origin for local variants of Postclassic redware traditions would still be found further to the south in the Belize Valley and the Peten Lakes, however, according to the published chronologies.

The fact that Peten Postclassic redwares emerge in the tenth century, northern Belize–related wares emerge in the eleventh century, and Tulum and Mayapan redwares emerge in the twelfth century implies that directions of influence may move from south to north (Sanders 1960; Arlen Chase

1986; Pendergast 1985; Ball and Taschek 1989: 195; Schele, Grube, and Boot 1995: 11). Robles links El Meco and Mayapan Tases wares with the New Town complex of the Belize Valley (1986: Figure 21), which appears by A.D. 1200 at the north coast of Quintana Roo, at least two hundred years after its emergence in the Belize Valley. South-to-north waves of influence observed from the Peten to Belize suggested by these ceramic sequences loosely correspond to early interpretations of the chronicles that describe migrations ("descents") into northern Yucatán that may have come from Peten (Lothrop 1924; Barrera and Morley 1949; Schele, Grube, and Boot 1995) during the Late Classic period and afterward. The stratigraphic analyses of Robles at El Meco indicate a minimal significance of redwares in the earlier Hocaba-Sotuta complex of this site prior to A.D. 1200 (1986c: Figures 23, 25, 29, 32).

Sanders (1960) presents compelling evidence for a south-to-north direction of influence on Tulum redwares that supports the chronological patterns summarized above. Comparing the ceramic assemblages from the Chetumal Bay site of Ichpaatun to those of Tulum, he notes that Ichpaatun (the more southern site) had a greater variety of redware ceramic forms and decorations. He suggests that this pattern indicates that Ichpaatun was closer to the center of the sphere producing these ceramics and that Tulum was more peripheral to this sphere. This hypothesis applies the distance-decay principle to evaluate the direction of ceramic emulation.

Comparable patterns are described in a recent discussion of the identification of craft specialization in the archaeological record at individual sites by Costin (1991: 29–32). Costin suggests that ceramic production localities may be determined within individual sites by the following two criteria: (1) a greater frequency of ceramics will be present at producer households compared to nonproducer households, and (2) a greater diversity of ceramic forms and types will be present at producer households compared to nonproducer households. If these criteria can be transferred from interhousehold comparisons within a community to intersite comparisons within a region, then Ichpaatun, with its greater percentage of decorated wares and greater diversity of redware types, would more closely resemble Costin's "producer" profile. In contrast, Tulum would more closely resemble a "nonproducer" profile, according to Costin.

The literal application of the term "producer" is probably inappropriate for these intersite comparisons, as each site may have produced a significant proportion of its own ceramics or obtained them from more proximate neighbors. However, an increased level of innovation in ceramic decoration may be exhibited at Ichpaatun due to its closer proximity to the center of this sphere of stylistic emulation. Although most ceramics from Ichpaatun and Tulum were probably not exchanged from site to site, their production

Figure 3.1 — Postclassic ceramic sequences for Maya Lowlands sites

yrs AD	Peten Lakes Macanche	Peten Lakes Tayasal	Peten Lakes Topoxte	Belize Valley Barton Ramie	N. Belize Colha	N-central Belize Lamanai	N. Belize Laguna de On	N. Belize Santa Rita	N. Belize Cerros	Q. Roo coast Tulum	Q. Roo coast El Meco	N. Yucatan Mayapan	yrs AD
1650													1650
1600													1600
1550													1550
1500		Kauil								Aguada Grande		Chikinchel (N=114)	1500
1450						Yglesias	Colonial						1450
1400			Topoxte										1400
1350						Cib							1350
1300					Ranas	Buk/Cib		Late Facet Xabalxab	Late Facet Kanan				1300
1250				Late Facet New Town		Buk/Cib	Late Facet Laguna				Late Tases		1250
1200	Early Facet Dos Lagos	Cocahmut				Late Facet Laguna				Tulum			1200
1150			Paxcaman		Canos			Early Facet Xabalxab	Early Facet Kanan		Early Tases	Hocaba/Tases	1150
1100						Early Facet Laguna	Early Facet Laguna						1100
1050	Late Facet Aura	Late Facet Chilcob		Early Facet New Town		Buk							1050
1000													1000
950				Spanish Lookout	Yalam				Sihnal	Vista Alegre			950
900	Early Facet Aura	Early Facet Chilcob	Augustine			TC/RPC	TC/RPC	Ihilk					900
source:	Chase & Chase 1986:Fig.4	Chase & Chase 1986:Fig.4	Chase & Chase 1986:Fig.4	Chase & Chase 1986:Fig.3	Valdez 1994: Figure 1	Graham 1987		Chase & Chase 1988:Table 1	Walker 1990	Sanders 1960	Robles 1986	Smith 1971	

Terminal Classic/Early Postclassic

Early Postclassic, Middle Postclassic, or Early Facet Late Postclassic

Late Postclassic, or Late Facet Late Postclassic

Terminal Postclassic &/or Colonial

3.1. Postclassic sequences published for Maya Lowlands sites. Note that these independently derived site sequences indicate the onset of the Early Postclassic (and associated ceramic complexes) at progressively later points in time from south to north. The southernmost locations are located to the left of the chart, and the northernmost are located to the right (compiled from Chase and Chase 1985: Figures 3, 4, and other sources as noted).

diversity may still reflect aspects of "emulation decay," in which diversity and elaboration may decrease with distance from the center of the production sphere. Ceramic production diversity would dissipate along a continuum at sites located at increasing distances from the central area, in a manner similar to certain types of exchange systems outlined by Renfrew (1975). Sanders's model is testable and quantifiable, if representative ceramic samples could be obtained from sites in Quintana Roo and Belize, and if the analysis were performed by a single individual to ensure consistency. Sanders had such an opportunity for regional comparisons, and his preliminary indications evocatively parallel the general spatial and chronological patterns observed in Figure 3.1. Waves of influence and perhaps elite migrations from south to north probably stimulated local production and contributed to the "spread" of the redwares further north with each generation, as suggested by Ball and Taschek (1989) and Schele, Grube, and Boot (1995). Further investigations are needed on the regional level to continue to document and evaluate this patterning.

Despite the evidence for south-to-north waves of influence prior to A.D. 1200 and north-south directions of emulation that percolated down from Mayapan after A.D. 1300, some regionally specific ceramic forms are reported from the Peten, Belize, the east coast of Quintana Roo, and Mayapan. This variation suggests that more than one center of emulation was operating in the Maya Lowlands during the Postclassic. Region-specific variations include Peten painted polychrome wares and red-on-cream ceramics (Bullard 1970; Rice and Rice 1985: Table 1), Lamanai chalice vessels (Pendergast 1981; Graham 1987; Graham and Pendergast 1989: 11), Santa Rita figurines (Gann 1918; Chase and Chase 1988: 78–79), and black-slipped or black-painted creamwares from the north (Sanders 1960; Smith 1971). A most notable difference in Peten Lakes assemblages includes the addition of unique Ixpop Polychromes that are not reported for Belize (Bullard 1970; Rice and Rice 1985: Table 1; Rice 1987a: Table 6). Other differences in paste, slip, and modal design elements are noted for Belize (Graham 1987; Chase and Chase 1988: 77–78). It is probable that producers from different sites used locally available clay sources that could account for slip and paste differences, which are less important for broad regional comparisons of typological templates that ceramic producers were trying to replicate with available materials. Site-based variation in clays suggests that producers were operating from individual communities, while participating in a broad pan-lowland interaction sphere. Utilitarian forms are shared at most of the sites mentioned above for the Peten, Belize, Quintana Roo, and Yucatán.

When does the transition from orange-red to deeper red-slipped ceramic assemblages occur in the southern lowlands? At Lamanai, this transition is thought to have occurred around A.D. 1300 with the Cib phase (Graham

1987), and at Santa Rita, this transition occurs around A.D. 1350 (Chase and Chase 1988: Table 1). These dates mark the rise of Mayapan to power in northern Yucatán and these changes incorporate ceramic attributes associated with this center. The emergence of Mayapan as a political center is associated with the full emergence of Postclassic redwares in the northern lowlands by A.D. 1200, after they initially made their way up from the Peten through Belize and the east coast. After Mayapan's rise to power, waves of influence began to pulsate in the opposite direction from north to south, resulting in changes in Belize sequences around A.D. 1300–1350 (Diane Chase 1984; Chase and Chase 1988: 78). Mayapan's influence on Belize and the Peten is also expressed in the emulation of Chen Mul–modeled effigy censers.

An Argument for Functional Variation

A pervasive issue in site-specific chronologies has been the temporal placement of Late Postclassic "Mayapan style" effigy censers, effigy vessels, and figurines. These ritual ceramics are found at the very end of the Postclassic sequence (late fourteenth and fifteenth centuries). The presence of abundant censer ceramics in surface levels at some sites is attributed to "pilgrimage" or other postabandonment activities (Sanders 1960; Sidrys 1983; Valdez 1987; Walker 1990) because they are not generally found in association with Tulum-style utilitarian assemblages and appear to be ritual deposits.

Several lines of evidence, however, suggest that these censer deposits are contemporary with Tulum-like wares found in domestic contexts at these same sites, and the isolation of Chen Mul effigies from these deposits is due to functional variation of ritual versus domestic use of different areas of the site. First and foremost, these effigy censers are found at Tulum, in association with Tulum redwares (Sanders 1960). Other compelling evidence for the temporal association of Late Postclassic effigy censers with the continued manufacture of red-slipped and unslipped ceramics like those made in previous centuries comes from the site of Mayapan itself. It makes sense, after all, that "Mayapan style" censers would be contemporary with the site of Mayapan and its utilitarian traditions, where the effigies are found in greatest number. An increase in the manufacture of these censers is observed over time at Mayapan (Smith 1971; Appendix I, this volume) and at other sites with good stratigraphic seriation such as El Meco (Robles 1986c). This increase is observed alongside continued manufacture of Mayapan or Tulum-style red-slipped and unslipped wares representing occupations of these sites. The recovery of Tulum redwares in middle and late lots along with locally more prolific Mama Red at Mayapan (Smith 1971: Figure 48 caption remarks) illustrates that these wares are contemporary. Differences in these wares, which are primarily in incised decoration style and paste characteristics rather than vessel form, are associated with geographic location with Tulum-like wares found more commonly at east-coast sites such as El Meco, Tulum, Ichpaatun, and Laguna de On, and Mama Red wares found in greater quantity at Mayapan and sites to the west of the east-coast region.

In Smith's (1971: 193–245) careful efforts to distinguish two phases of the Late Postclassic (Hocaba and Tases), he determined that the later Tases phase was distinguished from Hocaba based primarily on specialized ritual effigy ceramics, particularly Chen Mul–modeled. In controlled stratigraphic units of late deposits at Mayapan (Smith 1971: Tables 5, 6, 24), Hocaba and Tases ceramics co-occur (Figure 3.2). Furthermore, most of the Tases ceramics identified in these late stratigraphic levels are Chen Mul–modeled censers (Figure 3.3), indicating that Tases represents more of a functionally distinct assemblage than a temporal one. Recent work at El Meco in northern Yucatán lumps Mayapan Hocaba and Tases into a single Late Postclassic phase (Robles 1986c: Figure 21).

Careful stratigraphic analyses at El Meco have also shown that Tulum-like Payil Red ceramics are temporally associated with Chen Mul–modeled censers (Robles 1986c). Robles's seriations indicate that in some localities, the emergence of Chen Mul–modeled censers is accompanied by the emergence of Payil Red and Mama Red ceramics (Robles 1986c: Figures 23 and 25), while in other areas of the site, the censers overlay the redware deposits (Robles 1986c: Figure 27) indicating a probable shift in functional activities at these localities.

If redware ceramics continued in northern Belize into colonial times as some scholars have suggested (Pendergast 1977: 130; Sidrys 1983; Chase and Chase 1985: Figures 2 and 3; Graham 1987), then they are almost assuredly associated with effigy ceramic manufacture and use as described for Mayapan and El Meco above. If such redwares were not analytically classified as belonging to the Late Postclassic, then it is easy to see how investigators might attribute two functionally distinct Postclassic assemblages to two sequential periods at a single site. In such an instance, utilitarian red-slipped wares and unslipped wares would be recognized as belonging to the "Middle Postclassic," and censer wares would be recognized as belonging to a "Late Postclassic." Having dismissed utilitarian vessels as belonging to an earlier period, the "pilgrimage" interpretation is used to explain the representation of the Late Postclassic by ritual effigy ceramics or censers alone.

To illustrate this problem, a study of diligently quantified ceramic types by level at sites tested in northern Belize by Sidrys (1983: Table 7) is examined. Sidrys's careful reporting of this data allows the reader to note that wherever "Late Postclassic" components are recognized, associated ceramic diagnostics are represented by over 93 percent effigy censers (and over 96 percent in most units). This pattern is consistent with other analyses,

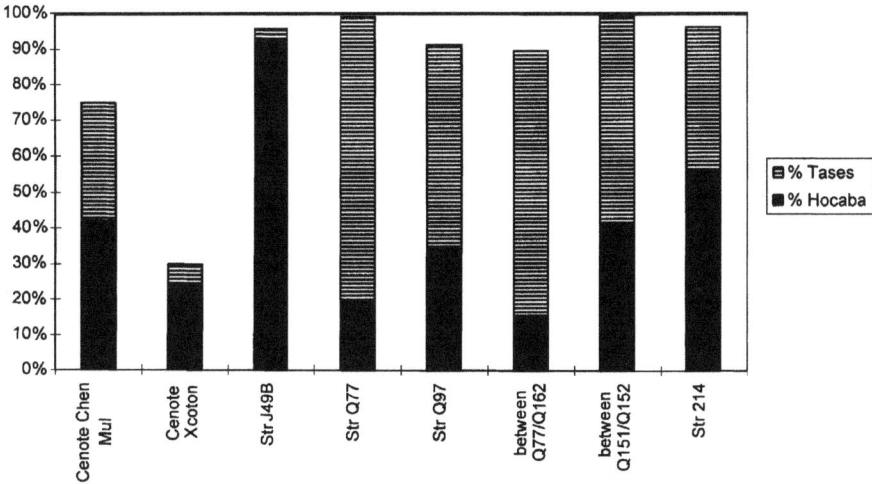

3.2. Percentage of Hocaba and Tases ceramics in late lots at Mayapan, showing the co-occurrence of Tases forms with Hocaba forms in most areas tested (compiled from Smith 1971: Tables 5, 6, 24).

including the "post-Mayapan" component at Tulum and other sites in Quintana Roo (Sanders 1960) and Belize (Walker 1990), which are identified primarily by ritual ceramics. As censers are located close to the surface and often ritually broken or smashed (Sidrys 1983; Valdez 1987), securing radiocarbon dates for these deposits is exceedingly difficult and the absolute determination of their age in these circumstances is hard to verify.

Stratigraphic evidence described above for Mayapan and El Meco suggests that northern Belize scholars are correctly attributing effigy censers to the latter portion of the Postclassic period, and only the issue of whether they represent site abandonment is a question that remains open for debate. Populations responsible for producing and depositing effigy censer wares and figurines must also have been living in the area and performing a host of domestic and economic activities involving ceramics. A more plausible interpretation attributes the distribution of effigy ceramics to functionally distinct, synchronic behavior, a possibility raised initially by Walker (1990: 26). Late Postclassic ritual ceramics would thus be temporally associated with populations making traditional Postclassic red-slipped ware (including Tulum-like wares) and unslipped utilitarian pottery. In cases where effigy wares are found stratigraphically above redwares, this pattern probably represents a change in use of particular areas of a site. In cases where effigy ceramics are found without redwares, this pattern probably reflects a functional segregation of activities within a site.

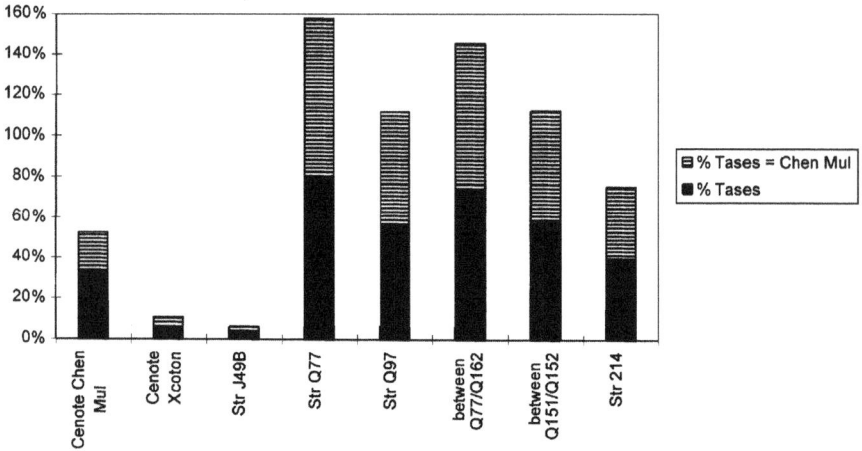

3.3. Late stratigraphic lots at Mayapan, showing the percentage of Tases ceramics in the late lots and the percentage of those Tases ceramics represented by Chen Mul–modeled effigy censers (compiled from Smith 1971: Tables 5, 6, 24).

Post-Mayapan or Colonial Diagnostics

In addition to the issue described above for defining Late Postclassic assemblages as distinct from Middle Postclassic ones in northern Belize, further difficulties have been encountered in attempts to identify post-Mayapan or colonial ceramics from sites between A.D. 1450 and 1650. At Mayapan, low numbers of sherds hindered this attempt. Robert E. Smith (1971: 247–248) defined four types of ceramics as post-Mayapan, amounting to 114 total sherds. Of these, thirteen sherds are a Fine Orange tradeware, twenty-three sherds are unslipped jars (N = 8) and bowls (N = 15), four brownware sherds comprise a comal (N = 3) and a bowl (N = 1), and seventy-one sherds are classified as Abala Red Ware, which Smith (1971: 248) claims to be colonial rather than pre-Columbian. Thus, of 398,921 "late" sherds analyzed at Mayapan (Smith 1971: Chart 3) there remain only forty-three sherds that define four types that could qualify as post-Mayapan and precontact (Fine-Orange Cunduacan Group, Ochil Unslipped, and Bolon Brown) and four forms (thick-walled vessel, low-neck jar, two restricted-orifice bowls, and a comal). This sample size is simply too small to define a "post-Mayapan" diagnostic assemblage of ceramics or to demonstrate that ceramics changed significantly between A.D. 1441 and 1517.

Sanders similarly struggles with identifying a ceramic component after A.D. 1441. Although he terminates the majority of Tulum's occupation at A.D. 1441, this is not based on radiocarbon or stratigraphic evidence at Tulum or any of its contemporary sites and appears to be based on the assumption that Tulum "fell" and was abandoned at the ethnohistorically derived date of the fall of Mayapan. Sanders defines a "Post-Mayan" period that begins at this time, but the only "Post-Mayan" ceramics identified are two forms of censers (Sanders 1960: Chart 3) at a single site on Cozumel Island, Aguada Grande, and a black paste censer found at Tulum.

More recent work at Lamanai (Pendergast 1977; Graham 1987: 91) has recovered colonial Maya ceramics from residential and church structures known to have been occupied in the sixteenth and seventeenth centuries. This work has succeeded in identifying the Yglesias phase of historic ceramics, which include the continued manufacture of redwares such as sag-bottom dishes, strap-handle jars, and high-necked jars from precontact times (Graham 1987: 91). Orange redwares, buffwares and black-slipped wares are also reported. Censer forms continue from the past, including forms that resemble Chen Mul and Cehac Hunacti Composite (Graham 1987: 91). In this complex, redware flanges are said to diminish to a notched ridge, and vessel feet in general are bulbous, ovoid, tapered, phalliform, and have large vents (Graham 1987: 91). The Lamanai assemblage demonstrates that aspects of indigenous redwares and unslipped wares continued to be manufactured into colonial times, perhaps as late as A.D. 1650 (Pendergast 1977: 130), attested to by the recovery of colonial Maya ceramics from secure historic contexts. The starting date for the Yglesias complex has not been absolutely determined, and many sherds from this assemblage closely resemble their pre-Columbian antecedents.

CERAMICS FROM LAGUNA DE ON ISLAND

This chapter has assembled the foregoing information on Postclassic Maya Lowland ceramic chronologies for the purpose of interpreting the ceramics trends and radiocarbon dates from Laguna de On in a regional context. As the discussion above indicates, Postclassic ceramic chronologies embrace a number of complicated issues and merit continued careful comparative examination. The interpretations presented here of ceramics from Laguna de On Island represent a first assessment based on field laboratory identifications performed by project ceramicist Shirley Mock (1997, 1998) and ongoing examinations by the author and Georgia West. The ceramic assemblage at Laguna is highly eroded and fragmented (Mock 1998), similar to the condition of ceramics reported from Tulum (Sanders 1960). No whole vessels have been recovered in three seasons of excavation and 45 percent of the sherd sample was too eroded for Mock to classify to type (Table 3.2). Due to the condition of this assemblage, it is less suitable for definitive temporal analysis than sites such as Lamanai or Santa Rita where whole vessels have been found. Diane Chase (1982) suggests that fine-grained temporal classifications are more appropriately made on whole vessels, rather than sherds, and her identifications of Rita Red are based on whole vessels at Santa Rita, which often occur in low numbers. Whole vessels have been used primarily to define the Lamanai sequence as well (Graham 1987; Pendergast 1981).

The perspective offered here from Laguna de On is thus that of the sherds, by default in having recovered no complete vessels from this site. However, this perspective represents a different and complementary alternative to the view of ceramic assemblages offered by the analysis of whole vessels. Perhaps for this reason the perspective from Laguna is that of a "lumper" rather than a "splitter," as fragments in this analysis tend to emphasis the recognition of commonalities rather than differences. Table 3.2 outlines the frequencies of ceramic types identified by Mock from ceramics recovered from the 1996 and 1997 seasons. Like the sites of Mayapan and Tulum, the classifiable assemblage at Laguna is largely comprised of a few major type groups of utilitarian ceramics, primarily Santa Unslipped (18.6 percent) and Payil Red (58.8 percent). Due to fragmentation and erosion of many sherds, it was difficult to distinguish Payil Red from Rita Red. The relative percentages expressed in Table 3.2 are not interpreted as a temporal indication that Laguna de On was occupied earlier than the site of Santa Rita or that its utilitarian assemblage differs significantly from Santa Rita.

Ceramics from Laguna de On fall into three major categories: slipped, unslipped, and "specials," or rare anomalous sherds probably representing tradewares. Classifications are provisional, based on cross-referencing to established types at Santa Rita, Cerros, Colha, and Tulum (Mock 1998: 193). Based on Mock's classifications (1998: 193–202), slipped redware sherds fall into three major ceramic groups: Rita Red, Payil Red, and Zakpah Orange (following Valdez 1987; Chase 1982; Walker 1990). Ceramic attributes used to identify these groups include a variety of criteria, including paste, slip, incision, flanging, appliqué, modeling, or form. Red-slipped wares consist of commonly found sag-bottom, tripod, vented-foot dishes (incised and plain, with occasional flanges), grater bowls, incurving-rim bowls, small jars, and large, lug-handled long-neck jars. Some of these ceramics are illustrated in Figures 3.4 and 3.5.

Unslipped ceramics include three groups: Cohokum, Tsabak, and Navula (following Chase 1982; Walker 1990: 2.1; Valdez 1993). The Cohokum group consists of two ceramic types at Laguna de On: Santa Unslipped (decorated or plain and coarse or flannel-textured varieties) and Kol Modeled (Mock 1998: 199–200). Santa Unslipped wares include primarily folded-rim ollas with occasional bowls or jars. Kol-modeled types include effigy figurines or censer vessels. Tsabak Unslipped forms at Laguna de On consist of large, crudely constructed direct rim ollas. Navula Unslipped wares include Cehac-Hunacti Composite censer vessels and perforated "colander" censers. Some of these ceramics are illustrated in Figure 3.6.

The co-occurence of Payil Red, Rita Red, Zakpah Orange Red, Santa Unslipped, Cehac-Hunacti Composite and Kol Modeled through stratigraphic levels across the site suggests that these types generally belong together as part of its contemporary Late Postclassic assemblage (Masson and Stafford 1998). The identification of Payil, Kol Modeled (a local version of Chen Mul; Chase 1982; Walker 1990), and Cehac-Hunacti wares tie Laguna de On into the northern interaction spheres of Tulum and Mayapan (Mock 1998). The presence of Rita Red and Santa Unslipped link Laguna de On to Santa Rita, and the presence of low numbers of Zakpah Orange Red indicates shared traditions with Lamanai Buk-phase ceramics (Mock 1998).

Table 3.2 compares ceramic frequencies found in three arbitrary stratigraphic levels assigned across the site. These frequencies serve the primary purpose of indicating the co-occurence of ceramic types from the beginning to the end of the site's occupation and use. These stratigraphic levels are based primarily on genuine (but gradual) natural changes observed in the soil across the island that are associated with changes in cultural features. Generally speaking, Level 1 represents the surface topsoil across the site, a 10–15 centimeter zone of dense artifact concentration locked in humic root mat. Level 2 represents an underlying 30-centimeter zone of brown-to-gray clay loam. Level 3 represents a 10–15 centimeter transition zone of the clay loam that interfaces with limestone bedrock. There is no evidence that substantial horizontal stratigraphy is present at the site that might compromise the vertical examination of these frequencies and the principle of superposition that these temporal comparisons are based on. These levels thus facilitate a preliminary examination of temporal patterns in artifact assemblages at the site.

Some temporal trends may be indicated in changing ceramic frequencies in the levels represented in Table 3.2. The most notable pattern is that a decline in the percentage of Payil Red ceramics (70 percent in Level 2, 49 percent in Level 1) appears to be affected by an increase in the percentage of Santa Unslipped (10 percent in Level 2, 28 percent in Level 1). The reason for this pattern is unclear, but it is possible that a significant proportion of Santa Unslipped may be unclassified in earlier levels. A number of ceramic concentration features containing diagnostic rim sherds of unslipped wares were found in Level 1 (around Structure I) in 1996 (Masson, Shumake, and Moan 1997), which may have contributed to the easier identification of unslipped types compared to body sherds present elsewhere at the site. Through the past two seasons of investigations, increased acuity has been achieved in making ceramic identifications, particularly of harder-to-identify unslipped body sherds (Shirley Mock, personal communication 1997), and reanalysis of lots recovered from the beginning of Laguna investigations is an ongoing project. For these reasons, it is better to refrain from basing

Table 3.2—Sherds from Laguna de On Island (from field form identifications made by Shirley Mock). Percentages shown are calculated based on number of classifiable sherds by level. Eroded, unidentified sherds are listed separately at bottom of table.

	Level 1	%	Level 2	%	Level 3	%	Total	%
UNSLIPPED WARES								
Cehac-Hunacti Composite	76	2.3%	18	0.7%	2	0.3%	96	1.5%
Unclassified sandy-paste censers	23	0.7%	35	1.4%	23	4.0%	81	1.3%
Unclassified striated	5	0.2%	32	1.2%	1	0.2%	38	0.6%
Unclassified unslipped	55	1.7%	47	1.8%	9	1.6%	111	1.7%
Tsabak Unslipped	88	2.6%	81	3.2%	2	0.3%	171	2.6%
Santa Unslipped	930	28.0%	275	10.7%	2	0.3%	1,207	18.6%
Unclassified colander censer	2	0.1%	2	0.1%	1	0.2%	5	0.1%
Kol Modeled	156	4.7%	62	2.4%	10	1.7%	202	3.6%
Cohokum Modeled	0	0.0%	3	0.1%	0	0.0%	3	0.0%
Unclassified comal	79	2.4%	10	0.4%	0	0.0%	89	1.4%
SLIPPED WARES								
Payil Red	1,655	49.7%	1,814	70.6%	337	58.4%	3,806	58.8%
Rita Red	130	3.9%	73	2.8%	38	6.6%	241	3.7%
Zakpah Orange Red	117	3.5%	112	4.4%	35	6.1%	264	4.1%
Canton Incised	2	0.1%	0	0.0%	0	0.0%	2	0.0%
Palmul Red Incised	9	0.3%	1	0.0%	0	0.0%	10	0.2%

Unclassified red	0	0.0%	0	0.0%	114	19.8%	114	1.8%
White/Buff paste	0	0.0%	4	0.2%	0	0.0%	4	0.1%
							0	0.0%
Total classifiable sherds	3,327	100.0%	2,571	100.0%	577	100.0%	6,475	100%
Eroded sherds	2,641	44.3%	2,137	45.4%	666	53.6%	5,444	53.6%
Total sample (classifiable and eroded shards)	5,968		4,708		1,243		11,919	

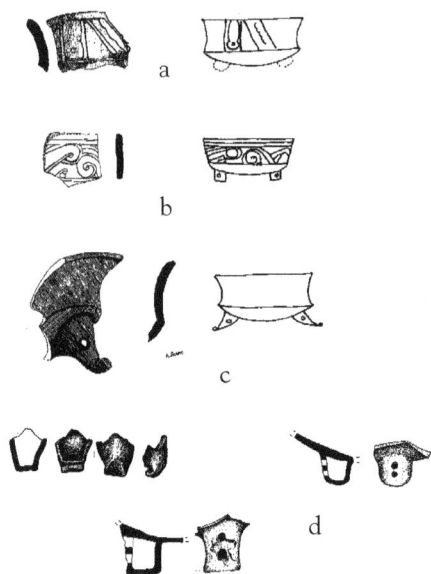

3.4. Palmul Incised red-slipped ceramic rim sherds from tripod sag-bottom bowls, Laguna de On Island (a, b); scroll-footed plain red-slipped tripod sag-bottom bowl (c); three variations of feet on tripod sag-bottom bowls (d). Sherds drawn by Anne Deane. Hypothetical reconstructions of vessels shown to the right of a, b, and c represent composite perspectives from a number of fragmented sherds in the Laguna de On type collection (not to scale).

conclusive interpretations on the variable frequency of Payil versus Santa at the site at this time.

Other ceramics show slight increases in Level 1 compared to Level 2, including Rita Red (increased by 1.1 percent), comals (increased by 2 percent from almost 0 percent), Kol Modeled (increased by 1.5 percent), and Cehac-Hunacti (increased by 1.6 percent). Some of these increases probably represent significant temporal trends, as Kol-modeled (Chen Mul–like) ceramics increase over time in all Postclassic sites from which they are quantified (Sanders 1960; Smith 1971; Sidrys 1983; Robles 1986c). The increase in comals is also a potentially significant pattern. It is also notable, however, that these forms are also present in deposits below Level 1 at the site, in association with Payil Red ceramics. These ceramics indicate that Laguna de On was a Late Postclassic site at which ceramic assemblages were very similar from the beginning to the end of its occupation. Radiocarbon dates discussed below suggest that these ceramic wares date from the eleventh through fifteenth centuries.

Radiocarbon Dates from Laguna de On

Radiocarbon dating of sites in northern Belize and Yucatán has supplemented ceramic chronologies at a few significant sites such as Santa Rita, Lamanai, and Colha, as summarized in Table 3.3. Obsidian hydration has also provided Postclassic dates for deposits at such sites as Macanche Island in the Peten (Rice 1987a: Table 2) and Colha (Hester 1985: 40). However, a recent

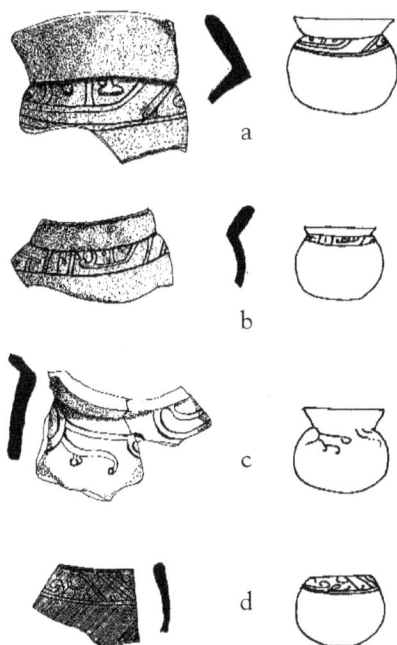

3.5. Palmul Incised red-slipped ceramic rim and neck sherds from small collared jars (a–c) and an incurving rim bowl (d). Sherds drawn by Anne Deane. Hypothetical reconstructions of vessels shown to the right of the sherds represent composite perspectives from a number of fragmented sherds in the Laguna de On type collection (not to scale).

critique of the reliability of this dating method by Braswell (1992) suggests that such results be interpreted cautiously until further refinement is accomplished. Unfortunately, three of the most significant sites north of Belize, including Tulum, Mayapan, and Chichén Itzá, have not been subjected to intensive chronological analysis utilizing absolute dating techniques. As their extensive investigation history and their prominent political role in late lowland Postclassic society causes the ceramic assemblages from these sites to serve as indices for comparison, it is most unfortunate that their chronologies are primarily based on stylistic, relative, or ethnohistoric measures. New data from Chichén Itzá (Bey, Hanson, and Ringle 1997) and the Chikinchel province (Kepecs 1998) has begun the important process of revising the northern chronology.

At Laguna de On, radiocarbon dating has provided the primary basis for reconstructing occupation history, in combination with stratigraphic feature analysis. Dates for Laguna de On are presented in Table 3.3 and Figure 3.7 (from Stafford 1998), along with selected published dates from contemporary sites. Nine accelerator mass spectrometer (AMS) samples have yielded Postclassic dates for Laguna de On (Table 3.3). Of these, calibrated ranges (2 sigmas) of five dates (Figure 3.7) fall within a time bracket of around A.D. 1000/1050–1280; three dates fall within a time range of A.D. 1250–1420

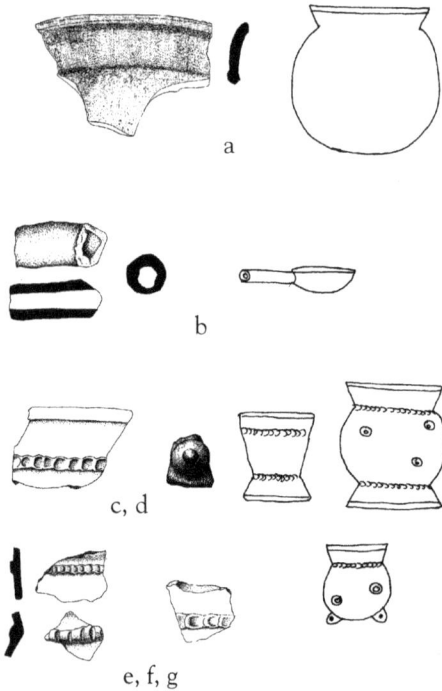

3.6. Unslipped ceramics from Laguna de On Island, including a Santa Unslipped folded rim olla (a), an unslipped ladle censer (b), fragments of Cehac-Hunacti Composite vessels with filleted-impressed appliqué and a rosette or "button" appliqué (c–g). Sherds drawn by Anne Deane. Hypothetical reconstructions of vessels are shown to the right of the upper two sherds (not to scale) and are based on composite perspectives from a number of fragments in the Laguna de On type collection. Three forms of filleted-impressed unslipped "censer" vessels known in the literature are shown to the right of fragments c–g, which are difficult to identify to form.

(Figure 3.7), and one date falls between A.D. 1439 and 1643. Compared to the substantial number of 14C dates published from the nearby site of Santa Rita (Figure 3.7; Chase and Chase 1988: Table 2), Laguna de On appears to have been occupied during the same time span and somewhat earlier. Laguna has two discrete clusters of dates. The first date cluster encompasses the eleventh, twelfth, and the first part of the thirteenth centuries, and the second date cluster is centered on the late thirteenth through early fourteenth centuries.

The dates published for Santa Rita do not exhibit a discrete early cluster. However, sampling design directly affects the nature of radiocarbon results at both sites. At Laguna de On, radiocarbon samples were selected from features that were distinctly separated into earlier and later stratigraphic contexts, particularly those that lay above and below easily identified construction features such as walls, cobble platforms, and terraces. This sampling was undertaken with the aim of identifying early and late sets of feature clusters. Additional dates from more nebulous or intermediary deposits would probably yield date ranges overlapping with each cluster, as suggested by the fact that the upper sigma ranges of the early cluster and the lower ranges of the later cluster actually do overlap in Figure 3.7. At Santa Rita, the inves-

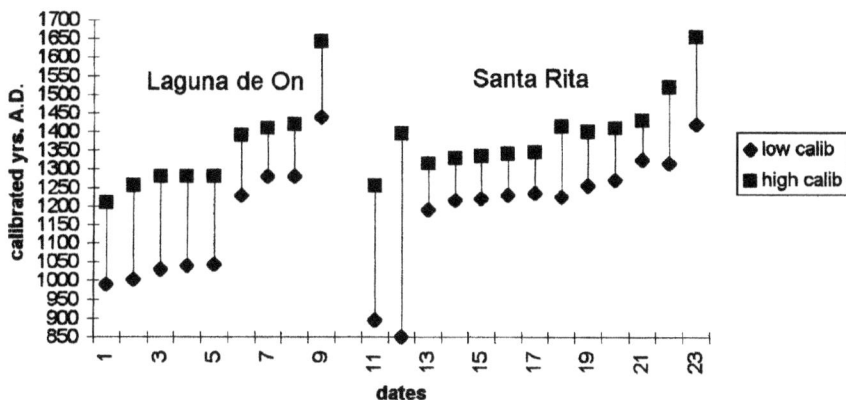

3.7. Postclassic C-14 dates for Laguna de On (nos. 1–9 on left, from Stafford 1998) compared to those reported from Santa Rita (nos. 11–23 on right, from Chase and Chase 1988: Table 2).

tigators targeted late deposits at the site according to their research design to ascertain its contact-period significance (Chase and Chase 1988: 78–79). Although fully aware that earlier deposits were present at the site, the investigators focused their 14C dating efforts primarily on the latest features of the site (Chase and Chase 1988: Table 2). This approach has yielded a tightly defined cluster of dates at the site that fall within the calibrated range of A.D. 1190–1430 (Figure 3.7), with a couple of dates falling earlier and later than this range (Chase and Chase 1988: Table 2).

The date clusters at Laguna de On are used to refer to Early (A.D. 1050–1250) and Late (A.D. 1250–1450) Facets of the Late Postclassic at the site in Chapters 4 and 5, where facets are employed primarily as an analytical device for examining diachronic patterning at this site. Generally, these temporal divisions follow the definition of an Early and Late Facet of the Xabalxab complex at Santa Rita (Chase and Chase 1988: Table 1) and an analogous chronology at Cerros (Walker 1990), although the A.D. 1250 division between Early and Late Facet Laguna de On differs slightly from the A.D. 1300 division at Santa Rita and the Early Facet at Laguna de On begins at A.D. 1050 rather than A.D.1150, as at Santa Rita. It is notable that Laguna de On is located to the south of Santa Rita, a factor that may account for its earlier sequence. As A.D. 1000 and 1050 merely represent the lower parameter of the 14C sigma ranges, it is not certain that Laguna de On was actually occupied this early, although it may have been. Ceramics that are found at the site during the twelfth century (where the mean dates of the earlier cluster are concentrated) presumably were developed by prior generations, so a late eleventh-century origin for these wares is not unreasonable to postulate.

The designation of Early and Late Facet chronological components at Laguna de On is also supported by ceramic frequency data (Table 3.2), which suggest that a continuum of linked ceramic production characterizes Laguna de On from its earliest occupation levels to its latest. Radiocarbon dates suggest this occupation extended from around A.D. 1050 until at least 1450 (but probably until Spanish contact). As Laguna de On is not linked to a strongly definable ceramic chronology at this stage of the analysis, the examination of chronological trends in subsequent chapters relies on dating of features according to their stratigraphic position and the 14C dates from feature clusters associated with earlier and later deposits at the site. The reliance on stratigraphic superposition for feature analysis and diachronic interpretations follows a similar approach employed at Isla Cerritos (Andrews et al. 1988).

SUMMARY

Ethnohistoric sources, ceramic chronologies, and radiocarbon dates have been used in the Postclassic Maya Lowlands to ascertain site-based and regional temporal patterns that form the basis for interpretations of cultural change during this dynamic era. This chapter has summarized selected issues in Postclassic ceramic chronologies, which provide the basis for the interpretations of ceramic and radiocarbon temporal evidence from Laguna de On. While considerable efforts have focused on individual sites across the lowlands, the time is ripe for intersite comparisons and collaboration to establish regional sequences following Sanders's (1960) and Sidrys's (1983) pioneering regional-level precedents. Ethnohistoric information has commonly been substituted for chronometric data, but the mythohistorical accounts of native chronicles need to be augmented and clarified with independently analyzed archaeological data.

Despite depositional obstructions to chronological analysis shared by the northern and southern lowlands, such as shallow or intermingled stratigraphy, highly eroded ceramic assemblages, and impacts to surface deposits by development, it is clear from sites such as Lamanai (Pendergast 1981; Graham 1987), Santa Rita (Chase and Chase 1988), Mayapan (Robert Smith 1971), Tulum (Sanders 1960), El Meco (Robles and Andrews 1986), Isla Cerritos (Andrews et al.1988), and Laguna de On that features and deposits amenable to chronometric dating or stratigraphic seriation can be found.

Table 3.3—Radiocarbon dates from selected Postclassic sites.

Site	Material/location (if specified)	Date (mean in parentheses), LAB (if specified)
DATES CLUSTERING IN THE 11TH–12TH CENTURIES		
Aventura (Sidrys 1983: Table 3)	shell	1025±80 B.P. (A.D. 1000) UCLA
Mayapan (Proskouriakoff 1962a:111)	charcoal? from floors at base of and below Castillo	(A.D. 1015)
Santa Rita (Chase & Chase 1988: Table 2)	P6F/33-1	930±110 B.P. A.D. 895–1255 BETA 18079
Santa Rita (Chase & Chase 1988: Table 2)	P6F/9-1	880±190 B.P. A.D. 850–1395 PENN 3076
Tipu (Graham 1987: 86)		(A.D. 1155±39)
Tipu (Graham 1987: 86)		(A.D. 1163±28)
Laguna de On Island (Stafford 1998)	Turtle bone, S.O. 12g Lot 42, bone conc. on Str. II	820±50 B.P., or A.D. 1043–1280 calibrated NSRL
Laguna de On Island (Stafford 1998)	Tapir bone S.O. 12b Lot 199, fire pit under Str. II	900±50 B.P., or A.D. 1003–1256 calibrated NSRL
Laguna de On Island (Stafford 1998)	Human bone Subop 5c Lot 86, burial	0950±50 B.P., or A.D. 990–1210 calibrated NSRL
Laguna de On Island (Stafford 1998)	Crocodile bone S.O. 8c Lot 27, censers next to St. I	830±60 B.P., or A.D. 1030–1280 calibrated NSRL
Laguna de On Island (Stafford 1998)	Homo sapiens S.O. 8, Lot 20, burial	840±50 B.P., or A.D. 1040–1280 calibrated NSRL
Santa Rita (Chase & Chase 1988: Table 2)	P6F/9-1	880±190 B.P. A.D. 850–1395 PENN 3076
Colha (Hester 1985: 40)	charcoal (base of midden, Op 2037)	820±50 B.P. A.D. 1060–1110 BETA 11584

Continued on next page

Table 3.3—continued

Site	Material/location (if specified)	Date (mean in parentheses), LAB (if specified)
Colha (Hester 1985: 40)	charcoal above base of Op 2037 midden	865±50 B.P. or A.D. 1037–1257, calibrated BETA 11585
Patchchacan (Sidrys 1983: Table 3)	bone collagen	760±110 B.P. UCLA

DATES CLUSTERING IN THE 13TH–14TH CENTURIES

Tipu (Graham 1987: 86)		(A.D. 1201±50)
Aventura (Sidrys 1983: Table 3)	shell	680±80 B.P. UCLA
Patchchacan (Sidrys 1983: Table 3)	bone collagen	760±110 B.P. UCLA
Santa Rita (Chase & Chase 1988: Table 2)	P2B/9-2	780±70 B.P. A.D. 1190–1315 BETA 18068
Santa Rita (Chase & Chase 1988: Table 2)	P8C/9-1	1273±50 B.P. A.D. 1215–1330 PENN 3073
Santa Rita (Chase & Chase 1988: Table 2)	P8C/62-1	730±70 B.P. A.D. 1220–1325 BETA 18082
Santa Rita (Chase & Chase 1988: Table 2)	P8C/76-1	710±70 B.P. A.D. 1230–1340 BETA 18083
Santa Rita (Chase & Chase 1988: Table 2)	P8C/76-1	700±50 B.P. A.D. 1235–1345 PENN 3075
Mayapan (Proskouriakoff 1962a: 111)	wooden beam from colonnaded hall	(A.D. 1360)
Laguna de On Island (Stafford 1998)	carbonized wood disk, S.O. 12k, Lot 113, on Str. II	700±50 B.P., or A.D. 1228–1390 NSRL
Laguna de On Island (Stafford 1998)	Human bone Subop 5, Lot 9, burial	620±40 B.P., or A.D. 1280–1410 NSRL
Laguna de On Island (Stafford 1998)	Turkey bone, collagen 1mg, Subop 8d Lot 34, fire pit under Str. I	620±50 B.P., or A.D. 1280–1420 calibrated NSRL

Continued on next page

Table 3.3—continued

Site	Material/location (if specified)	Date (mean in parentheses), LAB (if specified)
Santa Rita (Chase & Chase 1988: Table 2)	P8C/48-8	660±80 B.P. A.D. 1225–1415 BETA 18081
Santa Rita (Chase & Chase 1988: Table 2)	P6F/33-3	650±40 B.P. A.D. 1255–1400 PENN 3074
Santa Rita (Chase & Chase 1988: Table 2)	P6F/19-1	610±60 B.P. A.D. 1270–1410 BETA 18078
Santa Rita (Chase & Chase 1988: Table 2)	P3B/75-1	530±60 B.P. A.D. 1325–1430 BETA 18076

15TH CENTURY OR LATER MEAN DATES

Santa Rita (Sidrys 1983: Table 3)	charcoal	475±50 B.P. or (A.D. 1425) UCLA
Santa Rita (Chase & Chase 1988: Table 2)	P6F/51-8	490±100 B.P. A.D. 1315–1520 BETA 18080
Santa Rita (Chase & Chase 1988: Table 2)	P37A/23-31	330±70 B.P. A.D. 1420–1655 BETA 18087
Laguna de On Island (Stafford 1998)	Crocodile bone collagen 1mg, S.0. 8c Lot 27, censer conc. next to Str. I	360±40 B.P., or A.D. 1439–1643 calibrated NSRL
Sarteneja (Sidrys 1983: Table 3)	bone collagen	<300 B.P. or (>A.D. 1650) UCLA BETA 18076

4

Community Patterns at Laguna de On

POSTCLASSIC SETTLEMENT STUDIES AT LAGUNA DE ON

Laguna de On has a long history of twentieth-century explorations. When Thomas Gann first visited Laguna de On in 1927 (1928), he noted the presence of a "pavement of stone" on the mystical isle from which he collected numerous offerings. He also described ancient-appearing stone wharves around the lagoon's shores that remain to this day. He also tested and reported some mounds on the shore of the lagoon. Meighan and Bennyhoff visited the site in 1955 and Thomas Hester's observations (notes on file, Texas Archeological Research Laboratory) of lithic collections from this reconnaissance indicated the presence of Archaic, Preclassic, and Classic components at the lagoon's shore. Thomas Kelly and John Masson returned to Laguna de On as part of the Colha Regional Survey of the University of Texas and they reported the Postclassic nature of the island's debris (Kelly 1980).

The southwest shore and island of Laguna de On were investigated by the author and Fred Valdez in 1991 (Figure 4.1; Valdez, Masson, and Santone 1992; Masson 1993). Island testing during that season suggested that a range of domestic deposits were located, intact, just below the surface of the island's topsoil. Two small islands in the southwest vicinity of the lagoon were recognized as artificial platforms built of sterile lagoon sediment (Figure 4.1; Masson 1993, 1997). They were largely disturbed by looting, but exclusively Postclassic materials were recovered from test pits placed on these features. Investigations on the shore focused on three domestic structures located on a single residential platform group at the southwest corner of the lagoon (Figure 4.1, Masson 1993, 1997). The structures were built in the Terminal Classic, but were later occupied during the Postclassic period as indicated by the presence of artifacts of this date in surface levels (Valdez et al. 1992; Masson 1993, 1995, 1997). Limited probing of this platform and documentation of looter's trenches reveals that this residential group has

Early Classic and Late Preclassic components within it that have not been fully explored.

Two subsequent seasons of investigation have targeted the island community of Laguna de On in 1996 and 1997 (Masson and Rosenswig 1997, 1998a). Extensive exposure of domestic and ritual features and testing of midden zones has provided a more robust view of community patterns at this site (Figure 4.1). Shore surveys have located a zone of Postclassic occupation that extends along the north and west bluffs of the lagoon that was contemporaneous with the island's occupation (Figure 4.1; Waid and Masson 1998). This chapter outlines the settlement history of Laguna de On that has been reconstructed from research of the 1991, 1996, and 1997 seasons and represents a synopsis of initial research reports (Masson and Rosenswig 1997, 1998a).

POSTCLASSIC OCCUPATION OF LAGUNA DE ON SHORE

As described above, the shore of Honey Camp lagoon is the site of at least two Postclassic occupations. These components take the form of a sheet midden that covers bluffs on the west and north sides of the lagoon (Figure 4.2; Waid and Masson 1998) and surface topsoils recovered within and around household structures built in the Terminal Classic period (Figure 4.2; Masson 1993). The shore was occupied for the full duration of the Postclassic (A.D. 1050–1500). Laguna de On Island was occupied during the Preceramic (Rosenswig and Stafford 1998) and Postclassic periods exclusively.

The shore deposits are less suitable for addressing issues of Postclassic community life than the island deposits, for two reasons. First, shore sites are mixed in some locations with Late and Terminal Classic period debris. In contrast, most stratigraphic contexts on Laguna de On Island are not temporally mixed. The second advantage of the island is that these deposits are circumscribed. Due to the limited area for settlement, approximately five hundred years of Postclassic debris is concentrated in a relatively small 200 x 60 meter area. In contrast, strip settlement zones along the shore are thin and dispersed. This consolidation of island material and lack of temporal mixing allows for more-controlled sampling of Postclassic assemblages. Traditionally, nondiagnostic features and artifacts, such as faunal bone or human skeletal remains lacking grave offerings, can be assigned to the Postclassic with greater confidence. Despite the limitations of the shore deposits, they offer valuable information about the extent of Postclassic settlement.

Laguna de On Shore, Op 1: Terminal Classic/Early Postclassic Occupation

Three household structures of Terminal Classic/Early Postclassic date located at the lagoon's southwest shore were explored in 1991, including Structures I-2, I-3, and I-6 (Masson 1993, 1997). Two isolated mounds of

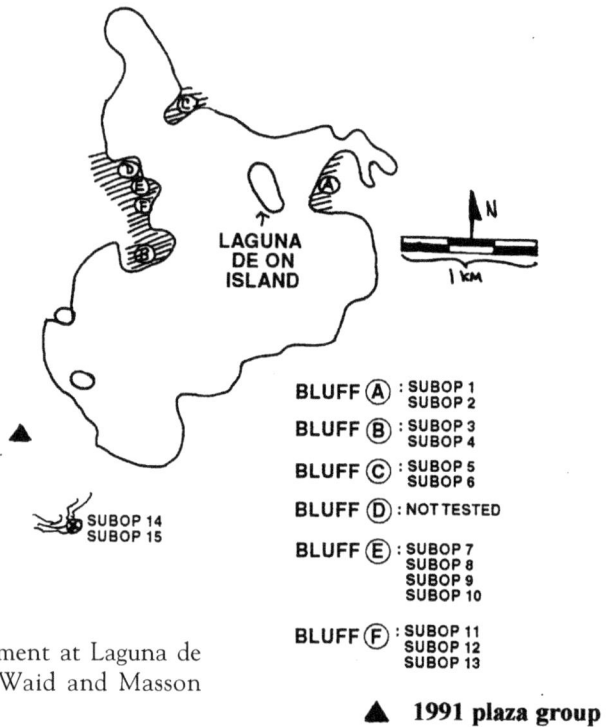

BLUFF Ⓐ : SUBOP 1
           SUBOP 2

BLUFF Ⓑ : SUBOP 3
           SUBOP 4

BLUFF Ⓒ : SUBOP 5
           SUBOP 6

BLUFF Ⓓ : NOT TESTED

BLUFF Ⓔ : SUBOP 7
           SUBOP 8
           SUBOP 9
           SUBOP 10

BLUFF Ⓕ : SUBOP 11
           SUBOP 12
           SUBOP 13

▲ **1991 plaza group**

4.1. Postclassic settlement at Laguna de On (redrafted from Waid and Masson 1998: Figure 34).

Classic period date were mapped near the residential plaza (Structures II and III), and artifacts observed in the road that encircles the lagoon suggest that more structures were present in this location that have been destroyed for construction. As described in Chapter 2, Postclassic surface components are quite vulnerable to development efforts at this lagoon and elsewhere.

Of the three houses excavated, two were lined with single-coursed house walls (I-2, I-3), and one earthen mound (I-6) lacked permanent wall foundations altogether (Masson 1993, 1997). The stratigraphy of these structures consisted of 20cm of topsoil. Marl inclusions in topsoil are thought to represent the eroded remains of house floors. Postclassic materials were found intermingled with Terminal Classic artifacts within wall foundations and in soil covering the interior and exterior spaces of these domestic structures, suggesting to this author that they were continuously occupied through the Terminal Classic/Early Postclassic to Late Postclassic periods (Masson 1995, 1997). Ceramic sherds were examined from all shore contexts by Fred Valdez (1993a) and form part of the basis for chronological assignments. Other artifacts, such as special finds and lithic tools, also indicate Terminal Classic through Late Postclassic occupation (Masson 1995).

4.2. Line of stone construction "box shrine" (Subop 11) on the west bluff (F) shore of Laguna de On.

Shallow graves were recorded in all three structures at Op 1 of Laguna de On Shore (Structures I-2, I-3, and I-4), represented by incomplete concentrations of human remains (Masson 1993; Rosenswig 1998). The topsoil was heavily disturbed by tree roots, and it is not known whether the graves were incomplete due to disturbance or secondary mortuary practices. Two of these burials are thought to date to the Terminal Classic period, based on fragmented ceramic sherds and stemmed chert blade fragments found with two individuals.

Laguna de On Shore, Ops 2 and 3: Postclassic Occupation

Prominent elevated bluffs along the north and west shores of the lagoon were the location of a sheet midden of Postclassic living debris, including lithic tools, flakes, ceramic vessels, ceramic beads, and a mano observed on the surface (Figure 4.2; Waid and Masson 1998). Both bluffs were the target of test pit investigations by Alice Waid (Waid and Masson 1998). The north bluff area represents the smaller of two areas, but it is covered with dense debris. The west bluff area is more extensive, and a thin veneer of Postclassic materials was observed over a 300 x 100–meter survey strip along the bluff edges (Figure 4.1). These areas were suitable for settlement due to their proximity to the island and high, dry locations. A bluff along the northeast shore of the lagoon was also surveyed, but deposits yielded primarily Classic period remains (Waid and Masson 1998). A thin scatter of materials of various periods was present in many areas inspected around the lagoon, but survey results suggest that the west and north bluff zone was the nucleus of Postclassic shore settlement. A stone shrine structure was also found in the west bluff area (Figure 4.2, Suboperation [Subop] 11; Waid and Masson 1998).

To test these deposits, several 1 x 2 meter units were placed at intervals along the west and north bluffs (Waid and Masson 1998). Identified Postclassic ceramics include Santa Unslipped, Kol Modelled, Cehac-Hunacti Composite, and Payil Red (Shirley Mock, personal communication). Cultural deposits on these bluffs are confined to about 30cm of topsoil that overlies bedrock. Two *chultuns* or wells were located along the west bluff (Waid and Masson 1998). The shrine structure (Subop 11, Structure V) on the west shore bluff was fully excavated (Figure 4.2). Ceramics from this feature almost exclusively include Kol-modelled effigy censers and ollas, and other censer vessels that date to the Late Postclassic (Diane Chase 1982; Walker 1990). The feature is a "box shrine," consisting of a square alignment of vertical slabs (2.5m x 2.5m in dimension) that retained a soil and rubble fill. Concentrations of effigy ceramics were found on all four exterior sides of this feature, as well as on top of it. No reconstructable vessels were found, and each concentration included intermingled pieces of different vessels. The largest concentrations were from the south and north sides. This shrine contained the greatest amount of Kol-modelled censers recovered from any context at Laguna de On. It is perhaps significant that it is not located on the island, which is more difficult to reach. It is not known whether this shrine was used primarily by occupants of the shore, or whether it served the greater lagoon community, including the occupants of the island. As it is unique at the site, I favor the latter interpretation.

SETTLEMENT AT LAGUNA DE ON ISLAND

Two temporal facets (Early and Late) have been defined for the Late Postclassic occupation of Laguna de On Island, as outlined in Chapter 3. The Early Facet, represented by deposits from 16cm below the site's surface to bedrock (30cm) and having radiocarbon dates clustering within A.D. 1050–1250, is characterized by a series of domestic deposits and features that suggest the site was probably a hamlet or small village-sized settlement, when the shore component is considered (as such settlements are defined in Flannery 1976: 164). The domestic production of ceramics, textiles, lithic tools, and subsistence items was common at the site at this time, and other types of activity, such as ritual or public works construction, appear absent. This occupation is found in a domestic sheet midden deposit that covers bedrock in most locations tested across the island. This sheet midden generally consists of grey-brown soil that is intermingled with small pieces of the limestone bedrock. Artifacts within this sheet midden consist of large utilitarian tools, used flakes, and utilitarian ceramics. Large fire pit features are found in these lower deposits. Few signs of domestic architecture have been identified, as buildings were made entirely of perishable materials on dirt floors during the island's Early Facet occupation. Hints of this type of construction have been encountered at Subop 5 (Figure 4.3). During the Early Facet, skeletons were interred in seated, flexed, west-facing positions with few variations (Rosenswig 1998; Sheldon 1998).

The Late Facet Postclassic component is defined with

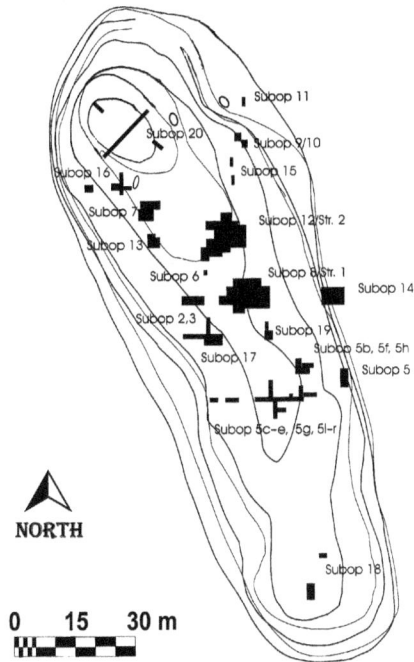

4.3. Map of Laguna de On Island showing location of test units (from Masson 1998: Figure 1, prepared by Pam Headrick).

the aid of radiocarbon dates clustering from A.D. 1250 to 1450 in deposits within 15cm of the site's surface. A suite of domestic features and artifacts in this component suggest that the island continued to be occupied. The Late Facet settlement, including the shore, was of the same size or larger than that of the Early Facet. Greater labor investment in domestic architecture is observed at this time, and stone wall foundation alignments, cobble platforms, plaster surfaces, and modified bedrock floors are several forms of domestic space construction observed at this time. This increased effort in the construction of domestic architecture is accompanied by public feature construction, including Structures I and II (Masson, Shumake, and Moan 1997; Masson 1999b; Rosenswig and Becker 1998), a possible ballcourt (Barnhart 1998a), a dock (Masson and Gonzalez 1997), and terraces that extend and level off the east upper contour of the island (Barnhart and Howard 1997; Rosenswig and Stafford 1998). Platforms of lagoon sediment on small isles in the lagoon are probably contemporary with the Late Facet features on the large north island (Masson 1993). Ritual behavior and the construction of public works thus increased during the Late Facet of the island's occupation. Notably, a decline in the standardization of burial patterns is also observed (Rosenswig 1998).

Only a hint of post–A.D. 1450 occupation is present at the site. As features of this age are likely to lie immediately on the site's surface, where few deposits are encountered that are suitable for radiocarbon dating, this issue represents a methodological barrier to identifying Terminal Postclassic or colonial components at sites such as Laguna de On. One sixteenth-century 14C date is reported from faunal bone in a ritual concentration of remains near the site's surface (Stafford 1998). Low numbers of diagnostic Colonial period unslipped utilitarian wares, such as those recently identified at Laguna Seca, are present at Laguna de On (Shirley Mock, personal communication). The presence of these materials suggests the site continued to be occupied through at least the sixteenth century.

Early Facet

Domestic Architecture and Features. The construction of domestic dwellings of perishable materials during the Early Facet makes the detection of this type of architecture exceedingly difficult in topsoil deposits or sheet middens located within 30cm of the site's surface. With few soil contrasts noted within these deposits of brown humic topsoil and midden, postmolds are largely invisible unless they penetrate white bedrock below these soils. Postholes have been identified in Subop 17 (Aguilera 1998: Figure 3) and Subop 5 (Sheldon 1998: Figure 10) that are thought to reflect the remains of Early Facet domestic (or other) structures. Middens and features are more frequently found than the domestic structures they are likely to be associated with. Analysis of domestic assemblages from this site (see Chapter 5) is thus based on midden and other feature materials. Middens provide assemblages of discarded artifacts and ecofacts that help reconstruct domestic production patterns at the site. The Early Facet domestic features are described below.

Middens. Ceramic, lithic, and faunal debris have been recovered from a 15cm grey-brown loam deposit resting on bedrock across the site. This layer of soil represents a sheet midden of largely domestic debris that is attributed to the Early Facet occupation. This midden was encountered in almost every unit excavated at Laguna de On, including Suboperations 2, 3, 5 (except 5a, 5b), 6, 7, 8, 9, 10, 11, 12, 13, 15, 16, 17, 18, and 20. Figure 4.4 shows a stratigraphic profile of excavation units around Structure I (Subop 8) Beneath Structure I's stone alignment (pedestalled at top), midden deposits are documented beneath the structure and overlying bedrock, at a depth of 40–50cm below the alignment in this photo. The photo also shows the contents and outline (foreground) of a partially excavated fire feature that underlies the stone alignment. The analysis of artifacts found within these middens

4.4. Photo of stratigraphy at Laguna de On Island shows view of section of Structure I, pedestalled stone alignment at the surface, with midden soils shown beneath the structure and above bedrock and partially excavated fire feature (Lot 34) beneath the structure in foreground (note dark stain parameter of feature intruding into bedrock and pit contents pedestalled behind the sign).

provides clues to their domestic nature. Lithic tools and debris are particularly diagnostic of domestic function (Masson 1999b). Large stone tools such as cores (used and unused), bifaces, unifaces, and used flakes that were employed in a variety of utilitarian tasks are found in these lower deposits. The density of lithic debitage is an additional indicator of the domestic nature of this midden. Lithic debitage forms a proportion of 44.9 percent of the site's debris, in deposits that are primarily middens such as the one below Structure II (Masson 1999b: Table 3). In contrast, lithic debris forms only 5.8 percent of the surface deposits associated with Structure II, a ritual feature (Masson 1999b: Table 3).

Fire Features. In Early Facet deposits at Laguna de On, distinctive fire features are found that provide intriguing clues about domestic production. The most common type of feature found at the site is a large fire pit (Figure 4.5). These pits originate within the midden, at an average depth of 15cm below the surface. They range from 1m to 1.5m in diameter, and are on the average 75cm deep. They intrude into bedrock. The soil within these features is dark brown, black, or grey, and has ash inclusions (Masson, Shumake,

4.5. Profile perspective of Lot 34 fire feature in midden soils beneath Structure I.

and Moan 1997; Wharton 1998). Artifacts and ecofacts within these features vary considerably, and include large ceramic sherds (including slipped sherds and vessel feet), net weights, spindle whorls, broken mano or metate fragments, obsidian blades, burned and unburned *Pomacea* shells, faunal bone, marine-shell implement manufacturing debris, lithic tools, and lithic flakes. These artifacts may have been deposited in these features through processes of cultural or natural infilling, and they may or may not be related to feature function. This artifact density and the darkening of soil color are two characteristics that lead to the detection of these features in the soils of Laguna de On. The broad range of artifacts found within the pits confounds their functional interpretation.

Eight large fire features have been found at the site during excavations of Subops 8, 7, 12, 17, and 19a (Table 4.1). Plan maps of one these features (Lot 295) from Subop 7 are provided in Figure 4.6 (after Wharton 1998: Figures 20–23). Lot 295 was located in a brown loam beneath a wall and marl platform in Subop 7a, b, and c (Wharton 1998). This pit was lined with upright oblong stones (including recycled metates and manos and natural limestone rocks) and had two charred, flat tabular pieces of limestone placed at the base (Wharton 1998). Another feature, Lot 199, was located in a grey-brown midden beneath the platform of Structure II in Subop 12 (Rosenswig and Becker 1997). It contained a complete, uncharred tapir humerus, which was dated to A.D. 1030–1280±50 (Stafford Labs #3501, Stafford

View 1   View 2

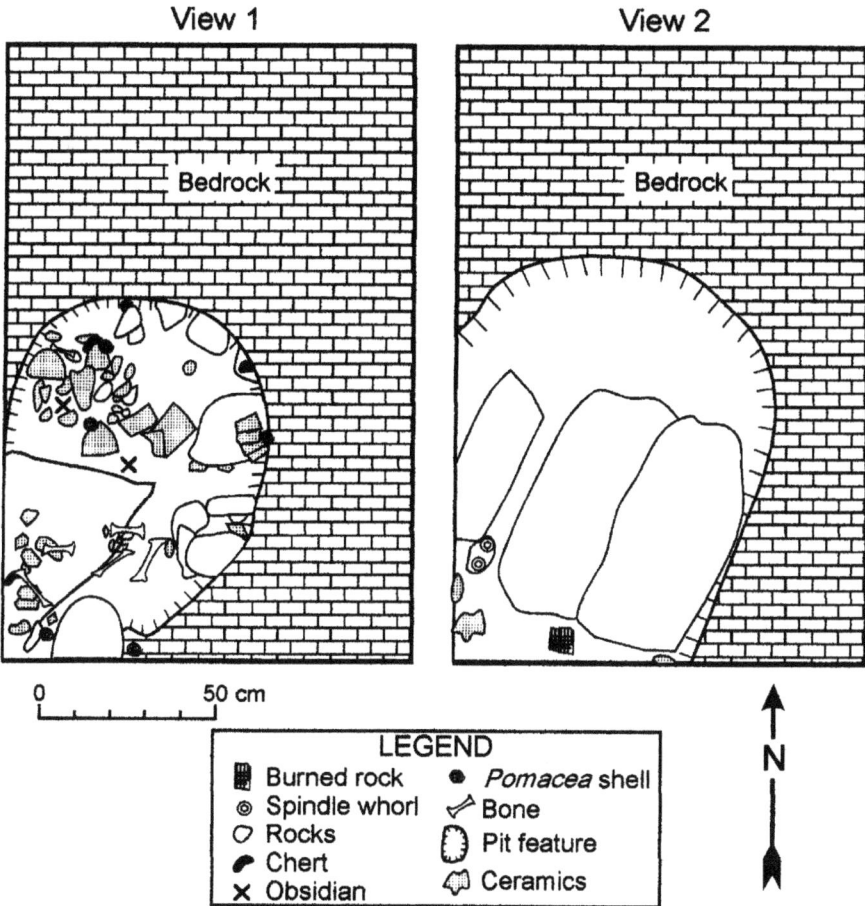

0   50 cm

LEGEND

🔳 Burned rock	● *Pomacea* shell
◎ Spindle whorl	✍ Bone
⌀ Rocks	🅿 Pit feature
➤ Chert	ᗡ Ceramics
✕ Obsidian	

N

4.6. Plan of Lot 295 fire feature and contents (redrafted from Wharton 1998: Figures 23 and 23). View 1 shows the feature midway through excavation and the variety of materials recovered within it. View 2 shows the base of the feature, which consisted of two charred limestone slabs.

1998). In Subop 17, Lot 245 was found in a grey-brown midden beneath the topsoil (Aguilera 1998: Figure 3). It was below a cobble platform that may represent a domestic house floor in this unit. Lot 245 is thought to be earlier than the cobble platform (Lot 256) due to its stratigraphic position. At the surface of Lot 245 (15cm below surface), a broken metate fragment was found (Aguilera 1998: Figure 3). In the west profile of Subop 19, an additional fire pit was identified. It was not fully excavated, but a large piece of abraded, red mineral pigment was mapped in profile and collected from the surface of this feature. Three fire features were encountered in the Subop 8 excavation units around Structure I. All were encountered at levels beneath the wall

Table 4.1—The contexts and dimensions of fire features identified at Laguna de On Island

Subop	Evidence for Household Architecture	Fire Features	Dimensions of Fire Feature	Citation
Subop 7	Late Facet wall alignment outcropping on surface, plaster floor surface extending east of wall	Lot 295, beneath Late Facet architecture	1m x 80cm, 70cm deep	Wharton 1998
Subop 8d	Late Facet wall alignment, domestic and ritual Structure I	Lot 34, beneath Late Facet architecture	1.5m x .80cm, 80cm deep	Masson, Shumake, and Moan 1997
Subop 8p	north of Late Facet wall alignment, domestic and ritual Structure I, originates beneath 15cm topsoil	no Lot # assigned, identified in profile	.90cm x .90 cm, 40cm deep	Aguilera 1998
Subop 8q	beneath Late Facet wall alignment, domestic and ritual Structure I	not excavated, corner of feature identified in profile	not known	Aguilera 1998
Subop 17	adjacent to and deeper than Late Facet cobble house platform, at same horizontal level as plaster floor and postholes, originating 15 cm below the surface	Lots 241, 245	1.5m x 1m (est.), .60cm deep	Aguilera 1998
Subop 19a	beneath 15cm topsoil	no Lot # assigned, identified in profile	.70cm long in profile, .50cm deep	field notes on file
Subop 12	beneath Late Facet cobble shrine platform	Lots 193, 197	1.2m x 1m, .70cm deep	Rosenswig and Becker 1997

foundations of Structure I. In Subop 8p, Lot 360 was documented along the north exterior edge of Structure I (Aguilera 1998: Figure 5). Another fire feature was encountered at the base of Subop 8f, but it was intruding from the wall of Subop 8q and was not excavated. A large fire feature of later date was excavated beneath Subop 8d, Lot 34, beneath the northwest wall foundation alignment of Structure I. Faunal bone from this feature yielded a 14C date of A.D. 1280–1420±50 (Stafford Labs #3500, Stafford 1998). The stratigraphic position of Lot 34, originating at 15cm below the surface, suggests that it should be associated with the Early Facet, yet the 14C date fits within the Late Facet at the site. It is possible that the faunal bone is intrusive. Alternatively, the use of fire features continued in the Late Facet and the construction of Structure I is very late.

These fire pits may be related to ceramic production. Their size suggests that they were created for some type of industry, as their depth appears excessive for mere domestic cooking purposes. The presence of large ceramic sherds in these features is notable (as large as 13–15cm in length), especially compared to the average ceramic sherd size in midden deposits across the site (2–3cm in length). The large stone slabs and recycled metates in a couple of these features may have been used to support or protect ceramic vessels during firing. The large quantities of ash and burned soil is also another characteristic that might be explained by ceramic production. The presence of a range of other materials might also be expected for a ceramic-firing feature. As ceramics are often covered in soil during firing, the deposits within firing features would be repeatedly removed and returned to the feature. During such deposition cycles, a number of domestic artifacts could have easily found their way into the pits with the soil. Alternatively, after a feature is no longer used, they may have been filled or used as trash receptacles.

Evidence of clay quarrying at Laguna de On also suggests that a ceramic industry was in place at the site. In Subops 19 and 19a, a series of pit intrusions were documented in the east profile of a 1 x 4 meter by 2.2-meter-deep trench that intrudes into fine white clays that occur above bedrock in this location (Rosenswig and Stafford 1998: Figures 30 and 31). The pitted intrusions are observed along the entire 4m section of the east profile of Subops 19 and 19a, and their base is 2m below the current ground surface. These pits originate at a depth of at least 1.25–1.5m below the surface, and were filled in during terrace construction in this area in the Late Facet occupation. A number of disturbed deposits above the pits suggest that the overlying soils are terrace fill in this area of the island. Further complicating this stratigraphic record, a Preceramic component was identified in the white clays overlying bedrock into which these intrusive pits were placed (Rosenswig and Stafford 1998).

The white clay detected at the base of Subop 19 is of excellent quality, and it is easily molded even without preparation. When fired, this clay turns a grey color, according to field experiments performed by project artist Anne Deane (1999). The color and quality of this clay when fired matches that of the unslipped (Santa Unslipped) utilitarian wares recovered at the site. As noted previously, a fire feature was present within the overlying fill soils at Subop 19a (west profile), in which chunks of red pigment were recovered. The pigment was smoothed and appeared to have been prepared (pulverized and formed into a small rectangular cake) and used. Experiments by Deane indicated that this pigment formed a suitable slip that matches the reddish brown color found on Payil Red slipped ceramics from Laguna de On. This evidence for clay quarrying at the site combined with the presence of a number of fire features at Laguna de On suggests that ceramic production was an important activity during the Early Facet occupation.

The problem of locating ceramic production features, such as kilns, has long perplexed Maya ceramicists (Rice 1987a). Predicted characteristics of ceramic kilns include high quantities of large-sized ceramic sherds (manufacturing failures), large numbers of overfired or burned sherds possibly used as wasters (Shepard 1957: 214; Stark 1985), pieces of accidentally fired raw clay, and pigment. At Laguna de On, few of these characteristics are represented in the fire features. However, they are not interpreted to be proper kilns. They may represent subsurface firing pits, filled with ashy, burned soil and a range of secondary midden debris, some of which is burned and some of which is not burned. Midden debris can easily work its way into a pit feature, especially if the characteristics of that pit's use include repeated emptying and filling of the pit with soil. Non-kiln potting hearths are also discussed by Rice (1987a: 153–158). Possible analogs to the ceramic production pits at Laguna de On have been reported by Willey et al. (1965: 97, Figure 38), who describe a fire-hardened clay pit containing charred limestone fragments at Barton Ramie. The Barton Ramie feature, of Late Preclassic date, was of an analogous size to those at Laguna de On (about 1.45m across and 45cm deep), and contained burned limestone, ash, and sherds within it.

To test the effectiveness of these pits for ceramic firing, Anne Deane created a pit of similar dimensions outside of the field laboratory in San Estevan, Belize (1999). Lining the base of the pit with pieces of cinder block (similar to the rock-lined pit in Subop 7), Anne placed ceramic tiles made from white clays found at Laguna de On atop the cinder block slabs and piled firewood around them. A small amount of pigment recovered from the pit in Subop 19 at the site was dissolved into a slip and brushed onto one of the tiles. The firewood was lit and the pit was filled with the soil that had been excavated from it. The following day, the soil was removed. The tiles were completely fired and the slip had adhered to them. The experiment demonstrated that the fire features from Laguna de On represent viable facilities at which ceramics may have been fired at the site.

Ethnoarchaeological research on ceramic production by Deal (1988a: 124) also outlines criteria for identifying "ceramic firing hearths" from "cooking hearths." Criteria for ceramic production include the presence or proximity of metates (often recycled metates) and manos used to grind pigment or temper (Deal 1988a: 124). At Subop 17, a possible recycled broken metate was found on the surface of a large fire pit. The fragment found was a portion of a large trough-shaped metate made of coraliferous limestone. At Subop 7, in fact, one metate found in the fire pit was made of sandstone. Such an implement would be useful for grinding ceramic tempers and other materials. Deal notes that potters at the Maya Highland community of Chanal had an average of 2.1 metates per household compared to 1.4 per households not engaged in ceramic production (1988a: 117). Deal (1988a: 124) states that the extent to which ceramic production features are used directly affects our ability to recognize them in the archaeological record. Features used only a few times will not accumulate large amounts of diagnostic waste related to production. Deal notes that domestic potters make and fire fewer vessels and create less production waste (1988a: 124).

Another indication of ceramic-producer households may be the presence of a greater diversity of vessel types and greater numbers of vessels at potter households (Becker 1973: 399). This hypothesis was tested and supported by Deal's study at the modern community of Chanal (1988a: 129), in which producer households had 34 percent more vessels than nonproducer households. Costin (1991: 20–21) also notes that increased ceramic densities at production localities may be used as one criteria for distinguishing producer from nonproducer or consumer household assemblages. At Laguna de On, such types of comparisons are not possible, as most of the substantial domestic zone investigations revealed the presence of fire features.

Limited Evidence for Early Facet Structural Remains. Three postholes have been recorded at Laguna de On Island during the Early Facet. Postholes are difficult to detect due to the similarity of their fill with surrounding soils. Despite these difficulties, at Subop 17 a posthole was recorded in a layer of brown loam mixed with flecks of marl, which is presumed to represent a living floor at a depth of 29cm below the surface (Lot 244; Aguilera 1998: 13, Figure 3). Adjacent to this loam/marl surface (originating at 24–29cm below surface) was a large fire pit feature (Lots 241/245) in which a broken metate and large amounts of debris were found. In a nearby unit, at the same depth (24cm) a concentration of probable domestic debris was recovered in Subop 17c (Lot 306; Aguilera 1998: 15, Figure 3). The concentration

contained *Pomacea* shells, turtle bone, crocodile bone, lithic flakes, and ceramic sherds. No other postholes were found in this unit, but the marl
surface is thought to represent an initial domestic construction at Subop 17
that was capped by midden topsoils adjacent to a Late Facet cobble platform
recorded in Subop 17a.

Two postholes and a possible hearth were recorded in Subops 5g/j and 5e
respectively (Sheldon 1998: Figure 10). In Subops 5g/j, one posthole showed
up below the grey-brown midden layer in which it was thought to originate,
and penetrated 15cm into white bedrock below. A posthole observed in the
east profile of Subop 5g is thought to be associated, and a possible hearth
feature in Subop 5e at a related elevation may also be part of this feature. The
hearth feature was about 75cm in diameter and 25cm deep. It contained ashy
loam soil and few artifacts except for large ceramics of an incomplete unslipped
vessel and the articulated skeleton of a frog (probably not cultural). Dirt
floor surfaces in topsoil or loam deposits at Laguna de On Island provide
evidence that entirely perishable domestic structures were present at the site
during the Early Facet occupation.

Early Facet Mortuary Patterns. Three mortuary populations have been recognized at Laguna de On (Masson 1993; Rosenswig 1998). The first of these
consists of nine individuals found in domestic structure topsoils of the Group I
residential platform at Laguna de On Shore, and the other two populations are
identified at Laguna de On Island. These skeletal groups are dated from the
Terminal Classic/Early Postclassic (A.D. 900–1000, Laguna de On Shore), the
Early Facet Late Postclassic (A.D. 1050–1250, Laguna de On Island), and the
Late Facet Late Postclassic (A.D. 1250–1450, Laguna de On Island). Terminal
Classic/Early Postclassic and Early Facet Late Postclassic burials are described
in the section below. Late Facet burials are discussed later in this chapter.

The burials from the Terminal Classic/Early Postclassic shore consist of
fragmented, incomplete remains of individuals (Masson 1993: 92–98, 185–
190). The fragmentary nature of these remains is likely due to poor preservation and bioturbation by the forest floor. Due to the fragmentary nature, no
patterns are identified in burial positioning with the exception of one
extended burial. One individual was buried with broken Terminal Classic
lithic tools (Burial #1), and another was interred with a fragment of a Terminal Classic vessel (Burial #7). All other burials, better described as "bone
concentrations," were not interred with burial offerings. The count of nine
individuals was based on a "minimum number of individuals" (MNI) calculated from teeth. All interments recovered were those of adults between the
ages of eighteen and twenty-five (Masson 1993).

A second mortuary population is represented by the Early Facet sample
from Laguna de On Island. These individuals were placed in seated-flexed,

or flexed, side-lying, west-facing positions in circular pits that originate a few centimeters above bedrock about 30–50cm below the surface (Rosenswig 1998). Nine individuals have been recovered in the seated-flexed position (#3, #4, #5, #7, #8, #10, #11, #14, #20) and two were in flexed side-lying positions (#9, #17) that are attributed to this period. Temporal placement is based on radiocarbon dates and the stratigraphic position of each burial. Two individuals, Burial #7 (Subop 5c) and Burial #9 (Subop 8), have been respectively radiocarbon dated to A.D. 990–1210±50 and A.D. 1040–1280±50 (Stafford Lab #3505 and #3507). Other seated-flexed burials at this depth are dated to the Early Facet by association with these samples. Of the twelve seated-flexed Early Facet individuals, three have filed teeth and one was associated with grave offerings (Burial #17, Subop 5j/p). The grave offerings of Burial #17 included a greenstone bead, a carved peccary bone, a ceramic effigy face, and an eroded ceramic vessel (Rosenswig 1998: Table 16, Figure 58; Sheldon 1998: 28, Figure 7). This individual, an elderly male with cranial deformation, may represent a village leader or another important individual within the community (Rosenswig 1998: 153). The eleven individuals that comprise this burial population were recovered from four areas of the site (Subops 5, 8, and 9, and 18). Two females and one child were among these individuals, four were adult males, and four were undetermined. The placement of these individuals is consistent and appears formalized in their flexed, predominantly seated, west-facing positions (Figure 4.7). West-facing positions are most common in the Postclassic at Tulum (Miller 1982: 48, Table III), and flexed positions are most common at Santa Rita (Diane Chase 1982), Sarteneja (Sidrys 1983: 182), and Playa del Carmen (Marquez Morfin 1982).

An additional patterned behavior associated with this Early Facet burial population is the tendency to place interments in linear clusters along east-west or north-south axes (Rosenswig 1998; Sheldon 1998). At Subop 5, an east-west row of five individuals was found, and three individuals were generally placed in a north-south cluster at Subop 8. Such patterned interments suggest that mortuary areas were carefully maintained, perhaps by lineage groups, within a time period short enough to ensure that interments did not intrude into one another. Late Facet burials are described below.

Late Facet

Architecture and Midden Debris. The surface topsoils of the site contain materials that date primarily to the Late Facet, according to radiocarbon dates of features found within these soils. These topsoils consist of dark brown, loosely packed organic humic soil riddled with root intrusions. The top 10–15cm of the island's surface is covered in this topsoil layer, which represents a sheet midden capping the top of the site. This soil blends gradually with lower

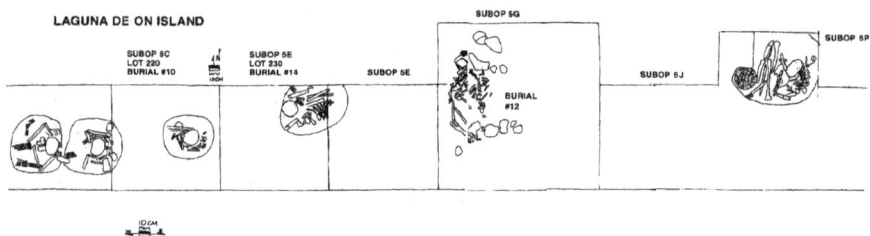

4.7. Row of burials excavated in Subop 5 trench (from Sheldon 1998: Figure 7, drafted by Masson). Adjacent areas tested to the north and south of this trench revealed no interments. Early Facet burials (originating at 50cm below surface) are in seated-flexed positions. A single extended Late Facet burial is shown in center (#12) that originated at 15cm below the surface.

midden loam deposits at the site, and it represents a more recent, humic version of the same soil. The Late Facet thus represents an arbitrary stratigraphic and temporal division. Within these soils, midden materials and artifact concentrations of varying densities have been recorded and wall alignments and cobble platforms are found that are associated with the Late Facet occupation of the site. Adjacent to these structures, concentrations of ceramics or *Pomacea* shell are often recovered.

Cobble surfaces found at Laguna de On Island represent both domestic platforms and paved residential courtyard areas. In Subop 17a, a surface of flat cobbles (Figure 4.8; Aguilera 1998: 14, Figure 3) is interpreted to comprise the floor of a domestic structure. At this location, extension units to the west and north indicated that the cobble surface was 4m wide, ending abruptly at the line dividing Subops 17b and 17c (Aguilera 1998: Figure 3). Its full north-south dimension was not determined by the excavation, but it extends 3.75m through Subops 17a and 17d before ending in an abrupt, straight alignment detected in Subop 17d (Aguilera 1998: Figure 3). A hearthlike feature comprised of burned rock (Lot 257; Aguilera 1998: Figure 3) intruded into the southeast corner of this platform. The feature was 50cm in diameter and 15cm deep. Six meters to the north of Subop 17a, a cobble surface (5cm below the surface) was recorded near the surface in a 2m x 8m unit excavated as Subops 2 and 4 (Masson 1993, 1997). The broad area of this cobble surface was originally interpreted as a paved courtyard in this area. Alternatively, it was the surface of a very large structure.

Broad, flat structures marked by cobble alignments or paved surfaces are characteristic of the Late Facet Postclassic in northern Belize, as determined at Santa Rita (Chase and Chase 1988: Figures 10, 23, 28, 34). A 4m x 2m section of a cobble surface was also identified at the edge of a terrace in

4.8. Cobble surface of Late Facet domestic structure, Subop 17, Lot 256. Note pit features and metate in soils adjacent to the surface in foreground.

Subop 5 (Masson 1993). An ovoid, burned cobble feature associated with Late Facet surface topsoils was identified in Subop 5b/h/f (Lot 236; Sheldon 1998: Figure 9). This feature is stratigraphically dated to the Late Facet, as it sits upon a level of terrace fill that was constructed from A.D. 1250 to 1450. Its dimensions were 2.2m by 1.4m, and the stones comprising it were burned. Little debris was recovered on this feature or adjacent to it, and it is not interpreted to represent a domestic dwelling. A burial (#15) was found partially beneath this structure on its southwest side (Sheldon 1998: Figure 9). Due to the burial's offset location relative to the feature, there is no clear evidence that the burial is associated with the feature's construction (Sheldon 1998: 31).

A concentration associated with the Lot 256 cobble platform was identified in Lot 212 of Subop 17, and the contents of this feature testify to the domestic function of this cobble platform. The concentration (Lot 212) had Santa Unslipped olla fragments, incised and undecorated red-slipped Payil sherds, net weights, a spindle whorl, a slipped ceramic lug handle, obsidian blades, biface fragments, lithic flakes, faunal bone, and *Pomacea* shell (Aguilera 1998: 12). Censer fragments were not present. Comparisons of censer frequencies in units across the site suggests that these vessels were used primarily in confined, specialized ritual areas at the site, and they are infrequently recovered in other locations (Masson 1999b; Chapter 5, this volume).

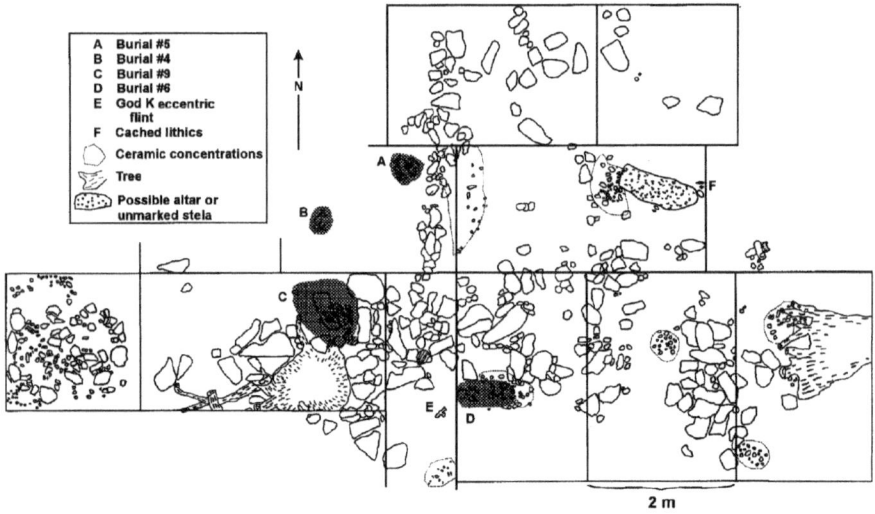

4.9. Plan map of Structure I (Subop 8) and associated features (redrafted from Masson, Shumake, and Moan 1997: Figure 3, by Tim Hare).

An additional form of architecture that is interpreted to be at least partially domestic is a stone wall alignment, Structure I (Subop 8, Figure 4.9; Masson 1999b), that was partially visible on the site's surface prior to excavation. No evidence of flooring was associated with these stones, and the structure may have had a dirt floor. Interpretation of the function of this structure is difficult, as the associated artifact assemblage suggests a mixture of domestic and ritual activities at this location. Comparisons of Structure I's assemblage to more purely ritual or domestic features at the island suggest that this feature is probably a dwelling of an upper-status family who hosted rituals in this location (Masson 1999b). Alternatively, the function of this structure changed over time, from a domestic to a ritual facility. There is some stratigraphic evidence to support the latter hypothesis. Most of the ritual materials, including concentrations of broken censers (Masson 1999b), large game animal crania (Masson 1999a; Wharton and Stanchly1998), a God K eccentric flint, and other artifacts (Masson 1999b), were encountered within 5–10cm of the surface (Figure 4.10). Domestic debris, in lower quantities at Structure I than at purely residential localities (Masson 1999b: Table 3), had greater quantities of utilitarian stone tools and flakes below the top 5 to 10cm.

Four burials were recovered from the vicinity of Structure I (Masson, Shumake, and Moan 1997). Three of these, seated-flexed adults, were found well below the building outside the west wall (Burials #4, #5, #9) and are thought to belong to the Early Facet based on position, stratigraphic loca-

4.10. God K eccentric flint found 15cm below the surface at the southwest corner of Structure I.

tion, and radiocarbon dating. One Late Facet child burial (#6) was placed in shallow deposits outside the south wall, within 40cm of the eccentric flint. It is possible that the structure's placement and the focus of ritual activities performed at this location were linked to the presence of these interments, though their association is difficult to assess. The west wall of Structure I parallels the row of three adult burials, and their orientation could have been a consideration in the building's design. No burials were located beneath the wall or within the structure's interior. The association of the child burial with the eccentric flint is uncertain, as both were recovered in topsoil deposits and a pit outline was not discernable for either deposit. Their horizontal proximity and comparable depth suggest they may be associated.

Late Facet Limestone Marl Surfaces and Modification of Bedrock. Landscape modification at Laguna de On Island is a characteristic of Late Facet community efforts at the site. In addition to cobble surfaces described above, limestone

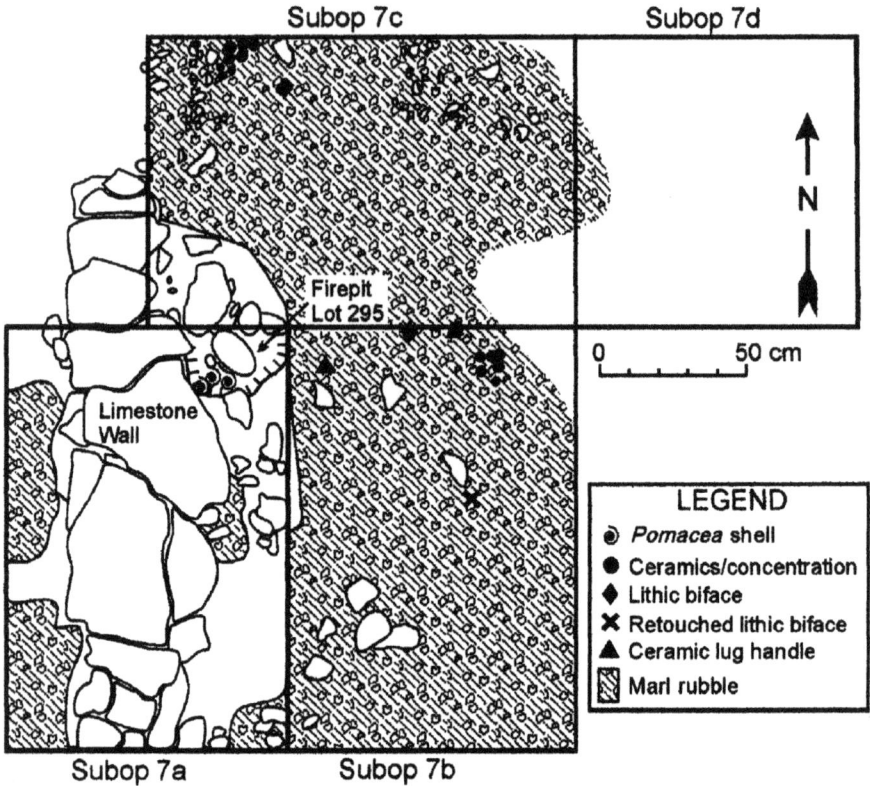

4.11. Plan map of Subop 7, Late Facet marl limestone surface (redrafted by Pam Headrick from Wharton 1998: Figure 20). Pit feature (Lot 295) shown in this map originates below the marl surface and is associated with the Early Facet.

marl floors and modified bedrock are also used as living surfaces (Subops 7, 13, and 16). These marl or bedrock surfaces are encountered in shallow topsoil deposits within 10cm of the surface and are thus assigned to the Late Facet. Limestone marl floors are encountered in the form of eroded and uneven deposits near the surface. They overlie deposits of loam, midden, or fire features (Barnhart and Howard 1997: Figure 24; Wharton 1998: Figures 20 and 21). At Subop 7, one such surface (Lot 263) is recorded from the east and west sides of a large tabular boulder wall alignment (Figure 4.11). Test pits beneath this surface indicate that at least 30cm of underlying brown loam separates the near-surface marl floor from bedrock below (Subop 7c), affirming the artificial origin of the marl surface (Barnhart and Howard 1997; Wharton 1998). At Subop 13, similar thick limestone flooring was encountered beneath surface soils and above 30cm of underlying brown loam (Barnhart and Howard 1997: Figure 26).

In one area of the site (Subop 16a, Lot 222), bedrock actually rises to the surface of the site, where it was difficult to recognize initially as it had decomposed and resembled a limestone marl surface (West 1998a: Figures 16, 17). Excavations in Subop 16a determined that no underlying deposits existed within a 1.5m-diameter area of this bedrock dome, and adjacent soils to this outcrop were surfaced with limestone marl that overlay around 30cm of loam soils above bedrock. Essentially, bedrock represents an uneven surface at Laguna de On, and in the Subop 16 area where it protrudes at the surface it was expanded by marl flooring to create a domestic structure in an opportunistic manner (West 1998a: 49). Such use of bedrock is also noted for Late Postclassic construction at Mayapan and at Santa Rita (Proskouriakoff 1962a: 92; Diane Chase 1982) and in earlier periods in northern Belize at the site of Nohmul (Pyburn 1989: 98).

The limestone floors represent the surface of domestic structures or courtyard areas. Attempts to follow these surfaces horizontally at Subops 7a–d and 16a–d were unable to locate an edge where the surface terminated. In Subops 7a–d, the lack of an edge may be due to the limits of the excavation. In Subops 16a–d, trenches extending east from the modified bedrock and limestone surface were disturbed by uprooted trees, and the surface was continuous in the extent of a 1m x 3m north-running trench (West 1998a: Figure 17). The recovery of a similar surface at Subop 13 also implies that the edge of the upper contours of the west side of Laguna de On Island were covered in limestone flooring. It is not known whether this surfacing is continuous and represents a paved courtyard edge in the central area where limestone floors were encountered in many units or whether these floors form parts of different dwelling areas. It is conceivable that domestic structures and their associated patios would use the same limestone surfacing. Artifacts of a domestic nature were recovered from all three locations, but only Subop 7 had an associated wall and fire feature from a level below the limestone surface.

Limestone marl inclusions are observed throughout the site in topsoil. They often take the form of small (2cm in diameter) clumps. It is possible that thin floors were previously constructed in other areas that have since decomposed. Much of the island's surface may have been plastered in the past, with only the better-constructed floor surfaces lending themselves to preservation and documentation.

Late Facet Burials. Nine individuals are associated with Late Facet deposits at Laguna de On (Rosenswig 1998). This burial population was present within the upper soil levels of the site, encountered within 15cm of the surface. Four of these burials were lying on their sides in a semiflexed position (#2, #6, #12, #16), one was seated-flexed (#15), one was disarticulated (#18), one was lying on its back or side with disarticulated or disturbed legs (#11), and the position could not be determined due to poor preservation for the two remaining burials (#1, #13). The direction of skull placement among these individuals varies (Rosenswig 1998), but three of four semiflexed burials faced west (#2, #12, #16, including two females and one male) and the child burial faced north (#6). The seated-flexed individual, a male, faced northwest (#15). Altogether, two females, one child, and two males were identified and four were unsexed (Rosenswig 1998). Three of these individuals were interred with grave offerings, two of which had freshwater snail shells (#1, #2; Masson 1993; Rosenswig 1998) and the other had a crystal bead near its hand (#15; Sheldon 1998: Figure 9). This burial was placed into surface soils of a terrace built after A.D. 1250. Two interments probably represent sacrifices. Located in the center of a linear depression feature that is interpreted to be a ballcourt (Subop 20), Burial #16 was missing its skull and Burial #18 was disarticulated (Barnhart and Howard 1998: Figures 27 and 28; Rosenswig 1998).

Eight of these nine individuals were placed in shallow graves within 15–20cm below surface. One of these individuals (#1) was buried beneath a low (35cm) mound of earth, and another (Burial #2) is buried beneath a layer of terrace soil fill. This latter burial dates to A.D. 1210–1480±40 (Stafford Labs #3499), and the overlying 1.5m of terrace fill above it is thus at least this old. Other more shallow Late Facet semiflexed, side-lying burials are thought to be contemporary with Burial #2 or later based on their proximity to the surface and their shared preferred burial position with #2. A decline in the formalized treatment of mortuary remains is thus observed from the patterns described for the Early Facet period to those summarized above for the Late Facet (Rosenswig 1998). Late Facet direction of burial orientation and burial position is not consistent, and individuals do not occur in spatial clusters. Little care was taken to inter individuals deeply below the surface. Few funerary offerings are found with Late Facet burials, but this pattern is common to both periods (Rosenswig 1998). As three burials were incomplete, and one was missing its head, perhaps secondary mortuary practices were more common later in the site's history. One burial had cobble-sized burned rocks placed at the skull area (#12) that crushed the skull after interment.

Ongoing analyses of these burials is exploring the variation observed in Late Facet mortuary treatment (Rosenswig 1998). Sampling error may be a factor in the Late Facet patterning at Laguna de On, as lavish Late Postclassic interments were found at Santa Rita (Chase and Chase 1988) and Lamanai (Pendergast 1981). Alternatively, the site of Laguna de On was at the lower end of the northern Belize political hierarchy and few individuals of distinguished status inhabited this community. However, the mortuary patterns are at odds with other evidence from the site that suggests an acceleration in public works construction, investment in domestic architecture, ritual practice, and exchange (Chapter 5), trends that imply that greater status differentiation was in effect at this site in the Late Facet compared to the Early Facet.

Structures II, V, and Island Platforms—Late Facet Shrines. During the Late Facet, the construction of ritual architecture is observed at Laguna de On Island. One feature, a rubble platform and patio complex designated as Structure II (Figure 4.12), served as a shrine or some other type of ritual facility. Structure II represents the "pavement of stone" referred to by Gann during his 1927 site visit, from which he collected several whole vessels (1928). The feature was partially visible from the surface and is located at the high point of the island. Structure II is located only 5m north of Structure I, and ritual activities at these two features are thought to have been contemporary and integrated. An additional line-of-stone "box shrine" was identified on the west shore of Laguna de On (Op 3, Subop 11; Waid and Masson 1998). Island platforms were also identified at the south end of the lagoon. They were artificially constructed of lagoon sediment. Extensive looting of these structures destroyed much of their surface deposits, but the lack of substantial amounts of domestic debris suggests these island platforms may have also served as shrines.

Structures I and II are located at the point of highest elevation of the island, along the east edge of a north-central plateau that is thought to represent a courtyard area. These structures are functionally linked by the recovery of Late Facet ceramic concentrations found around their parameters (Masson, Shumake, and Moan 1997; Rosenswig and Becker 1997; Masson 1999b). As noted previously, Structure I exhibits signs of domestic and ritual activity. In contrast, Structure II has been used exclusively for ritual (Masson 1999b). This feature was largely clear of debris and has a number of discrete, small burned-rock concentrations that were used for specialized burning activities. Artifact frequencies from Structure II differ from Structure I and other domestic assemblages (Chapter 6, this volume; Masson 1999b), in that Structure II has far more ceramics and fewer of other types of debris than any other area examined on the island. The construction of Structures I and II and the ritual activities associated with them are part of a general increase in public focus of ritual at the site during the Late Facet period. The original construction of Structure II in the Late Facet is dated by a radiocarbon date from a carbonized wooden disk (Figure 4.13) embedded into its rubble surface of A.D. 1228–1390±50 (Stafford Labs #3508). Structures I and II appear to have been used for ritual during the Late Facet and perhaps into colonial times. Possible Colonial period use of Structure I is suggested by a radiocarbon date of A.D. 1439–1643±40 (Stafford Labs #3500) and use of

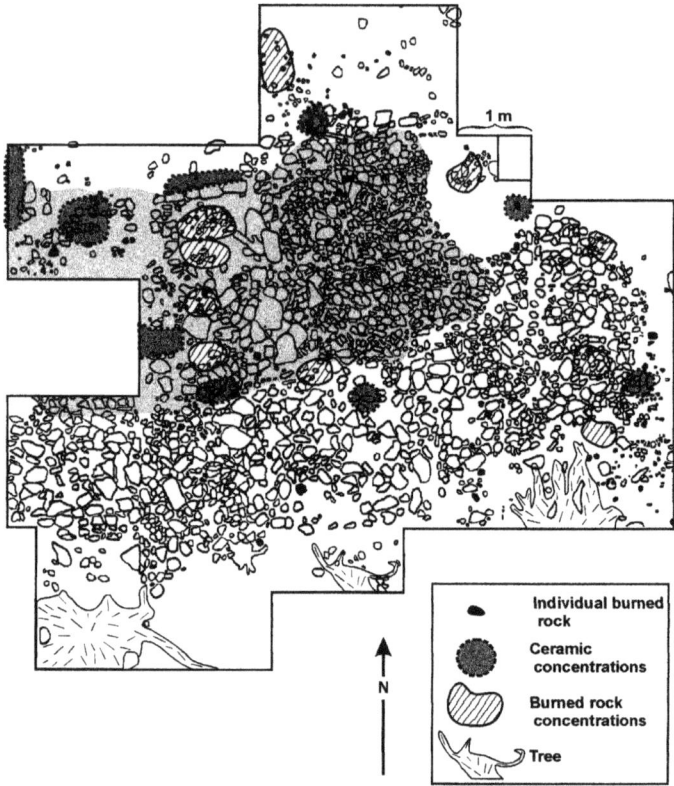

4.12. Plan of Structure II (Subop 12) and associated features (redrafted from Rosenswig and Becker 1997: Figure 12, by Tim Hare).

Structure II at this time is suggested by Gann's 1927 recovery of a ceramic effigy vessel like those of the colonial era in Belize (Gann 1928; Thompson 1977; Masson 1997; Elizabeth Graham, personal communication 1994).

Structure II is a rubble platform of 30cm (Figure 4.12), oriented 20 degrees west of north. It is constructed of softball-sized cobbles, within which are numerous concentrations of small, cube-shaped, intensively fire-blackened rocks (Figure 4.12). In front of the platform on the south side, a rectangular cobble patio extends (Figure 4.12). The burned rock features on the platform may be due to burning of incense or igniting fires. A carbonized disk of wood (13cm in diameter) was recovered from the surface rubble of Structure II, but its specific function is unknown (Figure 4.13). Gann collected over two hundred offerings from the surface at Laguna de On Island, presumably from Structure II, including copper bells, ceramic effigy figurines, ceramic incense burners, ceramic bowls, jade beads, and obsidian blades (1928). His collec-

4.13. Carbonized disk found embedded in rubble platform of Structure II.

tion was apparently thorough, as few materials were recovered from the sur-face of this structure when it was excavated in 1996 (Rosenswig and Becker 1997). There is no evidence that Gann excavated into the structure or around its periphery. Although the large quantity of cranial fragments of large game were not found at Structure II during our excavations, Gann reported them (1928). These materials represent an important similarity with Structure I.

Structure V, a line-of-stone box shrine located on the west shore of the lagoon near the edge of a prominent bluff (Figure 4.2, described previously), is a Late Facet construction as indicated by associated ceramics. Island plat-forms were identified on two islands at the lagoon's south end that also date to the Late Facet (Masson 1993; Chapter 2, this volume). Structure V and the two island platforms provide further indications of the acceleration of public works and religious features during the later occupation at Laguna de On.

Ballcourt. A linear depression cut into bedrock at the north end of Laguna de On Island (Structure IV, Subop 20; Barnhart 1998a) is interpreted to be a sunken ballcourt feature. The depression is 12m long in a north-south direc-tion, 8m wide (east-west), and 1m deep at its lowest point from surrounding terrain (Barnhart 1998a). The central "alley" of the depression is flat, and the northern end is shallower (.50cm) than the southern end (1m). The feature was tested by a cross-section trench that bisected it east-west at its center point and a couple of other test trenches bisecting the northern and

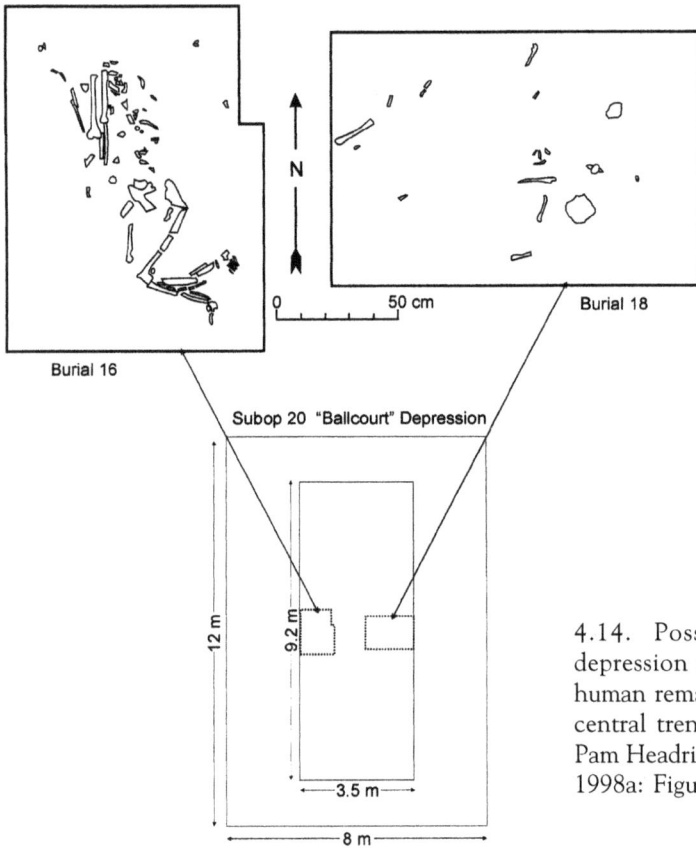

4.14. Possible ballcourt depression feature showing human remains recovered in central trench (compiled by Pam Headrick from Barnhart 1998a: Figures 25, 27, 28).

southern ends (Barnhart 1998a). As many types of architectural spaces can be designated as ball-playing areas (Freidel, Schele, and Parker 1993), the small size and lack of elaborate architectural investment in this feature does not inhibit its interpretation as a ballcourt. Two primary forms of evidence support this interpretation. First, the feature is not explained naturally. It is not a sinkhole, or a drainage gully. It is completely enclosed. Second, a primary characteristic of ballcourts in Mesoamerica is their association with sacrifice. Ballcourts are also often dedicated or made sacred through ritual offerings in their center (Eaton 1982). The center trench placed in this feature by Barnhart (1998a) tested the hypothesis that this anthropogenic feature was a ballcourt by trenching its center to look for a feature of ritual significance. Within this trench, Barnhart found two adult burials (Figure 4.14). Only one was identifiable to gender, a male. It was decapitated, and the skull was missing. The second burial was disarticulated, and the full skeleton was not present. The decapitated skeleton was lying on its side, semiflexed, facing west, in the Late Facet tradition. Both burials were

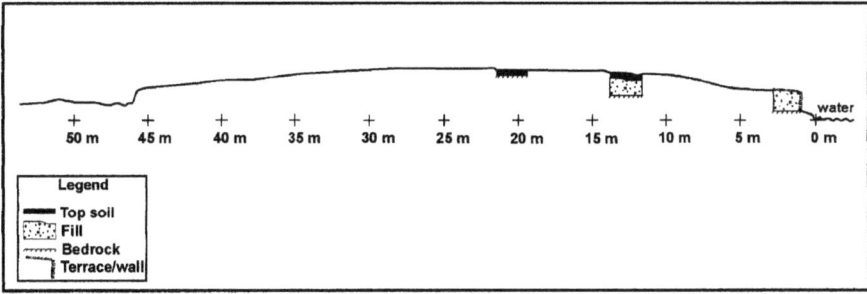

4.15. Cross section of Laguna de On Island at Subop 5, showing terrace construction fill on the island's east side (drawn by the author, reproduced from Barnhart and Howard 1998: Figure 18).

located 15cm below the surface, also a Late Facet trait. These burial characteristics and the behavior of landscape modification suggest that the ballcourt dates to the Late Facet.

Minimally, there is evidence of mortuary ceremonialism in association with the use of the central space in the depression as a burial place. Burials were not encountered in the trenches at the north and south ends of this feature, nor on the central slopes of it in the center. Ballcourts are a critical element to the *Popul Vuh* Quiche Maya creation myth that has its roots in the Classic period or earlier (Coe 1989). In this myth, the ballcourt is the context for themes of ritual sacrifice (through decapitation) and rebirth. These themes played pivotal roles in the first creation of the world and the reenactment of these rituals was considered critical to the maintenance of Maya society, or so rulers claimed (Freidel, Schele, and Parker 1993: 355–372). The anthropogenic nature of this odd linear depression feature at Laguna de On Island and the recovery of two uncharacteristic (for the island) skeletons buried in its center suggest that this feature was conceptualized as a ballcourt for inhabitants of this site during the Late Facet.

Terraces. Terrace facilities were built along the central east edge of the island at this time (Barnhart and Howard 1997; Figure 4.15). These terraces extend the island's upper contour and create more elevated surface area suitable for habitation. They represent considerable efforts in earthmoving and serve as an index of public works at the site. A stone rubble canoe dock was also constructed along the east edge of the island (Masson and Gonzalez 1997). As few artifacts are located on the dock, and deposits surrounding it are inundated, the postulated Late Facet date for this feature is not secure.

Investigations indicate that terraces were constructed at Laguna de On to artificially modify the island's topography along its central east sector

(Figure 4.15). The date for the terrace fill is derived from an extended burial (Burial #2) found in a midden beneath the fill, which was radiocarbon dated to A.D. 1280–1410±40 (Stafford Labs #3499). At Subops 5 and 19, terraces connect the high central contour eastward to the waterline in a nearly horizontal plane. Bedrock is highly uneven, and drops sharply in elevation just east of the upper east contour. Bedrock is 40cm below the surface at the top of the east upper contour at Subop 5c, and it plummets to 1.4m below the surface at a distance 5.6m to the east at Subop 5b. Terrace fill placed over bedrock at 5b thus effectively raises the ground surface in this area to a nearly equivalent elevation as the center of the island (Figure 4.15). Bedrock is 1.5m deep at the shore of the island at a distance 8m further to the east at Subop 5 (Barnhart and Howard 1997: 18). Overlying terrace fill in Subop 19a also raises the island's surface 133–160cm above bedrock (and above a Preceramic living surface; Rosenswig and Stafford 1998). As observed for Subops 5b and 5c, the depth of bedrock in Subop 19a is contrasted by a bedrock depth of only 40cm in nearby units in Subop 17 (8m to the west) and Subop 8 (5m to the north). Essentially, Late Facet fill has elevated the island's surface 1–1.5m above bedrock for an area at least 13m long from the island's highest east contour to the shore in two areas tested. These efforts made the island more inhabitable. The surface topsoils of these areas contain scatters of domestic debris that suggest living surfaces were created atop the terraces. Along the edge of this east-extending terrace, masonry walls are preserved in a few places. No modification of the western slope has been documented at Subop 5 (Sheldon 1998), but at Subops 2 and 3, levelling of the upper contour in a westward direction through the addition of 50cm of cobble and boulder fill is documented (Masson 1993).

The construction of the stone dock (Subop 14) may date to this period (Masson and Gonzalez 1997), when modification of the eastern side of the island occurred. It is notable that the east side of the island is closest to the shore. The construction of terraces and retaining walls had the effect of making the east side of the island steeper. A fortified palisade may have been built around this terrace edge and the construction of a dock suggests controlled access to the island. As postholes are difficult to detect in Laguna de On topsoils, the documentation of a palisade is problematic.

SUMMARY

Interesting contrasts emerge when Early Facet features are compared to those of the Late Facet. Domestic architectural remains in the lower levels suggest that constructions were entirely of perishable materials. Fire features appear far more common in the Early Facet lower stratigraphic levels, but one radiocarbon date suggests the use of one of these features during the Late Facet. Mortuary patterns are more standardized in the Early Facet, based on the current sample of burial features and radiocarbon dating. A rigid pattern of seated-flexed (or side-lying flexed) west-facing pit burials is observed during the Early Facet, and the favored position in the Late Facet appears to be side-lying, semiflexed, and west-facing. More variability is observed among Late Facet interment positions. Late Facet burials were also placed in shallow deposits, where they were more easily disturbed. They were more commonly disarticulated, and two of these burials were located within the ballcourt feature, perhaps as sacrifices. It is possible that some of these characteristics were common to both periods, as not all features and burials have been AMS dated.

The Late Facet marks an acceleration in construction of a diverse range of features, including domestic platforms, shrines, terraces, a possible ballcourt, and small island platforms. The construction of these public works implies the exercise of persuasive or coercive power that is absent in the Early Facet. Enhanced religious activities suggested by the shrines and the ballcourt reflect increased effort at community or regional integration. Evidence for intensified social hierarchies is expressed by the increased investment in domestic architecture (at Subops 7, 8, and 17), yet social status differentiation is not implied by Late Facet mortuary patterns. It is possible that an insufficient sample of mortuary remains is providing a misleading picture from this site. Regional lines of evidence such as settlement (Chapter 2) and economic development (Chapter 5) suggest that the Late Facet was a time of florescence and growth for northern Belize, presumably in response to an economic and demographic surge felt all along the east coast of Yucatán through accelerating world system trade networks.

The construction projects in the Late Facet at Laguna de On raise some interesting questions regarding the type of political authority that controlled this site. According to Renfrew and Bahn (1991: 178–180) this amount of earthmoving is easily accomplished among loosely organized, kin-based tribal societies. However, it is known that Maya Postclassic cultures were organized into secondary states (Blake 1985; Fox 1987), with full knowledge of highly stratified societies that existed in Mesoamerica in close spatial and temporal proximity. Perhaps more curious is the lack of more substantial construction at Laguna de On, considering the impressive architectural works in evidence at the nearby capitals of Lamanai (Pendergast 1981) and Caye Coco (Barnhart 1998a; Masson and Rosenswig 1998b). The public works at Laguna de On do not represent overly conspicuous expenditures of cooperative labor investment.

One might then ask, why was it necessary to expand the habitation space upon the surface of Laguna de On Island (through terracing) and was this need related to an increase in shrine-centered ritual practice? There may have been a demographic expansion at this time, as the west-bluff shore settlement has yielded primarily Late Facet–type ceramics and features. Changing regional conditions such as acceleration in warfare may have made island habitation more attractive for defense. The construction of steep-walled terraces and perhaps wooden palisades may have added to this advantage. Perhaps the shallow, cursory graves of the Late Facet reflect a violent end to this community. Religious revitalization may have played a centralizing role in response to such regional changes. The lines of evidence outlined above suggest that comparisons of the Early and Late Facet occupations at Laguna de On reflect important changes in northern Belize Postclassic political and economic systems that affected this agrarian village. These themes are examined in regional context at the conclusion of Chapter 6.

5

Economic Production and Exchange at Laguna de On

THE MERCANTILE MODEL AND ECONOMIC PATTERNS AT LAGUNA DE ON

A model describing the mercantile nature of Postclassic Maya society was developed during investigations at Cozumel Island on the east coast of the Yucatán peninsula (Rathje 1975; Sabloff and Rathje 1975; Freidel 1981; Freidel and Sabloff 1984). The decrease in hierarchical organization during the Postclassic period is interpreted in this model as an efficient attribute of a more commercial-oriented society. Commercial activities of this period were linked to expanded international markets and a maritime trade network. An increased degree of community autonomy facilitated greater direct participation of producers in the exchange of a variety of commodities, to an extent far beyond levels observed in the Classic period. These changes followed the collapse of the Classic period southern kingdoms and the heavy tribute demands they placed on supporting populations (Rathje 1975; Sabloff and Rathje 1975; Kepecs, Feinman, and Boucher 1994).

According to this model, opportunities for exchange at markets and trading ports were open to many members of society, and a greater degree of economic affluence resulted. Communities such as Laguna de On can directly test this model through examining wealth and status distinctions among members of Postclassic Maya society. Rathje's interpretation of a more broadly affluent society proposed that its members were less disposed toward the outward display of status signifyers, such as large monumental architecture or finely made crafts (1975: 416–417). In this model, material culture is geared toward efficiency, and harnessed labor and energy were channeled toward mass economic production rather than toward quality aesthetic craft production (Rathje 1975; Rathje, Gregory, and Wiseman 1978; Sabloff and Rathje 1975).

Elements of this model are best considered independently for their relative merit in the analysis of the economy of Laguna de On and its regional context. Specifically, the notion that production "efficiency" promoted a decline in aesthetics of Postclassic products such as ceramics for the purpose of mass export in commercial enterprise is debatable. The Laguna de On data do not support this contention but do suggest that diminished invest-ment in architectural works and decreased intracommunity social status dis-tinctions were characteristic of this period. These trends marked part of a societal transformation that placed a new emphasis on commercial exchange. Evidence for active participation in broad-ranging long-distance commercial spheres, even at peripheral, small, rural production communities such as Laguna de On, provides a window into the full impact of commercial systems of Late Postclassic Maya society initially identified by Rathje and Sabloff (Rathje 1975; Sabloff and Rathje 1975).

Aesthetics and Efficiency of Postclassic Ceramic Production

The unfavorable assessment of the relative aesthetic value of Postclassic craftsmanship versus that of the Classic period claims that the degree of skill was allegedly compromised over time in favor of "efficiency" (Rathje 1975). This notion may have been influenced by the nature of highly eroded and fragmented surface Postclassic ceramics and the unfortunate use of the term "decadent" to describe Postclassic period crafts (Proskouriakoff 1955). The identification of attributes used to measure aesthetics is a problematic issue that has yet to be defined for comparing changing ceramic styles over time for the Maya, though Prudence Rice (1980) has pioneered such efforts with paste characterizations. Indeed, it may be argued that some of the most resplendent and finely made ceramic vessels of any Maya period are repre-sented in the Postclassic period. One fine example of workmanship is ob-served in various vessels of the Buk phase at Lamanai (Pendergast 1981). The general quality of slips and pastes even on common slipped Postclassic serving wares is equivalent or superior to those of earlier periods (Webb 1964: 571; Masson and Mock n.d.). This pattern is also noted for Payil Red wares of northern Belize as well (Masson 1999c; Masson and Mock n.d.), as the highly fired fine pastes of Payil Red and the quality of this ware's slip compare favorably to some of the finest ceramics ever made in the Maya area.

Evidence for the "efficient" mass production of ceramics as proposed by Rathje and Sabloff (Rathje 1975: 431, 433; Sabloff and Rathje 1975: 82) has yet to be recovered archaeologically. Most ceramic assemblages of Late Postclassic age consist primarily of footed dishes, small bowls, and jars used in food preparation and consumption in household and ritual contexts. These are generally analogous to utilitarian domestic assemblages of earlier periods. No evidence for mass production and transport of perishable commodities in vessels designed for this purpose has been quantitatively reported or de-scribed, nor have facilities been found where such containers and their commodities would have been warehoused. Rathje and colleagues (Rathje 1975; Sabloff and Rathje 1975; Rathje, Gregory, and Wiseman 1978) proposed that the common Postclassic period "sag bottom" of tripod-footed dish forms was a design amenable to stacking and transport, but paste characteristics suggest that such ceramics were made and used on a primarily local basis (Sanders 1960; Prudence Rice 1980; Mock 1998; Masson and Mock n.d.). Ceramics were probably not the most efficient medium for the transport of commodities such as honey, when less-destructible containers such as gourds were available. Based on current evidence, it is not possible to confirm whether Postclassic Maya ceramics were more "efficient" for commercial purposes than those of earlier time periods.

Processes of Postclassic Mercantile Development at Laguna de On

Other aspects of the mercantile model are directly testable and are reflected in the Postclassic archaeological record. The decreased investment in architecture compared to the Classic period is one sign of efficient Postclassic strategies that is observed at centers such as Mayapan and Tulum (Webb 1964: 573; Rathje 1975: 421). The reinterpretation of the downsizing trends observed in Postclassic architecture as a reflection of an emphasis on commercial enterprise and other organizational transformations rather than as a sign of devolution represents a significant interpretive breakthrough for understanding Postclassic Maya developmental processes. While Postclassic architecture may not preserve as well, Webb notes that one cannot judge a society by the quality of the enduring ruins they create, and the incredibly thick walls needed to support vaults that created "ridiculously small" rooms of the Classic period were a highly inefficient way to build (Webb 1964: 573). In fact, Webb cites an architectural study of Maya structures (Roys 1934; Webb 1964: 580) that concluded that the structures at Tulum incorporated the most sophisticated combination of building techniques of all sites examined in the Maya area.

The lack of investment in public or private architecture at Postclassic centers, relative to the Classic period, thus correlates with an amplified emphasis on commercial enterprise. To what degree did commercial production and exchange accelerate within the Postclassic period Maya provinces over time? This process is not well understood, and it forms the foundation of Rathje and Sabloff's model for the rise of mercantilism. Several types of evidence reflect the development of thriving commercial activities during the Late Postclassic. Documentary sources describe such activities at Spanish contact (Pina Chan 1978). Eastern and northern coastal trading centers and ports are established during this period, implying the amplification of maritime exchange from earlier periods (Andrews et al. 1988). Changes in settlement patterns in northern Belize exhibit a greater number of communities and increased elite construction projects at this time (see Chapters 2 and 6 of this volume). An increase in the quantity and diversity of long-distance imports at small Maya Postclassic sites such as Laguna de On would also reflect the growth of mercantile activity. These patterns are considered in this chapter in the diachronic assessment of economic activity at this site.

Along the east coast of Yucatán, Quintana Roo, and Belize, a number of trading ports appear during the Postclassic period that would have based their economy on the exchange of long-distance commodities and inland or locally produced goods (McKillop 1980; Andrews and Vail 1990; Guderjan and Garber 1995). After A.D. 1200, the sites of El Meco, Cozumel, Tulum, Ichpaatun, and Santa Rita reached their maximum florescence (Sanders 1960; Robles and Andrews 1986; Freidel and Sabloff 1984; Chase and Chase 1988). The ceramics of the east coast are closely linked to the center of Mayapan (Connor 1983), and it is probable that exchange centered along the east coast formed a primary foundation of Mayapan's economy (Freidel and Sabloff 1984). A paucity of Late Postclassic settlements along the west coast of Yucatán (Andrews 1977: 73) may support this suggestion that Mayapan's economic strengths lay to the east, a trend that Pollock (1962) and Roys (1962) also ascertained from documentary evidence. The east coast centers may have emerged in a vacuum of power created by the fall of Chichén Itzá around A.D. 1200 (Andrews 1993), which had wielded much influence in regional economy during the Early Postclassic (Andrews et al. 1988; Kepecs, Feinman, and Boucher 1994). An acceleration in the scale of international trade and exchange is reported throughout Mesoamerica after A.D. 1200 (Blanton and Feinman 1984; Carmack 1996). The east coast of the Maya Lowlands actively participated in this world of trade (Sabloff and Rathje 1975; Pina Chan 1978). The collapse of Chichén Itzá may have created new opportunities for emerging east coast centers at this time.

Commercial activity has been linked to religious integration in the "pilgrimage fair" model proposed for Cozumel Island (Freidel 1981). Religious shrines are also thought to be closely connected to trading activity at Tulum (Miller 1982). The complex of shrines at these coastal trading centers is thought to have served as a cult of integration for international traders convening at neutral religious centers (Miller 1982). Sacred places constructed at these sites may have helped to defuse potentially hostile encounters among traders from different Mesoamerican cultures by providing a meeting place on sacred ground. This interpretation follows Victor Turner's (1974; Miller 1982: 95–96) characterization of ports of trade as sacred, neutral places that discourage conflict and facilitate diplomacy. Sites along the east coast of Yucatán such as Tulum and Santa Rita invested considerable effort in religious mural art, perhaps for this reason. Attributes of coastal Postclassic

Maya murals, which contain a mixture of iconographic elements that resemble both the Maya codices (Taube 1992) and "Mixteca-Puebla" (Robertson 1970) or "international style" (Smith and Heath-Smith 1980) motifs, were designed to appeal to diverse, cosmopolitan cultural audiences.

Laguna de On provides a view of Postclassic society from a site that is neither a political center or a coastal trading port. The economy of this site is thus probably typical of hundreds of inland sites whose production and consumption energies fueled the international Late Postclassic exchange sphere. Laguna was located near the headwaters of the Freshwater Creek drainage that leads to the Caribbean Sea. Freshwater Creek was one of several aquatic avenues to the interior along which commercial items probably made their way in and out of inland communities. Due to its inland position, Laguna de On's location probably occupied a lesser role in coastal exchange, although it probably brokered items to and from smaller inland settlements that were not close to a waterway linked to the sea. The small size of this site suggests it would have held a lower-rung position in regional prestige economies. Occupants of Laguna de On probably participated in regional markets, although the extent to which these systems operated is difficult to ascertain based on current data. Sites such as Laguna de On represent marginal locations of little political advantage that serve as a highly useful gauge for determining the full effects of Late Postclassic "mercantile" transformations. Laguna's relative affluence and access to useful local and long-distance items, described below, provides a useful comparison to the distribution of commodities at central communities such as Mayapan, Tulum, San Gervasio, and Santa Rita.

The Chetumal province is referred to as an affluent one in documentary sources (Roys 1957; Pina Chan 1978: 39; Jones 1989). This province produced textiles, cacao, honey, flints, and other tropical products and it represented an important zone that lay between the northern Yucatán centers and the Peten Lakes and Honduras to the south. Island sites along the coast of Belize are linked into this Late Postclassic exchange sphere by the identification of Tulum-related ceramics (McKillop 1980; Guderjan and Garber 1995) at sites such as Moho Cay that served as trading nodes for obsidian and other items (McKillop 1980; Dreiss and Brown 1989).

Evidence presented in Chapter 4 suggests that during the last half of the Late Postclassic at Laguna de On, after A.D. 1250, acceleration in public works and ritual activity is observed. On a small scale, this community reflects an upward developmental trend observed at coastal centers in league with Mayapan. Diachronic economic changes between the Early Facet and the Late Facet of Laguna de On are examined in this chapter, with the goal of addressing two primary issues. First, what changes are observed in Laguna de On's economy over time that might reflect the community's participation in the developing Late Postclassic Mesoamerican world of trade? Second, what evidence is observed for interhousehold status differences at this site during the Early and Late Facets? What affects did changing regional political and economic organization have on the development of status hierarchies within this community?

ECONOMIC PRODUCTION AND EXCHANGE SPHERES AT LAGUNA DE ON

Production activities at the Laguna de On settlement were diverse, consisting of subsistence agriculture, inferred cash crops including cacao and cotton, hunting and fishing, textiles, ceramic vessels, lithic tools, and lithic raw materials. This product list is derived from ethnohistoric sources and artifacts recovered from the site (Pina Chan 1978). The production of these commodities was geared toward one or more of three spheres of consumption or exchange, including: (1) domestic production, consumption, and household maintenance, (2) local exchange spheres within the Chetumal and Dzuluinicob province regions, and (3) long-distance exchange with regions outside of northern Belize/Quintana Roo as indicated by the presence of exotic materials at the site.

Domestic production and consumption at the site are defined as those economic activities taking place within the community for the purpose of maintenance of the members of households comprising the settlement. The household is assumed in this analysis to have been the primary organizational institution through which labor was integrated. The degree to which household production units engaged in surplus production for local exchange is not determined at Laguna de On, due to the limited preservation of domestic architecture and the difficulty in locating or defining discrete domestic units. It is probable that local surplus production was closely linked to household producers, as indicators of formalized craft specialization beyond the household level in the form of specialized facilities and abundant concentrations of craft production debris (as defined by Shafer 1982) have not been found at the site.

Local exchange systems examined at Laguna de On are defined as intercommunity economic relationships of a reciprocal down-the-line or regional-market variety (as defined in Renfrew and Bahn 1991: 322–323). Some form of community redistribution may have been practiced, as evidence for differential access to such resources as large game suggests (Masson 1999a). Despite hints of slightly privileged access to finer items observed in distributions of formal tools at the site, no evidence for exclusive monopolies or excessive control over local commodities is observed at Laguna de On. Utilitarian objects are of local northern Belize manufacture and were probably obtained through intercommunity exchange or they were made at the site. Strict control of the flow of commodities is not observed and multiple systems of exchange probably operated in Belize simultaneously as has been suggested for previous periods (McAnany 1991; Hester and Shafer 1984).

The role of village leaders in mediating the local economy is not known, and their role may have been more significant in the realm of long-distance exchange. The term "local" is loosely defined, given the paucity of regional economic studies for the northern Belize or southern Quintana Roo regions during the Postclassic period. Generally, local exchange refers to exchange among communities within regions estimated to approximate the size of ethnohistoric provinces as defined by Roys (Figure 2.2; Roys 1957). Laguna de On's position on the southern edge of the known extent of the Chetumal province (Figure 2.2; Jones 1989: Map 2) placed it in a boundary position with special opportunities for exchange with the Dzuluinicob province to the south. Exchange among communities within these provinces probably varied with proximity to raw-material sources as well as terms of interprovince political relationships. Evidence suggests that resource diversity in this area existed, as observed in flints and chalcedonies around individual sites (Oland 1998, 1999). This diversity affected community assemblages and intersite exchange relationships. For example, Laguna de On's proximity to the site of Colha probably enabled it to have a more advantaged exchange relationship with this site than communities located further away from Colha such as Caye Coco.

Regional exchange probably also existed among neighboring or more distant lowland provinces. The need for such exchange was generated by resource heterogeneity among interacting provinces (Graham 1994; Rathje, Gregory, and Wiseman 1978). Lithic quartz and other common, but nonlocal, lithic raw materials found at Laguna de On were probably obtained through exchange from communities within the Chetumal province or neighboring provinces. These lithics are consistently present in low proportions, and their natural origin has not been found in the chert and chalcedony beds located to date near Laguna de On (Oland 1999). These materials are found in domestic contexts and expedient tools are made from them, suggesting that they were not highly valued or difficult to obtain. Further work is needed to determine the source of such materials, and distribution data is needed for understanding community and regional exchange.

Long-distance exchange in this study is defined as exchange beyond the parameters of the Maya Lowlands, represented archaeologically in the form of commodities not obtainable in the lowlands. Laguna de On's long-distance exchange and emulation networks were linked to coastal economic trade that operated around the Yucatán peninsula, from the central Mexican liason port of Xicalanco, Tabasco, to Honduras (Pina Chan 1978: 45; Scholes and Roys 1948: 34–35). Some artifact styles appear earlier outside the Maya Low-lands during the Terminal Classic or Early Postclassic periods, including spindle whorls, lenticular knives, and side-notched projectile points (Thompson 1939; Shafer and Hester 1983). These styles are attributed to maritime-facilitated interaction with the Gulf Coast or other Mexican enclaves. Obsidian blades come from the highlands of Guatemala, primarily from the Ixtepeque source (Sidrys 1983; Dreiss and Brown 1989; McKillop 1980; Henry Chaya, personal communication 1998). Other exotic raw-material objects such as volcanic or sedimentary rock metates (Sidrys 1976), greenstone celts, greenstone, crystal, or mineral beads, copper bells, and even a fleck of gold represent imported valuables obtained via long-distance networks that extended south to the Maya Mountains, Honduras, and west to the Gulf Coast (Scholes and Roys 1948: 29–30).

Ideas that flowed from the Peten to Belize and northern Yucatán (and the reverse) are expressed in stylistic emulation of ceramics such as engraved redware vessels, effigy censers, and various undecorated forms found throughout these regions (Mock 1994). Although differences in paste and slip are definitely observed from type sites such as Mayapan (Smith 1971), Cozumel (Connor 1983), Tulum (Sanders 1960), Santa Rita (Diane Chase 1982, 1984), Lamanai (Graham and Pendergast 1989: 11), and the Peten Lakes (Bullard 1973; Prudence Rice 1980, 1987a), these changes are attributable to differences in local raw materials available for the manufacture of paste and slips. General conformity of common utilitarian redware and unslipped forms ties Laguna de On and other northern Belize sites to pan-lowlands spheres extending from the Peten to northern Yucatán. The circum-Yucatecan trade route of the Late Postclassic assuredly fostered long-distance stylistic emulation that had its roots in economic symbiosis and promoted a sense of pan-lowland ethnic integration.

Local and long-distance exchange spheres, while they can be examined separately, are unlikely to have operated in isolation from one another. In many ethnographic cases, subsistence and utilitarian exchange operate simultaneously at intercommunity or interpolity gatherings when more formalized gift-giving of nonutilitarian valuables is practiced ceremoniously among elites (Mauss 1925; Malinowski 1922; Renfrew 1986: 8). Elites thus have a role in utilitarian exchange by providing the venue for intervillage interaction (Freidel 1981). An additional difficulty in defining local exchange as utilitarian exchange is the mixture of cultural contexts for the use of "utilitarian" and "nonutilitarian" artifacts in the Postclassic period. There is considerable use of utilitarian artifacts in Postclassic ceremony, as indicated by the inclusion of unslipped olla fragments and serving bowls in concentrations of smashed censers at Laguna de On (Masson, Shumake, and Moan 1997; Masson 1999b) and the depiction of such vessels in New Year's rituals on Postclassic codices (Diane Chase 1985, 1988; Masson 1999b) and murals (Ball 1982; Miller 1982).

In this chapter, patterns of domestic production, local exchange, and long-distance exchange are examined at Laguna de On Island. This data is presented in order to understand the integration of Laguna's economies, and to examine developmental trends in the economy of this community that are related to regional processes of mercantile development and social change. For each class of data examined in this chapter, the assemblages of the Early Facet and Late Facet are described. As volumetric dimensions of the Early and Late Facet vary across the site, comparisons over time are accomplished through the examination of relative frequencies or ratios within each set of deposits. In general, the Early Facet deposits are volumetrically greater than those of the Late Facet, as soils and features comprising the lower 20–30cm of soil in each unit comprise the Early Facet, and features confined to the top 15cm of each unit comprise the Late Facet, though some variability is observed in these depths. The assignment of stratigraphic deposits to the Early or Late Facet has been accomplished with the aid of 14C dates of associated features from across the site and cross-referencing of these dates to associated deposits as described in Chapter 4 (Stafford 1998; Masson and Stafford 1998).

Identifying artifact distributions that reflect patterns of economic organization and social differentiation is of particular interest to this study. Both utilitarian and nonutilitarian trajectories of production and consumption are examined for the entire site, as well as the manner in which various artifacts are distributed spatially across the settlement. The evidence for differential access to specific commodities is evaluated to determine whether economic advantages were linked to a social hierarchy in the Early or Late Facet occupations of the site. The analysis of economic data tests interpretations of patterns of features and architecture (Chapter 4), which suggest that more investment in these latter projects during the Late Facet may have distinguished the social status of some families beyond the degree observed for the Early Facet.

Table 5.1 summarizes the interpreted function and social status of zones tested across the island based on feature analysis. Essentially, two ritual Late Facet features are identified at the site: the Subop 20 ballcourt and the Subop 12 rubble shrine foundation. The ballcourt date is inferred from the stratigraphic context and anatomical position of burials found in its center, which matches patterns observed in Late Facet burials across the site. Beneath the rubble shrine in Subop 12, a domestic zone of features and midden is found, which 14C dates assign to the Early Facet. The rubble construction of the shrine itself is of Late Facet date. Across the site, five subops tested upper-status residental zones, identified from associated architecture and artifacts and their central position on the island. These include Subop 8 (Structure I), Subop 17, Subops 2 and 3, Subop 6, and Subop 5. All but Subop 5

Table 5.1—Functional variability of zones tested at Laguna de On Island (synopsis of Chapter 5 comparisons of artifact assemblage variability)

Ritual/Upper-Status Residential Zones	Early Facet	Late Facet
Subop 20	unknown	hypothesized function: ballcourt, burials
Subop 12 (Structure II)	rubble platform, underlying brown loam sheet midden; hypothesized function: shrine built over upper-status residential zone	topsoil and upper surface of rubble platform, burned rock features, ceramic concentrations; hypothesized function: shrine
Subop 8 (Structure I)	brown loam sheet midden, fire features, burials; hypothesized function: upper-status residential zone	line-of-stone three-sided wall foundation, east-facing structure, burial #4, God K eccentric, smashed censer/animal bone concentrations; hypothesized function: upper-status residence with abundant amount of ritual activity perhaps converted to shrine function over time
Subop 5	upper-status residential zone, south central part of site, burials, abundant mortuary ritual activity	upper-status residential zone, burials, with some mortuary ritual and scarce censer sherds
UPPER-STATUS RESIDENTIAL ZONES/NO RITUAL ACTIVITY		
Subops 2, 3	none (not completely excavated)	courtyard/patio surface, upper-status residential zone affiliated with Subop 8 with little ritual activity
Subops 17, 19, 6	upper-status residential zone, near Subop 8	upper-status residential zone, near Subop 8
RESIDENTIAL ZONES/MORTUARY ACTIVITY		
Subops 7, 13, 16	residential zone, northwest part of site	residential zone, northwest part of site, burial (Subop 7)
Subops 9, 10, 11, 15	residential zone, northeast part of site, burial (Subop 9)	residential zone, northeast part of site
Subop 18	residential zone, south part of site, burials (Subop 18a)	residential zone, south part of site, burials (Subops 18, 18a)
OTHER		
Subop 14	dock?/unknown	dock

are in the vicinity of Subop 8 (Structure I). Structure I is a location where increased ritual activities are recorded over time. It represents a domestic zone where ritual activity occurred, either simultaneously or sequentially (Masson 1999b). Other residential zones of lesser status are identified at the site, including Subops 13, 7, 15, 9–11, and 18. Subop 14 represents a dock with submerged deposits. Throughout this chapter, artifact assemblages will be compared among these zones to see if variation in quality of materials is patterned for higher-status residential zones and/or zones of ritual activity located near to upper-status domestic areas.

For each category of artifacts analyzed in this chapter, the usefulness of these data for understanding various systems of Laguna de On's economy is discussed. Each artifact class contributes variably to issues of local production, local exchange, or long-distance exchange relationships. The examination of artifacts begins below with a consideration of subsistence economy. Subsistence production is an aspect of Laguna's economy that was most closely linked to domestic maintenance. Ground stone, faunal bone, net weights, and projectile points reflect extraction of domesticated and wild resources. Local lithic tools attest to subsistence production and local exchange. Examinations of Laguna de On's craft production in textile, shell, and ceramic industries follow. The manufacture of such commodities was tied to local and long-distance exchange. A consideration of patterns of consumption of obsidian artifacts and exotic ornaments at Laguna de On is presented next. These items were obtained through networks of long-distance exchange and were not made locally. At the conclusion of this chapter, the variation of combined artifact assemblages at distinctive areas of the site is compared to search for evidence of economic differences that are tied to social status. Larger-scale patterns of economic change over time from the Early to Late Facet are evaluated at the end of this chapter, and their implications for organizational transformations of Postclassic Maya society are explored.

Ground Stone and Maize Processing at Laguna de On

A total of eleven manos and eight metates have been recovered from Laguna de On (Table 5.2). They are equitably distributed among the Early (N = 7) and Late (N = 12) Facets at the site. Most of the ground stone was made of local materials, including limestone and coral. Sidrys (1983: Table 11) notes a decrease in the use of Maya Mountains sedimentary sources in the Postclassic period (compared to the Classic period), and an increase in imports of volcanic ground-stone materials from Guatemala or Honduras. This pattern is not observed at Laguna de On, in which local materials predominate in both the Early and Late Facets. The type of ground stone found at Laguna de On may be an indicator of limited means for acquiring exotic ground stone at this site.

Table 5.2—Ground stone at Laguna de On

| | Late Facet | | | Early Facet | |
	Mano	Metate		Mano	Metate
		NORTH CENTRAL AREA			
Subop 8	0	0	Subop 8	1	0
Subop 12	0	0	Subop 12	0	0
Subops 2, 3	3	2	Subop 17	0	1
Subtotal	3	2	Subtotal	1	1
		SOUTH CENTRAL AREA			
Subop 5	1	3		0	0
		NORTHEAST AREA			
Subop 9	1	0		0	0
		NORTHWEST AREA			
Subop 7	1	0	Subop 7	3	1
		SOUTH AREA			
Subop 18	0	0	Subop 18	1	0
		DOCK			
Subop 14	0	1		0	0
Total Level 1	6	6	Total Level 2	5	2
Total Manos at Site: 11		Total Metates at Site: 8			

The distribution of manos and metates across the site supports the postulated identity of zones of domestic activity as summarized in Table 5.1. In the Early Facet deposits, ground stone was recovered from Subops 17, 7, and 18. One mano was also found from Subop 8. In the Late Facet deposits, ground stone was found in Subops 2, 5, and 7. Three metates were in secondary context, as they were reused in fire pits in Subops 7 and 17, including one broken trough-shaped metate in Subop 17. Metates are of the concave, trough, and flat varieties, and manos are of the planoconvex and circular varieties as defined by Jaeger (1988: Figures 53 and 54). Their presence at the site indicates that maize processing occurred on the island in a variety of domestic contexts.

Comals and Maize Processing

The preparation of maize is also implied by the recovery of comals at Laguna de On. The technology of tortilla making is thought to have spread from the Mexican highlands to the Maya area during the Terminal Classic/Early Postclassic period. A total of 319 comal fragments were recovered from the

Early and Late Facets at Laguna de On. They represent 7.5 percent of the unslipped-ceramic sample for the Early Facet (N = 275), but only .9 percent of the Late Facet (N = 44). Their use at the site occurs in limited distribution, as they are found primarily from ritual or high-status contexts. This pattern suggests that making tortillas may have been a privileged behavior limited to special occasions rather than an activity linked to the preparation of a daily staple consumed by all members of the community.

Procurement of Wild Faunal Resources— The Faunal Evidence

The subsistence base at Laguna de On was probably dependent on the cultigens of beans, squash, and maize. Wild botanical resources were also probably utilized for food, seasoning, and medicine, as they are today (Rathje, Gregory, and Wiseman 1978: Table 17, Figures 23–25; Voorhies 1982: Tables 1 and 2; Marcus 1982: Tables 1–12). Evidence for substantial exploitation of wild game at Laguna de On is provided from the recovery of 10,231 pieces of faunal bone (10,034 from nonfill contexts are listed in Table 5.3). Faunal analysis indicates that the following terrestrial animals were hunted locally and consumed at Laguna: white-tailed and brocket deer, peccary, tapir, turkey, armadillo, and numerous small mammals (Masson 1993, 1999a; Wharton 1998; Wharton and Stanchly 1998). While crocodiles were probably also hunted, other aquatic resources such as turtles and fish were extracted with nets from freshwater lagoons and rivers. Net weights representing these activities are recovered throughout the site.

Faunal remains were abundantly exploited in both the Early and Late Facets at the site, as 28.8 percent of the faunal sample was recovered from the Early Facet, and 71.2 percent was recovered from the Late Facet (Table 5.3). This distribution of animal bone suggests that reliance on wild game increased over time. Such changes could be due to an increase in habitation intensity on the island, a change in diet, increased availability of animal resources, or an intensified harvest of animal products during the Late Facet. No changes in the types of species being brought to the site is observed from the Early to Late Facet. Table 5.4 indicates the presence of all major species in each component based on the analysis of fauna from the 1991 season.

As discussed in Chapter 2, one characteristic of Postclassic sites in northern Belize is a local forest ecology that hosted abundant populations of terrestrial and aquatic fauna. This circumstance provided opportunities for Postclassic villagers to diversify their diets with the protein of wild game. Although issues of poorly understood Postclassic population levels are addressed in Chapter 2, the size of aquatic faunas, particularly turtles, suggests that human populations did not impact the animal populations to a significant degree (Masson 1999a). For example, at Laguna de On, pond turtles

Table 5.3—Faunal bone from Laguna de On Island

Subop	Early Facet		Late Facet		Total
NORTH CENTRAL AREA					
8	676	17.2%	3,249	82.8%	3,925
12	381	32.3%	799	67.7%	1,180
2, 3	0	0.0%	285	100.0%	285
17	546	48.7%	575	51.3%	1,121
19	72	82.8%	15	17.2%	87
SOUTH CENTRAL AREA					
5	433	27.1%	1,163	72.9%	1,596
NORTHWEST AREA					
16	47	23.5%	153	76.5%	200
7	247	61.8%	153	38.3%	400
13	10	5.0%	192	95.0%	202
NORTHEAST AREA					
9–11, 15	105	42.9%	140	57.1%	245
SOUTH AREA					
18	70	43.5%	91	56.5%	161
OTHER (BALLCOURT)					
20	92	73.0%	34	27.0%	126
(DOCK)					
14	206	40.7%	300	59.3%	506
Total	2,885	28.8%	7,149	71.2%	10,034

reach a considerable size, with carapace thicknesses of up to 1cm, suggesting that procurement pressures were not so great as to prohibit animals from reaching full maturity. Studies suggest that when human populations are overexploiting faunal resources, the majority of individuals in prey populations are immature (Klein and Cruz-Uribe 1984: 96–99). No pattern of overexploitation is observed among deer and tapir at the site, as mature teeth from individuals of each species have been recovered (Wharton and Stanchly 1998). Tapir are found in low densities in tropical forests, with each solitary individual requiring a relatively broad range of mature canopy (Matola 1995). The abundant numbers of tapir and deer at Laguna de On and their age ranges imply the presence of high canopy in this area and a moderate level of predation on game populations (Wharton and Stanchly 1998).

Other northern Belize sites such as Colha and Santa Rita also possess middens that contain abundant quantities of faunal bone (Scott 1981, 1982; Morton 1988; Shaw and Mangan 1994). In fact, middens with plentiful bone appear to be a hallmark of Postclassic deposits in this region, along with ceramic net weights, which are another subsistence indicator. The abundant faunal samples from Postclassic period sites suggests that demographic, ecological, or political variables were conducive to flourishing wildlife and hunting industries at this time.

Spatial Distribution of Faunal Bone and Status Hierarchies

When spatial distributions of fauna are compared within sites (Table 5.4), it appears that some species were accorded higher status and may have been incorporated into feasting or other redistributive ritual at the sites (Masson 1999a). It is improbable that hunting was highly controlled, given the apparent abundance of species, and households probably had the right to hunt and consume species they secured. Deer (white-tailed and brocket), peccary, alligator, crocodile, and tapir (and possibly bird) were manipulated in ritual at Laguna de On through decapitation and redistribution (Masson 1993, 1999a). Cranial fragments were found almost exclusively in areas of high ritual activity during the Late Facet, while postcranial fragments of the same "prestige" species were found in domestic middens across the site (Masson 1999a). The distribution of other species, including armadillo and other small mammals, turtles, and frogs, showed no evidence of manipulation. When interhousehold comparisons are made, zones hypothesized to have been occupied by families of upper status (Subops 2, 3, and 8) also exhibit a greater diversity of game (Masson 1999a: Table 5). Exotic faunas, such as tapir, are primarily found in upper-status or ritual contexts (Masson 1999a). The spatial distribution of faunal bone thus suggests that interhousehold status differences existed at Laguna de On and that the use of animals played an important role in the expression of such differences (Masson 1999a). This pattern concurs with Diego de Landa's (1941) description of calendric ceremonies and the elite households that hosted them in Colonial period Yucatán. The patterns described above are observed for the Late Facet (Masson 1999b).

At Laguna de On, a few differences are observed when the relative percentages of fauna are compared within units of the site from the Early to Late Facets (Table 5.4). Subops 20, 7, and 19 show a greater percentage in the Early Facet compared to the Late. Subops 8, 5, 16, and 14 contain a greater amount of fauna in the Late Facet. In certain areas these changing percentages may indicate important changes in the types of activities, such as butchering or the consumption of meat. The increase in fauna at Subop 8 is attributed to an increase in ritual in this location.

119

Table 5.4—Species identified (from 1991 season) in Early and Late Facets (other seasons under analysis by Wharton and Stanchly 1998)

Subop	Early Facet					Late Facet					
	2, 3	7	8	9–11	Total	2, 3	5	7	8	9–11	Total
Large Mammal	1	0	23	0	24	16	1	4	1	1	23
Mammal	0	0	16	3	19	5	0	2	4	1	12
Tapir	0	0	4	0	4	1	0	0	3	0	4
Deer	0	0	3	2	5	17	2	2	1	5	27
Peccary	0	0	4	0	4	12	0	0	1	0	13
Small/Medium Mammal	1	0	5	9	15	23	16	2	2	3	46
Agouti	0	0	1	0	1	1	0	1	0	0	2
Armadillo	0	0	1	4	5	31	5	0	1	56	93
Canid	0	0	1	0	1	13	0	1	0	0	14
Rodent	0	0	0	0	0	3	0	1	0	3	7
Alligator	0	0	20	0	20	5	0	0	17	1	23
Turtle	0	0	24	20	44	17	3	0	10	18	48
Iguana	0	0	1	0	1	0	0	0	0	0	0
Serpent	0	1	1	0	2	8	0	1	3	0	12
Frog	0	0	1	0	1	6	0	1	0	4	11
Bird	0	1	3	0	4	16	0	2	2	0	20
Fish	2	0	12	0	14	20	2	0	2	1	25
Unidentified	4	0	61	0	65	94	12	5	18	22	151
	Total Bone (Early) 1991 sample				229	Total Bone (Late) 1991 sample					531

Notched Weights and the Extraction of Aquatic Game

A total of 396 ceramic notched or "net" weights were recovered from Laguna de On, with 113 from the Early Facet and 283 from the Late Facet. Net weights at Laguna de On can be classified into two basic categories (Lisa Spillett, personal communication 1998): flat or bulbous (Figure 5.1). Flat weights can be made from modified sherds, in which grooves are made on opposite ends of a sherd. Modeled weights are formed into elliptical-shaped pods, with the grooves cut into them before firing. According to Spillett's classifications, 155 of the net weights at the site were of the flat variety, and 241 were of the bulbous variety. The modeled variety appears to gain in popularity over time, as 71 percent of the Late Facet weights are of this type compared to 35.4 percent in the Early Facet (Table 5.5).

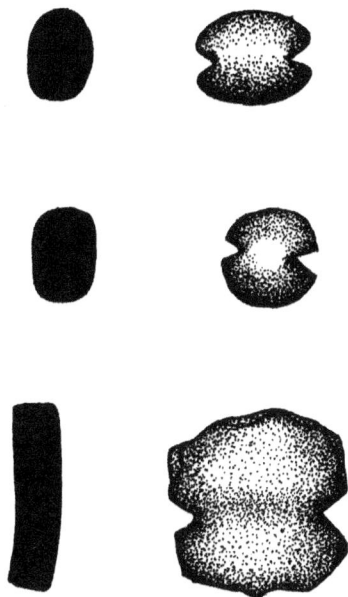

5.1. Net weights from Laguna de On Island (illustrated by John Labadie).

The distribution of notched weights at Laguna is summarized in Table 5.5. It is clear from this table that notched weights are found in many locations across the site. They do not appear to be exclusively distributed at high-status or ritual areas of the site. This distribution parallels that observed for spindle whorls at the site (discussed later), which are also found in a range of domestic and ritual contexts (Murray 1998).

Nonobsidian Flakes and Shatter

Quantities of unburned and burned flakes and shatter can be compared across the site as an additional clue to flintworking specialization and depositional processes (Table 5.6). In this analysis, flakes are defined as those pieces possessing a platform, and shatter includes those pieces that lack platforms. Flakes discussed here are of nonobsidian materials, primarily cherts and chalcedonies. Few differences are observed from the Early (N = 7,095) to Late (N = 12,220) Facets in the distribution of these materials (Table 5.6), which shared similar percentages of burned flakes (18.1 percent and 16.9 percent respectively), unburned flakes (23.7 percent and 24.6 percent respectively), burned shatter (22.3 percent and 22.6 percent respectively),

Table 5.5—Notched weights by subop/level at Laguna de On Island (classified by Lisa Spillett)

| | Level 1/Late Facet | | | | Level 2–4/Early Facet | | |
	Flat	Bulbous	Total		Flat	Bulbous	Total
NORTH CENTRAL AREA							
Subop 8	26.7%	73.3%	75		66.7%	33.3%	15
Subop 12	21.8%	78.2%	55		100.0%	0.0%	11
Subop 2	0.0%	0.0%	0		0.0%	0.0%	0
Subop 17	20.0%	80.0%	45		46.4%	53.6%	28
Subop 13	12.5%	87.5%	8		0.0%	0.0%	0
Subtotal	23.0%	77.0%	183		63.0%	37.0%	54
SOUTH CENTRAL AREA							
Subop 5	36.6%	63.4%	41		68.8%	31.3%	32
NORTHWEST AREA							
Subop 7	44.4%	55.6%	9		33.3%	66.7%	12
Subop 16	0.0%	0.0%	0		0.0%	100.0%	1
NORTHEAST AREA							
Subop 15	36.6%	63.4%	41		50.0%	50.0%	2
EAST DOCK AREA							
Subop 14	62.5%	37.5%	8		100.0%	0.0%	5
NORTH AREA							
Subop 20	100.0%	0.0%	1		100.0%	0.0%	3
SOUTH AREA							
Subop 18	0.0%	0.0%	0		100.0%	0.0%	4
Total: Level 1	82	201	283	Level 2	73.0%	40.0%	113
	29.0%	71.0%	100%		64.6%	35.4%	100%
Total for Entire Site					155	241	396
					39.1%	60.9%	100%

and unburned shatter (35.9 percent and 35.9 percent respectively). These remarkable similarities suggest that the site was not burned upon abandonment, an act that would have resulted in increased burned debris in the Late Facet surface materials. The ratios of all flakes to all shatter for each facet are identical (.71), suggesting that differences in flintworking are not observed over time. Increased proportions of shatter might have indicated a decline in flintworking skill at the site, or an increase in primary activities, but this is not the case.

Table 5.6—Flake and shatter frequency distributions for Level 1 Late Facet and Level 2–4 Early Facet deposits at Laguna de On Island

	Early Facet					Late Facet				
	BR flake	UnBR flake	BR shatter	UnBR shatter	Total	BR flake	UnBR flake	BR shatter	UnBR shatter	Total
NORTH CENTRAL AREA										
Subop 8	0.2%	28.4%	43.1%	28.3%	1,688	20.0%	24.9%	35.9%	19.2%	3,696
Subop 12	13.1%	47.0%	22.3%	17.5%	251	14.1%	49.4%	20.9%	15.5%	1,004
Subop 17	24.1%	26.9%	37.4%	11.5%	1,178	13.2%	15.2%	14.2%	57.5%	3,220
Subop 13	10.9%	1.7%	0.0%	87.4%	175	14.7%	43.9%	25.4%	15.9%	960
Subtotal	10.3%	27.9%	37.2%	24.6%	3,292	16.3%	26.2%	25.1%	32.4%	8,780
SOUTH CENTRAL AREA										
Subop 5	41.8%	16.5%	0.3%	41.5%	1,551	20.3%	12.6%	18.2%	48.9%	1,218
NORTHWEST AREA										
Subop 7	12.4%	33.7%	16.4%	37.5%	347	30.1%	23.5%	20.2%	26.2%	489
Subop 16	20.0%	21.1%	44.2%	14.7%	95	10.6%	22.3%	10.5%	56.6%	1,082
Subtotal	14.0%	31.0%	22.4%	32.6%	442	16.7%	22.7%	13.6%	47.1%	1,571
SUBOP 20										
Subop 20	13.5%	13.7%	9.1%	63.8%	563	24.6%	17.4%	17.4%	40.6%	138
NORTHEAST AREA										
Subop 15	10.8%	11.9%	16.3%	60.9%	453	6.8%	16.9%	11.9%	64.4%	59
EAST DOCK										
Subop 14	12.7%	31.1%	16.5%	39.8%	656	19.4%	31.9%	22.2%	26.6%	361
SOUTH AREA										
Subop 18	16.7%	25.4%	15.9%	42.0%	138	25.8%	50.5%	14.0%	9.7%	93
Total	18.1%	23.7%	22.3%	35.9%	7,095	16.9%	24.6%	22.6%	35.9%	12,220

During the Early Facet, proportions of burned flakes are not great in most subops (Table 5.6). Clear patterns are not indicated for the distribution of burned flakes (in greatest proportion in Subops 16 and 17), unburned flakes (highest in Subop 12), burned shatter (highest in Subop 8), and unburned shatter (highest in Subops 13, 15, and 20) across the site. Subop 13 has 87.4 percent unburned shatter, which is far greater than the proportion observed for any other zone. This pattern may suggest that flintworking took place at this location, also implied by other data on lithic distributions at the site.

During the Late Facet, no distinct spatial patterns are observed in the proportions of burned flakes (highest in Subops 7 and 18), unburned flakes (highest in Subops 12, 13, and 18), burned shatter (highest in Subop 8), and unburned shatter (highest in Subops 15, 16, 17). In both the Early and Late Facet components, Subop 8 has the highest proportions of burned shatter, perhaps due to the fire features found in this location (Chapter 4). Shatter, in addition to representing primary flintworking activities, can also be generated by exposure to heat. Much of the lithic debris from this subop exhibited heat fractures. Comparisons of these categories of debris provide little indication of changes in lithic industries over time at the site, and only a couple of hints about specialized activities associated with particular zones of the site. Relative quantities of lithic debris are more useful for assessing flintworking activities, and these patterns are discussed in the comparisons of frequencies of all artifact classes at the site at the end of this chapter.

Projectile Points and the Extraction of Terrestrial and Avian Resources

The distribution of projectile points at the community of Laguna de On may indirectly reflect hunting activities performed by households at this site. Side-notched arrow points associated with the Postclassic period are reported from Chichén Itzá (Sheets 1991), Mayapan (Proskouriakoff 1962b), Topoxte (Bullard 1973: Figure 17), Barton Ramie (Willey et al. 1965: Figures 267 and 268), Colha (Shafer and Hester 1983; Michaels 1987), Santa Rita and Wilson's Beach (Shafer and Hester 1988; Andresen 1983: Figure 162 [a, b, e, and f]), and many other sites. Lenticular bifaces and small triangular bifaces are also associated with this period (Shafer and Hester 1988). At Colha, stratigraphic patterns suggest that side-notched bifacial dart points appear earlier, and they are later joined in Colha deposits by lozenge-shaped forms and lenticular bifaces (Shafer and Hester 1983). At Laguna de On, these forms appear more contemporary.

Arrow points are very similar at the Postclassic period sites mentioned above. Five basic forms are identified, and three of these forms are side-notched varieties (Table 5.7). These forms include the following: side-notched square-base points, side-notched round-base points, side-notch concave-base points, contracting-stem "diamond"-shaped points and leaf-shaped points made on blades that may represent preforms for the previous four varieties. These types are named after those described in Shafer and Hester (1988: 112, Figure 57). Another critical morphological division are two basic shapes that can be recognized: elongate and triangular (Shafer and Hester 1988: 112). However, as base forms are shared between elongate and triangular forms, triangular forms may represent resharpened late-use–stage versions of elongate forms. Currently, little is understood about curation strategies that were applied to these artifacts.

At the colonial site of Tipu, Simmons (1995: Figures 4–9) also distinguishes a curved-base variety and variants with bases that follow technological attributes such as striking platforms or basal fractures. These types are not defined at Laguna de On. The manufacture of Late Postclassic points endures well into colonial times, based on the recovery of points from Tipu (Simmons 1995: 143–144). Simmons notes that these points were made on flakes or blades with a minimum of effort, and suggests that such expediency may have been conducive to their mass production in warfare. He notes their utility in hunting as well (1995: 144–145).

Scholars have suggested that side-notched obsidian arrow points date to the latter part of the Late Postclassic period (Thomas Hester, personal communication 1993). At Laguna de On, obsidian arrow points have been recovered primarily in the top 15cm of Late Facet deposits (except for one in Subop 9; Table 5.8), which supports their assessment as late additions to Belize Postclassic assemblages. Stratigraphic recovery suggests that chert or chalcedony dart points appear first in the sequence during the Early Facet, and are joined in the Late Facet by the manufacture of obsidian arrow points.

Of fourteen complete Laguna de On chert or chalcedony side-notched points, two are square-based, four are round-based, one is concave-based, one is diamond-shaped with contracting stem, two are leaf-shaped with slightly contracting stems, and four are distal portions of fully bifacial points (Table 5.7; Figure 5.2). Except for the four distal fragments, all other points are not fully bifacial and are made from trimmed flakes or blades.

Patterns over time are not evident in this small sample. Three points from the Early Facet include a square-based point, a round-based point, and a tip of a bifacial point. The Late Facet exhibits this range of styles, and some additional styles are also noted that may be due to the greater number of points recovered from these deposits (N = 11). Late Facet points identified include one square-based point, three round-based points, one diamond-shaped point, one concave-base point, two leaf-shaped points, three bifacial point tips, and four blanks. From the Laguna de On data, then, it is not possible to determine a temporal relationship between fully bifacial and non–fully bifacial point styles, as both occur in each component. Some points

5.2. Varieties of projectile points from Laguna de On Island, obsidian point shown third from the right.

listed above appear only in the Late Facet, however, and it is notable that the majority of the site's points are found in these later deposits. This pattern may reflect an increase in hunting activities or in warfare over time.

Although Simmons (1995: 143) suggests that multiplicity in point styles may be related to accelerated population movements in the colonial era at Tipu, the Laguna de On points suggest that multiple styles were in use by a single community during the Late Postclassic period. It is possible that intergroup social dynamics fostered the exchange of points or stylistic templates. It is also possible that a lack of standardization was acceptable among manufacturers of these points in the Late Postclassic. With minor additional retouch, square-based points can be converted into round-based points or concave points. Perhaps such variability occurred among different flintknappers according to the needs of the haft or rejuvenation of the haft element as Flenniken and Raymond (1986) have suggested for North American variable morphologies. As Simmons (1995: 145) notes, point manufacture was a relatively expedient technology that allowed for rapid and mass production, and it is possible that strict conformity to base configuration was not adhered to for similar reasons of efficiency.

Most points from Laguna de On are made of Colha chert. They could have been obtained from that site, or they could have been manufactured on

Table 5.7—Side-notched chert and chalcedony projectile points from Laguna de On

Site	Subop	Lot	Length	Portion	Type	Material
LATE FACET						
Island	5c	50	3.1cm	whole, missing distal tip	arrow, side-notched, square-based, narrow elongate shape, not fully bifacial	Colha chert
Island	5c	50	6.1cm	blank or knife	narrow elongate shape, edges trimmed and slightly dulled, not fully bifacial	chalcedony
Island	5p	342	4.1cm (incomplete)	whole, missing distal tip	small dart point or blank, side-notched, round-based, not fully bifacial	Colha chert
Island	51	284	2.6cm	whole	small arrow, side-notched, round-based, narrow elongate shape, resharpened, not fully bifacial	Colha chert
Island	5m	311	1.7cm	distal tip	small bifacial tip, probably arrow	material unidentified, heat damage
Island	5m	311	2.5cm	whole	small arrow, contracting stem, diamond shape, not fully bifacial	material unidentified, heat damage
Island	8c	32	3.9cm	whole	arrow, side-notched, concave-based, narrow elongate shape, not fully bifacial	Colha chert
Island	8a	11	5.1cm	whole, tip missing	arrow or small dart point, leaf-shaped with slight contracting stem, not fully bifacial	Colha chert
Island	8i	81	6.7cm	whole	leaf-shaped dart point or biface with slight contracting stem, not fully bifacial	Colha chert

Continued on next page

Table 5.7—continued

Site	Subop	Lot	Length	Portion	Type	Material
LATE FACET—*continued*						
Island	8o	187	4.2cm	whole, missing distal tip	arrow, side-notched, round-based, narrow elongate shape, not fully bifacial	Colha chert
Island	6	1	6.1cm	almost whole, missing base	bifacial dart point, base has been shattered off by heat damage	chert, heat damaged
Island	3	1	3.2cm	distal tip	appears fully bifacial, heat damaged	chalcedony
Shore	13	81	3.2cm	distal tip or blank	large arrow or small dart point, narrow elongate, not fully bifacial, medial snap break	Colha chert
Shore	13	83	3.3cm	blank	arrow, narrow elongate shape, not fully bifacial	Colha chert
Island	11a	41	4.9cm	blank	triangular shape, not fully bifacial, medial snap break	Colha chert
EARLY FACET						
Island	18	215	3.6cm	whole	side-notched, square-based, narrow elongate, not fully bifacial	Colha chert
Island	17	379	4.9cm	whole	large arrow or small dart point, side-notched, square-based, elongate, not fully bifacial	Colha chert
Island	51	293	3.3cm	distal tip	large bifacial tip, probably dart	chalcedony

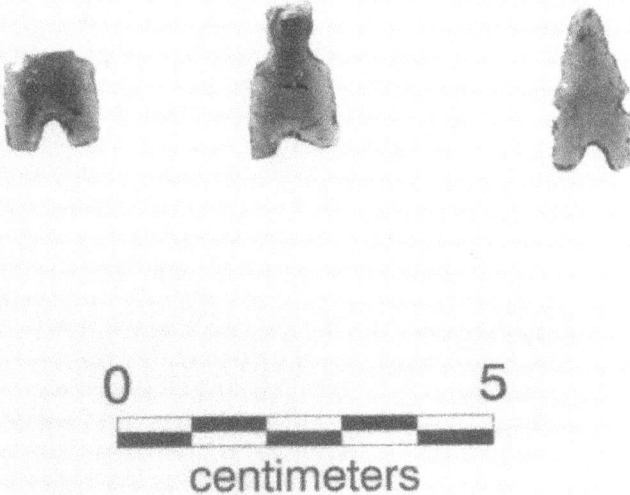

5.3. Obsidian points from Laguna de On Island.

flakes obtained from Colha. The lack of standardization in point shapes and sizes suggests this industry was not tightly controlled by a limited number of craft specialists.

Obsidian points from Laguna de On represent an additional form of weaponry that are limited primarily to the Late Facet, in which eleven point fragments were found in various stages of production and wear (Table 5.8, Figure 5.3). The points recovered in 1991 were originally classified by Valdez (1993b), and Table 5.8 represents an updated inventory with specimens from subsequent seasons. One obsidian point was found from Early Facet deposits. Two types of side-notched points are observed in the collection during the Late Facet: basal-notched (concave-base) and round-base points. The round-base side-notched point (N = 1) is identical in form and technology to the side-notched round-base chert points (not fully bifacial) also recovered from the Late Facet (described above). The side- and basal-notched points appear different from the concave-base chert point described above, however, in having a deeper and narrower notched concavity. Of the Late Facet sample, few specimens were complete. Only one basal-notched point was found and one round-base whole point was found, both under 2.7cm in length. Two basal-notched points (one Early, one Late) appear to have been heavily resharpened as suggested by their narrow medial widths, and may have been used as drills rather than points. As only the proximal halves are recovered,

129

it is impossible to determine their full configuration or function. Four basal-notched specimens were incomplete, lacking side notches, final edge trimming, or manufacture-related breaks. Three such manufacturing failures were recovered from Subop 3 and the other was from Subop 14f, which may have been an areas where obsidian knapping was performed.

The distribution of points across the site reveals important patterns of functional variability (Tables 5.7 and 5.8). During the Early Facet, each of the three chert or chalcedony points was recovered from a different domestic zone: the extreme south end of the island (Subop 18), the south central area (Subop 5), and the north central area (Subop 17). During the Late Facet, chert points were only found from two areas, those associated with upper-status residential zones including Subop 5 (N = 6) and the north central area including Subops 8, 6, and 3 (N = 6). This Late Facet distribution is similar to that of the Early Facet, although no points were recovered from the site's south end.

The distribution of obsidian points is more limited than that observed for chert and chalcedony points (Tables 5.7 and 5.8). Nine of eleven points or point fragments fall in the north central vicinity of the site (Subops 2, 3, 8, 17). One fragment was found in Subop 13, a location near the north central zone, and an additional fragment was found in the water at Subop 14. Obsidian points thus appear more spatially confined to the central area of the site than chert or chalcedony arrows, and their concentration in the upper-status domestic zone around Subop 8 suggests that obsidian points may correlate with prestige or ritual activity. An additional point was recovered from the surface occupation of a Terminal Classic/Early Postclassic house platform excavated on the shore of Laguna de On in 1991 (Masson 1993).

It has previously been suggested (Masson 1999b) that the limited distribution of points to upper-status residential zones and areas of high ritual activity at the site is closely related to the ritual manipulation of large game animals and incense burners. It is possible that the confinement of points to restricted areas of the site indicates areas where game was butchered, resulting in the increased loss of points that had been embedded in carcasses in butchering areas. It is not unreasonable to suppose that hunting might have been a collective and cooperative activity at this small settlement. The distribution of points may indicate areas where cooperative butchering occurred. Certainly, the distribution of points in the Late Facet correlates with the distribution of inedible elements of large game (crania). The recovery of primarily broken points (and two whole specimens) may also suggest that butchering was the activity responsible for their discard in the locations where they were recovered. Other points, including the three incomplete fragments at Subop 3 and the incomplete fragment at Subop 14, are not associated with animal cranial or foot elements.

Table 5.8—Obsidian points from Laguna de On

	Subop	Lot	Length	Description
LATE FACET				
Island	2	3	frag.	basal side-notched, bifacial
Island	3	3	frag.	blade fragment, basal notch made on blade
Island	3	3	frag.	basal, steep side notches
Shore	19	1	2.6cm	distal portion, base missing, not fully bifacial
Island	3	3	frag.	side notch
Island	17	225	2.9cm	whole, side-notched, square base, not fully bifacial
Island	13b	159	frag.	basal fragment
Island	8	9	frag.	basal notch, blade fragment
Island	14f	149	frag.	basal notch, blade fragment
FLAWED POINTS (MANUFACTURING FAILURES)				
Island	3	3	1.5cm	blade fragment, side notch, slight basal notch
Island	3	3	1.5cm	pointed and notched flake
Island	3	3	frag.	basal-notched blade
EARLY FACET				
Laguna de On	9	5		basal notch worked into a perf or scraper

In summary, the analysis of arrow (and dart) points from Laguna de On Island suggests that diversity is observed in styles of the basal haft element of Late Postclassic period. Despite the diversity in basal shape, technological similarities link most chert, chalcedony, and obsidian forms. Particularly, the tendency to modify flakes or blades into points by edge retouch without completely thinning the point bifacially unifies the various styles. As flakes and blades used for preforms are very thin to begin with, full bifacial trimming is not necessary. Full bifacial points are represented at the site, but only by distal portions. They appear thicker in cross section. There is no evidence from the Laguna de On assemblage of chert and chalcedony arrow points that they were made on prismatic blades. If blades were used, they would have been flake blades or percussion blades, which is why it is impossible to determine whether the points were made on blades or flakes. The distinction does not appear to have mattered. Obsidian points are made on prismatic blades, and occasional experimentation is observed on a flake fragment. These poorly executed specimens could represent "practice" notches (as identified for Bell-Andice points in Texas by Collins 1994) or simply unskilled workmanship. The recovery of various incomplete specimens and the fact that one obsidian point was made in a form identical to the round-base chert points from the site suggests that points were locally made on imported obsidian blades.

Despite the diversity of styles represented at the site, the distribution of points at Laguna de On is confined primarily to a couple of upper-status residential or ritual zones. This distribution may signal areas where cooperative activities, such as butchering, were conducted. It may alternatively identify communal spaces at the island where individuals gathered for social reasons and performed tool kit maintenance tasks such as refurbishing projectile points.

It is notable that an increase in the numbers of points is marked from the Early to Late Facet deposits for both chert/chalcedony and obsidian points. This increase may indicate an increase in warfare or in hunting activities. As an increase in animal bone across the site is observed from the Early to Late Facet as well, the latter interpretation is favored. However, other evidence presented in Chapter 4, such as the construction of the east terrace and dock at Laguna, suggests that inhabitants of the island took steps to restrict access to the settlement in the Late Facet, and it is possible that intergroup conflict posed a real threat. It is therefore possible that the increase in projectile points in the Late Facet are related to an increase in warfare or raids as well as hunting activities.

LITHIC TOOLS, AGRICULTURAL PRODUCTION, AND LOCAL EXCHANGE

Located in a rural setting, Laguna de On assuredly engaged in agricultural production. Although ethnohistoric descriptions of the orchards and fields of Chetumal province imply that agricultural activities were important (Jones 1989: 33–34), they are not highly visible in the material record of the island. Orchards and fields were probably located around the shores of the lagoon. The field-to-house distance would thus have been increased by the need for travel across the water, although gardens may have been present on the island. Agricultural activities are indirectly reflected at Laguna de On through lithic tools such as bifacial celts that were discarded after recycling in domestic contexts. Consumption of agricultural products is reflected in ground-stone artifacts recovered.

Oval biface celts have been identified at Colha, Pulltrouser Swamp, and Albion Island as tools of agricultural production (Shafer and Hester 1983; McAnany 1986; Eaton 1991; Hester and Shafer 1991) in the Preclassic and Classic periods. The use of similar celtiform bifaces is continued in the Postclassic at Laguna de On (Masson 1993, 1997) and Santa Rita (Shafer and Hester 1988). At Laguna de On Island, oval biface celts that are identical

Table 5.9—Total tools by deposit at Laguna de On (from Masson 1993 and 1997; Oland 1998)

	Level 1 (N)	% of Level 1 tools	Level 2 (N)	% of Level 2 tools	Total (N)	% of total tools
FORMAL TOOLS RECYCLED FROM OR RESEMBLING CLASSIC PERIOD FORMS						
Oval biface	29	9.7%	10	4.6%	39	7.6%
Tranchet tool	2	0.7%	1	0.5%	3	0.6%
Biface thinning flake	2	0.7%	3	1.4%	5	1.0%
Stemmed blade	1	0.3%	5	2.3%	6	1.2%
Blade (percussion)	16	5.3%	6	2.8%	22	4.3%
General utility biface	1	0.3%			1	0.2%
Total	51	17.0%	25	11.6%	76	14.7%
POSTCLASSIC FORMAL TOOL FORMS						
Lenticular biface	13	4.3%	10	4.6%	23	4.5%
Triangular biface	2	0.7%	1	0.5%	3	0.6%
Knife/Preform	1	0.3%	1	0.5%	2	0.4%
Thin or parallel biface	9	3.0%	3	1.4%	12	2.3%
Projectile point	9	3.0%	4	1.9%	13	2.5%
Laurel-leaf biface	1	0.3%			1	0.2%
Total	35	11.7%	19	8.8%	54	10.5%
POSTCLASSIC EXPEDIENT TOOL FORMS						
Used flake	156	52.0%	124	57.4%	280	54.3%
Notched flake	1	0.3%		0.0%	1	0.2%
Biface	12	4.0%	15	6.9%	27	5.2%
Chopper	1	0.3%	2	0.9%	3	0.6%
Core	22	7.3%	15	6.9%	37	7.2%
Core tool	8	2.7%	8	3.7%	16	3.1%
Core hammerstone	3	1.0%	6	2.8%	9	1.7%
Hammerstone	8	2.7%	1	0.5%	9	1.7%
Uniface	3	1.0%	1	0.5%	4	0.8%
Total	214	71.3%	172	79.6%	386	74.8%
Grand Total	300	100.0%	216	100.0%	516	100.0%

to those made at Colha for local exchange in the Classic period are found in Postclassic deposits. It is possible that Laguna continued to receive this product from Colha in the Postclassic period. Alternatively, Laguna villagers may also have recycled oval biface celts scavenged from Classic period domestic sites in the area. Despite social and political changes that distinguish the Classic from Postclassic periods, milpa activities and the tools needed for agriculture may have been more resistant to change than other artifact classes (Masson 1997). The manufacture of oval bifaces occurs throughout all Maya periods at Colha (Shafer and Hester 1988: 116), and the recycling of oval bifaces made in earlier periods at consumer sites is also observed.

Nonobsidian chipped-stone tools are not numerous at Laguna de On Island (Table 5.9). I have suggested that obsidian blades were preferred at this site for many common domestic tasks, and that this preference reduced reliance on expedient or recycled tools made of local materials compared to the Classic period (Masson 1997).

The production of lithic tools at Laguna de On is visible archaeologically in examples of expedient tools made of low-grade raw materials recovered from domestic contexts. Chalcedony found in the vicinity of Laguna de On is one resource that could have been extracted for exchange. A quarry site (Locality 11) found near Laguna was littered with large primary flakes, cores, and tested cobbles (Oland 1998, 1999). Other raw materials, such as quartz-blend materials, appear at Laguna de On in low numbers and their sources have not been identified. Surveys of northern Belize sources have located a number of possible raw-material outcrops (Hester and Shafer 1984) that may be the origin of unidentifed cherts and chalcedonies found at Laguna de On.

Surveys around Laguna de On have located nine chalcedony outcrops around the lagoon's periphery or within three miles to the northwest of the site (Oland 1998, 1999). Although there is no evidence that Laguna de On specialized in the production of formal lithic tools for export, a nearby Postclassic production center is known at Colha, ten kilometers to the southeast of the lagoon (Shafer and Hester 1983; Michaels 1987). Colha sits on one of the finest outcrops of chert in the Maya world, and exported stone tools to many locations in the southern lowlands from Preclassic through Postclassic times (Shafer and Hester 1983; Hester and Shafer 1984, 1994; Hester, Shafer, and Berry 1991). Despite the abundant superior cherts available at Colha, artisans at this site chose to make formal tools out of chalcedony as well as chert during the Postclassic period (Shafer and Hester 1983; Hester and Shafer 1984; Michaels 1987). Chalcedony is not available at Colha, and the type used there was probably procured from the vicinity of Laguna de On, as it is comparable to the types identified in outcrops around this site.

Patterns of local exchange in lithic production may thus have been complex in the Postclassic period. At this time, Laguna de On may have provided Colha artisans with chalcedonies in raw-material form while manufacturing their own expedient tools from these materials and low-grade local cherts. Laguna de On obtained formal chert and chalcedony tools from Colha (Masson 1993, 1997). Chalcedony may have thus gone to Colha from Laguna de On in raw form and returned in the form of a finished product. This pattern is not documented in the preceding Classic period.

As Laguna de On chalcedony is more prone to shatter and is less homogenous than Colha chert, the motivation for Colha artisans to diversify their use of raw materials to include chalcedony is probably not due to functional or technological superiority of this material. Chalcedonies from Laguna do offer new aesthetically appealing alternatives, and perhaps this decision was motivated by stylistic considerations and a desire for variation.

Analysis of the types of tools made at Laguna de On and the types of raw materials used to make these tools documents important details of local economy during the Postclassic period at this site. A sample of 516 formal and expedient tools has been recovered (Table 5.9). Formal tools at the site can be classified into two categories: tools resembling those known to have been produced by craft specialists at Colha during the Classic period and perhaps beyond (Shafer and Hester 1983; Hester and Shafer 1984; Roemer 1984) and tools representing new diagnostic forms to the Postclassic as originally defined at Colha (Shafer and Hester 1983; Hester and Shafer 1984; Michaels 1987; Shafer and Hester 1988: 116).

As mentioned previously, formal Classic period forms may either have been continued during the Postclassic, or these forms may have been collected from Classic period contexts and recycled during the Postclassic (Shafer and Hester 1988: 114, 117). These forms found at Laguna de On (Table 5.9; Figure 5.4) that appear recycled include, in order of frequency: oval biface celts, tranchet tools or flakes, stemmed and unstemmed chert macroblades, general utility bifaces, and low numbers of large Colha chert bifacial thinning flakes. These forms are identified following the typology of Shafer and Hester (1983). Forms diagnostic to the Postclassic period as defined at Colha include lenticular bifaces, triangular bifaces, laurel leaf bifaces, and side-notched projectile points (Shafer and Hester 1983). At Laguna de On, low numbers of small, thin, oval bifaces and parallel-sided bifaces are also recovered, which are probably of Postclassic period design. Classic period forms at Laguna comprise 14.7 percent of the total assemblage, and Postclassic forms represent 10.5 percent of the sample (Table 5.9; Figure 5.4). Together, these formal tool categories (N = 130) form 25.2 percent of the site's nonobsidian lithics.

Expedient tools include a range of nonstandardized forms, including utilized flakes, bifaces, choppers, various utilized cores, core hammerstones, spheroid or discoid hammerstones, and unifaces (Table 5.9; Figure 5.5). These tools represent the majority of nonobsidian lithic implements at the site (N = 386), 74.8 percent of the sample.

The function of these lithic tools within the domestic economy of Laguna de On is an important factor for explaining the high percentage of expedient

5.4. Formal tools from Laguna de On Island (bottom two rows). Center row and bottom right examples show fragments of broken and recycled formal oval biface celts (Classic period tool forms used in Postclassic contexts). Bottom row shows thin Postclassic biface segment (left), proximal end of a Postclassic lenticular biface (center).

tools at the site. Almost all of the formal Classic period tools are in highly expended and fragmented states (Figure 5.5). It is probable that they were procured in expended states from Classic period contexts in the first place, and their use at Laguna represents a secondary recycling context. Having been procured through opportunistic scavenging, they are not thought to represent a valuable commodity gained through local exchange.

Formal Postclassic tool functions also help explain their low frequencies at Laguna de On. The most highly standardized forms—lenticular bifaces, triangular bifaces, and projectile points (Shafer and Hester 1983; Michaels 1987)—are known to have been manufactured at Colha, and thus they may represent valuable artifacts obtained through local exchange. No evidence for workshops that produced these artifacts locally at Laguna have been found. These objects are highly specialized in their function. Lenticular bifaces are suitable for mounting on staffs to be used as spear points (Thomas Hester, personal communication 1993). They also have the same basic outline as the Aztec and Mixtec glyph for "flint" and are occasionally shown in iconographic sources as knives used in sacrifice (Masson 1993, 1997). Edge dulling on specimens recovered from Laguna is not extensive, and this wear could have resulted from cutting of soft- and medium-textured materials (such as flesh or hide) or from hafting. All but two specimens are represented by fragments, so use wear is difficult to assess on lenticular bifaces. Few triangular

5.5. Examples of expedient tool forms from Laguna de On Island.

bifaces have been found at Laguna (N = 3), and only one was complete. It seemed to have been placed as an offering, unused, along the east edge of Structure II (Rosenswig and Becker 1997). Other formal Postclassic tools, such as projectile points and other thin bifacial knife or projectile-point blank forms, also suggest a specialized function and limited use arenas. Expedient tools were much more important than formal tools in activities conducted at Laguna de On.

The expedient assemblage of Laguna was comprised largely of utilized flakes (N = 280). A range of bifaces, core tools, cores, and hammerstones was also found (Figure 5.6). Most of the nonobsidian chipped-stone tools at the site were used in heavier tasks, as macroscopically visible edge damage is common. Expedient core tools, chopper tools, and bifaces were often made on modified cobbles. Flawed attempts at resharpening were also common, suggesting a lack of skill or concern for conservative curation of these categories of tools. Low-grade raw materials suitable for expedient tools are abundant in the vicinity of Laguna de On (Oland 1998, 1999). Tables 5.10 and 5.11 show that 20–21 percent of the expedient tools at the site were made of local chalcedonies and 9–12 percent were made of local weathered chert, illustrating the degree to which this community relied on local resources. The fact that 24 percent of the expedient tools from Laguna are made of Colha chert is also an important pattern. It is possible that many of

Table 5.10—Tool types by raw material for Level 1 Late Facet deposits at Laguna de On Island (from Masson 1993 and 1997; Oland 1998)

	Colha chert	Chalcedony	Weathered Laguna chert	Misc. chert	Coarse chert	Quartz blends	Other/burned	Total
FORMAL TOOLS RECYCLED FROM OR RESEMBLING CLASSIC PERIOD FORMS								
Oval biface	18	4	4	3	0	0	0	29
Tranchet tool	2	0	0	0	0	0	0	2
Biface thinning flake	2	0	0	0	0	0	0	2
Stem of stemmed blades	0	1	0	0	0	0	0	1
Blade (percussion)	8	2	1	1	0	1	3	16
General utility biface	1	0	0	0	0	0	0	1
Total	31	7	5	4	0	1	3	51

	Colha chert	Chalcedony	Patinated chert	Misc. chert	Coarse chert	Quartz blends	Other/burned	Total
POSTCLASSIC FORMAL TOOL FORMS								
Lenticular biface	5	2	0	4	0	0	2	13
Triangular biface	1	1	0	0	0	0	0	2
Knife/preform	0	0	0	0	0	0	1	1
Thin or parallel biface	4	4	0	1	0	0	0	9
Laurel leaf biface	1	0	0	0	0	0	0	1
Projectile points	3	3	0	2	0	0	1	9
Total	14	10	0	7	0	0	4	35

POSTCLASSIC EXPEDIENT TOOL FORMS

								Total
Used flake	38	28	18	23	33	10	7	157
Biface	2	4	1	0	0	1	4	12
Chopper	0	0	0	0	0	0	1	1
Core	2	5	0	11	0	1	3	22
Core tool	1	2	0	4	0	0	1	8
Core hammerstone	0	0	0	0	0	0	3	3
Hammerstone	0	2	0	1	0	2	3	8
Uniface	1	0	1	1	0	0	0	3
Total	44	41	20	40	33	14	22	214

Grand Totals

Formal (N)	45	17	5	11	0	1	7	86
Formal (%)	52.33%	19.77%	5.81%	12.79%	0.00%	1.16%	8.14%	100.00%
Expedient (N)	44	41	20	40	33	14	22	214
Expedient (%)	20.56%	19.16%	9.35%	18.69%	15.42%	6.54%	10.28%	100.00%
All (N)	89	58	25	51	33	15	29	300
All (%)	29.67%	19.33%	8.33%	17.00%	11.00%	5.00%	9.67%	100.00%

Table 5.11—Tool types by raw material for Level 2 and lower Early Facet deposits at Laguna de On Island (from Masson 1993, 1997; Oland 1998)

	Colha chert	Chalcedony	Weathered Laguna chert	Misc. chert	Coarse chert	Quartz blends	Other/burned	Total
FORMAL TOOLS RECYCLED FROM OR RESEMBLING CLASSIC PERIOD FORMS								
Oval biface	9	0	1	0	0	0	0	10
Tranchet tool	0	0	1	0	0	0	0	1
Biface thinning flake	3	0	0	0	0	0	0	3
Stemmed blade	1	0	1	0	0	0	3	5
Blade (percussion)	2	2	0	2	0	0	0	6
Total	15	2	3	2	0	0	3	25

	Colha chert	Chalcedony	Patinated chert	Misc. chert	Coarse chert	Quartz blends	Other/burned	Total
POSTCLASSIC FORMAL TOOL FORMS								
Lenticular biface	2	5	0	3	0	0	0	10
Triangular biface	1	0	0	0	0	0	0	1
Knife/preform	0	1	0	0	0	0	0	1
Thin or parallel biface	0	1	0	2	0	0	0	3
Projectile point	3	0	1	0	0	0	0	4
Total	6	7	1	5	0	0	0	19

POSTCLASSIC EXPEDIENT TOOL FORMS

							Total
Used flake	27	25	15	21	11	9	16	124
Biface	4	5	2	1	0	0	3	15
Chopper	1	1	0	0	0	0	0	2
Core	7	1	1	1	0	0	5	15
Core tool	2	1	1	1	0	1	2	8
Core hammerstone	0	4	0	1	0	0	1	6
Hammerstone	0	0	0	0	0	0	1	1
Uniface	0	0	1	0	0	0	0	1
Total	41	37	20	25	11	10	28	172
Grand Totals								
Formal (N)	21	9	4	7	0	0	3	44
Formal (%)	47.73%	20.45%	9.09%	15.91%	0.00%	0.00%	6.82%	100.00%
Expedient (N)	41	37	20	25	11	10	28	172
Expedient (%)	23.84%	21.51%	11.63%	14.53%	6.40%	5.81%	16.28%	100.00%
All (N)	62	46	24	32	11	10	31	216
All (%)	28.70%	21.30%	11.11%	14.81%	5.09%	4.63%	14.35%	100.00%

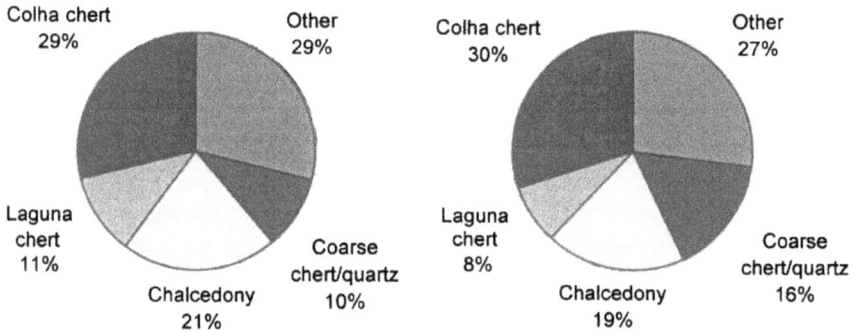

Colha chert 29%
Other 29%
Laguna chert 11%
Chalcedony 21%
Coarse chert/quartz 10%

Colha chert 30%
Other 27%
Laguna chert 8%
Chalcedony 19%
Coarse chert/quartz 16%

5.6. Types of raw materials from which local lithic tools are made in the Early (left) and Late (right) Facets of Laguna de On.

these tools represent recycled Classic period artifacts that have been reduced beyond the point of recognizing their original form, although other explanations are possible.

Low procurement costs are thus indicated by heavy reliance on local materials at Laguna de On. This strategy is an efficient one in terms of "consumer energy outputs," as Clark (1987) has noted. In this type of system, nonobsidian lithics circulate in economic spheres that are not tightly politically controlled and are not particularly significant for the purposes of social-status distinction. Expedient tools at Laguna de On thus reflect the place of chert, chalcedony, and quartz production and consumption in a strongly utilitarian realm of domestic maintenance.

Early and Late Facet Variability in Lithic Industries

Some general observations can be made when the lithic debris of Laguna de On is examined diachronically. A slight (5 percent) increase is seen from the Early to Late Facets in the amount of Classic period formal tools found in the assemblages (Table 5.9). The percentage of Postclassic formal tools also rises slightly (3 percent). These changes cause the amount of expedient tools in the assemblages to fall from 80 percent in the Early Facet to 71 percent in the Late Facet. As the Early Facet assemblage forms 41.9 percent (N = 216) of the total tools from the site and the Late Facet forms 58.1 percent (N = 300), sample size problems do not account for these differences. In both facets, Classic period formal tools are commonly in the form of oval bifaces and blades, and Postclassic formal tools are primarily lenticular bifaces and projectile points. The most frequent expedient tools in each assemblage include utilized flakes, bifaces and choppers, and hammerstones. Cores are also relatively common. These patterns suggest a possible intensification over

142

time of exchange relationships with Colha, or possible intensification of scavenging activities of Classic period components in the vicinity of Laguna de On for recyclable formal tool fragments. However, these differences are not marked, and significant changes in the domestic, utilitarian realm of nonobsidian chipped stone are not reflected over time at Laguna de On.

Differences in raw materials from the Early Facet to the Late Facet are not dramatic, and share important similarities (Figure 5.6). For both assemblages, Colha chert is more commonly identified for formal tools (29–30 percent), but is substantially represented among expedient tools as well (20–24 percent). Chalcedonies (19–21 percent) and local weathered and speckled patinated cherts (8–11 percent) account for similar percentages of formal and expedient tools (Tables 5.9 and 5.10) in each facet. Differences are not marked in the use of these materials for the manufacture of either formal or expedient tools, falling within three percentage points of each other or less during the Early and Late Facets (Figures 5.7 and 5.8; Tables 5.9 and 5.10). Coarse-grained cherts and quartz are an exception. For both samples, quartz-blend materials were used primarily for expedient-tool manufacture, probably due to advantages of this coarse material for heavier tasks. An increase is observed in the use of coarse cherts in the Late Facet (16 percent) compared to the Early Facet (10 percent). Sources for coarse cherts found at Laguna are not well known. Liberally, this increase in their number in the Late Facet may reflect an intensified sphere of regional exchange in northern Belize. Conclusive interpretation of this pattern awaits the identification of their sources (Oland 1998).

Spatial Variability of Lithic Industries in the Early Facet

When variability is examined within subop areas from across the site, most subops with sufficient sample sizes conform to the same patterns described above for the site as a whole. Particularly prevalent in all areas is an increase in the amount of coarse-grained raw materials from the Early to Late Facets. Some subops show increases in the amount of Colha materials and a decrease in chalcedony use (such as Subops 8 and 12), but these changes are probably linked to an increase in ritual activities at these areas over time.

Three variables are examined among subops from across the island during the Early and Late Facets. For each time period, the percentage of utilized flakes among the expedient tool sample, the percentage of formal versus expedient tools in each area, and the ratio of obsidian to expedient tools and flakes in each area are discussed. Comparisons of these variables are examined to determine whether areas associated with greater or lesser ritual activity or social status at the site (Table 5.1) can be distinguished by their lithic assemblages.

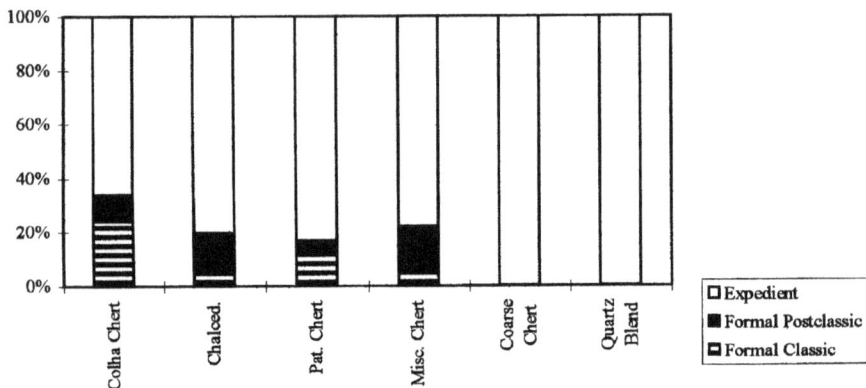

5.7. Early Facet raw materials by tool category.

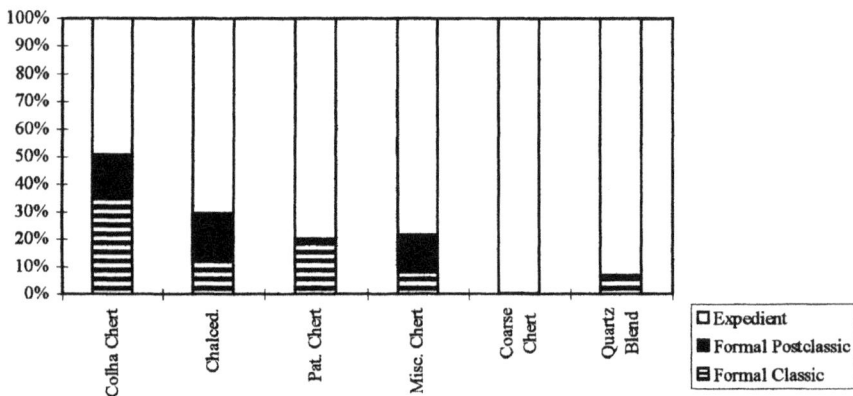

5.8. Late Facet raw materials by tool category.

Tables 5.12 and 5.13 and Figures 5.9 and 5.10 suggest that areas equated with higher status or with more ritual features (Subops 12, 8, 5, and 20) were the focus of differing activities than those areas with purely domestic deposits (Subops 17, 2 and 3, 13, 19, 9, 10, 11, 15, and 7). The first set of spatial comparisons, that of total lithic tools by area, indicates a contrast in areas with greater ritual activity and areas lacking ritual activity (Tables 5.12 and 5.13; Figures 5.9 and 5.10). In the Early Facet, Subops 8 and 12 exhibit greater percentages of formal tools or Colha products than the other subops. This distribution is accounted for by a higher number of lenticular bifaces and recycled Classic period oval bifaces and Colha bifacial thinning flakes in these subops compared to others. These numbers may reflect possible status differences among Late Facet domestic zones across the island, as ritual areas are associated with elite activity (Chapter 4; Masson 1999b). Similar results are reported from Terminal Classic households on the shore of Laguna de On (Masson 1993), in which house structures of greater size and elaboration had greater access to formal tools obtained through exchange with Colha. Further evidence of controlled access to formal lithics in the Early Facet is shown in Table 5.14, where Subops 8 and 12 have higher obsidian-to-expedient tool ratios than any other subop at the island. However, Subop 20 also possesses increased amounts of obsidian relative to expedient tools (Table 5.14), and this pattern is not easily explained. While percentage differences are noted, it is important to note that distributions across the site are not exclusive. Lenticular bifaces and blades were the most common formal tools present in the Early Facet deposits, and they were present in subops in many areas, including Subops 5, 7, 18, and 19 in addition to the "status" zones described above. Five nonobsidian projectile points were also found from areas not associated with indicators of elevated status or ritual activity (Subops 9–11, 18, and 14).

When percentages of utilized flakes are compared to other expedient tool (and core) distributions, Subop 12 (Early Facet) appears different from all other assemblages at the site with only 25 percent utilized flakes. In fact, the Subop 12 distribution closely resembles that reported for this area subsequently in the Late Facet deposits. Interpretations of the low frequencies of expedient flakes at Subop 12 are discussed for the Late Facet in the following section.

Little variation among other subops across the island is observed for the Early Facet in the percentage of utilized flakes compared to other expedient forms. Four areas (Subops 8, 5, 20, 9–11, and 15) exhibit utilized flake frequencies less than or equal to 72 percent in their Early Facet assemblages. Two samples exhibit frequencies of 81 percent or higher, including Subops 19 and 7. The high frequencies of utilized flakes in these units correlate with lower ratios of obsidian-to-expedient tool frequencies as shown in Table 5.14 (Figures 5.11 and 5.12). Conversely, Subop 12's low densities of utilized flakes correlate with high obsidian-to-expedient tool and obsidian-to-utilized flake ratios. Similar correlations are seen in Subops 8 and 20, which also appear to have fewer utilized flakes compensated for by the increased use of obsidian in these areas. Other areas (Subops 17, 5, 9–11, and 15) do not appear to have increased relative amounts of obsidian despite comparable lower densities of utilized flakes. As alluded to previously, these distributions and ratios suggest that a gradation of status differences is reflected in the frequencies of formal tools and/or higher obsidian densities at Subops 8, 12, and 20 at Laguna de On Island. These status differences appear to be linked with ritual features. It is perhaps more important to note that these

Table 5.12—Formal lithic tool frequency distributions by subop for Level 2–4 Early Facet deposits at Laguna de On Island (from Masson 1993, 1997; Oland 1998)

	Thin Biface	Lenticular Biface	Triangular Biface	Side-notched (biface) Point	Leaf-shaped (blade) Point	Blade	Oval Biface	Tranchet Tool	Tranchet Flake	Colha Bifacial Thinning Flake	Total	% of all tools (including utilitarian, N=216)
NORTH CENTRAL AREA												
Subop 8	0.0%	33.3%	0.0%	0.0%	0.0%	16.7%	41.7%	8.3%	0.0%	0.0%	12	5.6%
Subop 12	0.0%	0.0%	0.0%	0.0%	0.0%	0.0%	20.0%	0.0%	0.0%	60.0%	5	2.3%
Subop 17	0.0%	0.0%	0.0%	0.0%	0.0%	25.0%	75.0%	0.0%	0.0%	0.0%	4	1.9%
Subop 19	50.0%	25.0%	0.0%	0.0%	0.0%	25.0%	0.0%	0.0%	0.0%	0.0%	4	1.9%
Subop 13	0.0%	0.0%	0.0%	0.0%	0.0%	0.0%	0.0%	0.0%	0.0%	0.0%	0	0.0%
Subop 6	0.0%	0.0%	0.0%	0.0%	0.0%	0.0%	0.0%	0.0%	0.0%	0.0%	0	0.0%
Subtotal	8.0%	20.0%	0.0%	0.0%	0.0%	20.0%	36.0%	4.0%	0.0%	12.0%	25	11.6%
SOUTH CENTRAL AREA												
Subop 5	0.0%	25.0%	0.0%	0.0%	0.0%	75.0%	0.0%	0.0%	0.0%	0.0%	4	1.9%
NORTHWEST AREA												
Subop 7	0.0%	33.3%	0.0%	0.0%	0.0%	66.7%	0.0%	0.0%	0.0%	0.0%	3	1.4%
Subop 16	0.0%	0.0%	0.0%	0.0%	0.0%	0.0%	0.0%	0.0%	0.0%	0.0%	0	0.0%
Subtotal	0.0%	33.3%	0.0%	0.0%	0.0%	66.7%	0.0%	0.0%	0.0%	0.0%	3	1.4%
SUBOP 20												
Subop 20	0.0%	0.0%	0.0%	100.0%	0.0%	0.0%	0.0%	0.0%	0.0%	0.0%	1	0.5%

NORTHEAST AREA

NORTHEAST AREA												
Subops 9, 10, 11, 15	0.0%	0.0%	0.0%	100.0%	0.0%	0.0%	0.0%	0.0%	0.0%	0.0%	1	0.5 %
EAST DOCK												
Subop 14	50.0%	0.0%	25.0%	25.0%	0.0%	0.0%	0.0%	0.0%	0.0%	0.0%	4	1.9%
SOUTH AREA												
Subop 18	0.0%	50.0%	0.0%	50.0%	0.0%	0.0%	0.0%	0.0%	0.0%	0.0%	2	0.9%
Fill	0.0%	50.0%	0.0%	0.0%	0.0%	25.0%	25.0%	0.0%	0.0%	0.0%	4	1.9%
Total	4	10	1	4	0	11	10	1	0	3	44	20.4%

Table 5.13—Expedient lithic tool frequency distributions by subop for Level 2 Early Facet deposits at Laguna de On Island (from Masson 1993, 1997; Oland 1998)

	Biface	Uniface	Utilized Core	Chopper	Utilized Flake	Core	Core Hammerstone	Spherical or Discoidal Hammerstone	Total	% of all tools (including formal, N=216)
North Central Area										
Subop 8	11.1%	0.0%	0.0%	0.0%	66.7%	14.8%	7.4%	0.0%	27	12.5%
Subop 12	25.0%	0.0%	12.5%	12.5%	25.0%	25.0%	0.0%	0.0%	8	3.7%
Subop 17	9.1%	0.0%	0.0%	0.0%	72.7%	9.1%	4.5%	4.5%	22	10.2%
Subop 13	0.0%	0.0%	0.0%	0.0%	0.0%	0.0%	0.0%	0.0%	0	0.0%
Subop 19	0.0%	0.0%	12.5%	0.0%	87.5%	0.0%	0.0%	0.0%	24	11.1%
Subop 6	0.0%	0.0%	0.0%	0.0%	0.0%	0.0%	0.0%	0.0%	0	0.0%
Subtotal	8.6%	0.0%	4.9%	1.2%	70.4%	9.9%	3.7%	1.2%	81	37.5%
South Central Area										
Subop 5	8.8%	2.9%	8.8%	0.0%	70.6%	8.8%	0.0%	0.0%	34	15.7%
Northwest Area										
Subop 7	4.8%	0.0%	4.8%	4.8%	81.0%	4.8%	0.0%	0.0%	21	9.7%
Subop 16	0.0%	0.0%	0.0%	0.0%	0.0%	0.0%	0.0%	0.0%	0	0.0%
Subtotal	4.8%	0.0%	4.8%	4.8%	81.0%	4.8%	0.0%	0.0%	21	9.7%
Subop 20										
Subop 20	14.3%	0.0%	0.0%	0.0%	71.4%	0.0%	14.3%	0.0%	7	3.2%

NORTHEAST AREA										
Subops 9, 10, 11, 15	16.7%	0.0%	0.0%	0.0%	0.0%	66.7%	16.7%	0.0%	6	2.8%
EAST DOCK										
Subop 14	18.2%	0.0%	0.0%	0.0%	54.5%	27.3%	0.0%	0.0%	11	5.1%
SOUTH AREA										
Subop 18	0.0%	0.0%	0.0%	0.0%	91.7%	0.0%	8.3%	0.0%	12	5.6%
Total	12	3	4	2	71	14	6	1	172	79.6%

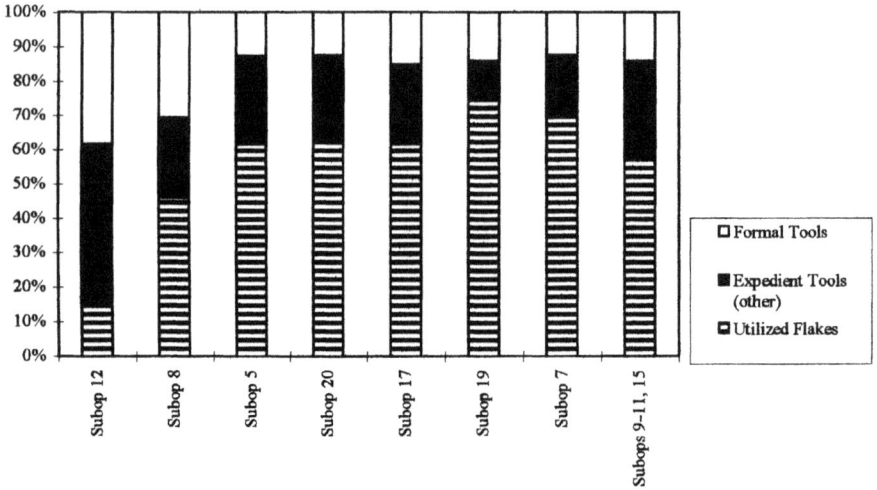

5.9. Early Facet percentage of lithic tool types by area.

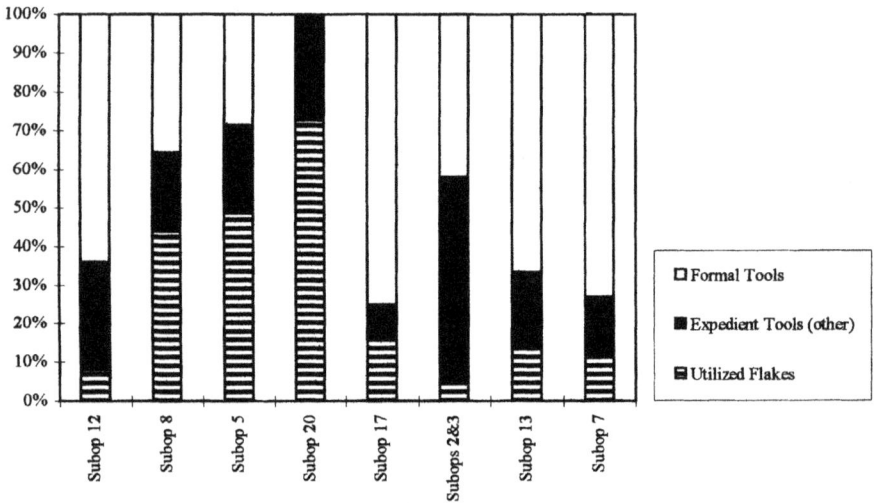

5.10. Late Facet percentage of lithic tool types by area.

distributions are not exclusive, and it appears that occupants of all areas of the island had access to the full range of local and long-distance lithic materials.

Spatial Variability of Lithic Industries in the Late Facet

Important changes are observed in the distribution of lithics during the Late Facet when compared to the patterns described above for the Early Facet

Table 5.14—Early Facet obsidian blades: Expedient chert tools ratios by subop

	Obsidian blades: all expedient tools	Obsidian blades: utilized flakes
Subop 12	4.7	19.0
Subop 8	3.0	4.6
Subop 20	2.5	3.6
Subop 9–11, 15	1.8	2.7
Subop 17	1.5	2.0
Subop 5	1.2	1.7
Subop 7	1.04	1.3
Subop 19	.12	.14

deposits. The distribution of nonobsidian chipped-stone formal tools is no longer primarily limited to Subops 8 and 12 (Figures 5.9 and 5.10). Higher frequencies are reported from zones where few ritual features have been identified (Subops 17, 13, and 7), in addition to Subop 12. No formal chert or chalcedony tools were recovered from Subop 20. These differences suggest that a greater range of activities may have been performed in the domestic zones listed above with the highest number of formal tools. Alternatively, these items were more more generally accessible to all individuals living at the site. With the exception of generally anomalous Subop 12, all other ritual feature areas show a decline in formal tools that may be related to an increase in specialized behaviors and a reduction of lithic assemblage diversity. Other lithic distribution patterns described below assist in interpreting patterns of the Late Facet at Laguna de On.

Examining the distribution of types of formal tools reveals that thin bifaces were recovered only at the north central area of the site. Points also seem to be concentrated in status or ritual areas during the Late Facet. They were recovered from Subops 8, 2 and 3, 6, and 17, which represent ritual and domestic localities comprising the north central area of the site. Points were also found from Subop 5 deposits. Only one triangular biface was found, at Subop 12. Oval bifaces and lenticular bifaces were commonly distributed at subops ac;ross the site. The frequencies of utilized flakes are distributed similarly across the site. Ritually associated Subops 12, 8, 5, and 20 have 72 percent or less utilized flakes in their expedient assemblages, while domestic zones lacking ritual indicators (Subops 17, 2 and 3, 13, and 7) have 80 percent or greater utilized flakes (Tables 5.15 and 5.16; Figures 5.11 and 5.12). Several of these latter subops also had higher frequencies of formal tools.

An examination of the ratios of obsidian blades to expedient tools and flakes in Table 5.17 provides further evidence of ritual/status functional

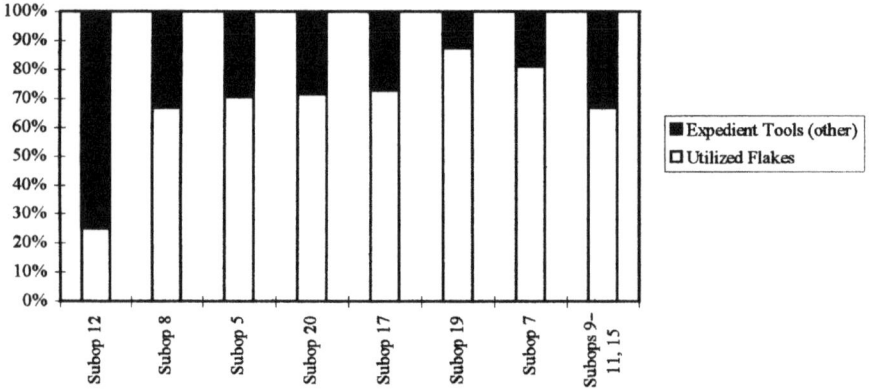

5.11. Late Facet percentage of utilized flakes comprising the expedient tool assemblage.

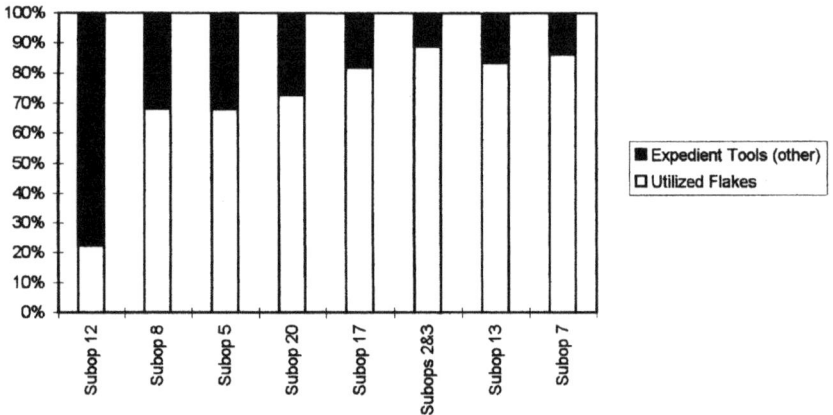

5.12. Early Facet percentage of utilized flakes comprising the expedient tool assemblage.

distinctions. Subops 2 and 3 have the greatest ratio of obsidian to expedient nonobsidian tools and flakes (with the exception of Subop 12, discussed below). This pattern is significant, especially considering the fact that this area also had a high percentage of utilized flakes (Figure 5.12). A use of obsidian in this upper-status domestic courtyard area thus supplemented rather than replaced the use of utilized flakes. As this area is not associated with ritual activity, the obsidian and expedient tool frequencies suggest that intensive economic activities occurred in this location. Though not a ritual area, Subops 2 and 3 are located immediately west of Subop 8 (Structure I), and a rubble patio foundation feature was found around 10cm beneath the surface at this location. Upper-status residential and ritual zones of the north central area as a group (Subops 2, 3, 8, and 12) have the highest obsidian-to-expedient tool and flake ratios of any other subops. Subop 17, located a few meters to the south of Subops 2 and 3 and also spatially associated with Subop 8, did not exhibit this amount of obsidian relative to expedient nonobsidian tools.

This patterning suggests that production activities involving lithics may have been concentrated in specific locations across the site, and that the use of obsidian appears to have been distributed more favorably in upper-status residential zones. Obsidian ratios are low for Subops 17, 7, 13, 5, and 20. While the first three subops listed are interpreted as zones of domestic activity, Subops 5 and 20 are associated with specific types of ritual features (mortuary remains at Subop 5 and the ballcourt configuration of Subop 20). Despite their ritual association, they do not exhibit high obsidian densities. This pattern suggests that obsidian distribution may be controlled by status factors rather than simply ritual considerations during the Late Facet, and that this material was used primarily for economic purposes. Despite differences in frequencies examined in this section that are used to tease out subtle patterns of status distinction at this site, a far more important pattern is that significant amounts of obsidian are found in all contexts examined. This resource was thus not tightly controlled, as it was apparently accessible to those living in all areas across the island.

The Use of Obsidian Blades in Domestic Activities

The abundance of obsidian at Laguna de On resulted in the substitution of the use of blades for a broad range of tasks related to household production in lieu of coarser chert and chalcedonies (Masson 1993, 1997). Although obsidian has a thinner edge that is more easily destroyed, use wear on obsidian blades from domestic middens at the site includes light, medium, and heavy edge damage. The abundance of obsidian at the site (N = 1,208; Table 5.18) and the heavy wear on many specimens suggests that it may have been easily obtainable and used indiscriminantly for a range of tasks without concern for conserving its edge (Figure 5.13). The wear reflected on obsidian blades is thus probably related to activities of domestic maintenance, including food preparation or the production of items such as leather or matting. Macroscopically observable use wear on obsidian blades consists of 61.9 percent light wear or undetectable wear, 30.6 percent medium wear, and 7.4 percent heavy wear of those blades examined (Valdez 1993b).

Obsidian was obtained through long-distance circum-Yucatecan merchant canoes that stopped at trading stations along the Belizean coast (McKillop 1980). Few cores were recovered at Laguna de On from the 1991

Table 5.15—Formal lithic tool frequency distributions by subop for Level 1 Late Facet deposits at Laguna de On Island.

	Thin Biface	Lenticular Biface	Triangular Biface	Side-notched (biface) Point	Leaf-shaped (blade) Point	Blade	Oval Biface	General Utility Biface	Tranchet Tool	Tranchet Flake	Colha Bifacial Thin Flake	Total
NORTH CENTRAL AREA												
Subop 8	11.5%	15.4%	0.0%	3.8%	3.8%	23.1%	42.3%	0.0%	0.0%	0.0%	0.0%	26
Subop 12	6.3%	12.5%	6.3%	0.0%	0.0%	25.0%	31.3%	0.0%	6.3%	0.0%	12.5%	16
Subop 17	0.0%	33.3%	0.0%	33.3%	0.0%	0.0%	33.3%	0.0%	0.0%	0.0%	0.0%	3
Subop 13	33.3%	33.3%	0.0%	0.0%	0.0%	33.3%	0.0%	0.0%	0.0%	0.0%	0.0%	3
Subops 2, 3	10.0%	20.0%	0.0%	10.0%	0.0%	20.0%	20.0%	10.0%	10.0%	0.0%	0.0%	10
Subop 6	0.0%	0.0%	0.0%	100%	0.0%	0.0%	0.0%	0.0%	0.0%	0.0%	0.0%	1
Subtotal	10.2%	16.9%	1.7%	6.8%	1.7%	22.0%	32.2%	1.7%	3.4%	0.0%	3.4%	59
SOUTH CENTRAL AREA												
Subop 5	0.0%	0.0%	10.0%	40.0%	10.0%	30.0%	10.0%	0.0%	0.0%	0.0%	0.0%	10
NORTHWEST AREA												
Subop 7	0.0%	0.0%	0.0%	0.0%	0.0%	0.0%	100%	0.0%	0.0%	0.0%	0.0%	4
Subop 16	0.0%	100%	0.0%	0.0%	0.0%	0.0%	0.0%	0.0%	0.0%	0.0%	0.0%	1
Subtotal	0.0%	20.0%	0.0%	0.0%	0.0%	0.0%	80.0%	0.0%	0.0%	0.0%	0.0%	5
SUBOP 20												
Subop 20	0.0%	0.0%	0.0%	0.0%	0.0%	0.0%	0.0%	0.0%	0.0%	0.0%	0.0%	0

Northeast Area

Subops 9–11, 15	0.0%	33.3%	0.0%	0.0%	0.0%	0.0%	66.7%	0.0%	0.0%	0.0%	0.0%	3
East Dock												
Subop 14	0.0%	0.0%	0.0%	0.0%	0.0%	100%	0.0%	0.0%	0.0%	0.0%	0.0%	1
South Area												
Subop 18	0.0%	0.0%	0.0%	0.0%	0.0%	0.0%	100%	0.0%	0.0%	0.0%	0.0%	1
		42.9%	14.3%	0.0%	14.3%	0.0%	0.0%	28.6%	0.0%	0.0%	0.0%	7
Total	9	13	2	9	2	17	29	1	2	0	2	86

Table 5.16—Expedient lithic tool frequency distributions by subop for Level 1 Late Facet deposits at Laguna de On Island

	Biface	Narrow, Parallel-sided Biface	Uniface	Utilized Core	Chopper	Utilized Flake	Core	Core Hammerstone	Spherical or Discoidal Hammerstone	Total	% of all tools (including formal, N=300)
NORTH CENTRAL AREA											
Subop 8	6.4%	0.0%	0.0%	0.0%	0.0%	68.1%	19.1%	2.1%	4.3%	47	15.7%
Subop 12	33.3%	0.0%	11.1%	0.0%	11.1%	22.2%	22.2%	0.0%	0.0%	9	3.0%
Subop 17	0.0%	0.0%	0.0%	0.0%	0.0%	81.8%	9.1%	6.1%	3.0%	33	11.0%
Subops 2, 3	11.1%	0.0%	0.0%	0.0%	0.0%	88.9%	0.0%	0.0%	0.0%	9	3.0%
Subop 13	0.0%	0.0%	8.3%	8.3%	0.0%	83.3%	0.0%	0.0%	0.0%	12	4.0%
Subop 6	0.0%	0.0%	0.0%	0.0%	0.0%	0.0%	0.0%	0.0%	0.0%	0	0.0%
Subtotal	6.4%	0.0%	1.8%	0.9%	0.9%	71.8%	12.7%	2.7%	2.7%	110	36.7%
SOUTH CENTRAL AREA											
Subop 5	4.0%	0.0%	0.0%	4.0%	0.0%	68.0%	4.0%	0.0%	20.0%	25	8.3%
NORTHWEST AREA											
Subop 7	0.0%	0.0%	4.5%	0.0%	0.0%	86.4%	9.1%	0.0%	0.0%	22	7.3%
Subop 16	18.2%	0.0%	0.0%	9.1%	0.0%	72.7%	0.0%	0.0%	0.0%	11	3.7%
Subtotal	6.1%	0.0%	3.0%	3.0%	0.0%	81.8%	6.1%	0.0%	0.0%	33	11.0%
SUBOP 20											
Subop 20	9.1%	0.0%	0.0%	0.0%	0.0%	72.7%	18.2%	0.0%	0.0%	11	3.7%
NORTHEAST AREA											
Subops 9, 10, 11, 15	0.0%	0.0%	0.0%	10.0%	0.0%	80.0%	10.0%	0.0%	0.0%	10	3.3%

										Total
EAST DOCK											
Subop 14	0.0%	0.0%	0.0%	16.7%	0.0%	50.0%	33.3%	0.0%	0.0%	2.0%	
											6
SOUTH AREA											
Subop 18	0.0%	0.0%	0.0%	50.0%	0.0%	50.0%	0.0%	0.0%	0.0%	1.3%	
											4
Surface	6.7%	0.0%	0.0%	6.7%	0.0%	86.7%	0.0%	0.0%	0.0%	5.0%	
											15
Total	12	0	3	8	1	157	22	3	8	71.3%	
											214

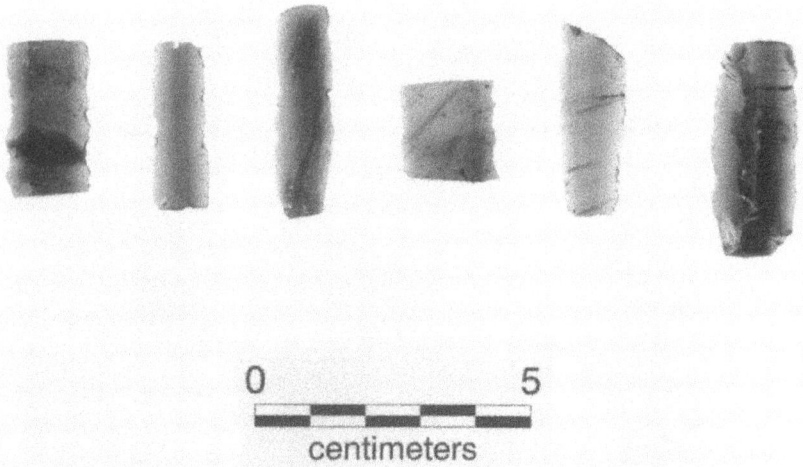

5.13. Examples of obsidian blades from Laguna de On Island.

and 1996 seasons. In fact, only four blade cores were found in the island and one occupations of this lagoon shore. Prismatic blade cores thus represent less than .3 percent of the 1,208 pieces recovered at the site (Tables 5.19 and 5.20). These cores from Laguna de On are small, measuring 5.5cm in length or less (Valdez 1993b). Most blades were probably obtained from merchants who stopped at trading sites such as those on Ambergris Caye or Moho Caye (McKillop 1980; Guderjan and Garber 1995), where most blades had already been removed from their cores. The mean blade width (Masson 1993: 233; Valdez 1993b) of measured proximal and medial fragments is 1.3cm and 1.2cm respectively. This small size of the blades indicates the peripheral position of Laguna de On in the long-distance coastal obsidian exchange sphere. Comparisons of blade widths at other sites in northern Belize may determine whether higher-ranking communities had first access to blade exchange, as blades removed earlier (from a larger core) would have a broader width (John Clark, personal communication 1993).

Low quantities of "chunks" of obsidian are also found across the site (Tables 5.19 and 5.20; Figures 5.14 and 5.15). These chunks represent small fragments (usually less than 3cm in diameter) of small flake cores, and appear to be the result of poor knapping skills. Flake removals are poorly and inefficiently executed, and the chunks exhibit no signs of having been former bifaces or formal cores that had entered a recycling stage. It is possible, based on these observations, to infer that raw obsidian material was also obtained through exchange for use as flake cores. However, as only fragments of these

Table 5.17—Late Facet obsidian blades: Expedient chert tools ratios by subop

	Obsidian blades: all expedient tools	Obsidian blades: utilized flakes
Subop 2, 3	21.4	24.1
Subop 12	6.7	30.5
Subop 8	3.7	5.5
Subop 17	2.3	2.8
Subop 20	2.1	3.1
Subop 13	1.1	1.4
Subop 7	.18	.25
Subop 5	.18	.21

remain at the site, they appear to have been heavily reduced and were probably in short supply. Chunks are relatively more common in the Early Facet assemblage (Table 5.19, 6.5 percent, N = 26) than in the Late Facet (Table 5.20, 3.8 percent, N = 31).

The site sample of obsidian includes 920 blades (305 from the Early Facet, 615 from the Late), 78 flakes (30 from the Early Facet, 48 from the Late), 149 chips (38 from the Early Facet, 111 from the Late), and 57 chunks (26 from the Early Facet, 31 from the Late) (Tables 5.19 and 5.20; Figures 5.14 and 5.15). Variability in the distribution of these categories of obsidian debris is observed in each component. During the Early Facet, Subops 7, 12, 8, 17, and 2 and 3 had the greatest percentage of blades (77–87 percent), followed by Subops 20, 5, and 9 (67–73 percent). Subop 13 had the least amount of blades (60 percent) and the greatest amount of flakes (13 percent) and chunks (18 percent) of any subop. No other subop (with a reasonable sample size) had this combined increased frequency of flakes and chunks, though Subop 5 had a comparable percentage of chunks (16 percent). The fewest chips and chunks recovered from any subop was at Subop 12, perhaps due to its ritual function. These distributions suggest that areas outside of the north central zone (Subops 12, 8, 17, 2, and 3) and Subop 7 were the focus of greater diversity in obsidian working and expedient activities that might result in chips, flakes, or chunks (Figure 5.14).

These patterns also suggest that chunks of obsidian raw material were not highly controlled, as they were recovered from a range of domestic zones. Subop 13 is the most likely location for knapping activities based on the increased recovery of chunks and flakes. Other lines of evidence (described previously) suggest it was also a location for local chert and chalcedony knapping on a modest scale. Subop 5 may also have been an area where working of obsidian flake cores was more common. The greatest

Table 5.18—Obsidian frequency distributions by subop for deposits at Laguna de On Island

	Level 1 Late Facet	% of subop total	Level 2–4 Early Facet	% of subop total	Subop Total
NORTH CENTRAL AREA					
Subop 8	219	66.4%	111	33.6%	330
Subop 12	73	61.3%	46	38.7%	119
Subop 17	81	62.3%	49	37.7%	130
Subop 13	23	51.1%	22	48.9%	45
Subop 19	0	0.0%	2	100.00%	2
Subop 2, 3	205	93.6%	14	6.4%	219
Subtotal	601	71.1%	244	28.9%	845
SOUTH CENTRAL AREA					
Subop 5	71	55.9%	56	44.1%	127
NORTHWEST AREA					
Subop 7	52	68.4%	24	31.6%	76
Subop 16	12	100.0%	0	0.0%	12
Subtotal	64	72.7%	24	27.3%	88
SUBOP 20					
Subop 20	6	18.8%	26	81.3%	32
NORTHEAST AREA					
Subops 9, 10, 11, 15	43	71.7%	17	28.3%	60
EAST DOCK					
Subop 14	20	42.6%	27	57.4%	47
SOUTH AREA					
Subop 18	4	44.4%	5	55.6%	9
Total	809	67.0%	399	33.0%	1,208

amounts of chips were recovered from Subops 2 and 3. The meaning of this pattern is not clear, and the small sample size of chips for the Early Facet (N = 14) is probably insufficient for meaningful analysis of their distribution.

During the Late Facet (Table 5.20; Figure 5.15), similar distributions of obsidian are observed. Subops 8, 12, and 17 continue to have high percentages of obsidian blades (77–80 percent), with Subop 5 joining this group (78 percent). Subops 2, 3, and 7 have lower frequencies of blades (68–71 percent) than in the Early Facet. Subop 13 continues to have a low percentage of blades (60 percent), and a high amount of chunks (13 percent) and flakes (26 percent) compared to the Early Facet. Subop 7 also has a notably high

Table 5.19—Obsidian type distributions by subop for deposits at Laguna de On Island—Early Facet

	Blades	Flakes	Chips	Chunks	Total Pieces
NORTH CENTRAL AREA					
Subop 8	79.3%	8.1%	11.7%	0.9%	111
Subop 12	82.6%	8.7%	4.3%	4.3%	46
Subop 17	77.6%	10.2%	8.2%	4.1%	49
Subop 13	59.1%	13.6%	9.1%	18.2%	22
Subop 19	50.0%	50.0%	0.0%	0.0%	2
Subop 2, 3	78.6%	0.0%	21.4%	0.0%	14
SOUTH CENTRAL AREA					
Subop 5	67.9%	3.6%	12.5%	16.1%	56
NORTHWEST AREA					
Subop 7	87.5%	4.2%	0.0%	8.3%	24
Subop 16	0.0%	0.0%	0.0%	0.0%	0
SUBOP 20					
Subop 20	73.1%	7.7%	11.5%	7.7%	26
NORTHEAST AREA					
Subops 9–11, 15	70.6%	0.0%	17.6%	11.8%	17
EAST DOCK					
Subop 14	77.8%	11.1%	3.7%	7.4%	27
SOUTH AREA					
Subop 18	100.0%	0.0%	0.0%	0.0%	5
Total	76.4%	7.5%	9.5%	6.5%	399

percentage of chunks (12 percent) and flakes (17 percent), and as this unit is close to Subop 13, informal obsidian-working activities may have been performed in each area as part of an expansion of activities that began earlier in the Subop 13 vicinity. Frequencies in Table 5.20 for Subop 14 are not interpreted due to the possible mixing of underwater deposits in this area. Subops 2 and 3 continue to have high numbers of chips (as do Subops 9–11 and 15). High frequencies of obsidian in general are seen in Subops 2 and 3 during the Late Facet, including relatively high numbers of points and incomplete points. Subops 2 and 3 may have been a locality that focused on obsidian-point production (as suggested previously) that could have generated greater numbers of chips.

Table 5.20—Obsidian type distributions by subop for deposits at Laguna de On Island—Late Facet

	Blades	Core	Flakes	Chips	Chunks	Total Pieces
NORTH CENTRAL AREA						
Subop 8	80.8%	0.0%	9.1%	6.8%	3.2%	219
Subop 12	83.6%	2.7%	6.8%	5.5%	1.4%	73
Subop 17	77.8%	0.0%	3.7%	6.2%	12.3%	81
Subop 13	60.9%	0.0%	26.1%	0.0%	13.0%	23
Subop 2, 3	68.3%	0.0%	0.0%	31.2%	0.5%	205
SOUTH CENTRAL AREA						
Subop 5	78.9%	1.4%	7.0%	7.0%	5.6%	71
NORTHWEST AREA						
Subop 7	71.2%	1.9%	17.3%	5.8%	3.8%	52
Subop 16	83.3%	0.0%	0.0%	16.7%	0.0%	12
SUBOP 20						
Subop 20	66.7%	0.0%	0.0%	16.7%	16.7%	6
NORTHEAST AREA						
Subops 9–11, 15	74.4%	0.0%	0.0%	25.6%	0.0%	43
EAST DOCK						
Subop 14	85.0%	0.0%	0.0%	5.0%	10.0%	20
SOUTH AREA						
Subop 18	100.0%	0.0%	0.0%	0.0%	0.0%	4
Total	76.0%	0.5%	5.9%	13.7%	3.8%	809

In all of these comparisons of temporal facet distributions, it is possible to generalize regarding several major points. The north central zone (Subops 8, 12, 17, 2, and 3) has greater percentages of blades or greater numbers of blades than most other subops in each component (Figures 5.14 and 5.15). In the Early Facet, Subop 5 appears more like Subop 13 (a domestic zone where increased knapping activities are indicated). This area more resembles the north central zone in the Late Facet, representing a domestic and ritual zone with a high percentage of blades and low numbers of other types of debris. Subop 7 appears more like the north central zone in the Early Facet (but lacks chips) and more like Subop 13 in the Late Facet. All other zones (with reasonable sample sizes) have 60–73 percent blades and various combinations of low numbers of chips, chunks, or flakes. These latter zones appear to represent domestic areas or features (such as the Subop 20 depression) in which nonspecialized residential debris may have fallen.

An increase in the amount of obsidian being brought into the site is observed over time. When the Early and Late Facet assemblages are com-

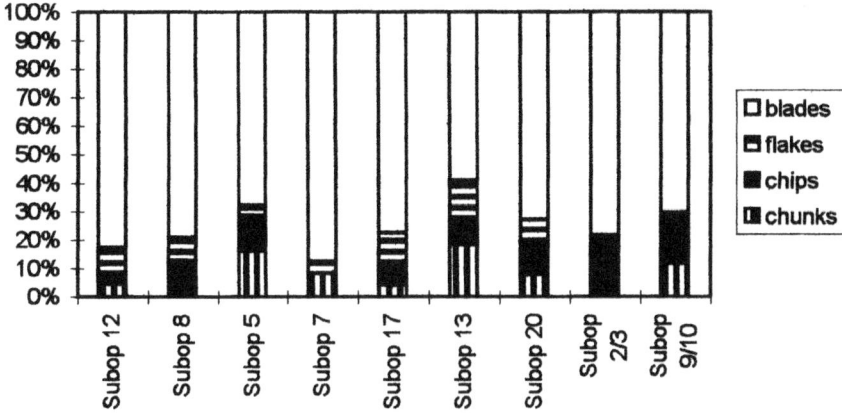

5.14. Types of obsidian pieces in Early Facet areas.

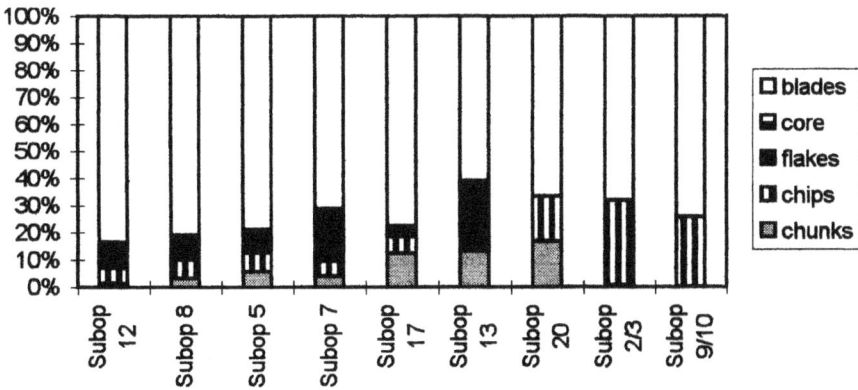

5.15. Types of obsidian pieces in Late Facet areas.

pared, the relative amount of obsidian at most subops appears to double in the Late Facet (Table 5.18, for sample sizes greater than 36). Subops that do not reflect this pattern either have unreliably small sample sizes, or they are from poorly controlled contexts such as the Subop 14 underwater dock deposits. The fact that the amount of obsidian doubles in the Late Facet is significant, especially as this component represents primarily the top 15cm of soil at the site, and the Early Facet deposits are represented by the underlying 30cm of materials. Volumetric considerations thus do not account for this change in frequency. This increase in obsidian during the Late Facet may thus signify an acceleration in the access to long-distance goods for Laguna de On. The Late Facet is tied to the amplification of the Mesoamerican world system after A.D. 1200 (Blanton and Feinman 1984; Carmack 1996), and it appears that the increase in obsidian brought into the site reflects Laguna de On's participation in this sphere of exchange.

When this increase in frequency of obsidian is examined relative to the amount of expedient and formal nonobsidian tools in the assemblage, important changes in the reliance on local versus long-distance lithic tools are observed over time. The pie charts in Figure 5.16 show that the percentage of obsidian among lithic tools at the site increased from 65 percent in the Early Facet to 73 percent in the Late Facet. From these figures, it is possible to observe the increased significance of obsidian tools in the Laguna economy over time. This increase can be assessed relative to other categories of materials at the site. Ceramic sherds are 25 percent more numerous in the Late Facet (7,363) than in the Early Facet (5,629) in the areas tested, and this comparison suggests an increase in occupational intensity over time at this site. However, unburned flakes are also over twice as frequent in the Late Facet (N = 3,006) than in the Early Facet (N = 1,681). The increase in lithic materials is not proportionate to the increase in ceramic materials. As ceramics provide a good gauge of occupational intensity (Rathje 1983), the disproportionate increase in lithic debris relative to ceramics implies that economic changes in local tool use and manufacture took place and that an increased amount of obsidian was brought in over time.

Most of the Postclassic period obsidian found at northern Belize sites that has been chemically sourced has been identified as Ixtepeque (Dreiss and Brown 1989), which appears to have arrived in Belize via routes of coastal exchange. Dreiss and Brown (1989) have conducted distribution studies that suggest Ixtepeque may have moved down the Motagua River to the Bay of Honduras before travelling north along the Belize coast, from which it was exchanged inland. In a regional study by Sidrys (1983), Ixtepeque (five out of five sites) and El Chayal (three out of five sites) sources were most common for the Postclassic. Sidrys also identified blades from San Martin Jilotepeque (N = 1), Pico de Orizaba (N = 1), and Pachuca (N = 3). Sidrys's samples are broadly attributed to a time period that extends from A.D. 1000 to 1550, which does not indicate whether patterns fluctuate over time. A greater variety of obsidian sources is reported for the Early Postclassic, including sources from highland Mexico (Andrews et al. 1989). The majority of Laguna de On obsidian blades appear to be from Ixtepeque (Geoffrey Braswell and Henry Chaya, personal communication).

These changing source frequencies reflect altered politics of extraction at highland sites near the raw-material outcrops. As no qualitative differences have been observed in obsidian from different sources, blades from various quarries were functionally interchangeable in consumer economies. Blades (and other commodities) were probably obtained by maritime mer-

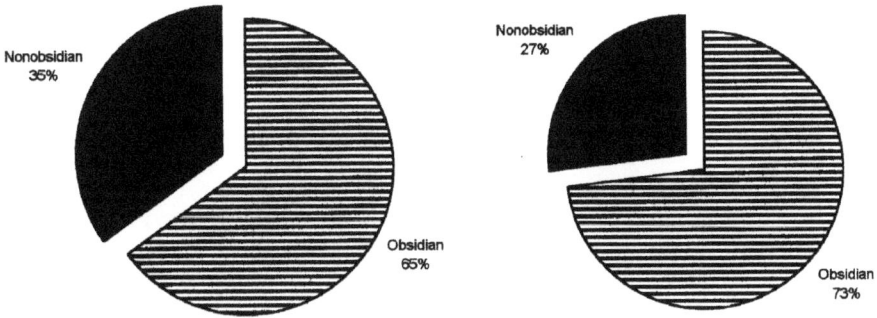

5.16. Obsidian blades/nonobsidian tool proportions in the Early Facet (left) and in the Late Facet (right) at Laguna de On.

chants from trading ports in the Gulf Coast or in the Bay of Honduras, and were then transported and exchanged around the coastal Yucatán circuit. While it is doubtful that the source of obsidian blades themselves mattered much to Maya consumers for aesthetic or technological reasons, this shift in trade routes lowered the cost of obsidian (Prudence Rice 1987b: 84) and greater quantities became available to consumer sites such as Laguna de On.

CRAFT PRODUCTION AT LEGUNA DE ON

Spinning

Evidence of cash-crop industries are scarcely visible in the archaeological record at Laguna de On. No evidence is observed of cacao growing, and some sources suggest that the heart of the cacao-growing region was further to the south and west (Rathje, Gregory, and Wiseman 1978: Figure 23; Graham 1994). Tools to process or consume cacao have not been identified archaeologically. Wax, honey, mamey apples, cohune palm, ramon, other fruits or nuts, and animal products were also available in this region and could have been extracted for sustenance or exchange (Rathje, Gregory, and Wiseman 1978: Figues 23 and 24). Cotton was also an important product that was probably grown by the Laguna de On community, reflected by the recovery of spindle whorls from middens and features at the site. While the remains of cotton plants and textile products are unlikely to be preserved and recovered archaeologically, they are indirectly accounted for from production activities. Ethnohistoric records list cloth as one of the items exacted in tribute throughout the province of Chetumal (Pina Chan 1978).

Spindle Whorls

The presence of spindle whorls at Maya sites is one of several hallmarks identified for the Postclassic period (Willey et al. 1965; Thompson 1939), along with comals, net weights, and obsidian blades (as discussed in Chapter 3). It is difficult to believe that the lack of ceramic spindle whorls in the Classic period represents a lack of textile manufacture. At some Classic period sites, perforated sherds are thought to have served this purpose, or perhaps spindle whorls were made of perishable materials. It is notable, however, that ceramic spindle whorls that bear resemblance to those of Veracruz, Mexico, are a signature of the Postclassic (Thompson 1939). This stylistic link reflects important economic ties to Mexico.

Thirty-four spindle whorls have been recovered from Laguna de On (1996 and 1997 seasons; Table 5.21; Figure 5.17). These have been classified into several types, including uniconvex and biconvex whorls with combinations of flat, curved, or concave superior and inferior surface configurations (Table 5.21, compiled from Murray 1998). Whorl diameters range from 24.51mm to 33.28mm in the Early Facet and from 25mm to 32.8mm (with one outlier, 37.78mm) in the Late Facet (Murray 1998: Tables 1 and 2). Differences in whorl diameters thus do not vary greatly from the Early to Late Facet. Other dimensions do not show much variation either. Hole diameter ranges from 8 to 10.1mm in the Early Facet and from 8.3 to 10.27mm in the Late Facet (Murray 1998: Tables 1 and 2). The average hole diameter for the Early Facet is 9.36mm, and it is 10.1mm for the Late Facet. The average whorl height is 14.39mm in the Early Facet and 14.89mm in the Late Facet. The whorl-diameter average for the Early Facet is 29.72mm and it is 30.24mm in the Late Facet. The similarities in dimensions suggest that these weaving technologies are closely linked over time at Laguna de On. Some variability is observed in the types recorded for the two facets (Table 5.21, extracted from Murray 1998: Tables 1 and 2). Greater diversity in whorl types is observed in the Late Facet. New types that appear in these levels include decorated whorls, concave/curved uniconvex whorls, and biconvex whorls. Types common to both facets include flat/curved uniconvex whorls, curved/curved uniconvex whorls, and flat/flat-sided uniconvex whorls (Murray 1998). Whorls were also recovered from most locations across the site, suggesting that weaving was a common household activity and not the prerogative of a few individuals (Table 5.21; Murray 1998: Tables 1 and 2). However, decorated whorls are limited to Subop 12, perhaps placed in this ritual locality as offerings (Murray 1998).

Spindle whorls are not as well made in the Belize Valley, where the more frequent forms are drilled sherds and only one manufactured specimen was reported (Willey et al. 1965: Figure 258 [a, b, c, g]). Further comparative work is needed to track intersite and interregional variability among Postclassic weaving traditions of the Maya Lowlands. The well-developed whorl industry at Laguna de On may be related to its proximity to coastal trading routes and more direct contact with foreign merchants.

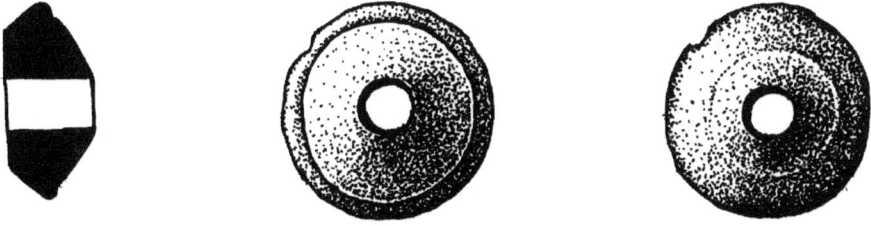

5.17. Example of a uniconvex spindle whorl from Laguna de On (illustration by John Labadie).

Shell Ornament Manufacture

Craft production was not limited to weaving at Laguna de On. Marine-shell ornament and ceramic production also took place. Raw materials for shell working were probably obtained through exchange with coastal sites in northern Belize. A total of forty-six pieces of marine shell were recovered at Laguna de On Island in 1996 and 1997 (Table 5.22). These pieces of shell were largely in the form of flakes and core debris from on-site shell-working industries. Shell working at Laguna appears to have involved the importation of whole shells in unmodified form, including whole whelk shells, conch shells, bivalves, and olive shells that were subsequently reduced at the site. Pieces of large marine gastropod "cores" and "debitage" are found at Laguna de On, including flakes and sections of the lip, whorl, and columella. (Table 5.22; Figure 5.18). Shell reduction involved the percussion removal of segments of the whorl and lip from the columella, and the subsequent abrasion of small pieces into beads or other ornaments. Such techniques are common in other regions of the Americas where shell-working industries are well developed (Eaton 1974; Luer 1986; Masson 1988). One whole shell ornament has been found at the site, along with shell beads. Incompletely abraded olivella shells and bivalves are also found in middens. Shell working represents a form of local craft specialization. It is most probable that the whole shells were acquired either directly or down the line from coastal trading villages along the Belizean Cayes. The majority of shell brought into Laguna was whelk (N = 23), and the next most common was conch (N = 13). Bivalves (N = 5), olivella (N = 2), and coral (N = 3) were less common (Table 5.22). One coral metate was also found. A similar shell-working industry that included marine gastropods and olivella shells is noted for the Postclassic period at Colha (Dreiss 1994: Tables 5 and 6).

There is an increase in shell working at Laguna from in the Late Facet (N = 30) compared to the Early Facet (N = 16). During the Early Facet, shell is more equitably distributed in a variety of contexts across the site (Table 5.22). One concentration of five pieces of shell was found in Subop 15a, a

Table 5.21—Spindle whorl types by subop/level at Laguna de On Island (extracted from Murray 1998)

	Uniconvex					Biconvex	
	Decorated Incised or Punctuated	Flat/ Curved	Curved/ Curved	Concave/ Curved	Flat/ Flat	Flat/ Flat	Flat/ Curved
LEVEL 1 LATE FACET							
NORTH CENTRAL AREA							
Subop 8	0	3	0	0	0	1	0
Subop 12	2	2	1	1	1	0	0
Subop 17	0	3	0	0	0	0	0
Subtotal	2	8	1	1	1	1	0
SOUTH CENTRAL AREA							
Subop 5	0	2	0	0	0	0	0
NORTHWEST AREA							
Subop 7	0	1	0	0	0	2	0
Total Level 1	2	11	1	1	1	2	1
LEVEL 2–4 EARLY FACET							
NORTH CENTRAL AREA							
Subop 8	0	1	1	0	0	0	0
Subop 12	0	1	0	0	1	0	0
Subop 17	0	3	0	0	0	0	0
Subop 19	0	0	0	0	1	0	0
Subtotal	0	5	1	0	2	0	0
NORTHWEST AREA							
Subop 7	0	4	2	0	0	0	0
Total Levels 2–4	0	9	3	0	2	0	0
Total All Levels	2	20	4	1	3	3	1

context not identified as an upper-status residential zone or area of ritual activity. Four pieces in the Early Facet were also found around Subop 8, and all other areas with shell had two pieces or less (Subops 19, 12, 5, 7, 17, and 20). In the Late Facet, not only does the sample size of marine shell double, but shell-working debris is limited in its distribution to upper-status residential zones or ritual activity areas. The majority of the Late Facet sample of marine shell was recovered from Subop 8 (twenty-four pieces out of thirty), and the remainder were found from Subop 5 or 17 (upper-status residential zones) or from Subop 12 or 20 (ritual activity areas). These patterns suggest that the value of shell as a status indicator increased from the Early to Late Facets, or perhaps the need to display status itself increased.

Ceramic Production

Although ceramics were probably produced at many communities during the Postclassic period (Prudence Rice 1980), it is also likely that communities such as Laguna de On produced some ceramics for local exchange. Differences reported among Postclassic redware ceramics suggest that the sites of Lamanai and Marco Gonzalez in northern Belize were affiliated with slightly different exchange and interaction spheres than Santa Rita Corozal (Chase 1984: 25; Graham and Pendergast 1989: 11). Regional comparisons are needed to refine understanding of intersite ceramic exchange and emulation spheres in northern Belize.

The analysis of ceramics from Laguna de On at this point also represents the perspective of a single community. It is possible at this preliminary stage to examine general categories of types of ceramics used across the site in the Early and Late Facets. Features that may signal the location of ceramic production at Laguna de On are described in detail in Chapter 4. Laguna de On had access to valuable white kaolin-type clays that have been located above marl bedrock substrate on the island itself (Rosenswig and Stafford 1998). The distribution of these pit-firing features across the site suggests that ceramic craft production may not have been strictly controlled by any household. They are found at upper-status domestic zones in Subops 8, 17, and the domestic component beneath Subop 12. One feature was also found at Subop 7, a domestic zone of undifferentiated status. As discussed in Chapter 4, ceramic firing pits at Laguna have been found primarily from Early Facet deposits. There is no evidence in the characteristics of ceramic assemblages from the Early to Late Facet that major changes occurred in production technology. Some of these firing pits may have continued to be used during the Late Facet (Chapter 4).

As described in Chapter 3, slipped wares do not show great variability over time between the Early Facets and the Late Facets based on current analyses (Mock 1997, 1998). Both components are comprised primarily of Payil Red ceramics (88 percent and 83 percent respectively). Tables 5.23 to 5.28 present quantifications of field classifications and typologies assigned by project ceramicist Shirley Mock (1997, 1998). There are more Rita Red ceramics in the Late Facet (7.3 percent compared to 4.5 percent; Tables 5.23 and 5.24), as should be expected given the fact that Rita Red is thought to have developed later than Payil in northern Belize (Diane Chase 1982). Zakpah Orange Red, a type related to earlier Postclassic wares at Cerros (Walker 1990), occurs only in the Late Facet of Laguna de On (Table 5.24). However, Zakpah slip tends to erode and make this ware harder to identify. At the site of Caye Coco, where preservation is superb, Zakpah Orange Red is clearly earlier than Payil Red (Masson and Mock n.d.). Few incised and "grater bowl" ceramics (N = 37 for the entire site) have been recovered at

Table 5.22—Marine shell at Laguna de On Island

Subop	Lot	Early Facet Type	Portion	N	Late Facet Type	Portion	N
8a	1	—	—	—	whelk	flake	1
8b	8	—	—	—	conch	flake	1
8b	8	—	—	—	whelk	flakes	2
8c	26	—	—	—	whelk	flakes	4
8c	27	—	—	—	conch	flake	1
8c	87	whelk	flake	1	—	—	—
8c	44	—	—	—	whelk	flake	1
8c	32	—	—	—	whelk	flakes	2
8d	130	conch	large whorl frg.	1	—	—	—
8d	34	—	—	—	conch	columella	1
8e	59	whelk	flake	1	—	—	—
8j	78	—	—	—	whelk	large whorl frg.	1
8i	81	—	—	—	whelk	flake	1
8i	84	—	—	—	conch	bead	1
8j	107	—	—	—	conch	flake	1
8j	96	—	—	—	coral	frg.	1
8j	95	—	—	—	conch	worked frg.	1
8l	115	—	—	—	conch	flake	1
8k	114	—	—	—	conch	flake	1
8k	130	—	—	—	whelk	flake	1
8p	336	—	—	—	bivalve	flake	1
8q	356	bivalve	flake	1	—	—	—
8f	45	—	—	—	whelk	flake	1
Subtotal Subop 8				4			24
19	232	conch	large whorl frg.	1	—	—	—
17a	256	coral	frg.	1	—	—	—
17a	264	—	—	—	whelk	flake	1
12i	110	bivalve	flake	1	conch	flake	1
Total North Central Area (inc. Subop 8)				7			26
5i	302	whelk	whorl frg.	1	bivalve	flake	1
5i	302	—	—	—	conch	columella frg.	1
Total South Central Area (Subop 5)				1			2
7abc	295	olivella	worked frg.	1	—	—	—
7abc	295	whelk	flake	1	—	—	—
Total Northwest Area (Subop 7)				2			0
20e	375	bivalve	flake	1	—	—	—
20d	338	—	—	—	conch	whorl frg.	1

continued on next page

Table 5.22—*continued*

Subop	Lot	Early Facet Type	Portion	N	Late Facet Type	Portion	N
20a	312	—	—	—	coral	frg. (burial)	1
Total Subop 20				1			2
15a	202	olivella	worked frg.	2	—	—	—
15a	202	whelk	worked frg.	1	—	—	—
15a	202	whelk	flakes	2	—	—	—
Total Subop 15				5			0
Total		Early Facet		16		Late Facet	30

Laguna de On. It has been difficult to establish Payil from Rita Red for many samples as they are comprised primarily of eroded body sherds that do not reveal vessel form.

Although some variability is observed among subops in the percentages of Payil and Rita Red (Tables 5.23 and 5.24), these patterns are not used here to interpret behavioral differences due to the possible overlap of classifications. It is notable, however, that incised sherds and grater bowls occur in postulated higher-status areas such as Subops 8, 12, and 5, as well as in lesser-status areas such as Subop 7 in the Late Facet. This pattern is observed for both facets, although different subops are involved. It suggests that incised redware ceramics do not strongly distinguish status or ritual areas at the site.

Interesting patterns are also observed for unslipped ceramics from Laguna de On. It must first be noted that a majority of ceramics from the Early and Late Facets were eroded or unclassified (66.2 percent Early, 65.8 percent Late). High numbers of eroded sherds from both facets suggests that Late Facet sherds were not more highly impacted by erosion than underlying deposits. Three groups of ceramics account for the majority of unslipped sherds not classified as "eroded" in Early and Late Facet samples (typologies following Diane Chase 1982; Walker 1990; Mock 1998), including the Navula and Cohokum Group (Cehac-Hunacti Composite and Santa Unslipped), the Tsabak Group (Tsabak Unslipped), and the sandy paste group (as yet an unnamed set of types). Other unnamed types in low frequency include those referred to in Tables 5.25 and 5.26 as striated wares, comals, and perforated-colander censers. Appliqué pieces (of unnamed types within the Navula and Cohokum groups) are also listed separately in Tables 5.25 and 5.26 as they follow distinctive distributions.

Most unslipped sherds from each period were classified as Santa Unslipped. The second most common types were those identified as comals and "sandy

5.18. Examples of worked marine shell from Laguna de On.

paste" sherds. These latter sherd types conform to distinctive distributions across the site that signify their importance in ritual use. All other types represent less than 1.9 percent of Early and Late Facet assemblages, making it difficult to assign meaning to their distributions. Santa Unslipped is more common in the Late Facet (21.7 percent, compared to 14.4 percent in the Early Facet). Sandy paste sherds are slightly more common in the Early Facet (7.4 percent compared to 5.1 percent in the Late Facet). High frequencies of comals in the Early Facet (7.6 percent compared to .9 percent in the Late Facet) are the primary distinguishing attribute of these lower levels. During both periods, this form has a limited distribution. In the Early Facet, all 275 pieces were recovered from Subop 8, and they were not found elsewhere at the site. This distribution suggests that they were used at Subop 8 for special purposes—perhaps upper-status families residing in this area used them to prepare special meals for feasting or ceremony.

During the Late Facet, several new forms appear in low numbers, and they have exclusive distributions that also seem to pertain to ritual use. Appliqué elements of Cohokum ceramics, generally associated with censers, are found at Subop 8 and Subop 5 only, and may be correlated with status and ritual at these locations. Comals are also limited in their distribution to Subops 8, 12, and 5, suggesting that the production of tortillas was a prerogative restricted to occasional use by privileged sectors of the community. They are neither common nor widespread, suggesting that tortillas were not a daily fare.

Slipped and unslipped ceramic ratios are examined across the site for the Early and Late Facets in Tables 5.27 and 5.28. For the Early Facet (Table 5.27), the highest ratios of slipped to unslipped sherds were found in Subops 8 and 12 (.77 and .96 respectively), the areas later correlated with ritual. Reasonably high ratios are observed for residential zones of Subop 7 and 17 also (.59 and .67 respectively), suggesting that access to red-slipped wares was not highly restricted. These areas (Subops 8, 7, and 17) are zones where ceramic production of redwares may have taken place, as suggested by the identification of fire features in their Early Facet deposits (Chapter 4). Production activities would perhaps explain the high frequencies of slipped ceramics in these zones. Subop 12, where only one production feature was located beneath Structure II, has a higher ratio than any other area. This pattern suggests a specialized function for Subop 12 for the Early Facet as well as the Late Facet at this location that follows other evidence described in this chapter. Areas with fewer or no domestic features at the site during the Early Facet (Subop 5, Subop 20, and Subop 18) expressed low ratios of redwares to unslipped wares.

In the Late Facet, ritual and upper-status zones (Subops 8, 12, and 17) retain high ratios of slipped to unslipped ceramics (Table 5.28). Subops 5 and 20 remain at the low end of the scale, newly accompanied by Subop 7. Subop 18 appears anomalously high, and this pattern is unexplained by factors of status or ritual. Generally, these patterns suggest a continued specialized focus of activity at Subop 12 compared to other locations, and individuals living near Subops 8 and 17 may have expressed a degree of upper social status through their possession of slightly more redware ceramics. Subop 18 indicates that the distribution of red-slipped ceramics was by no means exclusive at the site. Overall, these comparisons suggest that all families living on the island used similar ceramics, and while these artifact proportions hint at subtle differences in status among these groups, vastly different social divisions are not marked by ceramic distributions.

Miscellaneous Ornaments

Ornaments recovered from Laguna de On include those made of local materials and those made of exotic materials (Table 5.29; Figure 5.19). The distribution of these ornaments at the site over space and time suggests that they are of little use for determining status differentiation among domestic zones at the island. There is no pattern of increased frequencies of these objects at ritual areas such as Subop 12, Subop 8, or Subop 20, with the exception of pigments at Subop 12. This distribution suggests that most of these objects

Table 5.23—Slipped ceramic type frequency distributions for Level 2–4 Early Facet deposits at Laguna de On Island (based on field classifications by Shirley Mock in 1996 and 1997).

	Rita Group Rita Red	Payil Group Payil Red Plain	Payil Red Incised	Payil Red Grater	Zakpah Group Zakpah Red	Red-Slipped (untyped)	Other (buff, white)	Total
NORTH CENTRAL AREA								
Subop 8	2.8%	95.0%	0.9%	0.4%	0.0%	0.9%	0.0%	460
Subop 12	0.2%	79.6%	0.0%	0.0%	0.0%	20.3%	0.0%	592
Subop 17	9.2%	89.8%	0.0%	1.0%	0.0%	0.0%	0.0%	403
Subop 13	0.0%	0.0%	0.0%	0.0%	0.0%	100.0%	0.0%	1
Subtotal	3.5%	87.2%	0.3%	0.4%	0.0%	8.6%	0.0%	1,456
SOUTH CENTRAL AREA								
Subop 5	17.8%	80.0%	0.0%	0.0%	0.0%	0.0%	2.2%	180
NORTHWEST AREA								
Subop 7	3.3%	92.8%	3.9%	0.0%	0.0%	0.0%	0.0%	153
Subop 16	0.0%	0.0%	100.0%	0.0%	0.0%	0.0%	0.0%	2
Subtotal	3.2%	91.6%	5.2%	0.0%	0.0%	0.0%	0.0%	155
SUBOP 20								
Subop 20	0.0%	100.0%	0.0%	0.0%	0.0%	0.0%	0.0%	31
NORTHEAST AREA								
Subop 15	7.7%	84.6%	7.7%	0.0%	0.0%	0.0%	0.0%	13
EAST DOCK								
Subop 14	0.0%	99.3%	0.7%	0.0%	0.0%	0.0%	0.0%	149
SOUTH AREA								
Subop 18	11.1%	88.9%	0.0%	0.0%	0.0%	0.0%	0.0%	9
Total	90	1,754	14	6	0	125	4	1,993
	4.5%	88.0%	0.7%	0.3%	0.0%	6.3%	0.2%	

Table 5.24—Slipped ceramic type frequency distributions for Level 1 Late Facet deposits at Laguna de On Island (based on field classifications by Shirley Mock in 1996 and 1997).

	Rita Group	Payil Group			Zakpah Group		Other	Total
	Rita Red	Payil Red Plain	Payil Red Incised	Payil Red Grater	Zakpah Red	Red-slipped (untyped)	(buff, white)	
NORTH CENTRAL AREA								
Subop 8	1.9%	84.5%	0.7%	0.1%	12.4%	0.0%	0.5%	1,012
Subop 12	8.3%	80.4%	0.3%	0.3%	10.4%	0.0%	0.3%	616
Subop 17	7.4%	92.6%	0.0%	0.0%	0.0%	0.0%	0.0%	282
Subop 13	0.0%	100.0%	0.0%	0.0%	0.0%	0.0%	0.0%	18
Subtotal	4.7%	84.5%	0.5%	0.2%	9.8%	0.0%	0.4%	1,928
SOUTH CENTRAL AREA								
Subop 5	16.1%	74.1%	0.6%	0.3%	8.9%	0.0%	0.0%	347
NORTHWEST AREA								
Subop 7	43.1%	55.2%	1.7%	0.0%	0.0%	0.0%	0.0%	58
Subop 16	19.0%	76.2%	0.0%	0.0%	4.8%	0.0%	0.0%	21
Subtotal	36.7%	60.8%	1.3%	0.0%	1.3%	0.0%	0.0%	79
SUBOP 20								
Subop 20	50.0%	50.0%	0.0%	0.0%	0.0%	0.0%	0.0%	12
NORTHEAST AREA								
Subop 15	7.1%	92.9%	0.0%	0.0%	0.0%	0.0%	0.0%	14
EAST DOCK								
Subop 14	2.1%	96.5%	0.7%	0.0%	0.7%	0.0%	0.0%	144
SOUTH AREA								
Subop 18	0.0%	100.0%	0.0%	0.0%	0.0%	0.0%	0.0%	22
Total	186 7.3%	2,114 83.0%	13 0.5%	4 0.2%	222 8.7%	0 0.0%	7 0.3%	2,546

Table 5.25—Unslipped ceramic type frequency distributions for Level 2–4 Early Facet deposits at Laguna de On Island (based on field classifications by Shirley Mock in 1996 and 1997)

	Cohokum Group				Tsabak Grp.	Miscellaneous						Total
	Santa	Kol-modelled	appliqué (untyped)	other Cohokum	Tsabak Unslipped	striated	sandy paste	comals	perforated colander	other	eroded	
NORTH CENTRAL AREA												
Subop 8	16.8%	0.0%	0.0%	0.0%	0.0%	1.2%	4.5%	0.5%	0.0%	2.9%	74.1%	595
Subop 12	0.7%	0.0%	0.0%	0.0%	0.7%	0.0%	18.9%	0.0%	0.0%	0.0%	79.8%	615
Subop 17	11.5%	0.0%	0.0%	0.0%	3.0%	0.0%	0.8%	0.0%	0.0%	0.0%	56.0%	951
Subop 13	0.0%	0.0%	0.0%	0.0%	1.6%	0.0%	68.8%	0.0%	0.0%	0.0%	29.7%	64
Subtotal	9.6%	0.0%	0.0%	0.0%	1.5%	0.3%	8.8%	0.1%	0.0%	0.8%	66.7%	2,225
SOUTH CENTRAL AREA												
Subop 5	24.1%	0.6%	0.0%	0.0%	2.0%	2.6%	6.3%	0.0%	0.0%	0.0%	64.5%	664
NORTHWEST AREA												
Subop 7	24.5%	0.0%	0.0%	0.0%	2.6%	0.0%	0.4%	0.0%	0.0%	0.0%	72.5%	229
Subop 16	76.5%	0.0%	0.0%	0.0%	0.0%	0.0%	0.0%	0.0%	0.0%	23.5%		34
Subtotal	31.2%	0.0%	0.0%	0.0%	2.3%	0.0%	0.4%	0.0%	0.0%	3.0%	63.1%	263
SUBOP 20												
Subop 20	15.0%	0.0%	0.0%	0.0%	0.0%	0.0%	3.9%	0.0%	0.0%	0.5%	80.7%	207
NORTHEAST AREA												
Subop 15	5.2%	0.0%	0.0%	0.0%	3.4%	0.0%	0.0%	0.0%	0.0%	65.5%	25.9%	58
EAST DOCK												
Subop 14	0.0%	0.0%	0.0%	0.0%	0.0%	0.0%	10.9%	0.0%	0.0%	0.0%	89.1%	138
SOUTH AREA												
Subop 18	43.2%	0.0%	0.0%	1.2%	16.0%	0.0%	8.6%	0.0%	0.0%	0.0%	30.9%	81
Total	524	4	0	1	68	24	268	275	0	64	2,408	3,636
	14.4%	0.1%	0.0%	0.0%	1.9%	0.7%	7.4%	7.6%	0.0%	1.8%	66.2%	

Table 5.26—Unslipped ceramic type frequency distributions for Level 1 Late Facet deposits at Laguna de On Island (based on field classifications by Shirley Mock in 1996 and 1997)

	Cohokum Group				Tsabak Grp.		Miscellaneous					Total
	Santa	Kol-modelled	appliqué (untyped)	other Cohokum	Tsabak Unslipped	striated	sandy paste	comals	perforated colander	other	eroded	
North Central Area												
Subop 8	17.0%	0.0%	4.9%	0.0%	2.5%	0.4%	5.6%	2.2%	0.2%	0.5%	66.6%	1,649
Subop 12	17.2%	0.0%	0.0%	0.0%	3.1%	0.0%	5.3%	0.8%	0.0%	0.3%	73.3%	716
Subop 17	40.3%	0.0%	0.0%	0.0%	4.4%	0.0%	3.3%	0.0%	0.0%	0.0%	51.9%	360
Subop 13	90.4%	0.0%	0.0%	0.0%	0.0%	0.0%	0.0%	0.0%	0.0%	0.0%	9.6%	146
Subtotal	23.7%	0.0%	2.8%	0.0%	2.8%	0.2%	5.0%	1.5%	0.1%	0.4%	63.6%	2,871
South Central Area												
Subop 5	12.7%	2.0%	0.2%	0.0%	5.5%	0.6%	7.2%	0.1%	0.0%	0.0%	71.6%	1,340
Northwest Area												
Subop 7	45.7%	0.0%	0.0%	0.0%	3.6%	0.0%	1.8%	0.0%	0.0%	0.0%	48.9%	221
Subop 16	35.2%	0.0%	0.0%	0.0%	0.0%	0.0%	1.9%	0.0%	1.9%	0.0%	59.3%	54
Subtotal	43.6%	0.0%	0.0%	0.0%	3.3%	0.0%	1.8%	0.0%	0.4%	0.0%	50.9%	275
Subop 20												
Subop 20	0.0%	0.0%	0.0%	7.4%	2.5%	0.0%	1.2%	0.0%	0.0%	0.0%	88.9%	81
Northeast Area												
Subop 15	0.0%	0.0%	0.0%	0.0%	0.0%	0.0%	0.0%	0.0%	0.0%	0.0%	0.0%	0
East Dock												
Subop 14	31.8%	0.0%	0.0%	0.0%	0.5%	0.0%	0.5%	0.0%	0.0%	0.0%	67.3%	217
South Area												
Subop 18	9.1%	0.0%	0.0%	0.0%	3.0%	0.0%	0.0%	0.0%	0.0%	0.0%	87.9%	33
Total	1,046 / 21.7%	27 / 0.6%	83 / 1.7%	6 / 0.1%	166 / 3.4%	15 / 0.3%	247 / 5.1%	44 / 0.9%	4 / 0.1%	11 / 0.2%	3,171 / 65.8%	4,817

Table 5.27—Slipped/unslipped ceramic ratios—Early Facet

	Red Slipped	Unslipped/Eroded	Ratio
Subop 8	460	595	0.77
Subop 12	592	615	0.96
Subop 5	180	664	0.27
Subop 20	31	207	0.15
Subop 17	403	679	0.59
Subop 7	153	229	0.67
Subop 18	9	81	0.11

were personal adornments that belonged to inhabitants across the site and that such adornments were not used to signify differential status. In other archaeological contexts (Clark 1987; Clark and Blake 1993; Nassaney 1996: 182–184), such ornaments can be used to distinguish prestige, especially when they are in short supply.

Little difference is observed over time in the quantity or types of ornaments at the site. For example, clay beads, clay balls, ceramic ornaments, and modified bone, all made from local materials, were found in both Early Facet and Late Facet deposits (Table 5.29). Exotic materials, including greenstone beads and greenstone miniature celts (possibly from the Maya Mountains) are also recovered from both facets of the Late Postclassic. A single fleck of gold (5mm in diameter) was recovered from the sheet midden deposit at Subop 5 assigned to the Early Facet. However, this fleck was recovered near the transition of Early and Late Facet deposits around 15cm below the surface, and its temporal affiliation is unclear. The fleck of gold was not associated with any features. A crystal bead (Subop 5f) and an iron-ore bead (Subop 8c) were recovered from the Late Facet. Beads of these materials were not found in the Early Facet. Based on this small sample, the diversity of exotic-material beads does increase in the Late Facet at the site (Table 5.29).

This trend at Laguna de On may reflect increased long-distance mercantile activities over time in the Late Postclassic, as the increase in obsidian (discussed previously) also suggests. While this trend is seen at the site in terms of obsidian, a utilitarian item, there are surprisingly few nonutilitarian exotics at the site. Postclassic capitals such as Lamanai (Pendergast 1981), Sarteneja (Sidrys 1983), and Santa Rita (Chase and Chase 1988: Figure 30) have recovered burials of upper-status individuals with greater quantities of long-distance exotic objects, particularly metal pins, bells, or ornaments. The lack of such materials at Laguna may be due to its relatively low position in the regional political hierarchy in northern Belize/southern Quintana Roo during the Late Postclassic. It is also notable that Gann (1928) col-

Table 5.28—Slipped/unslipped ceramic ratios—Late Facet

	Red Slipped	Unslipped/Eroded	Ratio
Subop 8	1,012	1,649	0.61
Subop 12	616	716	0.86
Subop 5	347	1,340	0.26
Subop 20	12	81	0.15
Subop 17	282	350	0.81
Subop 7	58	221	0.26
Subop 18	22	33	0.67

lected some exotic ornaments (such as copper bells and jade beads) from the top of Structure II in 1926. It is still odd, however, that other such materials were not recovered in other archaeological contexts in recent investigations. Despite the small size of this settlement, occupants of Laguna de On clearly had access to utilitarian long-distance objects such as obsidian and exotic ornaments, and these are not exclusively distributed. It is possible, however, that nonutilitarian exotic ornaments may be more hierarchically distributed on a regional level, as greater quantities have been recovered from regional centers than from Laguna de On. Alternatively, their greater cost in the marketpace was prohibitive for residents at this site.

SUMMARY COMPARISONS OF ARTIFACT ASSEMBLAGE PATTERNS AT LAGUNA DE ON

The examination of Laguna de On artifacts above presents much information regarding the economic basis of this community. These materials reflect the subsistence base and different patterns of production and exchange at the site over time. Changes observed represent probable responses to regional economic changes and relationships with the world of trade. A summary of findings for each data class is reviewed below, followed by a comparative examination of the assemblage composition of each subop to examine variability in artifact frequencies relative to each other across the site.

Ground stone was found from a range of contexts at Laguna de On, and these reflect maize processing at the site. Ground stone was not differentially distributed in special status or ritual zones, and some broken pieces were found in secondary context in fire pits. No ground stone was found at ritual features Subops 12 (Structure II, shrine) and 20 (Structure IV, ballcourt). Low numbers of ground-stone artifacts were found at the site, and most of this material was locally procured. Laguna de On did not obtain much exotic ground stone, unlike the nearby contemporary site of Santa Rita (Jaeger 1988).

Table 5.29—Ornaments of local and long-distance origin and other miscellaneous items at Laguna de On

	clay bead	clay ball	ceramic ornament	pigment (or polished stone)	modified bone	stone bead (exotic)	green-stone celt	gold
LATE FACET								
Subop 17	4	2	0	0	2	0	0	0
Subop 8	0	0	0	0	0	1	0	0
Subop 5	1	0	0	(1)	0	4	1	0
Subop 16	0	0	0	0	0	1	0	0
Subop 7	0	0	1	0	0	0	0	0
Subop 14	1	1	0	0	0	0	0	0
EARLY FACET								
Subop 12	0	0	1	10	0	0	0	0
Subop 7	1	2	0	(3)	0	0	1	0
Subop 5	0	0	1	(3)	2	2	0	1
Subop 16	0	0	0	0	0	1	0	0

Comals represent additional evidence of maize processing and preparation on the island. These forms appear in relatively low frequency at the site, however, and they are more common in the Early than the Late Facet. Their low numbers suggest that tortilla making may have been more of a specialized activity, rather than an act linked to the production of a dietary staple. Comals are also limited in their distribution, recovered entirely from the upper-status residential zones in both the Early Facet (Subop 8) and in the Late Facet (Subops 8, 2, and 5). It is possible that comals were used to prepare ritual festivity foods for gatherings sponsored by occupants of this part of the site.

Faunal bone was recovered in high quantities in both facets, indicating the consumption of ample quantities of terrestrial, aquatic, and avian species throughout the site's occupation. The amount of fauna nearly doubles from the Early to Late Facets. It is possible that game became more regionally abundant at this time or that hunting activities were intensified. Further ecological research is needed to explore this pattern. The range of species represented in the Early and Late Facets does not differ, and high-forest species such as tapir are found in both components. This pattern suggests that high-canopy forest returned to this area by the eleventh century.

When the ratios of ceramics to fauna and lithics (obsidian, nonobsidian debitage, and nonobsidian chipped-stone tools) to fauna are compared from the Early and Late Facets (Table 5.30), it is notable that both ratios decrease

5.19. Exotic ornaments from Laguna de On. From left to right, a greenstone miniature celt, a greenstone bead, and an iron-ore bead.

over time. This pattern reflects an important relative increase in faunal remains compared to other materials. The ratio of fauna to lithics increases by almost 30 percent in the Late Facet and the proportion of fauna to ceramics almost doubles. This trend indicates that this community harvested greater amounts of faunal resources during the Late Facet compared to the Early Facet. Faunal resources were used in important ways within the Laguna de On settlement. As discussed previously, large game, and particularly cranial fragments, are more concentrated at status or ritual zones such as Subops 8, 2, and 3 than elsewhere at the site. These large animals were sacrificed in ritual activities at this central area, and were consumed at residential zones across the island perhaps after meat was redistributed (Masson 1999b).

Further comparisons are offered in the ratio of ceramics to lithics shown in Table 5.30. This ratio remains almost constant from the Early to Late Facets, suggesting that the role of these broad categories in the domestic economy of the site remained comparable. The ratio of ceramics to obsidian declines, reflecting a relative increase in obsidian within the Late Facet assemblage. These ratios provide important comparisons for the relative increase in fauna over time at the site, as noted above.

Burning across the island as reflected in the amount of burned flakes and shatter indicates that Subops 8 and 5 were the location of greater burning in both facets than other localities examined. The meaning of this pattern is not clear, but may be related to an increase in incense-burning rituals conducted at these locations. The pattern could also be related to different activities in each facet. During the Early Facet, two fire features have been located beneath Subop 8, and one burned rock feature has been exposed within Late Facet deposits at Subop 5. The use of features such as these may have contributed to the higher frequencies of burned flakes at these locations. Subops 8 and 5 both represent areas thought to be upper-status residential zones with increased ritual activity.

Projectile points increase over time at the site, as only three are from Early Facet deposits, and the remainder are from the Late Facet. No changes in point styles are seen over time in nonobsidian specimens, except for an increase in the variety of types that may be attributed to an increase in sample size. Almost all (except one) of the obsidian points are from Late Facet deposits. Points also have a limited distribution at the site, as they are found in primarily upper-status residential zones in the Late Facet (Subops 8, 6, 2 and 3, 17, and 5). All but one point were in these subops, which are all within the central area of the site. It is possible that the distribution of points is related to the distribution of large-game crania at the site, as the location of discard for these objects may be linked to butchering of animals in the vicinity of Subops 2, 3, 17, and 8. Obsidian-point manufacturing in Subops 2 and 3 may also be responsible for some of the concentration of discarded points in this area.

When nonobsidian lithic tools are examined, the Early and Late Facets show some differences. In each facet, formal tools comprise a minority of each assemblage, and these tools were obtained from the flint-working site of Colha (Colha chert and Colha-worked chalcedony). Most of the nonobsidian tools from each assemblage are expedient forms, made either from recycled Colha tools or on local chalcedony or low-grade cherts. Some expedient forms are made on low-grade quartz-blend materials for which the source is yet to be identified.

The distribution of formal tools appears more controlled in the Early Facet, when these forms appear in greater frequencies at status and ritual contexts of Subops 12 and 8. Fewer utilized flakes at Subop 12 attest to the focus on ritual activity at this locale. Utilized flakes in general appear to be important signifiers of domestic zones at the site. Over time, status and ritual areas show greater relative amounts of obsidian in their lithic assemblages, and formal nonobsidian tools are no longer more frequent in status and ritual zones. Obsidian assumes a greater role as a valued utilitarian lithic item at this site in the Late Facet. Obsidian specifically appears to replace utilized flakes in some higher-status domestic assemblages. However, formal tools and obsidian are not exclusively concentrated at any one locality during either facet, so the differences in relative frequencies do not reflect strictly

Table 5.30—Ratios of materials at Laguna de On

	Early	Late
ceramics:obsidian	12.3	8.3
ceramics:fauna	1.7	0.9
all lithics:fauna	2.7	1.9
ceramics:all lithics	.6	.5

controlled access to lithic materials. Some privileged access may have been accorded those of higher status, though this was not a substantial advantage.

The overall amount of obsidian brought into the site doubles from the Early to the Late Facet deposits, but the relative increase in the percentage of obsidian relative to other lithics is only 8 percent. These figures suggest that an increase in the use of lithic materials in general, including nonobsidian tools, is seen in the Late Facet. The increased significance of obsidian over time is an important pattern. It is probable that this increase is due to a greater availability of obsidian during the latter portion of the Late Postclassic due to accelerated maritime trade networks. Laguna de On would have occupied a peripheral position in this network due to its inland location, the relatively small size of this settlement, and the probable low-ranked regional position of this community. Blade widths average 1.3cm at this site. Comparisons of blade sizes from other Postclassic sites are needed to reconstruct the system of obsidian exchange between inland and coastal communities and settlements of various political rank. Exhausted, discarded chunks of poorly flaked obsidian at the site suggest that residents of Laguna de On were also obtaining low numbers of obsidian flake cores along with finished blades and occasional blade cores.

Spindle whorls were recovered from both the Early and Late Facets, from a range of contexts. They exhibit no spatially distinct distribution patterns in either component, as they are found in upper-status and undifferentiated-status residential zones and at the ritual feature of Subop 12. Over time, a greater range of styles is exhibited among the whorls, but functional aspects as measured in dimensions of the whorls remain fundamentally unchanged. The distribution of these artifacts across the site suggests that most households were probably engaged in the weaving of textiles.

The amount of marine-shell debris increases in the Late Facet compared to the Early Facet. Shell identified at the site primarily includes whelk, conch, or bivalve debitage and incomplete ornaments, suggesting that a small craft industry was present. Marine shell is found in greater quantities at upper-status residential zones in the Late Facet. This distribution is not observed in the Early Facet, where less debris is found in a range of contexts and one concentration is noted in Subop 15, a residential zone of undifferentiated status. In the Late Facet, Subop 8 has far more marine-shell debris than other areas of the site. Other areas with shell include Subops 5 and 17, also upper-status residential zones. This distribution suggests that shell working and shell ornaments have a more clear association with upper-status individuals in the Late Facet.

Slipped and unslipped ceramics form equivalent portions of Early and Late Facet deposits at the site. No increase in slipped sherds is observed over time. The highest ratios of slipped to unslipped ceramics are found in upper-status residential zones (Subops 8 and 17) and in the ritual area of Subop 12. In the Early Facet, Subop 7 also has a high ratio. Ceramics may have been produced in fire features found in these Early Facet subops, which may explain the higher proportion of slipped wares at these localities. In the Late Facet, some subops (8, 12, and 17) continue to have higher slipped-to-unslipped ratios than other subops examined, as they did in the Early Facet. Higher ratios of slipped ceramics could be due to upper-status factors or to the continued use of fire features in these locations. The presence of slipped and incised sherds at all zones across the site indicates, much like obsidian distributions, that access to slipped wares was not highly controlled and these items were available to all. Nonetheless, certain households tended to have more of these than others. At Laguna de On, status is thus tracked as points along a continuum without clear divisions notable in the distribution of utilitarian items. In contrast, appliqué ceramics (portions of censers) are found exclusively in the Late Facet at Subops 8 and 5, the two residential zones with the greatest number of ritual features. Ritual practice thus provides a clearer indicator of upper-status contexts at this site than utilitarian items (Masson 1999b).

Relative Frequencies of Artifact and Ecofact Classes of Data over Time and Space

When the relative percentages of abundant items recovered at the site, including lithic tools and debris, faunal bone, slipped and unslipped ceramics, and obsidian, are compared from Early and Late Facet deposits (Figure 5.20), an overall proportionate increase from 19 percent to 26 percent of faunal bone is observed. The quantities of lithic debris and lithic tools remain more stable in relation to one another. Obsidian's relative significance increases over time (Figure 5.20) as previously noted, but the importance of this pattern is dwarfed by large data sets in Figure 5.20. Ceramics form slightly less of the assemblage during the Late Facet.

When categories of materials that occur in lower numbers at the site are compared in Figure 5.21, including obsidian, net weights, marine shell, spindle whorls, and expedient and formal lithic tools, it is possible to view the relative increase of obsidian when compared to more numerically equivalent

data sets. The increase in obsidian correlates with a decrease in local industries using local lithic raw materials. Net weights also form a greater part of
the Late Facet site assemblage (Figure 5.21), a pattern that correlates with
the greater relative amounts of faunal bone at the site. The relative quantities of marine shell and spindle whorls appear equivalent in each facet in
Figure 5.21.

The cumulative frequencies of various classes of data from Laguna de On
subops are displayed in Figures 5.22–5.29. This technique has proven useful
for determining functional variability in the composition of various areas
across a site (Binford et al. 1970: 12). Classes of data chosen for comparison
with one another were those that tended to occur in high (Figures 5.22,
5.23, 5.26, and 5.27) or low frequencies (Figures 5.24, 5.25, 5.28, and 5.29)
at the site. Obsidian is shown on both graphs. These graphs are useful for
determining the degree to which assemblages reflect upper-status residential
zones (north and south central areas of the site), zones with increased ritual
activity, and undifferentiated-status residential zones (those to the north
and south of the central area of the site). The degree of ritual activity and
domestic status was first determined by feature analysis in Chapter 4, and is
reexamined through artifact analysis here.

The results of the comparisons in some figures show that ritual areas
(Subop 12 especially) do exhibit different intra-assemblage frequency distributions compared to upper-status residential zones. The curve for an upper-
status residential zone with a high degree of ritual activity (Subop 8) falls
midway between a purely ritual feature assemblage (Subop 12) and an upper-
status residential area without ritual distributions (Subop 17), as might be
expected (Figures 5.22–5.27). Differences are also observed between inferred
upper-status residential zones and lower-status residential zones, at least in the
Late Facet (Figure 5.26). Trends are more strongly expressed in the Late Facet,
which suggests that status and ritual zones became better defined over time.

The Early Facet displays neglible interresidential distribution differences
in terms of abundant artifact categories (Figures 5.22–5.23), though these
comparisons are hindered by low sample sizes in some subops (16 and 13).
Differences observed in abundant artifact classes include a trend for greater
percentages of ceramics in upper-status zones of the site, and more obsidian
is present at the lithic-working area of Subop 13 (Figures 5.23 and 5.25).
Undifferentiated-status zones in the Early Facet also had slightly more expedient tools than upper-status zones, as shown in Figures 5.24 and 5.25, which
graph the frequency of exotic materials, obsidian, and lithic tools. Beyond
these observations, no dramatic differences are noted. Ceramics form a greater
percentage of status/ritual assemblages in the Early Facet (Figure 5.22), but
their role in the assemblages of the Late Facet (discussed below) appears to
diminish.

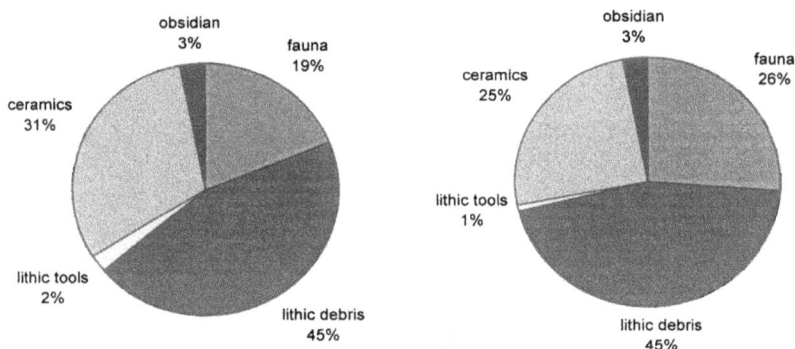

5.20. Relative proportions of materials that occur in large numbers at Laguna de On during the Early Facet (left) and the Late Facet (right).

During the Late Facet, abundant artifact classes (Figures 5.26 and 5.27) show important differences. In the upper-status/ritual graph (Figure 5.26), Subop 12 (primarily a ritual feature) has the highest relative frequencies of lithic tools, obsidian, and fauna and less debitage compared to other subops. Subop 17 (primarily an upper-status residential feature) is at the bottom of the graph (Figure 5.26), appearing least like Subop 12 and the most like undifferentiated-status zones in the companion graph (Figure 5.27). Subop 17 has the most debitage, as might be expected for a residential zone. Subops 8 and 5, thought to be upper-status residential zones with ritual activity, fall between Subop 12 and Subop 17, indicating the dual types of activities in these locations. Subop 8, where more ritual features are observed than Subop 5, has less debitage (Figure 5.26). Subop 20, a depression into which debris may have inadvertently accumulated, is more erratic. These graphs indicate that the percentage of debitage may be an important indicator to determine residential zones from ritual ones, and to determine varying status among residential zones.

When the upper-status/ritual graph is compared to the undifferentiated-status graph for the Late Facet, it is possible to see which classes of artifacts occur in greater percentages in each group of assemblages. Lithic tools and obsidian occur in greater quantities in zones associated with upper-status or ritual, and unslipped ceramics and debitage occur in higher frequencies in residential zones (that lack ritual activity) on both charts (Figures 5.26 and 5.27). Fauna forms a greater percentage of some, but not all, undifferentiated-status residences. Among these areas, Subops 9–11/15 have more relative quantities of obsidian and fauna than the others shown in Figure 5.27, which makes this area resemble the upper-status residential zone of Subop 8. It is

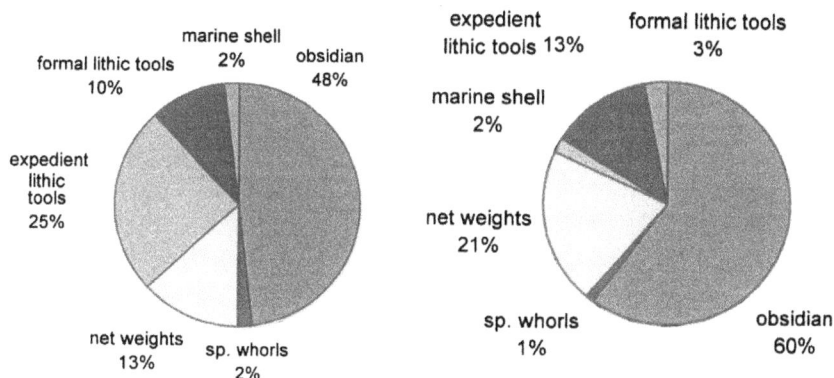

5.21. Relative proportions of materials that occur in lower numbers at Laguna de On during the Early Facet (left) and the Late Facet (right).

notable that ceramics form the smallest proportion of upper-status/ritual zones, and that unslipped wares are relatively more common in undifferentiated residential zones. When materials that occur in lesser quantities at the site are examined for the Late Facet (Figures 5.28 and 5.29), important differences are also observed. Most of the undifferentiated-status residential zones had far more expedient stone tools and obsidian than other materials, including marine shell, formal tools, net weights, and spindle whorls. While the amount of expedient tools is variable in the areas examined, most areas have more expedient tools than those examined in the upper-status/ritual graph. Subops 9–11/15 stand out from the groups in having proportionately more net weights within their assemblage (Figure 5.29). In this respect this area resembles the upper-status/ritual zones on Figure 5.28, as also noted in previous comparisons described above. Subops on the upper-status/ritual graph tended to have proportionately more net weights within their assemblages, and they have slightly more marine shell. Subops on both graphs do not exhibit pronounced differences in terms of the proportions of formal tools, spindle whorls, or obsidian during the Late Facet. Subop 20 appears anomalous on Figure 5.29, possibly due to the secondary origin of materials found in this feature.

SUMMARY

The examination of cumulative frequencies of artifact types from Laguna de On areas provides important information on the value of various artifact classes in this site's economy. It appears that upper-status and ritual assemblages are distinguished by greater proportions of net weights, marine shell, and obsidian and lesser proportions of expedient tools and debitage. Greater proportions of ceramics (particularly unslipped wares) and lithic flakes are noted in undifferentiated-status residential zones. Other than this trend, ceramics do not vary as much as other categories of artifacts and are one of the least-sensitive indicators of varying status and function at the site, at least in these most general terms of ceramic classification. More detailed attribute analysis may determine greater temporal and spatial variation within Laguna's ceramic assemblages. The role of some commodities such as marine shell and obsidian appears to change over time, in that they become more valuable and tightly distributed in status/ritual locations. Other materials, such as formal stone tools, become less tightly distributed over time. Certain utilitarian commodities, such as fauna and spindle whorls, are not sensitive to status or ritual indicators when counts alone are considered. Particular faunal species, such as large game animals, were probably manipulated by upper-status individuals. The possible identification of lithic manufacturing activities in the vicinity of Subop 13 is implied by the greater proportions of local and obsidian debris from this area.

Overall, these comparisons suggest that interhousehold status differences may have become more distinctive over time during the occupation of Laguna de On. Similar findings are reported from Santa Rita Corozal (Diane Chase 1992: 123) in which upper-status residences have high percentages of ritual indicators, such as incense-burner ceramics and projectile points. Similar to trends observed at Laguna de On, Chase and Chase (1988: 129) argue for a continuum in status differentiation within Santa Rita.

Subtle indications thus suggest the enhancement of interfamily status differences over time at Laguna de On. These differences were a matter of degree and were not pronounced. Slightly more nonlocal materials such as obsidian and marine shell, as well as the sponsorship of ritual activity, appear to signify the enhanced social status of those families that occupied the north central zone of Laguna de On. It is possible that leaders at communities such as Laguna de On played a role in the negotiation of intercommunity exchange or had better access to resources that resulted in subtle differences in their inventory of trade items relative to other members of the community.

The exact mechanisms of intercommunity exchange cannot be fully identified until comparisons among a greater number of Postclassic Maya sites are possible. As Hirth (1998; see also Smith 1999) has suggested for highland Mexico-Aztec period communities, the general distribution of long-distance items among households at a site probably suggests that such commodities were obtainable in an open-market system. In this sense, it is highly significant that no exclusive distributions of commodities are noted at Laguna de On. The pattern of broad distribution of long-distance

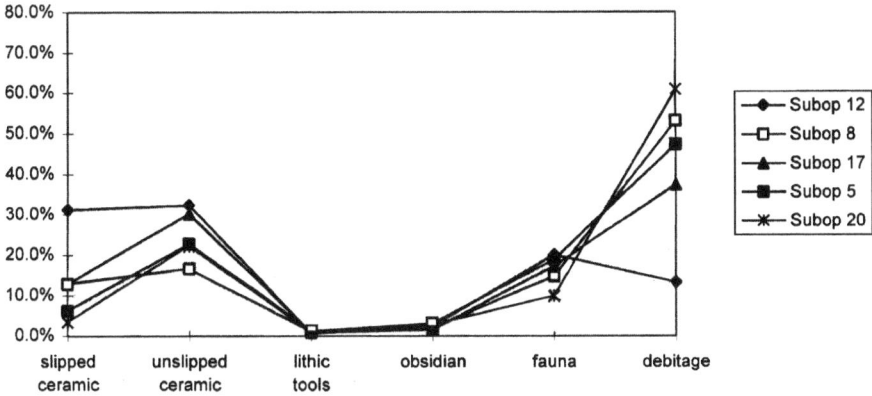

5.22. Frequency graph for materials that occur in large numbers at Laguna de On (Early Facet), showing proportions of these materials within areas identified as upper-status residential zones and/or areas with ritual indicators.

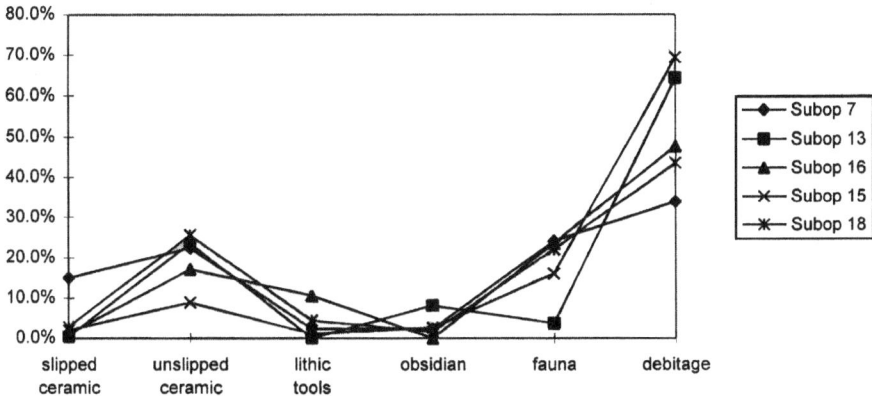

5.23. Frequency graph for materials that occur in large numbers at Laguna de On (Early Facet), showing proportions of these materials within areas identified as undifferentiated-status domestic zones that lack ritual indicators.

commodities in upper and lower social contexts at Maya sites is not new to the Postclassic, but is observed in earlier periods as well (Freidel 1986: 414). Quantitative comparisons are needed, however, in order to assess whether long-distance valuables such as greenstone and ground stone became more evenly distributed during the Postclassic than in earlier times, as is observed for obsidian. The Laguna de On data suggest that most trade items were more evenly possessed during the Postclassic period, but comparisons of household inventories across time and space are needed to fully address this question (Rathje 1983).

189

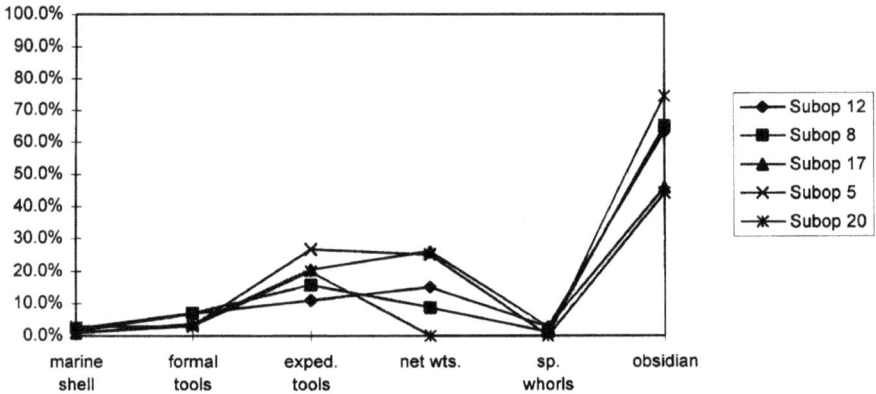

5.24. Frequency graph for materials that occur in low numbers at Laguna de On (Early Facet), showing proportions of these materials within areas identified as upper-status residential zones and/or areas with ritual indicators.

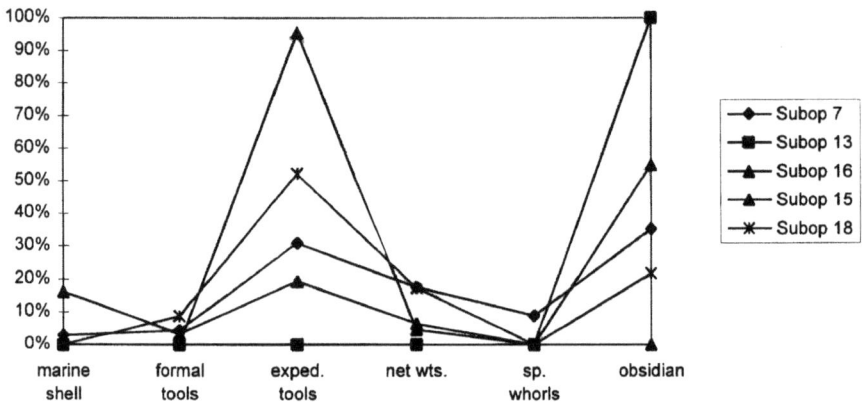

5.25. Frequency graph for materials that occur in low numbers at Laguna de On (Early Facet), showing proportions of these materials within areas identified as undifferentiated-status domestic zones that lack ritual indicators.

Obsidian is thought to have been obtained in open-market settings during the Postclassic period due to its broad distribution at communities of this period and considerable ethnohistorical evidence (Freidel and Sabloff 1984: 188–189). Long-distance commodities may have entered local markets through traders who obtained items such as obsidian from port of trade sites located along the east coast (Freidel and Sabloff 1984:189). This examination of economic patterns over time at Laguna de On illustrates the effects that the growth of a Mesoamerican "world system" (Blanton and Feinman 1984;

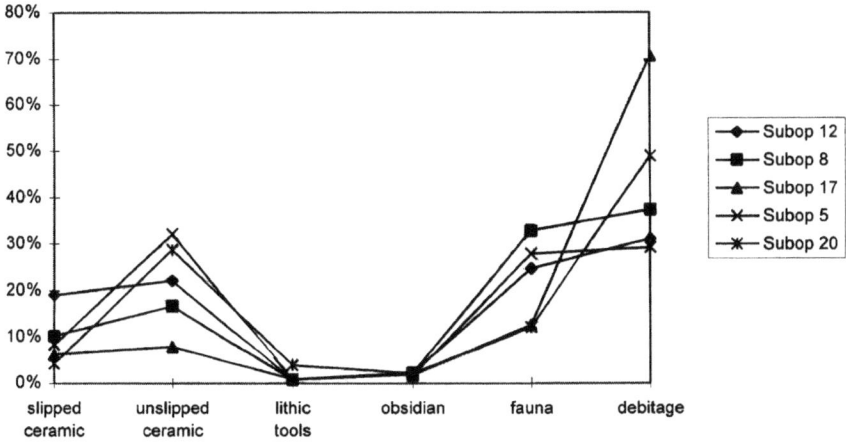

5.26. Frequency graph for materials that occur in large numbers at Laguna de On (Late Facet), showing proportions of these materials within areas identified as upper-status residential zones and/or areas with ritual indicators.

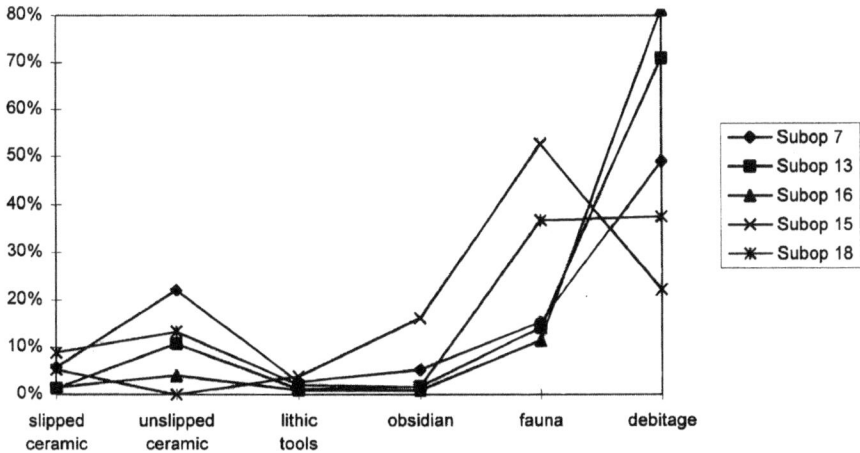

5.27. Frequency graph for materials that occur in large numbers at Laguna de On (Late Facet), showing proportions of these materials within areas identified as undifferentiated-status domestic zones that lack ritual indicators.

Carmack 1996) after A.D. 1200 had on a small inland community. This network provided Laguna de On with obsidian, which increased in importance over time. Greater differences in interhousehold status are detected after this point, and construction projects and ritual activity accelerated. The site's shore component may have expanded at this time. The Late Facet

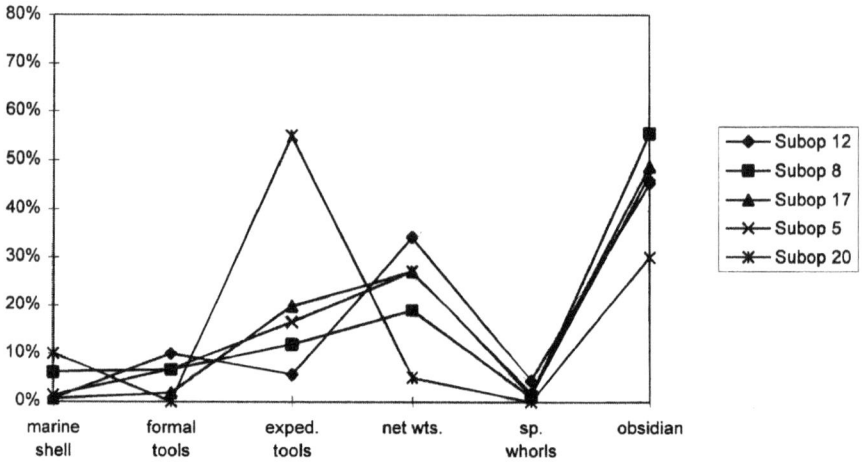

5.28. Frequency graph for materials that occur in low numbers at Laguna de On (Late Facet), showing proportions of these materials within areas identified as upper-status residential zones and/or areas with ritual indicators.

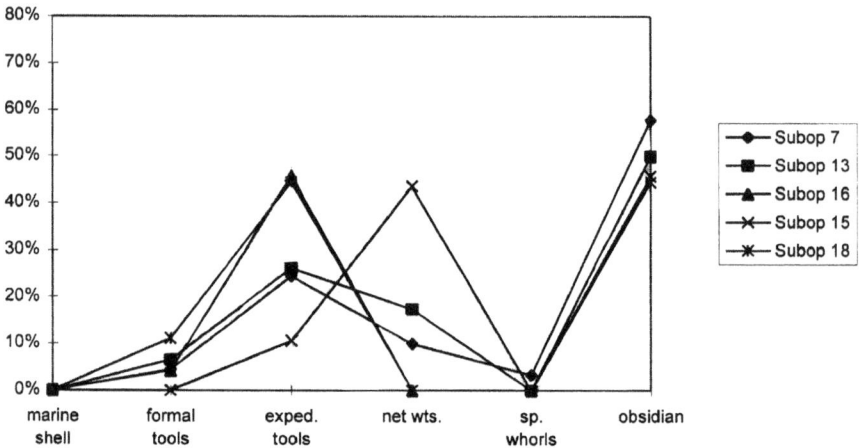

5.29. Frequency graph for materials that occur in low numbers at Laguna de On (Late Facet), showing proportions of these materials within areas identified as undifferentiated-status domestic zones that lack ritual indicators.

florescence of the Laguna de On community appears linked to the activities of its prominent families, who probably helped connect the site to regional networks of prestige and utilitarian exchange. While obsidian represents a highly visible indicator of long-distance exchange, historic records suggest that a great variety of local utilitarian products were being produced at Lowland

Maya sites that were also destined for coastal merchants (Freidel and Sabloff 1984: 188).The existence of an increased market for the site's lithic, ceramic, or textile industries, for export into circum-Yucatecan trade networks and beyond, may have been an important stimulant for growth at this site.

Despite indications that the development or amplification of interregional trading boosted Laguna de On's economy and modest social hierarchy, an additional point emerges from temporal comparisons. Many of the site's industries and trading networks appear to have been in place prior to A.D. 1200. It is clear that the Late Facet production patterns have their origins in the Early Facet component. Early Facet deposits show that a substantial amount of obsidian was brought into the site, and that all of its craft industries were well developed from A.D. 1050 to 1250. The impact of the "Late Postclassic world system" is thus primarily an amplification of earlier trends. This network intensified and expanded existing relationships with such communities during the thirteenth century. During the Early Facet, sites such as Laguna de On were linked to earlier Epiclassic or Early Postclassic world systems that were established through the activities of northern sites such as Chichén Itzá (Kepecs, Feinman, and Boucher 1994; Ringle, Negron, and Bey 1998) and Isla Cerritos (Andrews et al. 1988). The existence of such far-reaching economic systems in Mesoamerica prior to the Late Postclassic is an important issue (Smith and Berdan 2000). The rise of Mayapan, as discussed in Chapter 6, is also linked to the florescence of the east coast of the Yucatán peninsula during the thirteenth through fifteenth centuries. This site capitalized on the vacuum of opportunity left in the collapse of the Chichén Itzá polity and its allies. Laguna de On shares long-term cultural and economic links with east coast sites, and its Late Facet florescence accompanies their emergence as significant nodes of international maritime trade during the last three centuries before Spanish arrival.

6
Religious Institutions and Elite Power at Postclassic Maya Communities

It is the central thesis of this chapter that religious practices at Laguna de On and throughout the Postclassic Maya world in general closely reflected with social sources of kin-based power that formed important components of regional political institutions. However, politically dominant families were also articulated into crosscutting supra-kin institutions of assembly rule that were prevalent in Postclassic society. Recent examinations have refined our understanding of the degree of kin power in Classic and Postclassic political structure and the way that kin power found expression in hierarchical or decentralized regimes (McAnany 1995; Blanton et al. 1996; Fox et al. 1996; Chase and Chase 1996). The evidence presented in this chapter supports the argument that kin institutions were of primary importance in the power structure of Postclassic political organization (Carmack 1981; Fox 1987) and it explores the ways in which family power was negotiated, contained, and shared in Maya rule of this period.

Symbols of kin-based power are expressed primarily in the form of public art and architecture. Laguna de On, as a small agrarian settlement, is thus not the most useful place from which to examine dimensions of political rulership and associated elements of organized religion that originated from the top tier of Postclassic society. Nonetheless, ritual practice at Laguna de On was probably linked to religious structures that were "writ large" at political centers. The principle of replication of Maya religious institutions on various scales from the household to the monumental center is recognized as a fundamental characteristic of Pre-Columbian and modern communities (Vogt 1976: 572; Diane Chase 1986: 365–366; Deal 1988b: 72; Gossen and Levanthal 1993: 207; Masson 1999b). The context and meaning of ritual symbols at the sites of Mayapan, Tulum, and Santa Rita are explored in this chapter to shed light on the more modest evidence of ritual practice at Laguna de On. Types of religious practice associated with powerful and privileged sectors of society are examined, as well as types of ritual associated with domestic zones. The worship of ancestral gods and mythic heroes as a fundamental element in the legitimization of lineage power at Postclassic Maya centers is a theme that emerges in this evaluation. Religious art considered here includes architecture, stone sculptures, stucco façades, murals or frescoes, and ceramic effigy censers. These media comprise a critical set of symbols that encoded a revival and transformation of earlier religious institutions in Late Postclassic society. This religious revival accompanied economic growth and political trends of intensification that gripped the east coast lowland region during the northern reign of Mayapan from the thirteenth to fifteenth centuries.

Early examinations of Postclassic Maya religion suggested that it was practiced primarily at the household level, which was viewed as a symptom of a cultural collapse into decadence and a decline in the role of the formal priesthood (Thompson 1957: 624; Pollock 1962: 17; Proskouriakoff 1962a: 136). This interpretation was based on the identification of a large number of household altars and shrines at Mayapan, and a noted increase in the manufacture of ceramic effigies compared to earlier periods (Thompson 1970: 187–188). Since these early assessments at Mayapan, investigations of Maya residential groups from earlier periods have documented the fact that ritual practice at the household scale has always been a common component of this society (Levanthal 1983: 75–76; Gossen and Levanthal 1993: 211; McAnany 1995: 53). Residential platforms of the Preclassic and Classic periods commonly feature a "temple" or "lineage shrine" structure (McAnany 1995: 53) that served as a focal point for ritual, lineage integration, and the interment of important family members. Such residential facilities are directly analogous to the "household altars" of Mayapan. The thesis that religion was primarily a household phenomenon for the Postclassic has also been disputed with data from Cozumel, as Freidel and Sabloff (1984: 183–184) note that shrines were located in areas that were distinct from residential zones at Cozumel and they were part of the public domain at this site.

The degree to which Postclassic religion was practiced at the household level beyond the extent observed in the Classic period is open to debate. Mayapan was a political center of unrivaled magnitude in the Late Postclassic period, and domestic compounds within this city's walls represented the most privileged and upper-status sectors of society (Landa 1941: 25–26). Even if household practice of religion was more extensive at this site than in previous periods, it is an atypical political center that is not necessarily representative of domestic ritual practice among all Postclassic communities. The relative increase in censers as part of domestic and ritual assemblages in the Postclassic period compared to earlier times is an important pattern, however, and alternative interpretations are explored at the end of this chapter. The types and quantities of religious artifacts at Mayapan and

Tulum examined below identify ritual that is associated with public and elite sectors of society, as well as those shared by all social tiers of these communities. These patterns indicate that while household religious practice is common as the Mayapan investigators noted, evidence suggests that greater concentrations of religious activity were centered around elite and public features at the site. These concentrations of features and artifacts suggest the existence of internal social hierarchies within these communities and the association of the upper-status members of society with the sponsorship of ritual to affirm their positions. In this sense, social power, which was strongly rooted in lineage systems during the Postclassic period, overlaps considerably with political power. Such power is expressed and legitimated in the form of religious practice and public and private programs of religious art (Freidel and Sabloff 1984: 184).

An important element of lineage power for Postclassic Maya society is the institution of ancestor commemoration that is reflected in programs of public and private religious art and artifacts. This institution is not a new one for the Postclassic period, and its roots are traced to the origins of Maya society (McAnany 1995). However, with the removal of the institution of kingship during the Postclassic (Schele and Freidel 1990: 357–364), new opportunities would have emerged for kin-based segments of society to seize control. Dynamics of Maya leadership have perpetually been torn by contradictory segmentation and centralization tendencies (De Montmollin 1989), often acted out in the opposing interests of powerful lineage groups and other important factions (Webster 1977: 366–367; Freidel 1983a: 383; McAnany 1995: 133; Fox et al. 1996; Chase and Chase 1996; Demarest 1996).

The identification of ancestor commemoration in this chapter is based on several specific features. The definition of "ancestor worship" is adopted from McAnany (1995: 11) as "rituals and practices surrounding the burial and commemoration, by name, of apical ancestors of kin groups." Commemoration in this chapter is recognized in the construction of images of ancestors for public and private display in facilities designed for ritual practice invoking ancestors or celebrating ancestral history. Evidence for ancestor commemoration, thus defined, is examined in the contexts and contents of Mayapan sculptures, the themes of stucco façades and murals of Tulum, and in themes and contexts of Late Postclassic effigy censers. A potential source of confusion is addressed in the distinction between ancestors and "gods." These distinctions are not mutually exclusive in Maya religion, as Classic period ancestors often became deified or appeared "in the guise of" recognizable formal deities (Looper 1991). The theme of participation of multiple delegates of elite society in ritual celebrations, and presumably political rule, is also explored in the art of Mayapan, Tulum, and Santa Rita.

PUBLIC VERSUS DOMESTIC TYPES OF RITUAL PRACTICE

Forms of religious practice that occurred in domestic and public contexts in the Postclassic period may be assessed from comparisons of the contexts of ritual features and artifacts at various sites. As described in Chapter 4 for Laguna de On, religious features appear at this site in three major contexts and one domestic context: at the shrines represented by Structures II (island) and V (shore), at the possible ballcourt (Subop 20), and at one residence, Structure I, which appears to be the highest-status dwelling on the island. Most domestic areas do not possess ritual indicators in the form of censer fragments or shrine facilities (Chapter 5; Masson 1999b). Based on this distribution of ritual indicators at Laguna de On, it appears that religious practice did not occur at comparable levels in all domestic zones. Religious practice at this site was probably sponsored by community leaders (Masson 1999b). Investigations at Santa Rita and Mayapan also suggest that elite-sponsored ritual served as an important point of leverage for community leaders (Diane Chase 1988, 1992). The distribution of features and artifacts at Mayapan and Tulum are reviewed below to examine variation in ritual practice at these political centers, which provides an important basis for comparison to Laguna de On.

THE DISTRIBUTION OF RITUAL INDICATORS AT MAYAPAN

The distribution of four types of ritual features is examined at Mayapan, including the following: (1) the locations of sculptures at this site within and outside of its monumental center (Quad Q); (2) the variation in themes of sculptures according to location; (3) the distribution of religious architectural features including oratories, shrines, and altars at the site; and (4) the nature of artifacts and features associated with religious architecture. For the purposes of this examination, the ceremonial, public, elite sector of Mayapan is defined as the Q Square (Figures 6.1, 6.2, and 6.3), where the majority of large architectural buildings are concentrated at this site (Jones 1962). Outside of this central precinct, domestic structures and groups of various sizes are densely concentrated within a 4.2-square-kilometer area (Figure 6.1; Smith 1962: 264). A social hierarchy is implied at the site in the variation in architectural elaboration and number of rooms (Smith 1962: 265–266). While most of the religious architecture (96.5 percent; Smith 1962: 265) and elite residences (66 percent; Diane Chase 1992: Figure 8.4) are concentrated in the Q Square, the presence of some of these features outside of the center indicates that a perfect pattern of concentric settlement organization did not exist for this site (Diane Chase 1992: 128, 130, Figure 8.4). Scales of elaboration are also represented in the types of ritual features identified among Mayapan domestic groups by Ledyard Smith (1962). In descending order of magnitude, these include oratories, private shrine rooms, household altars, group shrines, and group altars (Smith 1962). The spatial clustering of sculptural themes at the site is considered below in light of this distribution of ritual features.

The Location of Sculptures at Mayapan

Of a sample of 189 sculptures recorded at Mayapan that were examined in this study (from Proskouriakoff 1962a: Figures 5–11; 1962b: Figures 1–7), 140 (74 percent) of them were located in the ceremonial center (Table 6.1; Figures 6.1 and 6.2). Of the remaining forty-nine sculptures recovered at Mayapan, twenty-two were concentrated in an outlying ceremonial group (Itzmal Chen) located outside the center in the H Square (Table 6.2; Figure 6.4). Twenty-seven additional sculptures were scattered in sixteen other contexts around the site, some of which were residential and some of which are in unknown contexts (Table 6.2; Figure 6.4; Proskouriakoff 1962a; Smith 1962). Outside the ceremonial center and the Itzmal Chen group, no single group or structure had more than three pieces of sculpture (Table 6.2). Two of these outlying groups had three sculptures, seven had two, and seven had one piece each (Table 6.2). In contrast, of the Q Square ceremonial group structures, seven had from two to five pieces, six had from seven to fifteen pieces, and two had twenty-one to twenty-five pieces (Table 6.1, compiled from Proskouriakoff 1962a: Figures 5–11). The concentration of sculptures in the Q Square of Mayapan and the higher frequency of sculptures at individual buildings in this area attests to the importance of ritual to the ruling factions of this center. These elites sponsored the creation and display of the majority of religious sculptures at the site. Examining the distribution of themes of these monuments below, other important patterns emerge that differentiate ritual practice in the center from that of outlying groups.

Thematic Distributions of Sculptures at Mayapan

The distribution of sculptural themes distinguishes elite from nonelite areas at Mayapan. Sculptures compiled from Proskouriakoff's illustrations (1962a) were grouped into twelve types (Table 6.1; Figure 6.5). Five types of sculpture are primarily found in public ritual contexts of Square Q, including buildings decorated with geometric friezes, banners, seated felines, serpent parts, and human body parts. The other seven types are found primarily in outlying (nonceremonial or non-Square Q) contexts, including ring sculptures, glyphic elements (recycled stones), turtle sculptures, mini-temples, zoomorphic *cuch*-type images, and miscellaneous unique items. While most of these categories are self-explanatory, the zoomorphic *cuch* category is an inclusive term adopted here for a set of figures that seem to display some type of crouching or crawling animal that is bearing a human or other figure on its

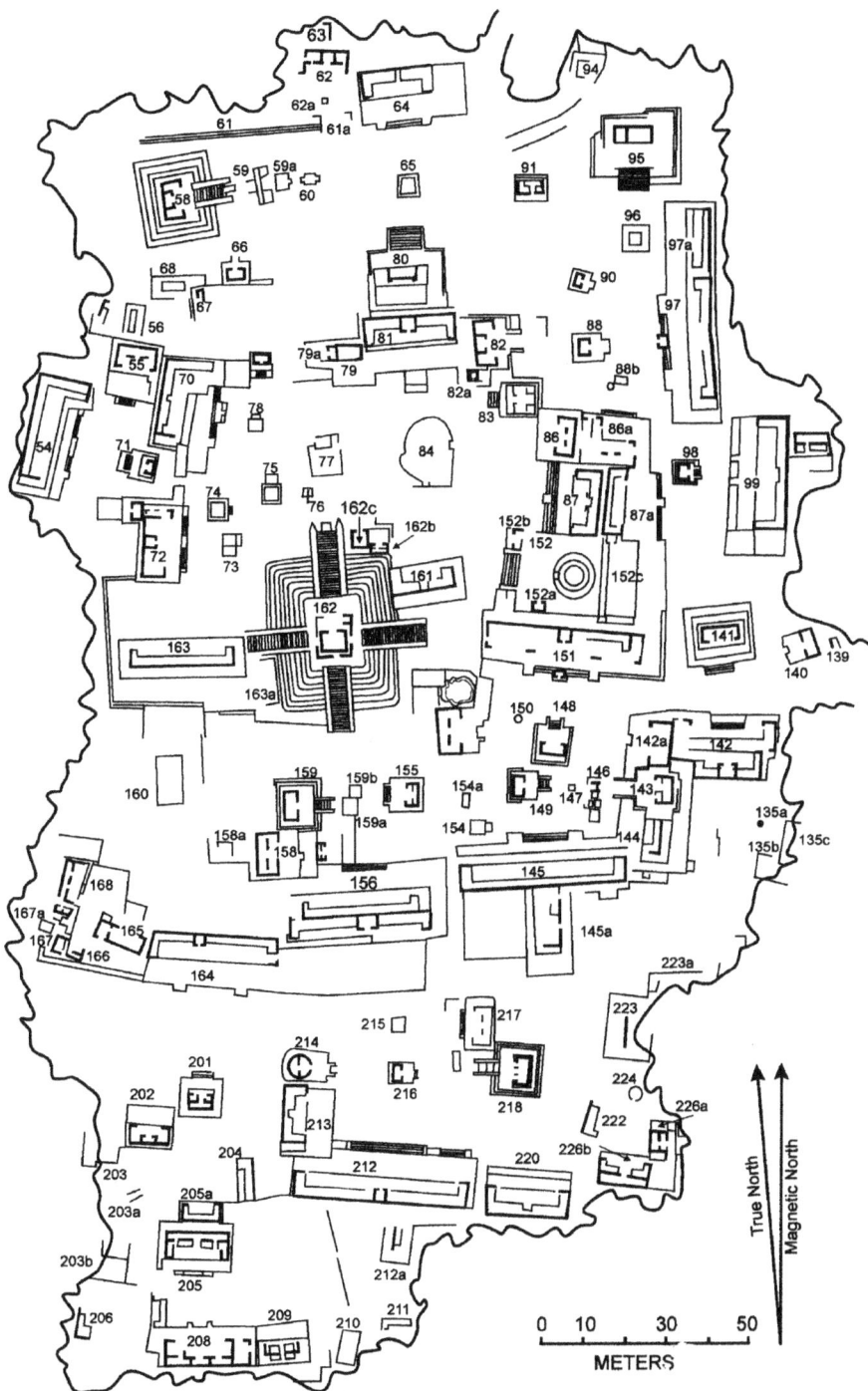

6.1. Map of Mayapan ceremonial center, Q Square (redrafted by Pam Headrick from Morris Jones 1962).

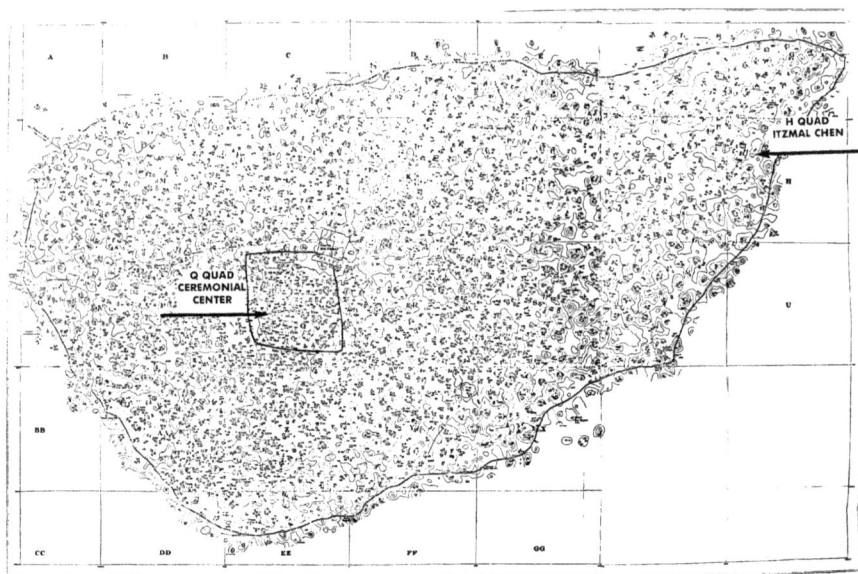

6.2. Map of Mayapan, showing areas discussed in the text (redrafted by Pam Headrick from Morris Jones 1962).

back (Proskouriakoff 1962b: Figure 4). Figures bearing loads on their back are documented in Classic period iconography and in the Postclassic codices as bearers of *cuch*, a term for cargo, tribute, or, metaphorically, for anthropomorphic beings who bring in the calendrical year (Taube 1988: 187–190, 227–228, Figure 73). Diving figures are referred to as "crouching" figures in Proskouriakoff's original description (1962b: Figure 3). As these figures could also be in a flying or diving position based on analogies to other images in Mesoamerican art (Masson and Orr 1998a), they are referred to as crouching/diving figures here. This association follows Taube's (1992: Figure 18b) identification of one of these Mayapan figures (Proskouriakoff 1962b: Figure 3g) as a "diving god."

Domestic Group Sculptures

Three categories of sculptures are found exclusively in outlying groups or dwelling complexes other than the Q Square of Mayapan (Figure 6.5). These include mini-temples (11.1 percent; Table 6.2), zoomorphic *cuch* figures (11.1 percent), and crouching/diving figures (11.1 percent). While they are exclusively distributed outside of the center, they are present in low frequencies (Table 6.2). The frequencies graphed in Figure 6.5 do not include the Iztmal Chen group, which represents a distinctive elite architectural group outside of the center. Figure 6.5 contrasts monuments recovered from the ceremonial center (Quad Q) to all others found at the site outside of Quad Q (except Iztmal Chen). Three other sculpture types are primarily from outlying areas of Mayapan (Table 6.2), including glyph blocks (14.8 percent), ring sculptures (7.4 percent), and turtles with human heads or humans emerging from their mouths (14.8 percent). The purpose of ring sculptures is unclear, and the representation of these objects in outlying zones of Mayapan is not fully interpreted here. Glyphic blocks may simply represent recycled monuments, and thus their context may be of little significance other than to suggest that families in zones outside of the Q group may have had less access to cohesive Postclassic sculptural programs and may have been more compelled to recycle earlier monuments. The turtles with human heads, mini-temples, zoomorphic *cuch* figures, and crouching/diving figures reflect some important dimensions of religious practice outside of the ceremonial center. These four types of sculptures are small, portable types (Proskouriakoff 1962b: Figures 1–5).

Two of the sculptural types common outside of the Q Square are probably associated with calendrical rituals, particularly tun or katun endings. The association of *cuch* images with year-bearers has been previously discussed. Some of the turtle sculptures at Mayapan bear series of "Ahau" glyphs on their backs (Proskouriakoff 1962b: Figure 1 [f, g, and h]), and the exterior carapace of one turtle is grouped into segments of twenty (Proskouriakoff 1962b: 2e), perhaps marking the twenty-year length of a katun. The Ahau glyphs mark tun or katun endings in the 260-day calendar. Ethnohistoric descriptions of the commemoration of tuns and katuns reveals that they are often rotated geographically around the landscape. Other associations of turtles with katun wheels and geography in the Postclassic period have been documented by Taube (1988). Even as year-bearers were rotated to bear the *cuch* of an incoming calendrical year (Taube 1988: 227–228), communities also rotated the duty (or privilege) of having the tun or katun stone "set" at their location. Tozzer (1941: 38) discusses several Colonial period references to the setting of katun stones at various communities. Setting the stone (also referred to as a tun) was a ritual connected with calendrical commemoration. Landa describes a number of calendrical festivals where feasts and rituals were hosted at various homes throughout colonial communities (Landa 1941: 153–156, for example). Coe (1965) and Diane Chase (1988) have pointed out that this practice of rotating ritual feasts throughout the homes of community leaders would have had profound integrative effects for Postclassic communities. Perhaps the wide distribution of turtle and zoomorphic *cuch* sculpture markers reflects this behavior at the site of Mayapan. This explanation accounts for the observation that these small sculptures are distributed inversely from other forms of sculpture at

Grp Q54 (Q71 shrine)

Q71

Grp Q64 (Q58, Q80)
  (Q58 serpent-column temple)
  (Q80 temple)

Q58

Q80

Q89

Q98

Grp Q97 (Q89,90,98,113,126,127a)
  (Q89, 90, 98 shrines)
  (Q113, 126 undet. structure type)

Q90

Q126

Q113

Q127a

Cenote Chen Mul (Q148, Q151)
  (Q148 shrine)
  (Q151 col. hall)
  (cenote area)

Q148

Q151

Grp Q145
  (Q143 serpent-column temple)
  (Q145 structure platform)
  (Q149 shrine)

Q143

Q145

Q149

Grp Q156 (Q156, 157a, 159)
  (Q156 col. hall)
  (Q157a statue platform)
  (Q159 serpent-column temple)

Q156

Q157a

Caracol (Q87/88, Q152)
  (Q87/88 col. hall/oratory)
  (Q152 Caracol)

Q87/88

Q152

Castillo (Q84, 161, 163, n.pza)
  (Q84 serpent-column temple)
  (Q161 col. hall)
  (Q163 col. hall)

Q161

Q84

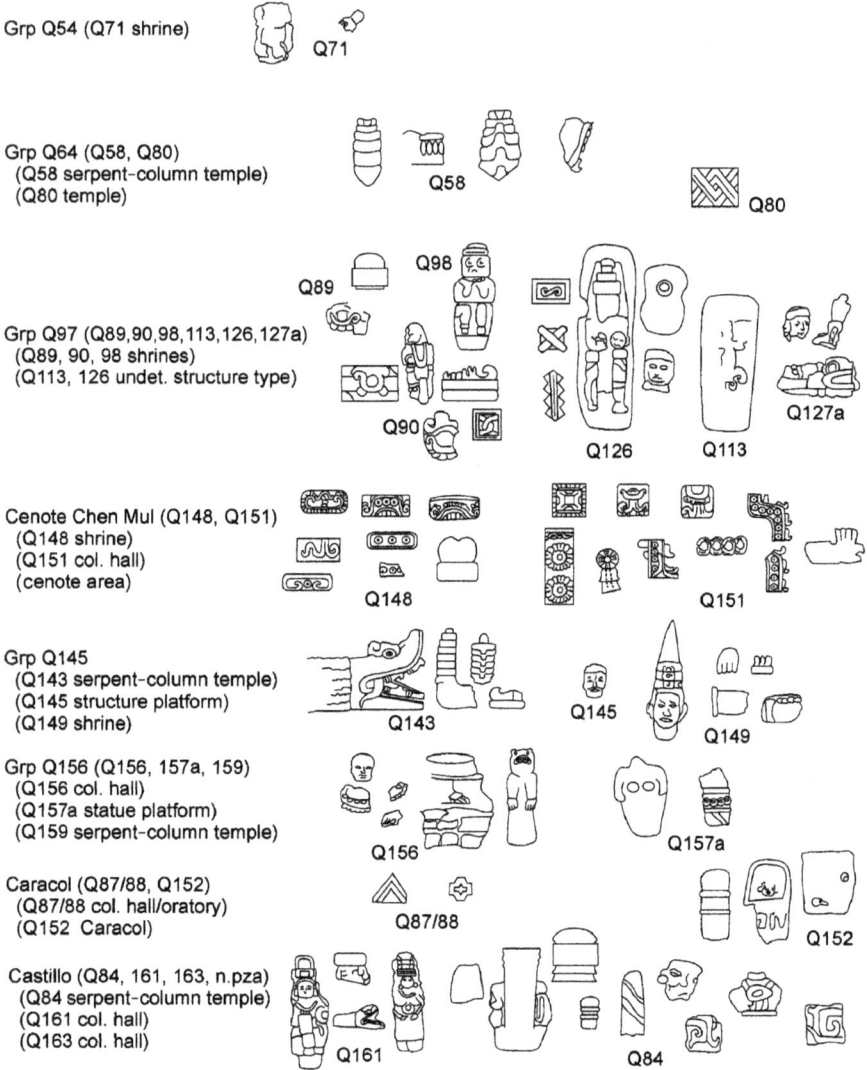

6.3. Sculptures from ceremonial center (Q Square) groups at Mayapan (traced from Proskouriakoff 1962a by the author, camera-ready work by Pam Headrick).

the site. Rotating tun or katun celebrations around the city would have served as an important mechanism to bind citizens together.

The mini-temple and crouching/diving figures also are found exclusively outside of the center, and no clear connection links them to calendrical festivities. It is probable that these images are related to household shrines and reflect a small-scale dimension of ancestor commemoration. Mini-temples might have served as symbolic substitutes for life-size versions. They resemble miniature

Group Q212 (Q214, 218, 244)
 (Q214, Q128 serpent-column temple)
 (Q244)

Q214

Q218

Q244

Group Q72 (Q73 platform)

Group Q169 (Q172, 173)
 (Q172 oratory, Q173)

Q172

Group Q142
 (Q141 temple, Q142 col. hall)

Structure Q112

Group Q70 (Q69 shrine)

Structure Q153 (oratory)

Structure Q83 (shrine)

Structure Q208

Q151

Cenote
Chen Mul

Q159

Q82

Q84

Q81

Q163

North Court
Castillo

Q163

Q163 North Court
Castillo

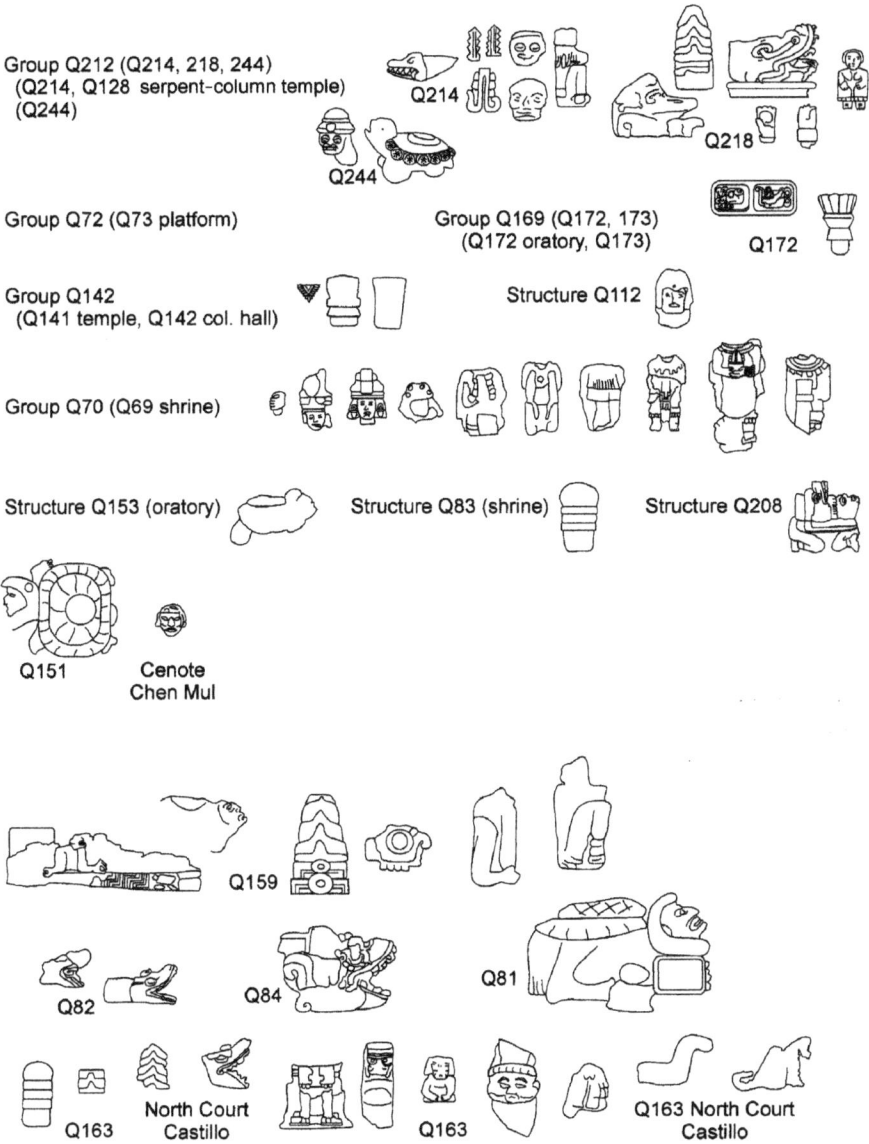

temples built at Tulum, and are identified as miniature shrines by Proskouriakoff (1962b: Figure 6 [a and b]). Similar miniature "lineage altars" are identified at Classic period Copan (Freidel, Schele, and Parker 1993: Figure 4.4a). The versions at Mayapan were recovered from burial fill and from a small altar (Proskouriakoff 1962b: Figure 6 [a and b]), also suggesting their association with ancestor commemoration. The crouching/diving or flying figures are referred to as "gods" by Proskouriakoff (1962b: Figure 3). These entities may also represent

Table 6.1—Sculptures by group within ceremonial center at Mayapan

	Human whole	Human head	Human torso	Human hands/ feet	Serpent eye/head/ tail	Seated feline	Bc f r
Group							
Grp Q54 (Q71)	0	0	1	1	0	0	
Grp Q64 (Q58, 80)	0	0	0	0	4	0	
Grp Q70 (Q69)	0	3	6	1	0	0	
Grp Q72 (Q73)	0	0	0	0	0	0	
Grp Q81 (Q81, 83)	0	0	0	0	0	0	
Grp Q97 (Q89, 90, 98, 113, 126, 127a, Q82)	3	2	0	1	6	0	
Grp Q142 (Q141, 142)	0	0	0	0	0	0	
Grp Q145 (Q143, 146, 149)	0	2	0	1	7	0	
Cenote Chen Mul (Q151, 148, Q153, cenote)	1	0	0	7	0	1	
Caracol (Q87/88, Q152)	0	0	0	0	0	0	
Grp Q156 (Q156, 157a, 159)	0	1	2	2	4	1	
Castillo (Q84, 161, 163, n.pza)	4	3	3	0	6	1	
Grp Q169 (Q172, 173)	0	1	0	0	0	0	
Grp Q208 (Q208)	0	0	0	0	0	0	
Grp Q212 (Q214, 218)	1	2	1	2	3	0	
Structure 244b, 244d	0	1	0	0	0	0	
Total	8	16	13	8	37	2	
% of total sculptures in ceremonial center	5.7%	11.4%	9.3%	5.7%	26.4%	1.4%	€

deified ancestors, which are but one category of Maya gods. Many do not bear the distinctive markings that have been used to identify specific gods (Schellhas 1904; Thompson 1957; Taube 1992) and each is individualized. A couple of these entities carry balls of incense, and the head of one emerges from a snake-mouth headress. It is curious that at Mayapan the "diving figure" imagery is confined to outlying areas of the site, whereas it is central at Tulum. This contrast attests to the variation in emphasis of different religious elements at two different Postclassic centers. Similar variations in emphasis are observed among Classic period centers (Schele and Freidel 1990).

Small numbers of fragmented human sculptures and even smaller numbers of serpent parts are also found outside the Q Square (Figure 6.5).

	Stela	Turtle w/wo human head	Glyph	Zoomorph carrying human	Mini-temple	Crouching or diving figure	Geometric	Other	Total
	0	0	0	0	0	0	0	2	4
	0	0	0	0	0	0	1	0	5
	0	0	0	0	0	0	0	0	10
	0	0	0	0	0	0	2	0	2
	1	1	0	0	0	0	0	0	3
	2	0	0	0	0	0	4	1	21
	0	0	0	0	0	0	1	1	3
	0	0	0	0	0	0	0	0	10
	1	4	0	0	0	3	3	21	
	4	0	0	0	0	0	2	0	7
	0	1	0	0	0	0	0	1	13
	4	0	0	0	0	0	2	0	25
	0	1	1	0	0	0	0	0	4
	0	0	0	0	0	0	0	0	0
	0	0	0	0	0	0	0	1	10
	0	1	0	0	0	0	0	0	2
	11	5	5	0	0	0	15	9	140
%	7.9%	3.6%	3.6%	0.0%	0.0%	0.0%	10.7%	6.4%	

Some overlap is to be expected when dichotomous contexts such as the ceremonial center and domestic zones are compared. Important trends are revealed in the proportions of imagery distribution—as well as exclusive distributions in some cases. Banner fragments were commonly found in both areas and do not appear particularly sensitive to context.

Ceremonial Center Sculptures

Imagery exclusively concentrated in the ceremonial center of Mayapan includes that of seated felines and geometric designs (Table 6.1; Figure 6.5). Stelae and human body parts are also common to this area. Images that denote power include seated felines and serpents (Table 6.1; Figure 6.5). The

Table 6.2—Sculptures by group outside of ceremonial center at Mayapan

	Human whole	Human head	Human torso	Human hands/ feet	Serpent eye/head/ tail	Seated feline	Ba fr m
Itzmal Chen elite group	3	0	0	1	2	1	
	13.6%	0.0%	0.0%	4.5%	9.1%	4.5%	4

Miscellaneous dwellings and structures of unknown function outside center

Y 2d	0	0	0	0	0	0	
Z50a, c	0	0	0	0	0	0	
Z8, 8b	0	0	0	0	0	0	
Cenote Xcoton	1	0	0	0	0	0	
Lot A166	0	0	0	0	0	0	
Lot A500	0	0	0	0	0	0	
Lot A—	0	0	0	0	0	0	
Lot A130	1	0	0	0	0	0	
S 133b	0	0	0	0	0	0	
R48	0	0	0	0	0	0	
R86	0	0	0	0	0	0	
R87	0	0	0	0	0	0	
R95–99	0	0	0	0	0	0	
P33b	0	1	0	0	0	0	
P110	0	0	0	0	1	0	
P39	0	0	0	0	0	0	
Total	2	1	0	0	1	0	
	7.4%	3.7%	0.0%	0.0%	3.7%	0.0%	7

greatest percentage of public sculptures is represented by serpent imagery (26.4 percent; Table 6.1) and human body parts (32.1 percent; Table 6.1). It appears clear that certain types of sculptures are concentrated in the ceremonial center of Mayapan, where the greatest number of public structures and elite residences are located. These patterns suggest that public/elite ritual emphasized different themes from those described for residential contexts outside the center in the previous section.

Serpent imagery, which has long been connected to Kukulkan myths (Landa 1941: 23–26), is found on at least five serpent-column temples that have been identified at the site (Table 6.3). Such serpents are also associated with warfare at Chichén Itzá (Freidel, Schele, and Parker 1993: 158).

A number of the human-body-part sculpture fragments are located at Structure Q69, Group 70. These sculptures appear to have been intentionally smashed and dismembered. Of twenty-five human or seated-feline figures

	Stela	Turtle w/wo human head	Glyph	Zoomorph carrying human	Mini-temple	Crouching or diving figure	Geometric	Other	Total
	0	5	0	1	0	0	5	1	22
%	0.0%	22.7%	0.0%	4.5%	0.0%	0.0%	22.7%	4.5%	
	0	0	0	0	0	0	0	0	2
	0	1	0	1	0	0	0	1	3
	0	0	0	0	0	0	0	0	2
	0	0	0	0	0	0	0	1	2
	0	1	1	0	0	0	0	0	2
	0	0	0	0	0	1	0	0	1
	0	0	0	0	0	1	0	0	1
	0	0	0	0	0	1	0	0	2
	0	0	1	0	1	0	0	0	2
	0	0	1	1	0	0	0	0	2
	0	0	0	1	2	0	0	0	3
	0	1	0	0	0	0	0	0	1
	0	0	1	0	0	0	0	0	1
	0	0	0	0	0	0	0	0	1
	0	0	0	0	0	0	0	0	1
	0	1	0	0	0	0	0	0	1
	0	4	4	3	3	3	0	2	27
%	0.0%	14.8%	14.8%	11.1%	11.1%	11.1%	0.0%	7.4%	

shown by Proskouriakoff (1962a: Figures 9 and 10), only eight are fully intact. Five disembodied heads are represented, and twelve severed torsos are shown. These images probably represented important ancestors of the ruling families of Mayapan. They may have been destroyed by residents of Mayapan or their foes when the site was defeated in A.D. 1441. It is possible that their locations recorded by the Carnegie project were close to the structures in which they were originally housed.

Seated felines may have been symbols of power or images of companion spirits of rulers or ancestors. It is possible to speculate that they may have represented companion souls, known as *uays* (Houston and Stuart 1989), of important humans. Jaguars are documented to have fulfilled this role for Classic period rulers, including a lord from Seibal (Houston and Stuart 1989), as well as for Zapotec rulers at Monte Alban (Masson and Orr 1998b). Their possible human identity is suggested by the fact that they were recovered in

Itzmal Chen

Y 2d

Z50a, c

Cenote Xcoton

Lot A166

Lot A501

R86

R87

P33b

P39

P110

H15 H18

H17

6.4. Sculptures from outside of the ceremonial center (Q Square) groups at Mayapan (traced from Proskouriakoff 1962a and 1962b by the author, camera-ready work by Pam Headrick).

the same contexts as human images and the fact that they were treated in a similar fashion, suffering the decapitation and ritual destruction described for human images above (Proskouriakoff 1962a: Figures 9 and 10). Human sculptural representations and perhaps their feline counterparts may be images of lineage ancestors of ruling families of Mayapan. Their primary

Z8, 8b

Lot A500

Lot A--

S133b

Lot A130

R48

R95–99

H6

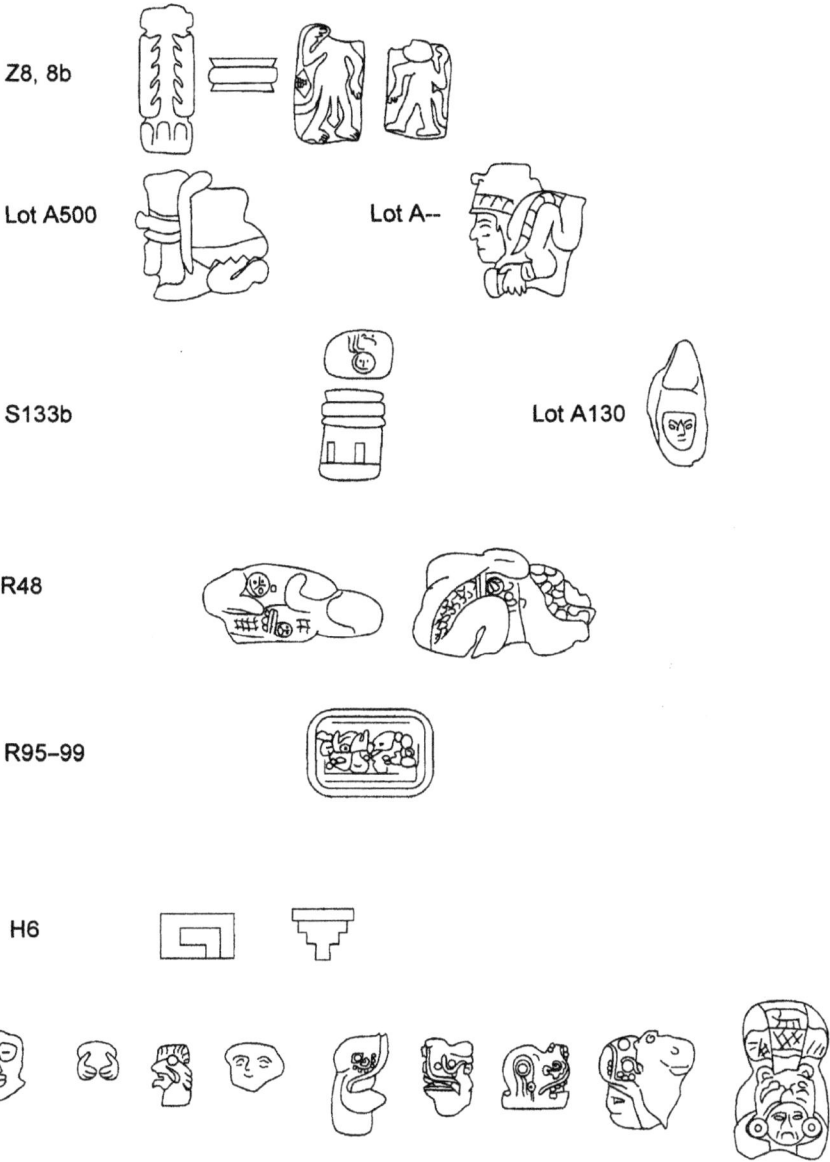

distribution within the site's ceremonial center may illustrate the significance of lineage ancestors in reckoning kin-linked power in the politics of the site.

Stelae are also confined to the Q Square. Stelae recovered from Mayapan are heavily eroded (Proskouriakoff 1962a: Figure 12). Scenes appear to depict lords seated on benches or standing on place signs. They are engaged in various rituals. The most well-preserved stela, Stela #1, bears a

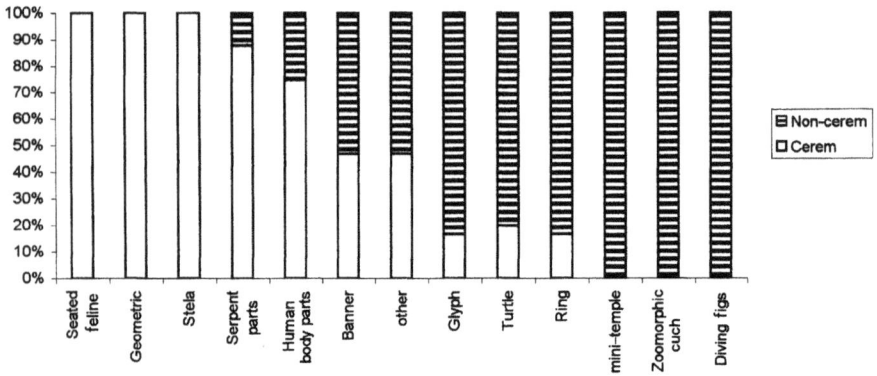

6.5. Distribution of sculpture by area at Mayapan.

10 Ahau date (Proskouriakoff 1962a). Sizeable eroded glyph panels above Stelae #1, #2, #4, #5, and #9 are unfortunately almost entirely illegible, except for a few calendrical day signs and numeric coefficients. Three stelae (#2, #3, and #4) were located on or near a "monument platform," Structure Q84. Fourteen monument fragments, many of them plain, may represent portions of stelae formerly located on this platform (Proskouriakoff 1962b: 107).

Mayapan Sculpture Themes by Structure Type

Some differences are observed in the distribution of sculptures by structure type within and outside of the ceremonial center (Tables 6.3 and 6.4; Figure 6.6). Figure 6.6 combines the sculptures associated with structures at the Izmal Chen group (Table 6.4) as well as those from the Q Square (Table 6.3), as the purpose of this graph was to examine patterns of sculpture by architectural type. Colonnaded halls were thought by Proskouriakoff to represent men's houses (1962a: 89) and they are also suggested to be council houses or lineage houses most recently in northern Yucatán (Bey, Hanson, and Ringle 1997). These interpretations are not mutually exclusive. Serpent imagery is the most common type of sculpture for the halls (30.3 percent; Table 6.3) and fragments of human images are the second most common type (24.2 percent; Table 6.3). Both of these images strongly suggest symbolism of descent. A range of other types of sculptures were present in low numbers (Table 6.3).

The most common type of sculpture associated with shrines is that of human image fragments, comprising 41.6 percent of the sample (Table 6.3; Figure 6.6). This association supports the interpretation that these images are those of ancestors. Ossuaries and isolated burials were associated with shrine rooms, altars, and oratories at Mayapan (Smith 1962: 221, 251),

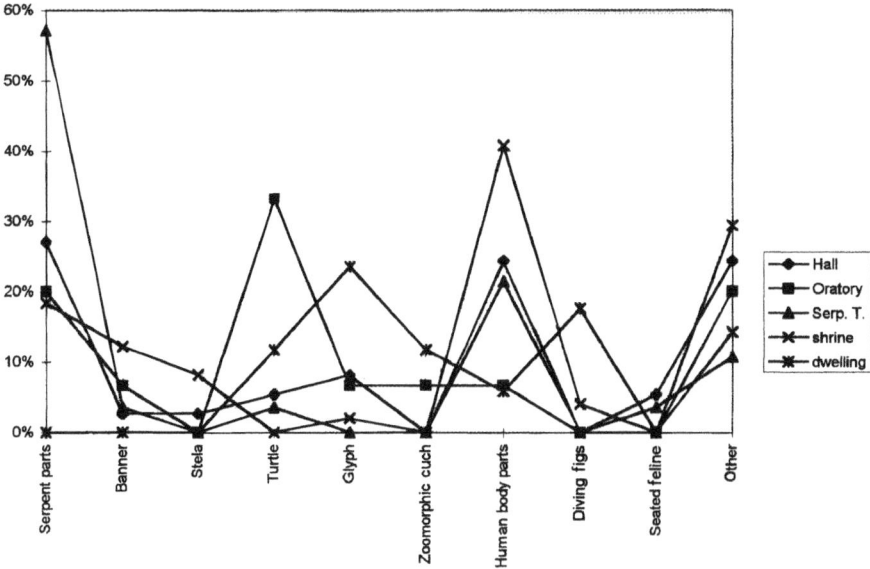

6.6. Distribution of sculpture by architectural type at Mayapan.

representing a further probable link to ancestor commemoration at these features.

Most of the images associated with oratories are turtle sculptures (Figure 6.6). Only one turtle sculpture was associated with an oratory in the Q Square of Mayapan (Table 6.3), and this building type had very few sculptures within the site's center. However, 80 percent of all turtles associated with oratories at Mayapan are from the Itzmal Chen group (four out of five; Tables 6.3 and 6.4). In fact, five out of the entire sample of nine turtles recovered from the site itself are from the Itzmal Chen group (Tables 6.3 and 6.4), which is an outlying ceremonial group in the H Square. This distribution of turtles and the association of turtles with oratories outside the center suggests that they may indeed correlate to rotating sponsorship of calendrical period endings by prominent citizens of the community as previously suggested. Few turtles were found in common dwellings (N = 2), confirming that their use was primarily a prerogative of the outlying elite.

Serpent temples, defined by their associated images, are obviously strongly associated with serpent sculptures (Table 6.3; Figure 6.6). They are also associated with significant amounts of human image fragments equivalent to those numbers observed for colonnaded halls. These associations strengthen the possibility that serpent images are closely equated with lineage at Mayapan. In Postclassic mural programs at Chichén Itzá, serpent imagery is used to delineate programs of descent and inheritance (Schele and Matthews 1998:

Table 6.3—Sculptures by structure type within ceremonial center at Mayapan

	Human whole	Human head	Human torso	Human hands/ feet	Serpent eye/head/ tail	Seated feline	Ba fr m
Q152: caracol	0	0	0	0	0	0	
Q214: caracol	1	2	1	0	0	0	
Total sculptures in caracol strs.	10	1	2	1	0	0	
% of each type of sculpture by structure type		10.0%	20.0%	10.0%	0.0%	0.0%	0.
CENOTE CHEN MUL: cenote	0	1	0	0	0	0	
Total sculptures in cenote	1	0.0%	100.0%	0.0%	0.0%	0.0%	0.
Q156: col. hall	0	1	1	2	0	1	
Q81: col. hall	0	0	0	0	0	0	
Q142: col. hall	0	0	0	0	0	0	
Q151: col. hall	0	0	0	0	7	0	
Q161: col. hall	0	2	1	0	0	1	
Q163: col. hall	0	0	1	0	2	0	
Q87/88: col. hall/oratory	0	0	0	0	0	0	
Total sculptures in col. hall strs.	33	2	2	2	2	10	
% of each type of sculpture by structure type		12.5%	12.5%	12.5%	12.5%	62.5%	6.
Q173: dwelling	0	0	0	0	0	0	
Total sculptures in dwelling	1	0.0%	0.0%	0.0%	0.0%	0.0%	0.
Q82: oratory	0	0	0	0	2	0	
Q153: oratory	0	0	0	0	0	0	
Q172: oratory	0	1	0	0	0	0	
Total sculptures in oratory strs.	6	0	1	0	0	2	
% of each type of sculpture by structure type		0.0%	33.3%	0.0%	0.0%	66.7%	0.0%
Q58: serpent-column temple	0	0	0	0	4	0	
Q143: serpent-column temple	0	0	0	0	3	0	
Q159: serpent-column temple	0	0	0	0	4	0	
CASTILLO PLAZA (NORTH): serpent-column temple	2	1	1	0	2	1	
Q218: serpent-column temple	0	0	0	2	3	0	
Total sculptures in serpent-column strs.	28	2	1	1	2	16	
% of each type of sculpture by structure type		14.3%	7.1%	7.1%	14.3%	114.3%	7.

Continued on next page

Ring culp- ure	Stela	Turtle w/wo human head	Glyph	Zoomorph carrying human	Mini- temple	Crouching or diving figure	Geometric	Other	Total
0	4	0	0	0	0	0	0	0	0
0	0	0	0	0	0	0	0	1	0
1	0	4	0	0	0	0	0	0	1
0.0%	0.0%	40.0%	0.0%	0.0%	0.0%	0.0%	0.0%	0.0%	10.0%
0	0	0	0	0	0	0	0	0	0
0.0%	0.0%	0.0%	0.0%	0.0%	0.0%	0.0%	0.0%	0.0%	0.0%
0	0	0	0	0	0	0	0	0	0
0	1	1	0	0	0	0	0	0	0
0	0	0	0	0	0	0	1	0	0
1	0	1	3	0	0	0	0	3	0
0	0	0	0	0	0	0	0	0	0
0	0	0	0	0	0	0	0	0	0
0	0	0	0	0	0	0	2	0	0
1	1	1	2	3	0	0	0	3	3
6.3%	6.3%	6.3%	12.5%	18.8%	0.0%	0.0%	0.0%	18.8%	18.8%
0	0	1	0	0	0	0	0	0	0
0.0%	0.0%	0.0%	100.0%	0.0%	0.0%	0.0%	0.0%	0.0%	0.0%
0	0	0	0	0	0	0	0	0	0
0	0	1	0	0	0	0	0	0	0
0	0	0	1	0	0	0	0	0	0
1	0	0	3	1	0	0	0	0	0
3%	0.0%	0.0%	66.7%	33.3%	0.0%	0.0%	0.0%	0.0%	0.0%
0	0	0	0	0	0	0	0	0	0
0	0	0	0	0	0	0	0	0	0
0	0	1	0	0	0	0	0	1	0
0	0	0	0	0	0	0	2	0	0
0	0	0	0	0	0	0	0	0	0
1	0	0	1	0	0	0	0	2	1
7.1%	0.0%	0.0%	7.1%	0.0%	0.0%	0.0%	0.0%	14.3%	7.1%

Table 6.3—*continued*

	Human whole	Human head	Human torso	Human hands/ feet	Serpent eye/head/ tail	Seated feline	Bar fre m
Q71: shrine	0	0	1	1	0	0	(
Q69: shrine	0	3	6	1	0	0	(
Q89: shrine	0	0	0	0	0	0	;
Q90: shrine	1	0	0	0	4	0	(
Q98: shrine	1	0	0	0	0	0	(
Q149: shrine	0	1	0	1	4	0	(
Q148: shrine	0	0	0	0	0	0	;
Q83: shrine?	0	0	0	0	0	0	;
Q146: statue platform	0	1	0	0	0	0	(
Q84: statue platform	0	1	1	0	1	0	;
Q157a: statue shrine	0	0	1	0	0	0	;
Q73: platform	0	0	0	0	0	0	(
Q80: temple	0	0	0	0	0	0	(
Q141: temple	0	0	0	0	0	0	(
Total sculptures in shrine/temple strs.	48	2	6	9	3	9	(
% of each type of sculpture by structure type	8.7%	26.1%	39.1%	13.0%	39.1%	0.0%	21.

Total ceremonial structure sculptures by function: 127
Sculptures not counted (unknown structure type): 13
(unknown structures include Q244d, Q244b, Q113, Q126, Q127)

218–219). An argument for this interpretation of serpent imagery for Tulum is made later in this chapter. Serpent imagery is also associated with segmentary political divisions for the Postclassic Peten Lakes (Prudence Rice 1989) and in the Maya Highlands (Fox 1987: 113–114, 127–135). As Rice notes (1989, following Houston 1984: 800), Maya homophones for "four," "snake," "serpent body," "sky," and the katun "head" link these concepts, and rulership in the Postclassic period was aligned with the periodicity of katun cycling (Prudence Rice 1989: 317). Schele and Kappleman (1998) pointed out the synonymous nature of words for "sky" and "snake" (*chan* or *kan*) in their discussion of "snake mountain" quadrupartite temples for the Maya and elsewhere in Mesoamerica and the important links between these temples, Mesoamerican origin myths, and symbols of power for Postclassic political leadership.

Three distinctive image associations are thus noted for three types of buildings within the ceremonial center of Mayapan: serpent temples with

ng ulp- re	Stela	Turtle w/wo human head	Glyph	Zoomorph carrying human	Mini-temple	Crouching or diving figure	Geometric	Other	Total
0	0	0	0	0	0	0	0	2	0
0	0	0	0	0	0	0	0	0	0
0	0	0	0	0	0	0	0	0	0
0	0	0	0	0	0	0	1	0	0
0	0	0	0	0	0	0	0	0	0
0	0	0	0	0	0	0	0	0	0
0	0	0	1	0	0	2	0	0	0
0	0	0	0	0	0	0	0	0	0
0	0	0	0	0	0	0	0	0	0
0	4	0	0	0	0	0	0	0	0
0	0	0	0	0	0	0	0	0	0
0	0	0	0	0	0	0	2	0	0
0	0	0	0	0	0	0	1	0	0
0	0	0	0	0	0	0	0	1	0
5	0	4	0	1	0	0	2	4	3
.0%	17.4%	0.0%	4.3%	0.0%	0.0%	8.7%	17.4%	13.0%	

serpent imagery and human images, oratories with turtle sculptures, and shrines with human images (Figure 6.6). Colonnaded halls do not exhibit a single most important sculptural type, but emphasize both serpent imagery and human body parts (Figure 6.6). Dwellings at the site have low numbers of crouching/diving figures (N = 3), mini-temples (N = 3), glyph blocks (N = 4), turtles (N = 2), zoomorphic *cuch* figures (N = 2), and one human sculpture (Table 6.4). No serpents, felines, stelae, banners, or geometric motifs were associated with dwellings, and few human images were found in household contexts either. These patterns indicate a dichotomous distribution of images at Mayapan, with certain types of sculptures apparently reserved primarily for lineage temples and lineage halls that were built and used by the site's elite. The association of serpent images and human sculptures at serpent temples and colonnaded halls indicates that these two architectural types are closely integrated. This link of snake symbolism and human ancestors is probably a reflection of a celebration of elite lineages and inheritance at Mayapan. Similar symbolism and emphasis on lineage power is also expressed in the art of Tulum.

Discussion

The distribution of sculptural themes at Mayapan indicates that the political elite emphasized certain themes of religious art in the site's center that are distinct from ritual indicators identified in outlying domestic contexts. Themes observed in the ceremonial center include serpent images at serpent temples and colonnaded halls, dismembered human and feline sculptures that probably represent important ancestors, and stelae that probably recorded events important to the site's elite history. Serpent temples were likely important symbols of various ruling elite lineages over time at the site (as proposed for the highlands by Fox 1987: 113–114), and colonnaded halls are interpreted as lineage long-structure "council" houses (Bey, Hanson, and Ringle 1997) or men's houses (Proskouriakoff 1962a). Such halls were probably the sites of important meetings among community leaders.

Other types of sculpture, such as small turtle images and burden-bearing *cuch* sculptures, were found primarily in outlying residential groups, including the elite group of Itzmal Chen. The turtles and possible year-bearer images were likely used in calendrical ceremonies that were hosted in various precincts of the community as observed in colonial times (Coe 1965; Taube 1988; Diane Chase 1988). The distributions of ceramics from the site of Tulum provide an additional perspective on the variation in ritual practice in domestic and public zones of a Late Postclassic Maya center.

THE DISTRIBUTION OF RITUAL FEATURES AND ARTIFACTS AT TULUM

Large amounts of sculpture were not recovered from Tulum as they were from Mayapan, so direct comparisons of data are not possible between these two political centers. However, the distribution of ceramics at Tulum (from Sanders 1960) provides a useful data set for the evaluation of variation in status and ritual activity at various contexts.

Tulum Ceramic Distributions in Residential and Ritual Contexts

Ceramic distribution patterns at Tulum suggest that the amount of ritual varied at domestic structures and temples at this site. Table 6.5 represents the manipulation of data extracted from Sanders's original report from Tulum (Sanders 1960: Table 2). Sanders's tabulations of ceramic types by excavation trench are grouped into areas and structures across the site in Table 6.5. Three broad categories are examined: domestic contexts, ritual contexts, and the "market" area proposed by Sanders (1960). Interpretations of structure function, such as "palace" or "temple," follow Sanders (1960), and the locations of these structures are shown in Figure 6.7. The distribution of

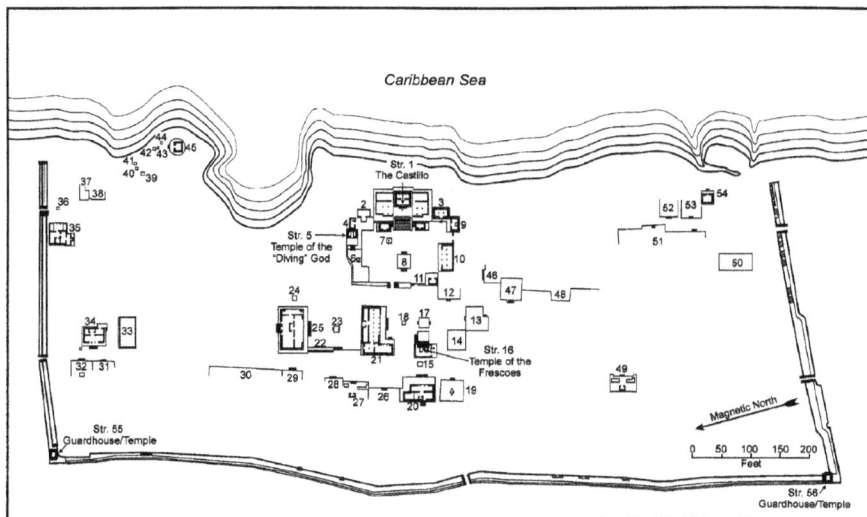

6.7. Map of Tulum, showing areas discussed in the text (redrafted by Pam Headrick from Lothrop 1924).

redwares, unslipped wares, and censer wares as defined by Sanders are examined for these architectural features at the site.

Among the residential "palaces" and platforms, differences are seen in the percentages of redware ceramics compared to plain (unslipped) wares. Residential "palace" Structures 21 and 25, 20, and 34 have at least 43 percent redwares, and Structure 10 approximates this amount with 38 percent (Table 6.5). In contrast, Structure 12 and Structure 35 (cenote house) have about half the amount of red-slipped wares (19 percent and 18 percent respectively). Differences in redware percentages may identify status differences among these residential zones, as these types of ceramics represent finer serving wares than their unslipped counterparts. Residences with the highest percentages of redwares are located along the "main street" thoroughfare of Tulum. The greatest percentages of Mayapan Red-on-Cream (ROC) partially overlaps with the distribution of redwares, found in higher numbers at Structures 21, 25, and 34 along the main street (Table 6.5).

Other interesting patterns are observed in the distribution of Tulum ceramics. Although censers occur in low numbers at all of these residential areas, Structure 12 (14 percent), Structure 21 (14 percent), Structure 25 (14 percent) and Structure 10 (10 percent) had greater proportions of censers than other dwellings (Table 6.5). Three of these structures (21, 25, and 10) also had higher proportions of redwares as described in the preceding paragraph (Table 6.5), but this pattern is not noted for Structure 12. Ritual

Table 6.4—Sculptures by structure type outside of ceremonial center at Mayapan

	Human whole	Human head	Human torso	Human hands/ feet	Serpent eye/head/ tail	Seated feline	Ba fr m
Z50c: col. hall	0	0	0	0	0	0	
Z50a: platform (roofed)	0	0	0	0	0	0	
Z8: undetermined	0	0	0	0	0	0	
Total sculptures	5	0	0	0	0	0	
% of each type for Z group		0.0%	0.0%	0.0%	0.0%	0.0%	0.
CENOTE XCOTON: cenote	1	0	0	0	0	0	
Total sculptures	2	1	0	0	0	0	
% of each type for Cenote Xcoton		50.0%	0.0%	0.0%	0.0%	0.0%	0.
ITZMAL CHEN (QUAD H ELITE GROUP)							
unknown structure type (H group gen.): undetermined	2	0	0	1	1	0	
H15: col. hall	0	0	0	0	0	1	
H16: col. hall	1	0	0	0	0	0	
H17: oratory	0	0	0	0	1	0	
H18: shrine	0	0	0	0	0	0	
Total sculptures	22	3	0	0	1	2	
% of each type for Itzmal Chen		13.6%	0.0%	0.0%	4.5%	9.1%	4.
DOMESTIC							
LOT A166: house	0	0	0	0	0	0	
LOT A500: house	0	0	0	0	0	0	
LOT A— (Proskouriakoff 1962b: Fig. 3g): house	0	0	0	0	0	0	
LOT A130: house	1	0	0	0	0	0	
S133b: house	0	0	0	0	0	0	
R48: house	0	0	0	0	0	0	
R86: house	0	0	0	0	0	0	
R87: house	0	0	0	0	0	0	
R95–99: house	0	0	0	0	0	0	
Total sculptures	15	1	0	0	0	0	
% of each type for dwellings		6.7%	0.0%	0.0%	0.0%	0.0%	0.
UNDETERMINED STRUCTURE TYPE							
Y2d	0	0	0	0	0	0	
P33b	0	0	1	0	0	0	
P110	0	0	0	0	0	1	
P39	0	0	0	0	0	0	
Total miscellaneous untyped structures	5	0	1	0	0	1	
	0.0%	20.0%	0.0%	0.0%	20.0%	0.0%	0.
Total sculptures outside center:	49						

Ring sculpture	Stela	Turtle w/wo human head	Glyph	Zoomorph carrying human	Mini-temple	Crouching or diving figure	Geometric	Other	Total
0	0	1	0	0	0	0	0	1	0
0	0	0	0	1	0	0	0	0	0
0	0	0	0	0	0	0	0	0	0
2	0	0	1	0	1	0	0	0	1
0.0%	0.0%	0.0%	20.0%	0.0%	20.0%	0.0%	0.0%	0.0%	20.0%
0	0	0	0	0	0	0	0	1	0
0	0	0	0	0	0	0	0	0	1
0.0%	0.0%	0.0%	0.0%	0.0%	0.0%	0.0%	0.0%	0.0%	50.0%
0	0	1	0	0	0	0	3	0	0
0	0	0	0	0	0	0	0	0	0
0	0	0	0	0	0	0	2	0	0
2	0	4	0	1	0	0	0	1	0
0	0	0	0	0	0	0	0	0	0
1	2	0	5	0	1	0	0	5	1
4.5%	9.1%	0.0%	22.7%	0.0%	4.5%	0.0%	0.0%	22.7%	4.5%
0	0	1	1	0	0	0	0	0	0
0	0	0	0	0	0	1	0	0	0
0	0	0	0	0	0	1	0	0	0
0	0	0	0	0	0	1	0	0	0
0	0	0	1	0	1	0	0	0	0
0	0	0	1	1	0	0	0	0	0
0	0	0	0	1	2	0	0	0	0
0	0	1	0	0	0	0	0	0	0
0	0	0	1	0	0	0	0	0	0
0	0	0	2	4	2	3	3	0	0
0.0%	0.0%	0.0%	13.3%	26.7%	13.3%	20.0%	20.0%	0.0%	0.0%
0	2	0	0	0	0	0	0	0	0
0	0	0	0	0	0	0	0	0	0
0	0	0	0	0	0	0	0	0	0
0	0	0	1	0	0	0	0	0	0
0	2	0	1	0	0	0	0	0	0
0.0%	0.0%	20.0%	0.0%	0.0%	0.0%	0.0%	0.0%	0.0%	

practice, as represented by the abundance of censers, is observed to occur in variable degrees among structures at Tulum. If the abundance of redware sherds provides a valid indication of status at this site, then higher proportions of censers may be associated with higher-status households at this center, although this pattern does not hold true for all structures with higher proportions of redware at the site. The distributions of redwares and censer wares may result, however, from a variety of processes including possible changing functions of structures over time. At Mayapan and Santa Rita, censer caches were recovered in structures that were inferred to have been abandoned elite residences (Thompson 1954: 623; Chase and Chase 1988: 25, 72). The amount of censers found in all domestic contexts at Tulum pales in comparison to the amount of censers found in public-ritual architecture at this site.

Ritual contexts at Tulum had the greatest proportions of censer wares at the site (Table 6.5). Ceramics associated with shrines in the vicinity of Structure 45 were primarily censers (82 percent), attesting to the specialized function of these structures. Temples and temple groups, including Structure 16 (Temple of the Frescoes) and the Structure 1 area (the Castillo and structures in its courtyard), had significantly greater percentages of censers (36 percent and 27 percent respectively) compared to the residences described above. Structure 5 (Temple of the Diving God) had fewer censer fragments (19 percent) than other temples, but this amount is still slightly greater than that observed for residences. Structure 54 had comparably few censers, and the ceramic frequencies of this building more closely resemble domestic Structure 10 than the other temples. Perhaps its functional interpretation as a "temple" is incorrect. Temples with the highest percentages of censers (Structure 16, Structure 1 court, and Structure 5) also have the greatest amount of mural and stucco art at the site. This pattern indicates that religious activity involving censers was more abundant in the public and elite contexts at this site, but the practice of censer rituals also occurred on a smaller scale in domestic contexts (some more than others). The fact that censers were most abundant in contexts associated with stuccos and murals is an important clue that supports parallels drawn below in the meaning of religious symbolism that co-occurs on these media.

In contrast to the recovery of abundant censers in ritual settings, the "market" area (according to Sanders 1960) has almost none of these artifacts. The market sample is comprised of 48 percent redwares and 40 percent plain wares, and only 1 percent of this area's sherds were censer fragments (Table 6.5). If indeed this area served as a market, this pattern suggests that censers were not distributed through market utilitarian exchange, but were produced and exchanged through specialized networks for specific ritual use.

Ancestors and Gods in the Tulum Stuccos and Postclassic Effigy Censers

During colonial times, a type of "community deity" is referred to in the "Relacion of Valladolid" (Tozzer 1941: 9–10). Entities with the names of Aczaquivae and Canpocolche were housed in temples of communities of the same name (Zacquivae, or Zaci, and Canpocolche), described by Scholes and Roys (1938: 609; also discussed in Tozzer 1941: 9–10). As Tozzer notes, Zaci was the original name for the city of Valladolid. These community gods were likely associated with prominent lineages or to have been controlled by them. Colonial references to specific "lineage gods" are summarized by Scholes and Roys (1938: 609) and Tozzer (1941: 9). Such entities described include Hunyxquinchac (god of the Ah Puces), Chocunqinchac (god of the Ah Kumun), and the "greatest" god, Cacaalpuc (Sacal Puc). The ritual of the Holpops described in the Chumayel manuscript is dedicated to lineage deities (Scholes and Roys 1938: 609; Tozzer 1941: 10). The identification of these deities verifies the fact that lineage gods existed, and also suggests that they were ranked in importance.

The deified ancestor (lineage god) Sacal Puc is described in a Postclassic Maya creation myth. He was the head of one of "four lineages which came from heaven" and he was the "first man to offer posole to the Chacs" (Scholes and Royes 1938: 609; Tozzer 1941: 9). Descending from the heavens is an apt term that describes the diving-god figures at Tulum. It is clear from these accounts that deified ancestors associated with places, creation myths, and powerful lineage segments were important aspects of the deity pantheon of the Postclassic Maya. It is therefore not unreasonable to suppose that the depiction of deified ancestors would be an important theme included in Postclassic Maya religious art, particularly at lineage temples.

One reference to an important legendary figure in Postclassic Maya mythology, Kukulkan, sounds suspiciously like that of a deified ancestor. Kukulkan, according to some accounts, was conceptualized as a historical individual who became deified (Tozzer 1941: 157). An annual festival, referred to as the Chic Kaban festival (Landa 1941: 158), was the occasion for Kukulkan to descend from heaven to receive the services of those celebrating the festival. Tozzer compares this festival to that of annual patron saint festivals in modern Yucatán (1941: 157). The broader mythical manifestations of Kukulkan are numerous and complex (Schele 1995; Ringle, Negron, and Bey 1998) and this account demonstrates one way in which this legendary character was appropriated and manipulated in ritual within a specific community. The notion of deified individuals "descending from heaven" is explicitly expressed in the diving-god figures at Tulum, and an argument is made below that these figures represent deified ancestors and perhaps even Kukulkan as a lineage-origin deity at this site.

Table 6.5—Distribution of ceramic categories at Tulum (manipulated from Sanders 1960: Table 2)

	Tulum Red Bowls	Tulum Red Jars	Tulum Red Misc.	Tulum Red Incised	Tulum Plain	Tulum Censer	Mayapan Red on Cream	V Fine OJ	Total	Tulum Red, All (Bowls, Jars, Misc., Incised)
DOMESTIC CONTEXTS										
Str. 21–25: palaces	76	108	566	10	634	251	86	7	1,738	750
	4%	6%	33%	1%	36%	14%	5%	0%	100%	43%
Str. 10: palace	29	25	180	5	313	61	1	4	618	234
	5%	4%	29%	1%	51%	10%	0%	1%	100%	38%
Str. 20: palace	18	34	233	4	228	46	10	4	577	285
	3%	6%	40%	1%	40%	8%	2%	1%	100%	49%
Str. 34: palace	20	12	236	2	200	21	33	3	527	268
	4%	2%	45%	0%	38%	4%	6%	1%	100%	51%
Str. 12: residential platform	1	0	34	0	121	26	4	0	186	35
	1%	0%	18%	0%	65%	14%	2%	0%	100%	19%
Str. 35: cenote house	14	61	236	15	1,357	17	43	10	1,753	311
	1%	3%	13%	1%	77%	1%	2%	1%	100%	18%
RITUAL CONTEXTS										
Str. 5: diving-god temple	5	3	61	2	147	56	15	3	292	69
	2%	1%	21%	1%	50%	19%	5%	1%	100%	24%
Str. 16: frescoes temple	4	1	75	0	84	99	6	5	274	80
	1%	0%	27%	0%	31%	36%	2%	2%	100%	29%
Str. 1, 2, 4, 9: Castillo court	48	70	598	6	749	580	94	11	2,156	716
	2%	3%	28%	0%	35%	27%	4%	1%	100%	33%

Str. 54: temple	23	28	252	4	489	94	29	3	922	303
	2%	3%	27%	0%	53%	10%	3%	0%	100%	33%
Str. 45: shrine	6	3	37	0	60	499	0	1	606	46
	1%	0%	6%	0%	10%	82%	0%	0%	100%	8%
"MARKET"										
Market	46	71	437	2	463	9	129	8	1,165	554
	4%	6%	38%	0%	40%	1%	11%	1%	100%	48%

Late Postclassic effigy censers closely replicate the imagery of the Tulum temples, and it is possible that they also represent lineage gods in the form of deified ancestors. This interpretation was originally proposed by Proskouriakoff (1955: 87), who suggested that some of the ceramic effigies portrayed "private ancestral gods." These ancestral representations are found in addition to other types of formal deities with recognizable attributes that are depicted in ceramic effigies, Postclassic Maya codices, and murals (Schellhas 1904; Thompson 1957; Taube 1992). This issue of ancestors versus gods is complicated, however, by the fusion of ancestor and deity identities in Maya religion (Looper 1991), as this distinction was blurred in antiquity. Ancestors, it seems, may appear "in the guise of" various deities in postmortem appearances to the living, as Looper (1991) has documented. Immediately prior to the Postclassic period, ancestors often appear in the guise of God K in very late monuments in the Maya Lowlands, summarized by Schele and Freidel (1990: Figures 10.3a, 10.4b, 10.5, 10.6). God K (*kawil*) is also an important deity in the Postclassic codices (Thompson 1970; Taube 1992; Love 1994).

The modern Lacandon interpret their effigy censers, called "god pots" (*lak-il k'uh*), not as actual gods or accurate depictions of gods, according to McGee (1990: 49, 51). They are viewed instead as abstract representations of humans, and serve as a medium through which offerings are submitted. Lacandon god pots dwell in god houses (McGee 1990: Figure 5.3) and when they are discarded they are taken to shrines, where bones of "gods" (i.e., ancestors) are also located (McGee 1990: 57). God pots are occasionally left at ancestral places as well, such as the Classic period centers of Palenque and Yaxchilan (McGee 1990: 57). Colonial Yucatec ceramic effigies were also housed in caves along with human skulls, according to accounts summarized by Tozzer (1941: 108).

It is difficult to know for certain whether Postclassic Maya effigies shared this function as an abstract "medium" for offerings associated with gods and ancestors, or if they were more specifically intended to portray such entities and to facilitate direct communication as has been suggested for previous censer traditions (Walker 1990). The Lacandon god pots exhibit considerably less stylistic detail than Postclassic effigies, especially in the distinguishing attributes of facial characteristics and accouterments. As these specific attributes facilitate the identification of the portrayed supernaturals (Thompson 1957), it is possible that such details have been lost in Lacandon censer ritual. Similarly, the greatest number of censers exhibiting specific attributes of Maya gods are found at the site of Mayapan during the Late Postclassic. With increasing distance from this site, specific deity assignations become more difficult, as the effigies are more generalized (Sidrys 1983; Walker 1990).

Replicating Structural Elements on Ceramic Effigy Censers and Tulum Stuccoes

Important ways in which ancestor commemoration is incorporated into themes of Postclassic religious art and artifacts are revealed in comparisons of elements shared in ceramic censers (found at all Postclassic lowland sites) and stucco or mural façades at Tulum. Further evidence of ancestor commemoration is indicated from an analysis of mural themes displayed inside Tulum Structure 16 and Structure 5. Parallel structural elements that co-occur in ceramic censers (effigy and noneffigy) and the Tulum façades are summarized in the following list:

1. diving figures (Figure 6.8);
2. seated or standing strong-faced males wearing elaborate feather headresses (Figure 6.9);
3. mat "lineage" motifs (Figure 6.10);
4. rosette or star motif (Figure 6.10);
5. trefoil motifs (Figure 6.10); and
6. serpent-eye motifs (Figure 6.11).

Figures 6.8–6.11 illustrate these structural replications on the media of ceramic art and Tulum façades. Ceramic censer elements are shown from Laguna de On, Mayapan, and other sites. Many more examples of the ceramic versions of these elements are published from the extensive Mayapan collections of Robert Smith (1971) and Ledyard Smith (1962), including a diving figure (Smith 1971: Figure 75e), strong-featured male figures with elaborate feather headresses (Smith 1971: Figures 32, 67, 73a), mat symbols (Smith 1971: Figures 31u, 63d, 73b), rosettes (Smith 1962: Figures 31 [c–d, u] and 62 [a–c]), trefoil "step-fret" symbols (Smith 1962: Figures 30 [p–r], 40, 43 [h, n]), and serpent-eye motifs (Smith 1971: Figures 32k, 73d). Mat and serpent symbols are also noted on slipped vessels among Peten Postclassic ceramics, though rarely together, and the significance of the ties of these symbols to rulership is recognized (Prudence Rice 1989: 311–313).

The ceramic diving-effigy vessels shown in Figure 6.8 were recovered from northern Belize in the vicinity of Progresso (Gann 1918: 81) and from Santa Rita (Chase and Chase 1988: Figure 16). One other example is reported from northern Belize (Sidrys 1983: 250). An additional diving-figure effigy vessel is reported from Coba (Miller 1982: 101). At a noble residence at Mayapan (Q208), two painted vessels with relief effigies of the diving figure were deposited, perhaps after the structured was burned and abandoned (Thompson 1954: Figures 2e and 2g; 1957: 623). A diving figure was also portrayed on a stela from the Peten Lakes site of Flores (Arlen Chase 1985: Figure 9), who appears in the guise of God K.

A reconstruction of Structure 16 from Tulum (Temple of the Frescoes) (Figure 6.12) shows the position of probable seated male ancestors in two niches flanking the central diving figure on the frontal external façade. Although these stuccoes are eroded today, the remains of their feather headdresses are still intact. This same program is replicated on Structure 1 (Castillo) as well (Figure 6.13), where two seated males flank a central diving figure. The male in the left niche of Structure 1 is well preserved (Figure 6.9 [a]), and this figure provides an indication of how the others at Structures 1 and 16 might have appeared. Although the external central diving figure is not shown in Figure 6.12, an additional, interior central diving figure is shown in a cutaway view. This interior diving figure penetrates the celestial band of the structure's internal mural. An additional seated male figure was present above the upper doorway of Structure 16 (Figure 6.12). It is probable that the niche figures and the diving figures portrayed in the roof positions of these temples represent deified ancestors, based on representations of other figures in celestial positions in Mesoamerican art.

Other Celestial Ancestor Programs in Mesoamerica

Comparisons to stucco themes in Maya architecture elsewhere in the lowlands support the case that these seated figures and the diving figure represent important lineage ancestors. Roof comb portraits of royal dynasts are reported, in eroded form, from the tops of lineage temples of Classic period Maya sites such as Temple 1 at Tikal or Labna Structure II, according to Proskouriakoff's reconstructions (1963: 8, 65). Commonly, ancestors are depicted in celestial positions in Maya mural and lintel programs (Schele and Freidel 1990: Figures 10.5, 10.7, and 10.8a), and roof comb façades are simply another expression of this tradition. In northern Yucatán, ancestor stucco portraits and mini-temples are shown along the upper portions of buildings such as the Nunnery Quadrangle at Uxmal (Headrick 1995: 4; for illustration, Proskouriakoff 1963: 73). The portrayal of ancestors in niches in roof positions at Tulum is directly analogous to these Classic period traditions. A diving figure is observed above a doorway of a Terminal Classic structure at the Puuc site of Sayil, showing time depth for this portrayal in Terminal Classic Yucatán prior to its expression at Tulum. Furthermore, as at Tulum, the Sayil diving figure is associated with a serpent (Proskouriakoff 1963: 55). Serpent imagery is also associated with diving figures and ancestral mural programs at Tulum.

Elsewhere in Mesoamerica, genealogical monuments of the pre-Columbian Zapotec portray conjured ancestors as diving figures (Figure 6.14), which descend from a celestial opening termed the "jaws of the sky" by Caso (1928). These images represent the visitation into this realm of conjured ancestors from their celestial dwelling place for the purpose of sanctioning important

a   b

c   d

6.8. Diving figures on effigy censers that are analogous to that of Tulum stuccoes. Figure (a) is a ceramic effigy from Progresso, Belize (redrawn by Jim Masson from Gann 1918: Figure 81). Figure (b) is from Tulum Structure 25 (drawn by Anne Deane from Miller 1982: Plate 41). Figure (c) is a ceramic effigy from Santa Rita (drawn by Anne Deane from Chase and Chase 1988: Figure 16). Figure (d) is a ceramic effigy from Mayapan (drawn by Anne Deane from Smith 1971: Figure 75e).

6.9. Strong-featured males with feather headdresses depicted in Tulum stucco niches (a and b) and in effigy ceramic form (c, d, and e). Figures (a) and (b) are drawn (by Jim Masson) from photos in Lothrop 1924. Figure (c) is from Laguna de On (Subop 11, Structure V, drawn by Anne Deane). Figure (d) is an example of feather headdress elements from Mayapan (drawn by Anne Deane from Smith 1971: Figure 73a), and Figure (e) is drawn by Anne Deane from Smith 1971: Figure 32.

a

b

c   d   e

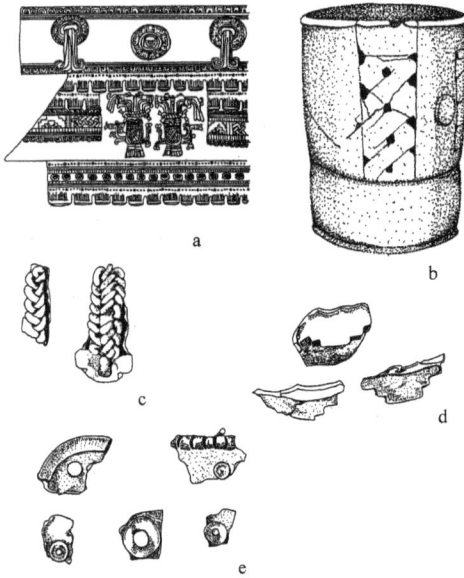

6.10. Representation of mat symbols, rosettes, and trefoil "step-fret" motifs on Tulum structure façades (Figure [a], Structure 5, drawn by Jim Masson from Miller 1982: Plate 25, and ceramic effigies [b–e] drawn by Jim Masson). Figure (b) shows a ceramic vessel with a mat symbol (from El Meco, Miller 1982: Figure 100), Figure (c) shows mat motifs from Mayapan censers (from Smith 1971: 73b), Figure (d) shows trefoil motifs from Laguna de On ceramic vessels, and Figure (e) shows rosette motifs from Laguna de On censers.

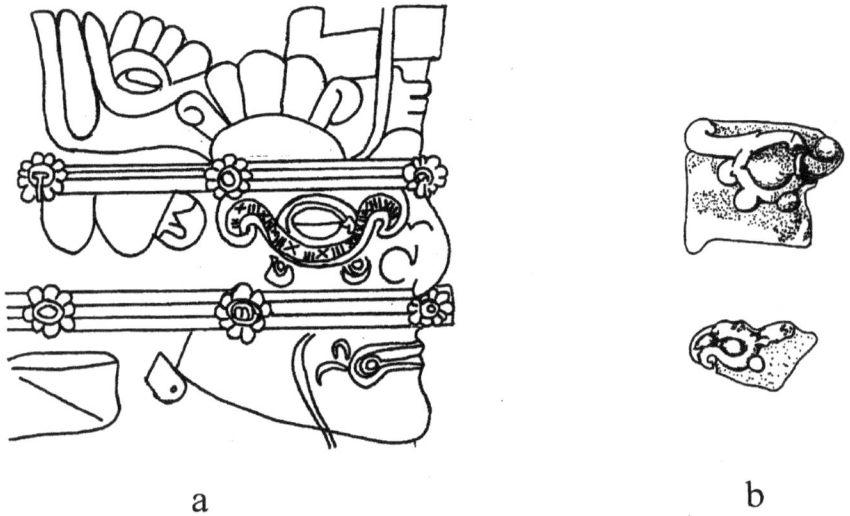

6.11. Representations of serpent-eye motif on Tulum structure façade (Figure [a], Structure 16, drawn by Jim Masson from Miller 1982: Plate 31) and ceramic effigies from Mayapan (Figure [b] drawn by Anne Deane from Smith 1971: Figure 73d).

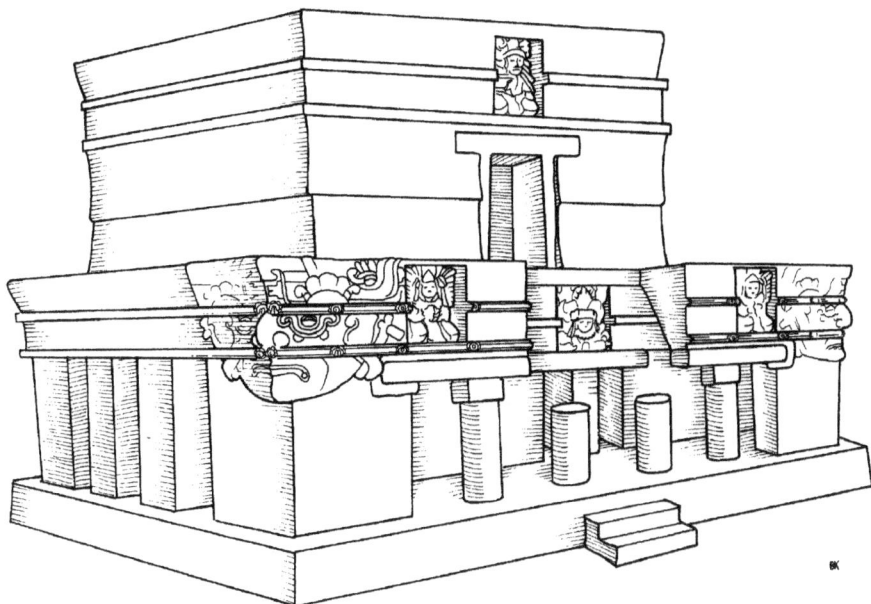

6.12. Reconstruction drawing (by Ben Karis, drawn from rendering by F. Davalos in Miller 1982: Figure 73) of Structure 16, Tulum, showing seated niche figures on either side of external façade (external diving figure in between them is not shown here). A seated niche figure in the upper building is also shown. An internal diving figure, which is at the center of Mural 2, is shown in cutaway view.

genealogical events such as marriages (Marcus 1983) and other events (Urcid 1991a; Masson and Orr 1998b). These Zapotec images are closely analogous to the diving figures shown at Tulum. It is probable that the Tulum temples were sanctuaries where rituals such as the conjuring of ancestors may have occurred.

Diving Figures as Gods

The identification of the diving figures at Tulum as deified ancestors is not incompatible with their identification as deities, due to the fusion of these two categories of supernaturals in Maya religion. As mentioned previously, ancestors often appeared in the vestments of particular gods. Miller (1974) suggests that Tulum's diving figures may be closely related to the celebration or commemoration of lineages in some way, based on the association of this image with twisted serpent chords. Other astronomical associations of the diving figures are explored by Miller (1982: 86), who compares the diving figures to the Venus "wasp star" of the *Codex Dresden*. Venus associations of the Tulum temples are also implied by Miller's (1982: 86–87) identification

229

6.13. Photo of Structure 1 (Castillo), Tulum, showing seated niche figures on either side of central diving figure.

of Venus in the sky band of Tulum Structure 5. Falling deities, like that shown on page 35 of the *Codex Madrid*, are interpreted by Miller (1982: 98) as Venus as morning star falling back into the underworld. The "rosette" motif, which has one circle encased in the other, resembles the "star eye" international symbol for Venus or star (Milbrath 1999: 148). It is prevalent throughout Late Postclassic art, and is found earlier in Classic period Oaxaca in the tomb murals of Monte Alban. The abundance of these motifs on temples at Tulum, especially Structure 16, affirms Miller's interpretations of the astronomical significance of these programs of art. Milbrath has recently provided further astronomical identifications on the Tulum murals (1999). The astronomical aspects of Tulum iconography do not conflict with interpretations of diving figures as deified ancestors, as the timing of important ritual events, often accompanied by the conjuring of ancestors to provide sanction, with astronomical cycles has a long history in the Maya Lowlands (Schele and Freidel 1990: 423, Figures 7.3b and 10.5; Freidel, Schele, and Parker 1993).

Taube (1992: 41) proposes that some Maya diving figures appear in the form of God E (maize god), and he suggests that Roys's (1933: 63) original identification of a "diving bee god" entity is not substantiated. Taube's identification of the God E deity is based on a maize-foliage motif that emerges from the head of the images (1992: Figures 17 and 18). He notes that this

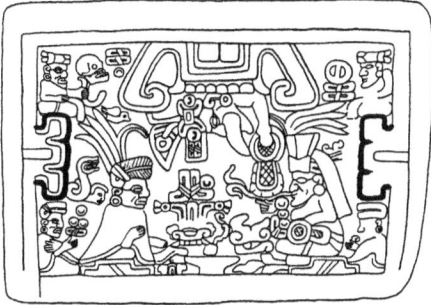

6.14. This diving figure from "sky jaws" on Zapotec genealogical register is analogous to the diving figures at Tulum (drawn by Javier Urcid).

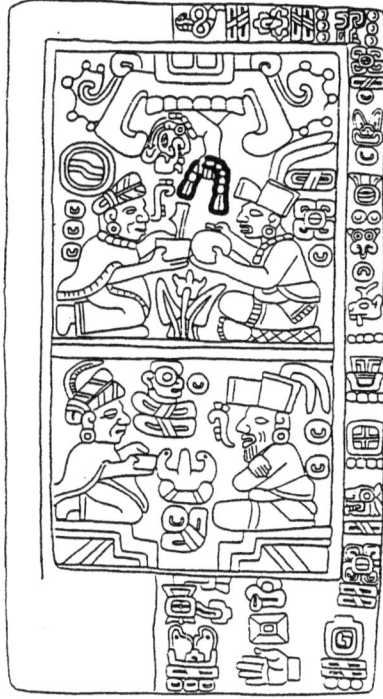

god is linked to the agricultural cycle, and has underworld and death associations (1992: 50). As most of the images of the diving figure at Tulum are currently too eroded to inspect their headdress insignia for maize-foliage motifs, with the exception of the images at Structures 16 (internal) and 25, it is not possible to know whether other diving figures at Tulum (Structures 1, 5, and 16 external) appeared in this guise. The murals of Structure 16 portray a number of figures and inanimate objects with this motif emerging from them (Figure 6.15). Since all of these individuals and objects do not represent God E, the occurrence of this motif is thus not limited to God E, but was more commonly utilized at Tulum. As such, not all images with this motif can be identified as God E. Thompson (1957: 607, citing Winters 1955: Figure 3 [o and p]) notes one instance where God B is shown in the diving position, suggesting that this position is not the exclusive posture of the God E supernatural entity. However, Taube (1992) argues that at least some diving figures appear in the form of the maize god, and it is argued here that these figures may also be ancestors. A notable Classic period precedent is the depiction of Pakal of Palenque in the guise of the maize god on this sarcophagus lid (Schele and Freidel 1990).

Several lines of evidence suggest that diving figures at Tulum may also represent manifestations of the Postclassic period mythic hero Kukulkan.

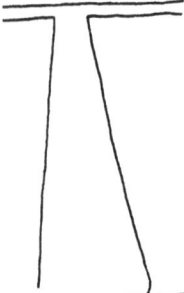

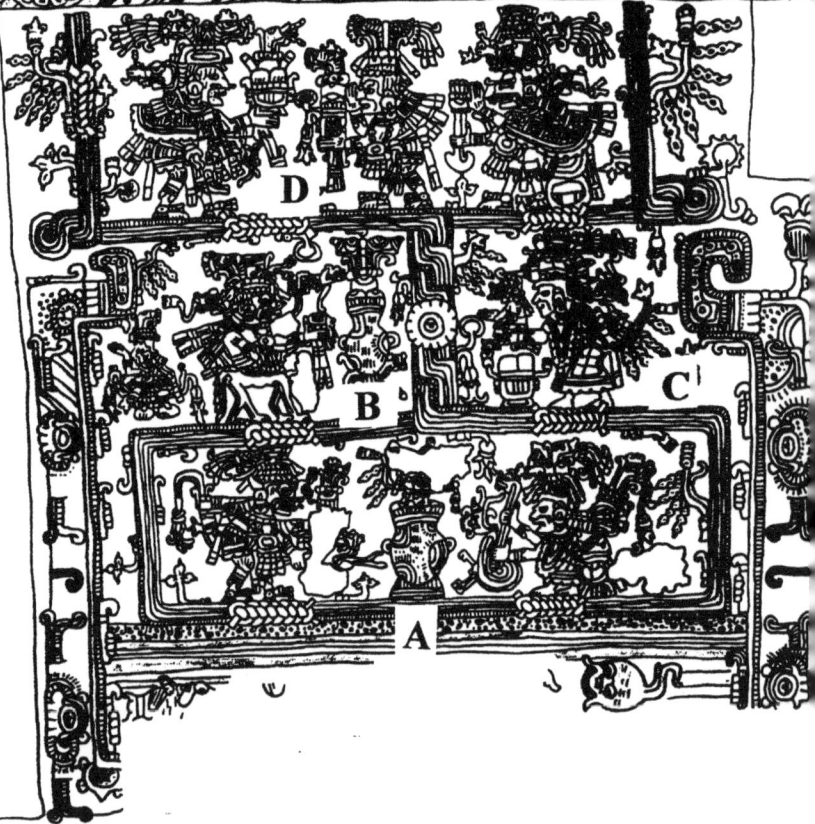

. Mural 2 from Structure 16 at Tulum (redrawn by Becky Adelman from F. Davalos
ition in Miller 1982: Plate 37).

This entity may have been claimed as the founding deity, or ancestor of elite
lineages, at this site. Evidence for this argument is best preserved at Structure 16. Two strong male faces form the corners of this building's exterior,
lower, frontal roof façade (Figures 6.11[a] and 6.12). The eyes of these males
are marked by the "serpent eye" and feathered-brow motif that Ringle, Negron,
and Bey (1998) identify as international symbols associated with the deity
Quetzalcoatl, of which Kukulkan is the Maya variant. The motif in the headdress of the Structure 16 interior diver that Taube (1992: 41) identifies as
maize foliage may alternatively represent twin serpent heads. Comparisons
of this element to numerous examples in the frescoes of this temple (Figure
6.15) indicate that this motif often exhibits the reptile-eye marking, the
brow, and the bifid tongue of serpents. An example of these markings is
found on the pair of serpent heads that emerge over the tamales that are
burped out of the serpent mouth to the right of the olla that is in front of
Scene E (Figure 6.15). Feathers are shown behind the Structure 16 diving
figure—or he emerges from a circle of them. The markings on his back (as
drawn by Davalos in Miller 1982: Plate 37; Figure 6.15 of this volume),
extending upward between his legs, may represent the rattle tail of a serpent.

These same markings are found on the rear of the diving figure of Structure 5 (Lothrop 1924: Figure 22). The step-terrace motifs (Figure 6.10[a]) that are painted into the celestial position on the frescoes of this temple represent the Ik glyph for wind that is internationally also associated with Quetzalcoatl/Kukulkan (Ringle, Negron, and Bey 1998: Figure 19). The diving figure on the Structure 25 façade (Lothrop 1924: Plate 23) actually shows a feathered serpent emerging behind it.

Thompson (1957) thought Kukulkan was portrayed as a youthful individual in censer imagery at Mayapan. This youthful characteristic is reflected in diving-god imagery, and recalls aspects of the maize god. Taube's identification of this figure as the maize god and Miller's Venus associations may thus also be correct as multiple aspects of this entity—perhaps Kukulkan—that represented an artful conflation of ancient and international symbolism. The Venus symbols that cover Structure 16 may reflect the ethnohistorically documented importance of Kukulkan as a renewal and origin deity. Numerous lineage mat symbols also present on the façade suggest that Tulum elites were appropriating this entity into their own lineage histories. Conjuring this figure "from heaven" may have been singularly important in the political and religious doctrine of this community.

Ancestral Lineage Murals at Tulum

The fresco murals of Structure 16 at Tulum represent the most extensive corpus of murals at this site, although other segments are preserved from Structure 1 and Structure 5 (Lothrop 1924; Miller 1982). Examination of the content of these murals provides further evidence for the close association of lineage, descent, and divine ancestors in the Tulum temples. A section of the Structure 16 murals published by Miller (1982: Plate 37, Murals 1, 2, and 5, drawn for Miller by F. Davalos) and redrawn here (Figure 6.15) shows a codex-style panel separated into segments in which a series of actors are depicted. This mural section is from the front wall of the inner chamber of Structure 16. An entwined serpent marked with mat signs and a central star-eyed rosette (Venus symbol) separates the scenes on the lower portion of the panel. The mural emerges from the jaws of a large serpent that frame the bottom of the panel. This "maw" is analogous to Classic period serpent portals such as that illustrated by Schele and Mathews (1998: Figure 3.18; see also Schele and Freidel 1990: Figure 6.3). Such maws are depicted in the contexts of death, passage to or from the underworld, and Uayeb ceremonies (Taube 1988: Figures 64 and 65).

The bottom of the panel (labelled Scene A, Figure 6.15) shows a male and female pair, facing each other, who are probably important ancestors. The female is identified by her cape, in a style that is analogous to the genealogical funerary monuments of Oaxaca (Marcus 1983; Urcid 1991b; Masson and Orr 1998b). A large pedestal-base lugged censer jar of a type found at Late Postclassic Maya sites is between this pair. Although partially eroded, each figure appears to hold a staff. The woman holds an object iden-tified by Taube as a serpent "aspergillum" (1992: 34, Figure 14). In the panel above (Scene B), a miniature figure and a four-legged zoomorphic figure are shown. Opposite to these figures and in a separate scene, a female holding a God K effigy is depicted (Scene C). Both figures in Scene C face vessels (a lug-handled jar and pedestalled vase respectively) in which tamales are vis-ible. Such vessels and tamale offerings are common elements in the Dresden and Madrid codices as well (Love 1989; Taube 1992: 41). The central figure in this mural appears to be a male (Scene D). He holds forward a vessel with tamale offerings in it comparable to offerings shown in the *Codex Madrid* (Taube 1988: 258). Two figures approach this central figure in Scene D, bearing staffs. The rear figure has been identified by Taube (1988: Figure 6c) as a Chac with a God K headdress.

An additional set of figures are shown above the chevron, star-marked, and rosette-marked sky band (Scenes E and F). These may be ancestors as well, perhaps more immediate ones. Alternatively, they may represent dei-ties (Milbrath 1999: 148). The gaping jaws of the two entwined serpents descend from the ceiling and produce offerings of tamales topped with double-headed serpent icons. The figure on the left (Scene F), a probable male, is seated on a bench and he holds a staff. The figure on the right (Scene G) is a female in a flying posture, with closed eyes suggesting she is deceased. She has possibly emerged from the serpent jaw on the right. Milbrath (1999: 148) argues that the women on this façade are aspects of moon goddesses or Goddess O. It is possible that female ancestors appeared in this guise. Two pairs of apotheosized ancestral figures may thus be shown in this segment of the Structure 16 murals, those at the very top and those at the very bottom. The depiction of ancestors in celestial, sky band, or upper portions of dynas-tic murals or carved inscriptions has much time depth in the Maya area (for example, Schele and Freidel 1990: Figure 8, 4.23, and 10.5). It is notable that all the prominent males (and one zoomorph) are shown on the left scenes of this mural, and all of the females are shown on the right. Two lords or deities are also on the right in the central Scene D.

The depiction of ancestors in lower scenes is less common in earlier monuments of the Maya Lowlands. This convention is observed in an earlier period (around A.D. 600–800) in "genealogical registers" of Zapotec Oaxaca such as the "Noriega" slab (Marcus 1983; Urcid 1991a, 1991b; Masson and Orr 1998b). Despite the origins of this convention, the Maya identity of these actors on the Structure 16 Tulum mural is clear. They bear close resemblance to figures in the Maya codices, as do most of the iconographic/glyphic symbols, such as the tamales. Other accouterments, such as ceramic vessels, are also those commonly found in the Postclassic Maya region.

The staffs carried by several figures in the Structure 16 murals may represent insignias of authority. In Scene D, the approaching figures (on the right) carry staffs. The first of these figures holds a serpent-headed staff. Such staffs are shown in three places on this mural: a partially eroded version held by the skeletal male in Scene A, a version held by a seated ancestor in Scene F, and the one in Scene D, which is perhaps the central male figure of this mural. Similarly shaped images emerge from vessels shown in Scenes B and F. They are also represented in the headdresses of figures in several scenes (B, C, and D). Their identification as "serpent" heads is shown in the double-headed serpents that emerge from the double jaws of the snakes in the upper panel that divide Scenes G and F. Forked tongues emerge from the mouths of these heads that are emerging from serpent jaws in Scenes G and F. These serpent heads are also associated with tamales on vessels and staffs shown throughout the mural. Many of these figures bear a serpent-eye motif and a stylized brow identifying them as serpent heads. One of the serpent bodies in this scene terminates in such a head with closed jaws (Scene F). Other such heads or double heads are shown in Murals 4, 5, and 6 of Structure 16 (Miller 1982: Plate 40). Some of these serpents have foliage emerging from their mouths, as in the headdresses of the approaching figures in Scene D (center and far right). These motifs bear a resemblance to symbols identified as maize foliage by Taube in the headdress of God D that is linked to diving figures (Taube 1992: Figures 17b, 17d, and 18e).

The subject matter of this mural segment from Structure 16 at Tulum, which is similar in content to other scenes at this structure, identifies a serious concern with lineage, descent, and ancestor sanction of historical ritual events such as the one probably depicted in Scene D. Mural 1 of Tulum Structure 5 similarly features two male-female pairs in scenes encased by entwined serpents (Miller 1982: Plate 28). The exact nature of the Structure 16 event shown in Figure 6.15 is difficult to know, but the central position of staffs and their limited distribution among prominent males suggests that authority is being recognized, if not assigned, to the key figure (far left) in Scene D.

The association of a God K title with accession to the office of Katun Lord has been noted in the *Codex Paris* by Love (1994) as one type of rotating office in Postclassic Maya society. The presence of a God K effigy (Scene C) and serpent staffs in the Structure 16 mural may indicate a similar type of ritual. The God K titles recognized by Love (1994) are associated with ascent to a rotating office. Serpents are closely associated with God K in Classic and Postclassic Maya belief systems (Taube 1992: 73–75). In fact, the serpent has been identified as the co-essence (*uay*) of God K of *k'awil* (Houston and

Stuart 1989: 8, as noted by Taube 1992: 79). God K was also strongly associated with lineage, rulership, ascent to office, and contact with the ancestors (Schele 1976; Schele 1982: 62–63, 118, 169; Coggins 1988; Taube 1992: 78–79; Grube 1992: 209–210). The celestial band in Structure 5 (Miller 1982: Plate 28), marked with lineage mat signs, is actually terminated at either end by a God K image (Taube 1992: Figure 34c).

At Laguna de On, a God K effigy eccentric flint was recovered at the corner of Structure I (Figure 4.10 this volume; Masson 1999b). This flint is identical to God K "manikin scepters" of political authority identified in Classic period iconography (Coggins 1988; Masson 1999b). It is interpreted to be an heirloom, as comparable artifacts have only been recovered from Classic period contexts, and it was perhaps obtained through looting of an ancestral monument during the Postclassic (Masson 1999b). This object was associated with the remains of broken censers and sacrificed game, and it was recovered above a concentration of burials that might have been the focus of associated rituals (Masson 1999b).

The interpretation that the central figures in the Tulum murals are lords engaged in ritual in the company of underworld characters was suggested by Miller (1982: 91). Entwined serpents are a convention known from Classic period Maya iconography, known as the *kuxan sum*, or "living chord," associated with death and birth (Miller 1974; Schele and Mathews 1998: 218, Figure 6.13). Miller (1974) has noted the use of serpent "chords" to tie together scenes in the Tulum murals, and he suggests that the use of this symbol connects the iconography of Tulum's murals and diving gods to lineages. Registers of descent showing "founding ancestors" at Early Postclassic Chichén Itzá are divided by entwined serpents (Schele and Mathews 1998: 218–219, Figure 6.14), in a manner directly analogous to that observed at Tulum. It is clear that rituals commemorating lineage and political authority are the key themes of the murals of Tulum. In this respect, they share a common purpose with the bulk of the legacy of Maya ceremonial-center art, i.e., the goal of political legitimization through framing inheritance and descent in terms of ancestral and supernatural ties (Schele and Miller 1986; Schele and Freidel 1990). Notably, a diving figure is centrally portrayed in the midst of the Structure 16 internal chamber murals (Figure 6.15). Additional external stucco portrayals of three seated figures and one diving figure are located on the building's exterior. Based on this context and the associations and analogies outlined above, these figures are most likely portraits of apotheosized lineage ancestors at Tulum, who assumed the attributes of certain deities such as the maize god (Taube 1992) or Kukulkan. It is probable that the interior spaces of Structures 1, 5, and 16 at Tulum were inner sanctums, analogous to the *pib nah* ("underground house") or *kunul* ("conjuring place") chambers identified in Classic Maya architecture, where sacrifices took place, offerings were made, and ancestors resided or were conjured for various purposes of ruling lineages (Schele and Freidel 1990: 239; Schele and Mathews 1998: 29). The recovery of censers in high numbers within these temples also suggests they were important places for communicating with the other world.

CONTEXTS OF EFFIGY CENSERS

The interpretations outlined above for Tulum mural/temple imagery have important implications for understanding the meaning and associations of effigy censers that are commonly found in concentrated deposits at Late Postclassic Maya sites. Two patterns of censer deposition are reported at these sites. Censers can either be smashed and deposited at different locations, or they can be deposited in reconstructable form as caches or offerings in altar or funerary settings (Chase and Chase 1988: 72). Broken censers have been dispersed over areas of four to eight square meters (Sidrys 1983: 242; Chase and Chase 1988: 72). These types of deposits are found at many sites in Belize including: San Andres, Saltillo, Consejo, Benque Viejo, Nohmul, Honey Camp/Laguna de On, Aventura, Carolina, Chowacol, Colha, Hipolito, Pozito, Indian Church/Lamanai, Betson Bank, Progresso (Caye Muerto) and Guinea Grass (Sidrys 1983: 244; see also Valdez 1987; Walker 1990; Masson 1997; Mullen 1999). Sidrys correctly proposes that these "Chen Mul–style" effigy censer deposits are contemporary with Mayapan, from A.D.1250 to 1450/1500 (1983: 241).

At Laguna de On, effigy censers are found around Structure I (island) and Structure V (shore). Single fragments of Kol-modelled (Chen Mul–like, as defined in Diane Chase 1982) effigies were found dispersed around the sides of Structure I on the island, and discrete deposits of incomplete censers were found around the sides and top of Structure V on the shore. Fully reconstructable vessels are not present at Structure V, which was excavated in its entirety. The ritual that took place at Structure V apparently involved bringing fragments of many previously broken censers to the shrine for deposition. This pattern of behavior has been previously identified (Adams 1953: 146; Sidrys 1983: 244), and such rituals may have served to integrate communities within a region or households within a community through the symbolic placement of fragments of the effigies from each place together in a central deposit. These vessels exhibit a variety of pastes with a range of tempering agents that suggests they were made by several different producers.

Thompson (1957: 601–602) lists the contexts of similar deposits at Mayapan, which are found in funerary, shrine, altar, and temple contexts. One burial cist had a deposit of 18,433 sherds (91 percent censers), which included only twenty-five effigy faces (Structure R86; Thompson 1957: 601–602, citing Proskouriakoff and Temple 1955: 327). An additional burial in

Structure Q208 had only six faces, broken into thirty sherds, from a deposit of 1,800 sherds. Only nine feet and ten arms were found in highly fragmented form as well, and Thompson notes that these effigy vessels were not complete when they were placed with the graves (Thompson 1957: 601–602). Censers are also associated with ossuaries, shrine rooms, burials, and stucco images of ancestors (Smith 1962: 193, 195, 221).

As these are sealed deposits, it is unlikely that incomplete vessel representation is due to postdepositional collection of distinctive faces and other objects as has been suggested for different types of surface deposits at Cerros by Walker (1990: 33–34). At Chichén Itzá, effigy censer deposits were found at the Monjas structure, the Red House, and the High Priest's Grave (Thompson 1957: 603). The latter represents one additional funerary context for censer deposition (Headrick 1990), and the Monjas structure has been identified as an ancestor-commemoration monument in recent reanalysis (Headrick 1995: 5). Perhaps significantly, effigy censers were not recovered from the Cenote at Chichén Itzá (Thompson 1957: 603).

The Identity of Effigies Portrayed on Ceramic Censers

The identification of entities portrayed on Postclassic effigy censers provides important information for the interpretation of rituals involving these objects. Thompson (1957) has identified a series of gods among the effigies at Mayapan, some represented by only one censer each (Table 6.6). He also noted that a variety of unidentified gods were represented. Thompson's list of deities was simplified to four types in subsequent studies (Smith 1971: 211; Sidrys 1983: 245), including old-faced, young-faced, death-faced, and Xipe Totec, as well as a host of unidentified types. Sidrys (1983: 245) also found one occurrence each of Thompson's Chac and Ek Chuah effigy types in northern Belize, and notes the uniqueness of all of the modeled and appliqué effigies he recovered. Censers were also difficult to assign to particular deities at Cerros (Walker 1990: 385).

It is notable that so few effigies take the form of identifiable "deities." Indeed, Thompson puzzled over the identification of only seven Chac faces, under 10 percent of the identifiable faces at Mayapan, which he compared to a representation of 53 percent for this deity in the *Codex Dresden* (Thompson 1957: 621). Similarly, "Itzamna," one of the most important Postclassic codaical entities (Thompson 1970; Taube 1992), is only identified in nine faces at Mayapan. If indeed the sample of 138,950 effigy-censer sherds from Mayapan (Smith 1971: 177, Chart 3) was closely linked with the worship of specific deities, it is remarkable that so few representations of actual deities are recognized at the site. It is thus likely that many of these effigies also represent deified ancestors. The censer effigy complex could thus represent combinations of deities, deified ancestors, and ancestors portrayed as deities,

Table 6.6—Gods identified by Thompson (1956: 608–612) in Late Postclassic effigy censers

God	Identifying Attributes
God D—Itzamna	toothless except for corner fangs, prominent cheekbones, occasional age grooves in face, large nose, sunken large eyes, scrolls sometimes under eyes, close-fitting cone-shaped skullcap
God B—Chac	trunk over nose, cross near eyes, teeth and corner fangs, eye goggles, snake or alligator headdress
God M—Ek Chuah "Whiskered" Gods	several varieties, long, pointed nose sometimes, whiskers, tusks, beard, bird headdress
Xipe Totec	closed eyes, vertical lines on lids, flat nose, dangling skins on arms and legs
Ixchel—Tlazolteotl	crescent symbol between eyes/in headdress
God E—Maize God	youthful face
Venus God	jawbones on lower face, hook Venus-shaped ear pendants
Kulkulcan	conch shell, face in puma jaws, peaked cap, bone dagger, hook Venus-shaped ear pendants
Death God	no lips, nose without flesh, sockets for eyes, death-head headdress
Old God	cleft chin

as Proskouriakoff originally suggested (1965: 87) and in a manner that may be analogous to that proposed for the Tulum stuccoes above. The most common effigy faces in the east-coast realm of the Yucatán peninsula (including Belize) are young-faced and mature-faced male individuals. Thompson (1957) felt that the former were associated with Kukulkan, and young-faced male deities are commonly associated with the maize god throughout Maya art of all periods (Taube 1992). The mature-faced individuals may represent Itzamna (Thompson 1957; Sidrys 1983). These dichotomous entities may have symbolized a foreign or exotic deity or a deity of origin (Kukulkan or the maize god) that was complementary to a local god of sorcery and antiquity (Itzamna). Important themes of renewal and rebirth surrounded the calendrical rituals that these censers were used to celebrate (Graff 1997). The sponsorship of such rituals would have helped to legitimate the power of families that hosted them (Diane Chase 1986, 1988).

The idea that effigy censers represent idols that were ritually destroyed and replaced with the commemoration of calendrical cycles was developed by Thompson (1957: 602), who notes that such ritual destruction of old images occurred in Chen or Yax months described by Landa (1941) as well as period endings of the 260-day almanac (Graff 1997). Diane Chase and Arlen Chase (Diane Chase 1985, 1988: 25; Chase and Chase 1988: 72) have pointed out further ethnohistoric analogies for the interpretation that effigy-censer caches and deposits represent offerings associated with the Uayeb cycle. Images of larger temple idols and portable ceramic images were fused in references to "idols" in Spanish accounts, but the two were probably related, according to Thompson (1957: 601). The close relationship of small ceramic effigies to larger temple images is reflected in the juxtaposition of structural elements of the effigy censers and stucco/fresco figures at Tulum.

The identity of these images as deities, ancestors, or combinations of the two does not alter their interpreted role in calendrical ceremonies. In Zapotec Oaxaca during colonial and pre-Columbian times, ancestors co-resided with the lightning deity, Cocijo, and ancestors are propitiated and asked to intercede with Cocijo and other deities on behalf of the living (Marcus 1983: 348; Masson n.d.b). The Zapotec effigy tradition is closely linked to funerary contexts and the practice of ancestor commemoration, and these effigies can represent deities, ancestors, or fusions of these categories (Marcus 1983; Masson n.d.b). It is one of the most well developed ceramic effigy traditions in Mesoamerica prior to the Postclassic Maya, and without disclaiming Maya ethnicity, Sidrys (1983: 139) has suggested that the Zapotec effigy "urn" may have served as an inspiration for the later Postclassic Maya effigy tradition. Other adopted forms, such as ladle censers, also may have been introduced from highland regions such as Oaxaca (Sidrys 1983: 139) or elsewhere. It is notable that the common recovery of these effigies in funerary contexts is a pattern observed in both ancient Oaxaca and the Lowland Maya area. Another shared pattern is the identities of these effigies, which blend aspects of ancestors and formal gods (Marcus 1983; Masson n.d.b).

SEATING THE TUN: RITUALS ON THE SANTA RITA MURALS

The Santa Rita murals represent a corpus of images associated with Late Postclassic calendrical tun-ending rituals indicated by a series of Ahau glyph dates recorded on the murals (Figure 6.16; Gann 1900: 663–677; Thompson 1965; Long 1919). These murals help to shed light on the types of rituals in which effigy censers might have been used, as the entities depicted on the murals share some general characteristics with those observed on portable effigy ceramics (Thompson 1957: 605, 609, 611; Gann 1900: 673–674, as noted by Chase and Chase 1988: 82). These murals also have important astronomical connotations that are summarized by Milbrath (1999: 230, n.d.: 6).

From left to right, the figures on the north wall can be described as

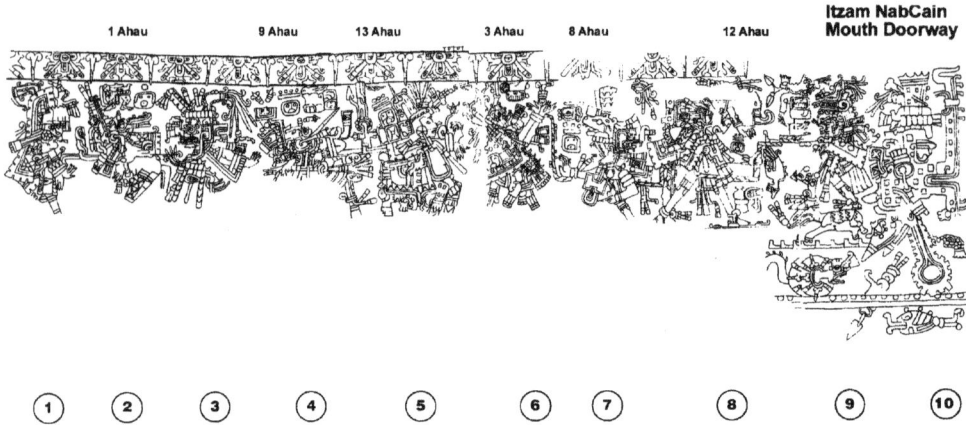

6.16. West half of north wall mural from Santa Rita, Structure 1 (drawn by Jan Olson from Gann 1900: 663–677).

follows. This partially recorded segment is but a portion of a larger mural that was destroyed (Gann 1900). The first of nine figures on the east half of the north wall is an older male (#1, Figure 6.16). Figure #1 is identified as God L by Taube (1988: Figure 31a). Most of these figures are bound together in a rope, which suggests captivity to some scholars (Taube 1988: Figure 26e; Milbrath 1999: 230, n.d.: 6). The rope alternatively may reflect lineage or political affiliation. The second figure (#2) from the left looks upward; his face emerges from a serpent-mouth headress, and he is associated with the glyph 1 Ahau. The third figure has been identified as God K (Taube 1988: Figure 26e). The fourth and fifth figures are associated with tun glyphs 9 Ahau and 13 Ahau respectively. They each have relatively youthful faces with distinctive mouth markings. A rope that binds them emerges from a tree that is linked to the sky band above this scene, probably signifying divine descent "from heaven." The images in procession from the left figure of this pair (#4, the 9 Ahau Lord) may thus be affiliated with this individual, and the images to the right of the right figure of this pair (#5, the 13 Ahau Lord) may be affiliated with him. The rope does not continue, however, from the 13 Ahau Lord to those figures to the right of him. He appears to be seated. A continuous rope connects the following figures to the right (#6, #7, #8, #9), associated with tuns 3 Ahau, 8 Ahau, 12 Ahau, and no glyph, respectively (Figure 6.16). The #6 figure wears a zoomorphic headress, and #7 appears to have a youthful face partially obscured by his headress. The last two figures in this group (#8, #9) have relatively youthful faces with distinctive mouth markings like the 9 Ahau and 13 Ahau lords. The 12 Ahau figure (#8) of this segment is not bound but appears to be pulling the

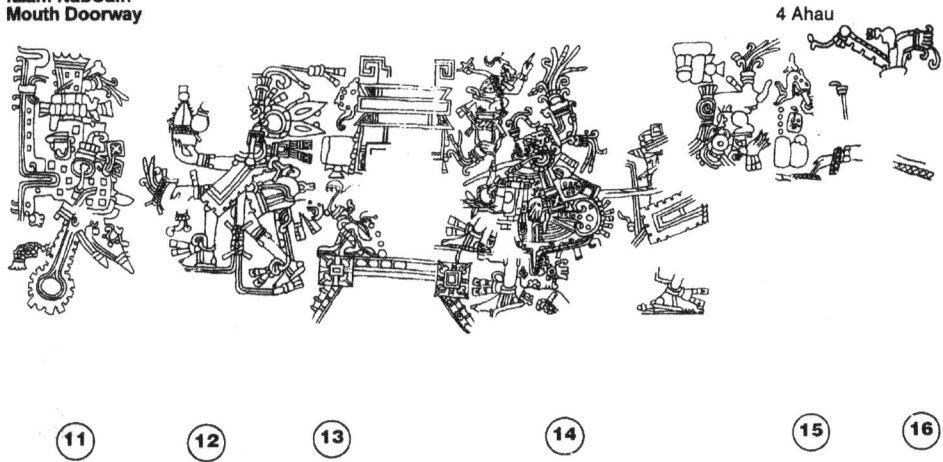

6.17. East half of north wall mural from Santa Rita, Structure 1 (drawn by Jan Olson from Gann 1900: 663–677).

rope. He stands in a doorway marked with serpent teeth. The far right figure (#9) stands on the back of a small mammal, perhaps a peccary. A bird awaiting sacrifice in a manner analogous to those shown on the New Year pages of the *Codex Dresden* and *Codex Madrid* (for example, *Dresden* page 26, *Madrid* page 37) hangs in front of this figure. A water band visible at the bottom of this segment may have underlain a greater portion of this mural segment, although it is not drawn. A feathered browed serpent (perhaps Kukulkan) is shown emerging from a sun or star circular portal beneath figure #9. The head of the snake is identical to that shown behind the diving figure of Structure 25 at Tulum.

This north wall mural is divided into two halves by a caiman mouth (portal) doorway that represents the mouth of Itzám Cab Ain (#10, #11; Taube 1992: 37), a caiman entity that wears the headress of Itzámna. A couple of other figures drawn by Gann (1900) on the west half of this doorway continue the procession scene observed on the east half (#12 and #13 in Figure 6.17). Immediately to the right of the doorway, two figures descend and ascend from either side of a temple (#12, #13), bearing offerings. The first, a departing figure (#12), carries a spiked incense cone in a matted vessel in one hand, and foliage or smoke emerges from a twin vessel in his other hand. This figure is not bound. The face of this figure is not visible. From the doorway of the temple behind this figure, the remains of a seated, feline figure is represented by three paws (#13). This figure is probably a temple deity or some sort of ruler in companion spirit transformation. It

243

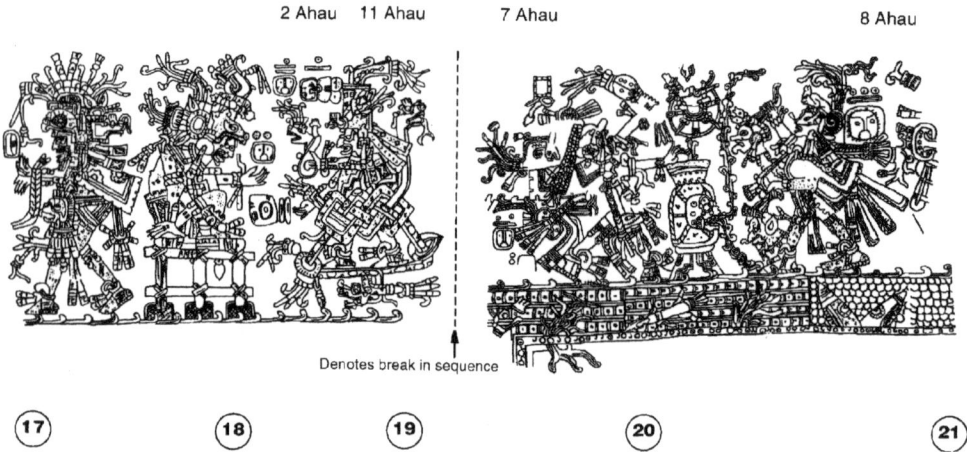

6.18. Discontinuous sections of west side of north wall mural from Santa Rita, Structure 1 (drawn by Jan Olson from Gann 1900: 663–677).

resembles jaguar lords portrayed at Monte Alban in the Classic period (Caso 1928; Masson and Orr 1998b). Jaguar costumes are common on lords of the Classic period Maya kingdoms, and jaguar protectorate spirits were also common during the Classic period (Houston and Stuart 1989; Schele and Freidel 1990). Ascending the other side of this temple is another youthful-faced figure (#14) carrying an animated, seated effigy that also has a youthful face. The remains of a rope binding this figure encircle his front arm and extend from his rear costume elements to the youthful-faced tun 4 Ahau figure behind him (#15), who faces another bound, eroded figure (#16).

Other (discontinuous) sections of the wall drawn by Gann (1900) show additional scenes (Figure 6.18). Figure 6.18 shows three more figures, including: one bound, departing individual (#17); one bound individual (#18, 2 Ahau Lord) seated on a scaffold wearing a possible peccary headress (a possible captive); and God D (Taube 1992: Figure 36d) associated with 11 Ahau and entwined in serpents (#19). Two figures shown on an additional segment are associated with tuns 7 Ahau and 8 Ahau (#20 and #21), and have been identified as Ek Chuah (or a whiskered deity) and a youthful entity holding the disembodied heads of God G and God M (Taube 1988: Figures 12d and 36b, 1992: Figure 22f).

Several figures are identified with place names in these murals, as indicated by phonetic glyphic elements accompanying figures on the east half of the wall (David Mora-Marin, personal communication 1998). Ten north-wall figures are accompanied by glyphs (either place names or personal names) that are not tun-ending Ahau glyphs (Table 6.7). An additional place sign may be represented by the shell icon marking the temple on the west half of the doorway. The shell icon may designate a coastal setting, perhaps even Santa Rita itself.

Only five of twenty-one figures of Santa Rita's north wall can be identified as "gods" that are analogous to those recognized in effigy censers or codices by Thompson (1957), and two additional disembodied god heads are present (Table 6.7). The five full figures that have deity insignia include two old gods (#1 and #19), two Ek Chuah/God M representations (#2 and #20), and one God K (#3). Two additional disembodied heads held by figure #21 represent Gods G and Ek Chuah/God M (Taube 1988: Figure 36b). In contrast, at least ten of the figures represent youthful-appearing adult males distinguished from one another by mouth markings (#4, #5, #7, #8, #9, #14, #15, #17, #18, and #21). These distinctions suggest that these images may represent historical individuals. Two other figures are eroded and unidentified (#12 and #16), and one is zoomorphic (#6). The head of the Itzám Nab Cain entity forms both sides of the doorway (#10 and #11), and one feline entity is seated in the temple (#13). The presence of ten unique name glyphs, which include a number of place names, suggests to this author that this mural records a procession of lords from different communities in the Chetumal province who may have alternated the "burden" or *cuch* of ushering in various tun cycles, as originally suggested by Long (1919) and Thompson (1963). This practice of setting tun and katun stones at various communities in northern Yucatán is documented in the *Books of Chilam Balam* and by Tozzer (1941: 38), and related calendrical rotation of offices among local lords may also be depicted in the Structure 1 mural at Santa Rita. Tun or katun confederations formed an important part of Highland Quiche communities as well (Fox 1987: 112–117).

While the "Mixtec" iconographic elements of these murals—including body painting, solar disks, the style of the temple, and the Venus sky band—have been heavily emphasized in previous analyses (Robertson 1970; Quirarte 1982; Sidrys 1983: 134), these figures have clearly Maya faces and are associated with Maya tun dates, place glyphs, and Maya portal doorways that clearly pertain to local phenomena. Chase and Chase (1988: 83–84) have previously argued for the Maya context and content of these murals, and have pointed out that these murals share clear iconographic themes with effigy censers from this site. However, the inclusion of elements common in highland Mexico as well as Maya elements is an important aspect of these murals, and reveals the outward-looking "international" focus of Postclassic Maya port cities such as Santa Rita (Smith and Heath-Smith 1980).

Characters portrayed in these murals probably represent important village leaders (either living or deceased) from the Chetumal province vicinity in the company of or in the guise of certain Maya deities. The act that draws

Table 6.7—List of figures on Santa Rita north wall mural

Figure	Description	Tun Glyph	Bound	Place Name (or additional glyph)
1	old face, God L (Taube 1988: Figure 31a)	none	yes	unknown
2	serpent-mouth headdress, figure with possible Ek Chuah nose	1 Ahau	yes	yes
3	God K (Taube 1988: Figure 26e)	none	yes	none
4	youthful face, mouth markings, binding rope emerges from tree descending from sky band (also #5)	9 Ahau	yes	yes
5	youthful face, mouth markings, binding rope emerges from tree descending from sky band (also #4)	13 Ahau	yes	yes
6	youthful face, mouth markings	3 Ahau	yes	yes
7	youthful face, mouth markings	8 Ahau	yes	yes
8	youthful face, mouth markings	12 Ahau	no	yes
9	youthful face, mouth markings	none	yes	yes
10	Itzám Cab Ain, caiman-mouth portal doorway (Taube 1992)			
11	Itzám Cab Ain, caiman-mouth portal doorway (Taube 1992)			
12	face obscured, holding twin mat bowls with offerings (*chord with mat sign emerges from him, stands on it)	none	no*	temple that has "shell" place sign
13	feline entity seated in temple	none	yes	temple that has "shell" place sign
14	youthful face, mouth markings, holding animated offering image in mat bowl	none	yes	temple that has "shell" place sign
15	youthful face, mouth markings	4 Ahau	yes	yes
16	eroded, headress only	unknown	yes	unknown
17	youthful face, mouth markings, owl headdress	none	yes	yes
18	youthful face, mouth markings, peccary headdress, seated on scaffold, tattooed captive?	2 Ahau	yes	yes
19	God D, old god, entwined with serpents, holds serpent object (Taube 1992: Figure 14e)	11 Ahau	no	yes
20	Ek Chuah, touching ceramic drum or censer	7 Ahau	no	maybe
21	youthful face, mouth markings, holds heads of two entities, Gods G and M (Taube 1988: Figure 36b)	8 Ahau	no	no

these entities together (symbolized perhaps by a binding chord) is that of ushering in the tuns. The calendrical web linked by these entitites and their associated dates underscores once again the importance of calendrical ritual as a rite of regional integration. Carefully timed regional rituals shared by contemporary communities of Maya have the same effect (Vogt 1976; Freidel, Schele, and Parker 1993: 123–134). On each side of the wall, unbound individuals (#8 and #12) appear to be pulling the chord that links these entities together. The unbound figure to the left of the Itzám Nab Cain doorway (#8) stands within a serpent-mouth doorway and the unbound figure on the west (#12) emerges from a temple that may represent Santa Rita. These actors appear especially important in this event. Perhaps the moment of office rotation is depicted, as one actor departs the temple even as another enters it from the other side. The seated jaguar may represent a temple oracle or some other housed supernatural, as is common in the Mixtec codices (Pohl 1994).

As observed for the effigy censers of Mayapan, the number of actual deities portrayed on the Santa Rita mural is less than the number of portrayals of individuals (or deified individuals) that lack distinctive deity insignia. This program offers additional evidence that the portrayal of historical personages (or ancestors) in the company or guise of gods was a critical element of Postclassic religion. Rituals evoking gods and ancestors were closely linked to the calendar, and arguments presented in this chapter suggest that these rituals were the focus of participation and integration within and between communities. Though effigy censers represent a different medium from these temple murals, they are used in the same types of calendrical events (Diane Chase 1988). Ceramic effigies are also, as noted above, used commonly in burials or ancestral shrines. The contexts of censers suggest that ancestors and gods are a critical focus of censer ceremonies, and these are the likely subjects portrayed in these effigies.

ELITE AND DOMESTIC RITUALS: A REASSESSMENT OF THE SECULARIZATION ARGUMENT

As mentioned at the beginning of this chapter, investigators at Mayapan suggested that religion had become "privatized," or primarily limited to household practice, in the Postclassic period (Thompson 1957: 624; Pollock 1962: 17; Proskouriakoff 1962b: 136). In this interpretation, effigy censers were thought to have been used in ancestor cults and family-based worship in the private sector. While the use of censers in conjunction with ancestor communication is probable, the earlier view that this practice was primarily private and domestic is contradicted by more recent work. The household practice of ancestor commemoration is a long enduring structure observed from the Preclassic period through colonial times (Levanthal 1983: 75–76; Gossen and Levanthal 1993: 211; McAnany 1995: 53). The above examination demonstrates that in addition to household scales of ritual, concentrations of particular types of ritual activities are found within public and elite sectors of Postclassic Maya centers. The maintenance of specific ritual zones administered by priests that were distinct from common residential zones has been reported from the Postclassic settlements of Cozumel Island (Freidel and Sabloff 1984: 184). At all Postclassic sites examined here, including Laguna de On, spatially distinct sacred features were reserved for ritual practice. It thus appears that Postclassic Maya religious practice was neither dispersed or confined to the household realm as originally thought.

Elite and public contexts have proportionately greater indications of ritual practice at Postclassic Maya central precincts than at outlying domestic zones, as reflected in architectural features, sculptures, and censers. However, some domestic zones do exhibit low numbers of censers and other types of effigies at Mayapan, Tulum, and Santa Rita (Smith 1962; Sanders 1960; Diane Chase 1982, 1988, 1992), and these materials suggest that the practice of rituals pertaining to ancestor commemoration or calendrical events was replicated at certain households (though not all of them) on a smaller scale. While some themes of the past are reflected in Postclassic iconography, a society with fundamentally changed organizational principles is reflected in the art. The coexistence of multiple political factions is seen in the presence of multiple ritual shrines or temples (Freidel and Sabloff 1984: 184). The serpent temples at Mayapan and multiple diving-figure temples at Tulum also reflect this multiplicity of competing, yet integrated, factions similar to those documented for the Highland Quiche Maya (Carmack 1981; Fox 1987).

The types of ritual that distinguish elite precincts from general domestic zones are found in temples, shrines, and colonnaded halls of Mayapan or Tulum. These themes primarily glorify the lineages of the political elite of these sites through the depiction of deified ancestors in the company of gods. Historical individuals, divine ancestors, and gods engage together in acts of accession to office and in the celebration of calendrical events. These figures are linked to serpent imagery in serpent-mouth portals, serpent cords, serpent columns, or feathered-serpent depictions in murals or stuccoes at Mayapan, Tulum, and Santa Rita. These strategies of elite legitimization can be recognized as Postclassic reproductions or transformations of very ancient religious institutions for the Maya Lowlands (Coggins 1979; Schele and Freidel 1990; McAnany 1995). Serpent imagery has long been linked to lineage descent (Miller 1974; Schele and Matthews 1998: 218–219). In the Postclassic period, serpent imagery symbolizes the links between founders of sites or new political regimes, lineages and conceptualizations of quadrupartite space, time, the heavens, and beings that dwell in the supernatural realm

(Houston 1984: 800; Fox 1987: 112–138; Prudence Rice 1989: 317; Headrick 1995; Schele and Matthews 1998: 218–219; Schele and Kappelman 1998). As these scholars have noted, Postclassic political iconography thus portrays elements of divine leadership that have their roots in past traditions along with newly redefined institutions that celebrate the importance of lineage power and the integration of multiple factions within communities and regions.

At Laguna de On, censer ritual is also concentrated only in a couple of locations, around Structures I and II in the north central zone of the island, and at a shrine on the west bluff of the lagoon (Structure V). Although the scale of ritual expression is reduced at Laguna de On compared to major centers, it reflects a similar pattern of control of ritual by probable leaders of the community. The ritual at all of these communities appears concerned with tying elites to the supernatural realm, and to the land, through celebration and glorification of lineage history. In these respects, Postclassic Maya ritual replicates historical institutions in a very deliberate way to meet the needs of emergent semiautonomous regional centers across the lowlands.

Although the discussion above emphasizes the local aspects of Postclassic period Maya religious traditions, this focus is not intended to deny the cosmopolitan nature of art of this period, as originally suggested by Robertson (1970) and Smith and Heath-Smith (1980). A recent important paper by Ringle, Negron, and Bey (1998) summarizes the transethnic spread of the feathered-serpent cult in the Epiclassic/Early Postclassic period in Mesoamerica. It is clear that centers during the Late Postclassic period were building upon earlier foundations in important ways. In the following section, I outline ways in which the myths of Kukulkan and other retrospective conceptualizations of ancient religious traditions were revitalized and appropriated for the purposes of Late Postclassic elites.

LATE POSTCLASSIC RELIGIOUS REVIVALS

The timing of the florescence of Late Postclassic centers along the east coast and Late Facet religious developments at Laguna de On coincides with the rise of Mayapan to power and expansionist tendencies generated by political regimes at this site. Mayapan lords had vested interests in attaining broad-scale lowland integration, as its political alliances and the foundation of its exchange economy lay in the eastern/southern realm of Quintana Roo and Belize. An argument is made below that the revival of earlier conventions, along with the introduction of new ones, in the art of Postclassic period Maya temples was generated by the polity of Mayapan. Furthermore, this ideological campaign was motivated by a desire to integrate, encourage, and influence distant provinces upon whose productivity the power of this late city depended. The patterns described here were briefly suggested by Thompson in 1945 (1945: 18), which he termed the Maya "resurgence" of Postclassic northern Yucatán. The long-term stability of the settlement at Laguna de On and the developmental trends observed in its exchange systems, ritual practice, and social hierarchy are inextricably linked to the Postclassic world of religion and trade that emanated from the northern center of Mayapan. A review of the political events and the strategies for development of the lowlands that were put into effect by this center provides important context for the changes observed over time at the rural community of Laguna de On.

"Revivalistic movements" were defined by Mooney in 1892 as movements that "emphasize the institution of customs, values, and even aspects of nature which are thought to have been in the mazeway of previous generations but are not now present" (Mooney 1889–1893, as paraphrased in Hicks 1999: 408). While revitalization cults are customarily attributed to cultures undergoing dramatic episodes of upheaval and destruction in the wake of colonial encounters, this definition is too narrow. Revival movements, as used here, can be initiated by powerful institutions, such as evangelical churches or nationalistic factions today—or they can represent the cultic doctrine of states formed by military coup, such as Mayapan. Revival movements do not necessarily have a grass-roots origin—although may claim to—and they may have strong grass-roots appeal as part of their cunning design. As Dahlin noted for Late Classic Tikal (1976: 331–332), state revitalization cults barely mask the strong desire of ruling factions to control trade and to centralize dissenting elements of society.

Postclassic religious institutions have earlier precedents in the practice of ancestor commemoration and conjuring, the portrayal of deities known from earlier times, reuse of symbols of accession to political power such as k'awil, and the connection of serpent and jaguar imagery to powerful lineages and political rulership. Another earlier behavior that returned to popularity during the latter part of the Late Postclassic is the construction of mound architecture at centers such as Mayapan (Pollock et al. 1962), Tulum (Lothrop 1924), Caye Coco (Masson and Rosenswig 1998), Lamanai (Pendergast 1981), Topoxte (Bullard 1973), and Zacpeten (Rice, Rice, and Pugh 1998). An additional former institution that became in vogue again in the Late Postclassic is that of stelae erection or reerection as indicated by the prevalence of such monuments that were newly inscribed, recycled, stuccoed and painted, or blank at the sites of Mayapan (Proskouriakoff 1962b: 107), Tulum (Lothrop 1924), Ichpaatun (Gann 1926: 53), Lamanai (Gann 1926: 65), Sarteneja (Sidrys 1983: 170–171), and Chan Chen (Sidrys 1983: 115–123). Resetting of earlier stelae was an important act of religious integration during the Classic period as well (Schele and Freidel 1990: 197).

The utility of revival movements is not limited to expiring cultures documented in the realms of nineteenth-century European colonial frontiers (Wallace 1956; Hicks 1999). Rather, the sponsorship of religious cultlike phenomena can directly support the aspirations of a political elite, precisely as Dahlin proposed for Ruler Hasaw-Kan-K'awil's late-seventh-century and early-eighth-century reign at Tikal (1976: 317, 324, 372, 367; also Schele and Freidel 1990: 197), which assisted in bringing this center back to prosperity from the brink of political and economic ruin. Revitalization movements in this latter sense can function as an important mode of integration during cyclic political upswings, as Dahlin (1976) suggests occurred in Tikal's Late Classic "comeback" to regional prominence. Demographic growth, the expansion and control of trading networks, and the intensification of local production accompany the conspicuous displays and rituals in state revitalizations that integrate supporting populations via the espousement of political ideology (Dahlin 1976: 331–332).

In northern Belize, a similar cycle is observed in the latter half of the Late Postclassic period. Religious intensification is observed in shrine construction and censer rituals (Chapters 4 and 6, above). An increase in regional populations is suggested by greater numbers of sites (Chapter 2) and evidence for hierarchical development is observed during the latter half of the Late Postclassic by the construction of mound architecture and a suite of other elite behaviors at contemporary, competing centers (Chapters 3 and 6, above). An acceleration in commercial activities is reflected by increased quantities of long-distance trade goods at sites such as Laguna de On. These trends imply that the eastern/southern lowland realm was gaining momentum during this latest of Maya developmental cycles.

This cycle was inspired by the actions of elites at Mayapan and in its allied provinces, who cajoled and manipulated local populations in the sponsorship of calendrical rituals and other periodic festivals and markets (Freidel 1981). The replication of ritual symbols and features at all levels of the settlement hierarchy, a trend that has its origins in earlier periods (Freidel 1983b: 41), was highly effective in bringing home elite ideology in the true sense of the word. The modest censer shrines at Laguna de On represent one local manifestation of this ideology at the lower end of the settlement continuum.

A primary characteristic of revival movements is the precondition of cultural depression or stress (Wallace 1956; Dahlin 1976; Hicks 1999: 407–408). More research must be done in parts of the lowlands before the evidence for such a state of being can be assessed prior to the Late Postclassic revival. Based on the Laguna de On data and reports of other thriving communities in the eleventh and twelfth centuries in northern Belize (Pendergast 1981, 1985, 1986; Sidrys 1983: Map 2; Michaels 1987; Andrews and Vail

1990), current evidence does not suggest that the Chetumal province subregion was suffering from depression or stress. To the contrary, the domestic features and artifact assemblages of the Early Facet of Laguna de On paint the profile of an affluent, growing settlement linked into well-established local and long-distance regional exchange systems. Similarities in the economic assemblages from the early and late stratigraphic deposits and features from this site indicate that while trade, political activities, and social distinctions may have intensified to a certain degree over time, the economic foundations of these late patterns have their origins in the site's earlier occupation. No evidence suggests that economic systems were disrupted or substantially altered over time at Laguna de On from A.D. 1050 to 1500, although burial patterns do indicate an unexplained decline in standardized mortuary behavior at this site.

It is possible to speculate on the meaning of these patterns reflected at this rural, and provincial, site in the Postclassic Mesoamerican international world of trade. Throughout the previous chapters of this book, it has been noted that two sequential major northern Yucatán centers are affiliated with "world systems" of trade and exchange with highland Mexico via a circum-Yucatecan maritime trade route. The first of these centers that was actively involved in the facilitation and control of a "multiple core" trading network for Yucatán is the site of Chichén Itzá (Andrews et al. 1988; Kepecs, Feinman, and Boucher 1994: 153–154). Certain provinces allied with Chichén Itzá, such as the Chikinchel province, experienced their maximum development and economic florescence along with this site during the earlier part of the Postclassic period (Andrews et al. 1988; Kepecs, Feinman, and Boucher 1994). The emergence of Mayapan follows the fall of Chichén Itzá (Landa 1941; Pollock 1962), and some trading networks came under Mayapan's influence in the thirteenth century (Freidel and Sabloff 1984). The rise of Mayapan to power is accompanied by the establishment of a number of Late Postclassic east-coast Quintana Roo centers and it is contemporary with the hierarchical processes observed at Laguna de On and contemporary sites in northern Belize. The early-fifteenth-century rise of the Aztec Empire is thought by some to have created a core-periphery dynamic of interaction between the highlands and the lowlands as part of a Late Postclassic world system (Blanton and Feinman 1984; Kepecs, Feinman, and Boucher 1994: 142, 153–154; Carmack 1996). It is probably too simplistic to conceive of the Maya Lowlands as a mere "periphery" of an Aztec sphere, as the Maya area was thriving for centuries prior to the rise of the Aztec Empire. However, it is likely that this central Mexican polity provided important impetus to commercial activities of affluent regions such as the Yucatán peninsula. These effects would have been very late, and could only have augmented an existing commercial florescence that was at that time linked to Mayapan's thirteenth-century rise to power and its subsequent two hundred years of rule in northwest Yucatán.

The degree to which the fall of Chichén Itzá would have affected distant, peripheral sites such as Laguna de On is negligible, especially if newly proposed revisions are current in suggesting that Chichén's position as a primary center was over by A.D. 1000 (Ringle, Negron, and Bey 1998; Bey, Hanson, and Ringle 1997), before Laguna de On Island was settled. Factional competition in northern Yucatán did lead to the rise of Mayapan after A.D. 1200, however, and this event appears to have more of an impact on northern Belize political and economic patterns. A series of revivalistic movements sponsored by the rulers of this center after the usurpation of "foreigners" in Yucatán, described below, greatly served the interests of Mayapan's elite. Some critical events associated with Mayapan's rise to power are outlined in Table 6.8, which summarizes documentary evidence and correlating archaeological trends.

The Chronology of Mayapan's Rise to Power

The history of northern Yucatán is complicated, controversial, and currently undergoing radical revision (see Chapter 3). Bey, Hanson, and Ringle's (1997) earlier chronology for Chichén Itzá may place the fall of this center to shortly before A.D. 1000, as the architecture of this site was completed by this date. The degree to which Chichén Itzá's earlier chronology affects the dating of Mayapan is unclear. It is known from Landa that Mayapan was occupied for five hundred years before Spanish arrival (Landa 1941), and the records suggest that Chichén Itzá and Mayapan were initially founded or refounded together by Kukulcan. Archaeologically, we know that Mayapan was occupied prior to A.D. 1200 (Pollock 1962; Proskouriakoff 1962a: 132; Smith 1971), and perhaps it was first "founded" as a minor shrine community by Kukulkan cult-related events as early as the tenth century, as the documents suggest (Landa 1941; Tozzer 1941). The sites of Chichén Itzá, Mayapan, Uxmal, and others had a long history of competitive skirmishes among rival factions during the Postclassic period that almost assuredly extended beyond Chichén's architectural construction dates discussed by Ringle, Negron, and Bey (1998), Bey, Hanson, and Ringle (1997), and colleagues. Regardless of these earlier events, evidence suggests that Mayapan emerged as the dominant center in western Yucatán after A.D. 1200.

The First Wave — Founding of Saclactun Mayapan

The founding of Mayapan took place over several katuns, following the defeat of Chichén's Itzá polity (Table 6.8). It occurred after the retreat of Itzá factions to Tan Xuluc Mul in the Peten, and their subsequent return, recharged, "from the east" (Roys 1962). If these accounts are right, then the

Table 6.8—Chronology of Mayapan (extracted from Roys 1962 {RY}; Barrera Vasquez and Morley 1949 {BVM}; Landa/Tozzer 1941 {LD, TZ, or LD/TZ}; Schele 1995 {SCH}; and Ringle, Negron, and Bey 1998 {RGL})

Katun	Year A.D.	Political Prophecy/History	Archaeological Correlations
8 AHAU	948	Morley thinks Mayapan founded as early as 948—not as a political center, but as a community {TZ}.	evidence of occupation of Mayapan during the Terminal Classic/Early Postclassic, though not a major center (Pollock 1962)
		Ringle et al. think Chichén's apocalypse occurred at this time {RGL}. This apocalypse may refer only to the Epiclassic polity centered at this site, or it may imply that the events listed for the next katun 8 Ahau (1185–1204) would have occurred at this time instead. It is not currently known whether this thesis affects dates for the founding of Mayapan but little data suggests that Mayapan's emergence as a Late Postclassic center during the 13th century is questioned by the new Chichén chronology. These scholars note that Chichén continued to be occupied and involved in the affairs of Yucatán after this date. If RGL are correct, then BVM's idea (below) that a League of Mayapan established in katun 2 Ahau resulted in 200 years of relative peace becomes attractive, as it bridges the time gap between the collapse of Epiclassic Chichén and the rise of Late Postclassic Mayapan.	
		BVM agree that the Itzá were expelled at this time {BVM: 33}.	
4 AHAU	968–987	Landa/Tozzer think Mayapan was founded in this katun, as colonial sources say it was occupied for 500 years before the Spanish came {LD/TZ}. This view is compatible with RGL (above).	ditto the above
		Eric Thompson and George Brainerd thought Chichén was settled at this time {BVM}.	

Continued on next page

Table 6.8—*continued*

Katun	Year A.D.	Political Prophecy/History	Archaeological Correlations
		Barrera Vasquz and Morley think Itzá returned around this time {BVM: 33}.	
		Roys places first coming of Kukulcan around this time, with the arrival of the Itzá {RY}.	
2 AHAU	987–1007	Xiu factions established at Uxmal and Chacnabiton, possible time of founding of League of Mayapan between these sites and Mayapan and Chichén Itzá— a 200-year peace follows {BVM: 33–35}.	
8 AHAU	1185–1204	Inter-Itzá conflict, faction departs Chichén Itzá (Pollock 1962), Chakanpu-tun attack, retreat to Tan Xuluc Mul in Peten {RY}, then re-emerge to establish Saclactun Mayapan over several katuns, coming back north from the east {RY}.	Stela 1 from Mayapan katun 8 Ahau (Morley suggested A.D. 1185, according to Proskouriakoff 1962a)
		Some scholars place the Hunac Ceel/Mayapan overthrow of Izamal and Chichén Itzá here {SCH; BVM: 34–35}, dissolving the League. Seven men of Mayapan are also involved in this—their names are largely nahuat {BVM: 35–36}.	A.D. 1100–1200: full development of eastern/southern redware and unslipped Postclassic traditions, which may evolve earlier than the Mayapan assemblages that they reresemble in fundamental ways, though local variation in decoration of certain vessels is observed.
6 AHAU	1204–1224	discontent with Chichén Itzá regime, heavy taxation, need to destroy evil leaders, prediction that after this "the earth shall face upward; then downward a second time" {RY}	ditto the above
4 AHAU	1224–1244	denial of obedience, half of katun is good, half is bad and miserable {RY}	ditto the above Stela 5 from Mayapan katun 4 Ahau (Morley thought dates to A.D. 1244, according to Proskouriakoff 1962a)
		Kukulkan comes to Chichén Itzá (a second coming) to restore order (the good half of katun).	

Continued on next page

Table 6.8—*continued*

Katun	Year A.D.	Political Prophecy/History	Archaeological Correlations
		Revival of Venus cult? Star names and references to dawn {RY}.	
		4 AHAU seen as major break with the past {RY}.	
		Itzá expelled treacherous lords of Mayapan and seized the land (in revenge of the Hunac Ceel event). The Itzá did this with the King of Izamal (Ulil) {BVM: 37}. The Mayapan lords were possibly the Cocom who had come with Kukulcan in the 10th century {BVM}, who were known for their Mexican allies in later times. The Cocom were probably from the same foreign faction as Hunac Ceel {BVM: 39}.	
13 AHAU	1263–1283	Founding of Mayapan by a faction of the Itzá—"Maya men they were named"—who came from Tan Xuluc Mul {BVM: 47}.	Stela 6 from Mayapan katun 13 Ahau (Morley thought dates to A.D. 1283, according to Proskouriakoff 1962a)
		Mats set in order, site organized with houses for lords—the land is divided among them. Kukulcan helps to establish this site and names it "standard of the Maya." Maya is the language spoken in the country {LD}.	Sometime in the 13th century, a shift appears in eastern/southern sites. Older centers are replaced by new ones in Belize, new centers such as Tulum are founded. As timing is imprecise, it is not known if these events are the result of ongoing local competition, or if they are tied more broadly to alliances/factions in the north.
			erection or re-erection of stela and altars or conspicuous reuse of stela in bldgs at eastern/southern sites—timing is difficult

Continued on next page

Table 6.8—*continued*

Katun	Year A.D.	Political Prophecy/History	Archaeological Correlations
			to assess—A.D. 1200–1500; candidates for re-dedication: Tulum stelae (orig. dates A.D. 564, 702), Ichpaatun Stela 1 (orig. date A.D. 593), and many uncarved stela at Belize sites.
			political founding or re-founding of centers such as Caye Coco, Santa Rita, Tulum, Cozumel in the late 13th or early 14th centuries.
11 AHAU	1283–1303	continued accounts of expulsion of foreigners in the two katuns before A.D. 1303 {BVM}	ditto
9 AHAU	1303–1323	period of terror, "sin is his katun," adultery {RY}	ditto
7 AHAU	1323–1342	erotic cult of *nicte*, "shame" {RY}	ditto
5 AHAU	1342–1362	things get worse, perversity, shame, few children born local lords lose power—possibly a reference to consolidation of Mayapan's power {RY} complaining lords resort to sorcery, turn into animals, predatory, predict rebellion—"the tame dog shall bite his master" {RY} dissension in assembly at Mayapan—"they bite one another, the snakes and jaguars" {RY}	New attributes join local utilitarian assemblages around A.D. 1250–1350. Deeper red-slipped pottery and new forms like those of Mayapan appear in addition to continued local wares. It is thought that eastern/southern pottery was the initial inspiration for Mayapan wares by the 12th century, but this center was an innovator and the direction of emulation soon began to also flow from north to east

Continued on next page

Table 6.8—*continued*

Katun	Year A.D.	Political Prophecy/History	Archaeological Correlations
			and south—close relationships of these areas with Mayapan.
3 AHAU	1362–1382	revolution during this katun and beginning of next one {RY}; "offspring of harlots" killed, noble lineage chiefs come to power (Cocoms)—Roys thinks another Itzá faction {RY}	ditto the above
		Cocoms claim descendancy from Kukulcan {RY}	
		Cocoms bring in Canul Mexican allies from Tabasco {RY}	
1 AHAU	1382–1401	Itzá faction exodus to Chakanputun—Roys thinks from Mayapan rather than Chichén Itzá {RY}	approximate timing of appearance of Chen Mul effigy censer complex at Mayapan (Pollock 1962) and throughout lowlands—new centers are "buying in" to this cult in a major way, probable time of Tulum Str. 16 (Temple of the Frescoes)
12 AHAU	1401–1421	happy time, "kind chiefs," "poor become rich" {RY} Mayapan sometimes referred to as Saclactun—its old name? {RY}	continued use of Chen Mul censer rituals? pilgrimage and stela activity?
10 AHAU	1421–1441		katun markers at Otzmal, Sisal
8 AHAU	1441–1461	expulsion of another group from Chichén Itzá	
		destruction of Mayapan, Mexican role in city blamed, taking locals as slaves	Mayapan abandoned
		Roys places Hunac Ceel/Mayapan treachery against Izamal and Chichén Itzá here	Belize sites continue to prosper

founders of Mayapan drew their strength from their Peten and east coast allies (or homeland; see Schele, Grube, and Boot 1995). The unresolved question at this moment is the precise timing of this event, but most scholars agree that the process of an Itzá faction's founding of Mayapan was completed during katun 13, A.D. 1263–1283. However, historical sources indicate that this site was one of several players in the northern Yucatán struggle for power for at least two hundred years prior to this date, and that the site was periodically controlled by local Itzá factions and rival groups in the company of their Mexican allies from the twelfth century forward. In their reading of the chronicles, Barrera Vasquez and Morley (1949: 33–35) propose that the League of Mayapan alliance was formed by Mayapan, Uxmal, and Chichén Itzá by A.D. 1007 (katun 2 Ahau), followed by two hundred years of relative peace. In katun 8 Ahau (A.D. 1185–1204), this alliance is dissolved, perhaps by Hunac Ceel of Mayapan's treacherous overthrow of Chichén Itzá and Izamal aided by Mexican mercenaries (Barrera Vasquez and Morley 1949: 34–36). The process of Late Postclassic Mayapan's difficult birth was begun.

Stela 1 from Mayapan has a probable date of A.D. 1185—the beginning of the rocky katun 8 Ahau (Morley's estimated date, quoted in Pollock 1962). The use of a stela was symbolic, I believe, of ancient Classic period roots (see also Proskouriakoff 1962a: 134). This stela may be retrospective, if Barrera Vasquez and Morley are correct in suggesting that Mayapan was in foreign hands during this katun. One of the first references to the founding of Saclactun Mayapan falls within this katun—although this act is said to take several katuns to accomplish. Roys (1962) feels Saclactun may have been the ancient name of Mayapan, another retrospective reference. The road ahead was rough at this time, however, as references of strife and struggle in northern Yucatán do not culminate in the dominance of Mayapan center until a hundred years later, in katun 13 Ahau or A.D. 1263–1283.

The Emergence of Mayapan as the Dominant Northern Center

Two other katun-ending dates are recorded on stelae from Mayapan (fifty-nine and ninety-eight years later), and these appear more directly related to the rise of this center to prominence. These are Stela 5 (A.D. 1244) and Stela 6 (A.D. 1283), which Morley placed in the thirteenth century, and there is no reason to believe he was incorrect. The first date (1244) marks the end of katun 4 Ahau, a katun described by Roys as seen as "a major break with the past" in the Maya chronicles (1962). He also notes numerous star names and references to the dawn in these sources, which he suggests may represent a "revival" of a Venus cult previously popular at Chichén Itzá.

The chronicles also refer to a second coming of Kukulkan to Chichén at this time. Perhaps this prophet was evoked to restore order in what was a very troubled katun. The Itzá expelled strangers living in the region during this katun (Roys 1962). It becomes evident that while Kukulkan was heralded in northern Yucatán as a foreign creator-deity associated with dynastic origins (Ringle, Negron, and Bey 1998: 223), this deity or priests/prophets in the guise of this deity were also invoked in the revitalization of troubled polities.

Kukulkan is also credited with helping to establish Mayapan as a center in katun 13 Ahau (Landa 1941), which may also be tied to this deity's second coming in A.D. 1263–1283. Stela 6 from Mayapan dates to the ending of this katun, and along with Stela 5 and twenty-five other plain stela, the archaicism begun a hundred years earlier with Stela 1 was continued (Proskouriakoff 1962a: 134). According to Landa's informants (1941), Kukulkan gave this center its name, "the standard of the Maya . . . because Maya is the language spoken in the country." Although cryptic, this reference may refer to local rather than foreign identity, as the language spoken in the country most likely refers to that of the majority of local, indigenous populations. Ironically, the chronicles state that a faction of the Itzá founded Mayapan at this time. However, this may have been a faction with strong local ties, referred to in the chronicles as "Maya men they were named," who came from the Tan Xuluc Mul Peten location and who expelled the foreigners (Barrera Vasquez and Morley 1949: 47). Their revival of the stela cult may reflect their heralded claim to local antiquity (see Schele, Grube, and Boot 1995 for further evidence of Itzá historical ties to the lowland Classic period). This katun 13 Ahau, then, reflects Mayapan's ultimate rise to dominance in northern Yucatán and its underlying legitimation, which appropriates both the foreign cultic icon of Kukulkan in foundation myths of this katun and local identity in the site's name, ruling personnel, and invocation of earlier stela traditions. The Castillo was most likely built or modified at this time as a revitalization of Epiclassic Chichén Itzá's Kukulkan cult (Proskouriakoff 1962a: 132). These rulers crafted a savvy identity of relatively recent Chichén icons, as well as more distant Classic period symbolism observed in the practice of stela erection.

Other Late Postclassic Maya centers founded by the thirteenth century followed suit in the erection of stela or circular altars (now plain, probably formerly stuccoed and painted) or the rededication or reuse of Classic period stelae from ancestral sites. This pattern is exhibited at Tulum (Lothrop 1924), Ichpaatun (Gann 1926: 53), Lamanai (Gann 1926: 65), Sarteneja (Sidrys 1983: 170–171), Chan Chen (Sidrys 1983: 115–123), and Caye Coco (Barnhart 1998b), among others. Resetting of earlier stelae was an important act of revitalization during the Classic period as well (Dahlin 1976; Schele and Freidel 1990: 197).

The characteristic red-slipped Mayapan ceramics and unslipped wares were most likely developed during the difficult birth of this center during the twelfth or thirteenth centuries, or slightly earlier (see discussion in Chapter 3). These wares are closely related to the assemblages of the eastern/southern realm of the Yucatán peninsula (Quintana Roo and Belize) (Robles 1986c; Connor 1983; Sanders 1960) and the institution of these new styles represented a clear break with the northern Yucatán immediate past. These wares originate earlier in the eastern/southern realm and develop from Terminal Classic southern traditions (Graham 1987). As such, the adoption of this style at Mayapan may have also emphasized connections to the more distant past as well as the eastern/southern provinces that formed a critical component of its economic empire (Robles 1986a, 1986b; Freidel and Sabloff 1984; Andrews and Robles 1986).

The Second Wave — The Cocom Usurpation and the Censer Cult

A second revitalization is recorded at Mayapan in the spread of the Chen Mul censer cult that emerges from this center toward the very end of its reign. Pollock (1962) and Roys (1962) document a hostile revolt in the historic records during katun 3 Ahau (A.D. 1362–1382) that marks the probable Cocom takeover of this site with the backing of allies from the Mexican Gulf Coast. Like many other previous regimes, the Cocoms claimed descendancy from Kukulkan (Roys 1962). Pollock (1962: 8) attributes the effigy-censer cult to this group, and given the likely traumatic effects of this usurpation and the growing dissent voiced in previous katuns (Table 6.8), Yucatán was again in need of revitalization.

Based on the numbers of these effigies at Mayapan, which far surpass those observed at any other site, it is clear that this tradition sprang from this center and was promoted by its leadership. The far-reaching effects of these rituals are reflected in the manufacture of these effigies as far south as the Peten (Bullard 1973). Their widespread geographic distribution reflects the degree to which the northern and southern lowlands were integrated during the Late Postclassic period, an observation that is also supported by architectural (Don Rice 1988), utilitarian ceramic, economic, and historic evidence (Pina Chan 1978; Masson 1999c). These entities closely replicate the imagery and symbolism shown on the Tulum and Santa Rita murals, which depict probable lineage ancestors and gods recognizable from the Classic period. Some imagery of the murals and effigy censers may also represent a late reinstitution of the Quetzalcoatl/Kukulkan cult that Ringle, Negron, and Bey (1998) suggest was originally sponsored by the center of Chichén Itzá between A.D. 800 and 1000. Symbolism such as the Ik glyph for wind (step-terrace motif) and the reptile-eye glyph associated with the censers and murals make this identification fairly secure, as described previously. As Kukulkan was known as a deity of origin and renewal, incorporating aspects of this earlier cult into Late Postclassic ritual practice fit well in a pan-lowland revival of local history.

The use of effigies that may have represented this hero, as well as depictions of community or lineage gods, would have reconciled foreign and local avenues of legitimation. The types of effigies found in provinces distant from the center of Mayapan indicate that local lords emulated this cult on their own terms, as the full pantheon of deities found in the Yucatán center are not found in outlying provinces. Many effigies are more generic, and they may have been conducive to more flexible interpretations of their identity to include local lineage ancestors and gods.

The result of the Cocom revitalization at Mayapan and its self-serving emulation in the eastern/southern realm was widespread integration and an economic boom that marked a new florescence for participating centers and their surrounding communities engaged in pilgrimage trading circuits (Rathje 1975; Sabloff and Rathje 1975; Freidel and Sabloff 1984). This revitalization thus achieved the goal of the state that sponsored it—at least for one brief shining moment before the final apocalypse of katun 8 Ahau, which ended in A.D. 1461 and marked the collapse of Mayapan. Eastern/southern sites in Belize continued to prosper (Chase and Chase 1988; Graham 1987), riding the wave of profit and interaction that this great center had set into motion until the Pacheco brothers annihilated the Chetumal province in 1544–1545.

The assistance of mercenaries from Xicalanco mentioned in the initial Hunac Ceel event that culminated in Mayapan's rise to power reveals important external influence in the affairs of Late Postclassic Yucatán. Xicalanco was a primary Mesoamerican trading port that facilitated interaction and exchange between highland Mexico and the circum-Yucatecan maritime trade route (Scholes and Roys 1948). The enlistment of mercenaries from such a place almost assuredly was linked to economic interests of factions from Xicalanco and Mayapan. Mexican "troops" were enlisted a second time during Mayapan's rule (Barrera and Morley 1949: Table 6), when the Cocom assumed power of this capital. These accounts reflect the strong interests and interference of outsiders in the political and economic matters of northern Yucatán from a few key historical events. Between the gaps left by these accounts, it is probable that substantial economic activities provided ongoing links between the reigning northern center and the Gulf Coast port. It is not known whether foreign traders or their mercenaries were present in great numbers, but they were pleased to provide assistance as needed to foster continued or improved economic symbiosis between Mayapan and the Gulf Coast.

These Late Postclassic political activities affected the Lowland Maya sphere far to the south at sites such as Laguna de On, where Late Facet developments are contemporary with Mayapan's reign and its religious proselytization. Later features at Laguna de On Island suggest that a wave of change affected this community sometime after A.D. 1250. Similarly, Late Facet Xabalxab ceramic changes at the nearby site of Santa Rita adopt some attributes of Mayapan ceramics after A.D. 1300 (Diane Chase 1984; Chase and Chase 1988). Late Postclassic sites throughout the lowlands possess local versions of Mayapan-style effigy censers (Sidrys 1983; Valdez 1987; Chase and Chase 1988; Robles 1986c; Smith 1971). Evidence reviewed above suggests that there was not just one effort at reviving and integrating Late Postclassic provinces, but rather that it was a process that began in the twelfth century and continued through the fifteenth century through various regimes.

The widespread geographic distribution of the Chen Mul ceramic effigies reflects the degree to which the northern and southern lowlands were integrated toward the end of the Late Postclassic period, an observation that is also supported by architectural (Don Rice 1988), ceramic (discussed in Chapter 3), economic (discussed in Chapter 5), and ethnohistoric evidence (Pina Chan 1978; Jones 1989). The entities depicted in effigy form are identifiable as primarily ethnic Maya individuals or gods, with a very small number (at Mayapan only) exhibiting characteristics of highland Mexican deities (Thompson 1957). This pattern makes sense, considering the role of Mexican allies in the founding events of the Cocom reign. The lack of Mexican deities identified in these effigies outside of the site of Mayapan in the eastern/southern realm reflects a more local basis of power at provincial communities.

It was noted in Chapters 4 and 5 that ritual artifacts and features increased over time at Laguna de On. This same pattern is observed for Mayapan (Smith 1971) and Santa Rita (Chase and Chase 1988). The relative increase in effigy censers in the latter portion of the Late Postclassic is a pattern observed at all sites where these artifacts have been recovered (Sanders 1960; Smith 1971; Bullard 1973; Diane Chase 1982; Sidrys 1983; Valdez 1987; Prudence Rice 1987a; Walker 1990), and they clearly represent an intensification in certain types of ritual activity. Prior to the advent of effigy censers, large numbers of appliqué, noneffigy forms such as Cehac-Hunacti composite are numerous in Postclassic assemblages (Smith 1971; Walker 1990), and these ceramics continue to be used along with the effigies throughout the Late Postclassic sequence (Walker 1990).

The acceleration of religious activities represented by the effigy censers is temporally associated with a late florescence of Mayapan and its affiliated east-coast and Belize-region sites. The symbolism of the effigies is replicated in religious temple art at Late Postclassic centers. Political regimes in power at these centers fostered and encouraged the acceleration of religious activities involving these effigies, which embody symbolism of deified ancestors or gods and the legitimation of the status quo. This state-sponsored cult served the purpose of revitalizing, integrating, and motivating participating polities, ideologically and economically, during the late cycle of growth that was experienced by the Mayapan/east-coast/Belize group of provinces in the lowlands.

The Late Postclassic intensification of religious practice in some respects represents a regional-scale revival of earlier Lowland Maya institutions in tandem with the adoption of a new set of symbols and rituals from a cosmopolitan milieux of interacting international elites. Links to the past were not direct, or literal, but were drawn by Postclassic community elites in an effort to legitimate their power through the manipulation and local interpretation of their own history.

7

Postclassic Maya Cultural Development in the Realm of Nachan Kan

This study of the Postclassic Maya realm of the community of Laguna de On provides an example of mature state development that contributes toward the revision of traditional notions of the life cycles of civilizations. A complementary relationship between village economics and the loose modes of political governance within the region is revealed at this time. During the Late Postclassic era, the degree of centralization, power, control, and hierarchy achieved by earlier city-states of the Classic period was no longer desirable or tolerated. As a result, many vertical aspects of the organization of Classic period Maya society were transformed to horizontal modes during the Postclassic period. Semiautonomy from centralized authority was enjoyed by communities and political territories throughout the lowlands. Although political control of the economy was relatively weak, this decentralized Lowland Maya society was nonetheless complex, affluent, and stable.

Variation is observed in the development of hierarchy and power across the landscape. Power is most concentrated during the Postclassic period at the center of Mayapan, although smaller centers were located along the east coast of the Yucatán peninsula and at some inland lacustrine sites such as Caye Coco, Lamanai, and sites of the Peten Lakes. The influence of Mayapan on distant affiliated territories is seen primarily in religious interaction that provided occasions for economic exchange and affirmed long-distance political alliances (Freidel 1981; Freidel and Sabloff 1984; Miller 1982). The emulation of Mayapan-like effigy-censer rituals throughout the lowlands region is a conspicuous example of the broad geographic extent of this interaction sphere. Attributes of utilitarian technology, such as the addition of new ceramic forms in the latter half of the Postclassic period, also reflect close economic relationships among eastern and southern provinces and Mayapan (Chapter 3; Graham 1987; Chase and Chase 1988).

Political power was expressed in various ways at major and minor centers of this era in different types of architectural, sculptural, or mural traditions (Chapter 6). This variation reflects a degree of autonomy and creativity exercised by local elites in the manner in which power was symbolized. Despite this variation, centers of this period exhibit a pattern of multiple, co-resident elite lineages and artistic traditions that celebrate lineage histories. The institution of *multepal* (Roys 1957), or group rule, is reflected in these configurations of art and architecture. Confederations of elites ruled Late Postclassic centers and their supporting territories. These assemblies provided checks and balances on the rise of hierarchy through mechanisms for power sharing such as office rotation (Love 1994). Although such leveling institutions were in place, Postclassic elite society was competitive, as numerous rivalries, conflicts, and skirmishes are noted in the documentary accounts (Barrera Vasquez and Morley 1949; Jones 1989, 1999). Variation is observed in the success of confederation rule and the degree of hierarchichal development in the ethnohistory of this region (Roys 1957; Marcus 1993; Jones 1999; Okoshi 1992; Quezada 1993; Alexander 1999; Kepecs 1998). Much archaeological research remains to be done before this variation can truly be assessed.

The study of Laguna de On suggests that the degree of elite competition and interaction in the Chetumal province during the Late Postclassic period did not disturb the stability of this territory's flourishing staple-goods economy, which developed steadily during the five hundred years before Spanish arrival. An increase in elite activities during the latter half of the Postclassic period at Laguna de On resulted in a surge of community development. This development is indicated by construction projects that expanded the island's living surface and created ritual facilities (Chapter 4). An increase in the acquisition of long-distance items at this site at all household areas also occurs (Chapter 5).

Utilitarian economy was probably under the control of community producers such as those of Laguna de On, who made and marketed their own commodities. There is little evidence for monopolization of production or privileged exchange of everyday products such as ceramics, local-stone tools, or textiles. A pronounced prestige economy that would have advertised elite distinctions is not evident, as distributions of exotic valuables among elite and nonelite residential areas are relatively equitable at Laguna de On. Upper-status living areas exhibit slightly greater quantities of obsidian blades and shell-working debris, but there are no exclusive distributions of any local or long-distance commodities at the site. A continuum of social-status differentiation is reflected in the distribution of economic items at Laguna de On domestic zones (Chapter 5). A greater degree of overall social affluence and a more equitable distribution of wealth during the Postclassic period compared to earlier times is one characteristic of the rise of "mercantile" society (Rathje 1975; Sabloff and Rathje 1975). Despite the lack of economic differentiation, at larger sites such as Santa Rita, elites possessed more prestige than other community members. This prestige was grounded in the organization and promotion of ritual and the possession of rare valuables such as metal ornaments (Chase and Chase 1988; Diane Chase 1992).

What was the role of elites in Postclassic Maya society? Freidel (1981: 378–381) proposes that elite sponsorship of a multitude of calendrical and other ritual celebrations provided important occasions for festivals, pilgrimages, and markets. As the location of various festivals was rotated among different communities, a phenomenon repeatedly documented by Landa's account (1941), these events were an important means for economic integration as they provided regularly timed opportunities for exchange (Freidel 1981: 378). Such exchange was accomplished through other ways as well, and true market towns existed at the time of Spanish contact (Roys 1957; Freidel 1981: 381). The documents suggest that elites were integral to market functions during the Postclassic period (Scholes and Roys 1948; Roys 1957; Freidel 1981; Miller 1982). The archaeological expression of elite status through various forms of ritual practice may thus indirectly reflect the sponsorship of important religious and economic events by this segment of society that facilitated integration and exchange.

POLITICAL AND ECONOMIC INSTITUTIONS FROM THE CLASSIC TO POSTCLASSIC PERIODS

In his introductory remarks to *The Sources of Social Power*, Michael Mann (1986: 63) points out that in the history of cultural development around the world, people only rarely submit themselves to coercive, centralized state power. They are reluctant to relinquish power to elites that they cannot recover, and always reserve the right to walk away (1986: 67). He classifies societies in terms of their effectiveness at constructing "social cages." Factors such as the boundedness of territories, intensive, tethering labor techniques such as irrigation, or the unequal distribution of locally accessible resources can result in concentrations of wealth and power that can lead to centralized, enforceable authority. In largely unbounded terrain, in which many pockets of cultivable land and other resources critical to survival are found, stringent social cages form with greater difficulty (Mann 1986: 63).

Mesoamericanists have long characterized the Maya area as relatively unbounded with dispersed, widely available resources suitable for the support of agrarian settlements. These characteristics inhibited the centralization of economic power during the Classic period (Sanders and Price 1968: 134, 145; Freidel 1981; Blanton et al. 1993: 163). Classic period centers were consumers of utilitarian items manufactured in the countryside, and they did not control the production or distribution of commonly used items (Rands and Bishop 1980; Prudence Rice 1987b). Utilitarian production remained largely under the control of a dispersed rural population throughout the Classic period (King and Potter 1994; Hester and Shafer 1994: 247; Potter and King 1995; Prudence Rice 1987b: 77–79; McAnany 1989: 363–364, 1993), and the basis for elite power lay primarily in a prestige-goods economy, political competition, and display (Demarest 1992; Ball 1993; Blanton et al. 1996; Reents-Budet 1994). Such display was costly in the Peten core region, and heavy tribute was required by some kingdoms to underwrite expenditures of political validation such as elaborate architecture, personal adornments, lavish gifts and ceremonies, and warfare. These elite pursuits heavily taxed the resources of lower-ranked members of urban and rural Maya settlements. By no accident, this form of political power was not enduring (Demarest 1992).

Political hierarchy of the Classic period was less pronounced in the Belize subregion than it was in the Peten core (Fry 1990), which resulted in a greater degree of rural autonomy in this peripheral zone and more blurred social class development during the Classic period (McAnany 1995; Potter and King 1995). In an important essay on political collapse, Yoffee (1988: 15) points out that the rate of development and linkage among various cultural institutions (social, political, economic, and ideological) is not constant, and in some cases it is possible for an economy to stay strong in the face of political fragmentation. Yoffee (1988: 11) agrees with Simon (1965), who observed that horizontal links in society can be far stronger than vertical ones. Such horizontal integration often endures after the collapse of vertical power structures to provide the seeds for establishing a new social order. More recently, well-developed horizontal networks of social and economic power have been recognized in the Belize region during the Classic period that are referred to as a form "heterarchy" (Potter and King 1995). Relatively less hierarchical, more autonomous areas such as northern Belize made an easy transition to the more mercantile-oriented, politically decentralized regional organization of the Postclassic period (Masson and Mock n.d.).

The fundamental difference between Classic and Postclassic period Maya society thus lies in the presence or absence of a vertical realm of charismatic kings whose power was based primarily on a prestige economy (Demarest 1992; Ball 1993; Blanton et al. 1996). This upper social tier was lobbed off at the end of the Classic period, which resulted in greater local autonomy and more collective distribution of wealth and social power during the Postclassic period. Despite this general trend that is broadly observed, considerable local variation is also observed in the nature of Classic to Postclassic transformations in different subregions of the lowlands (Freidel 1986; Culbert 1988: 87–88). Geographic pockets such as northern Belize or the Peten Lakes regions do not display the dramatic decline in populations noted for other parts of the Peten (Don Rice 1986; Pendergast 1986; Culbert 1988:

88; Fry 1990), and areas of rich resources maintained and attracted Postclassic occupants after the Classic period collapse (Diane Chase 1982; Rice and Rice 1985; Chase and Chase 1985, 1988; Graham 1985; Pendergast 1986; Masson and Mock n.d.). A new society was formed by the eleventh century, one that did not express drastic differences in social standing and wealth. Instead, its members invested greater social energies into commerce (Rathje 1975; Sabloff and Rathje 1975).

Decentralized State Societies

This transformation of Postclassic Maya society is relevant not solely for the Maya area but also for understanding long-term patterns of cultural change in other regions of the world. Conventional schemes of the evolution of "civilizations" have focused primarily on the emergence of primary states or the rise of highly centralized secondary states or empires (Service 1962). In reality, the "rise" of state societies represents only a small slice in time in the trajectories of civilizations and a small portion of the world archaeological record (Yoffee 1988; Cowgill 1988). Recently refined models examine long-term developmental trends of state formation in terms of processes of centralization and segmentation (De Montmollin 1989; Blanton et al. 1996; Blanton 1998). An argument put forth twenty-five years ago by Rathje (1975) entered a plea for the analysis of the Postclassic Maya period as a significant late trend in the evolution of civilizations that has not been adequately addressed in archaeological analysis. Complex decentralized states ensue after the collapse of initial state formations in many areas. Some of these states, like those of the Postclassic Maya Highlands or Lowlands, possess the capacity to centralize rapidly under the right circumstances (Carmack 1981; Blake 1985; Fox 1987).

Though less intensively studied due to the lack of conspicuous architectural works, decentralized state societies represent a critical development of maturing civilizations. In many regions, such "post-Classic" social formations often directly participate in expanded worlds of commerce (Yoffee 1988: 16; Eisenstadt 1988: 242). They represent mercantile societies that are fundamentally different from large, centralized regional states, as Rathje and Sabloff have emphasized (Rathje 1975; Sabloff and Rathje 1975). Maturing, less centralized secondary states often enter into the historical period where they become subsumed into world systems of empires, and thus are consigned to the realm of historians or classical archaeologists (Mann 1986; Cowgill 1988: 271). Certainly, the Postclassic Maya fall into this flickering shadow of history, and indeed, the rich ethnohistory of this region has generated many models of cultural organization and transformation that await archaeological evaluation (Barrera Vasquez and Morley 1949; Roys 1957, 1962; Jones 1989, 1999; Okoshi 1992; Quezada 1993; Kepecs and Alexander 1999).

In the context of the study of comparative civilizations, models presented by Malcolm Webb (1964) and William Rathje (1975) originally threw down the gauntlet for the assessment of developmental changes in Postclassic Maya society. Revisiting these models with regard to the developmental trends described in this volume revives the insightful perspectives of these scholars on the profound social transformations of the Postclassic Maya era compared to the earlier Classic period. Malcolm Webb (1964: 463–478) proposed that well-developed states did not evolve in Mesoamerica until the Postclassic period in the Mexican highlands and the Maya area. Webb (1964: 465–478) based this claim on criteria for "progressive" or advanced states established from comparative studies of Old World civilizations by White (1959), Steward (1955), Willey (1953: 344–359), Kroeber (1948: 298–304), and Childe (1959: 412–421, 1960: 88–112, 1954). The term "progressive" is an unnecessarily unilinear one, and the reference to these states as mature conveys the meaning intended originally by Webb in a less predetermined tone. Key criteria for identifying progressive or mature conditions of state development, according to Webb (1964: 478), include the following: (1) increasing technological innovation and efficiency, (2) increase in size of political units, (3) universality in ideological concepts, (4) increased political stability, (5) increased capacity for broad-scale warfare, (6) less investment of surplus into religious architecture ("secularization"), and (7) an increased amount of intersocietal trade that has the effect of breaking down social barriers. The increases in these trends are considered relative to earlier institutions of state development.

Based on these criteria, Webb suggested that Postclassic Mesoamerican society was at a more mature point of political and economic development than the preceding Classic period. In applying these criteria to Postclassic Maya societal characteristics, Webb, Rathje, and Sabloff have documented technological innovation in maritime transport and efficiency of building styles of this period, the decreased investment in religious architecture, and the acceleration of international trade (Webb 1964; Rathje 1975; Sabloff and Rathje 1975). Webb's (1964: 478) criteria of the increase in size of political units is also reflected in the broad distribution of ceramic styles across the lowlands. These ceramic similarities do not indicate sharp boundaries among subregions and suggest fluidity of economic interaction (Masson 1999c). In Chapters 3 and 6, I argue that the degree of pan-lowland integration during the Late Postclassic was more pronounced than during preceding periods. This trend increased from the twelfth century forward and is observed in similar ritual and utilitarian material assemblages from the Peten Lakes to northern Yucatán. In a very real sense, Lowland Maya geography was no longer divided by clearly delineated territories of kingly networks (Masson 1999c).

Webb's third criteria for mature state development, the spread of universal ideological concepts, is observed during the Postclassic period in the use of Chen Mul ceramic effigies across the lowlands. Related Quetzalcoatl/ Kukulkan censer-cult paraphernalia originates as early as A.D. 800–1000 (Ringle, Negron, and Bey 1998) and is revitalized during a late regime at Mayapan. The use of international symbols in Postclassic murals is another sign of universalizing, boundary-transcending development of international identity (Robertson 1970; Smith and Heath-Smith 1980).

Increased political stability, Webb's fourth criteria, is implied for the Postclassic Maya Lowlands as major societal disruptions are not seen at sites such as Laguna de On through long periods of occupation. This stability is also reflected in the persistence for four to six hundred years (in various zones) of Postclassic ceramic styles throughout the lowlands that indicates long-term conservatism in production practices, economic production and interaction, and group identity. Although ethnohistoric documents record political skirmishes (Landa 1941; Barrera Vasquez and Morley 1949; Roys 1962; Jones 1999), the economic data from small settlements such as Laguna de On suggests that these did not greatly affect patterns of daily life. While political regimes came and went, the production activities were not interrupted or substantially altered. This trend suggests that important aspects of the economy were controlled by rural producers who were little affected by political posturing. The evolution of a "mercantile" state may in fact be the triumph of a collective stability, conceived of and maintained by the grassroots producers of Maya society (Rathje 1975; Rathje and Sabloff 1975).

Mesoamerican political organization of the Classic period was viewed by Webb as weak, incipient, and poorly integrated (1964: 472, 554–555). Other scholars have come to similar conclusions about the unstable nature of Peten heartland Classic period polities (Sanders and Price 1968; Rathje 1973: 373–375; Demarest 1997). Webb correctly notes that the "beauty" and "durability" of Classic period architecture, and its size, have led archaeologists to fuse their models of political complexity with architectural aesthetics (Webb 1964: 573), and their temporal sequences with stages of evolution (Webb 1964: 468–469, 472). He and Rathje (1975: 421) both have described Postclassic period architecture as more efficiently constructed. The use of wood and plaster at Chichén Itzá and Mayapan was more efficient, and "releases social energy for other purposes," according to Webb (1964: 580), who observed that the buildings of the Puuc area and Mayapan were designed to incorporate greater numbers of people compared to the confining buildings of the Classic period. Webb (1964: 579–581) characterizes this social transformation as the "secularization" of society, or a move away from social investment in religious architecture and religious paraphernalia and a proportionate increase in investment in "secular" matters such as commercial profit, education, science, and other matters besides divine king-focused cults of Classic period society, which were a "sink" for social energies among members of the population. Erasmus (1968) similarly characterized the emergence of Postclassic society as an "upward collapse."

Corporate Cognitive Codes

I have recently suggested that relatively greater ceramic stylistic standardization across the lowlands during the Postclassic period, a trend first observed at Cozumel Island (Rathje and Sabloff 1975), is due to broad pan-lowland integration (Masson 1999c). An additional phenomenon is observed in assemblages of this date that contrast with the Classic period—a reduction in the overall diversity of types and forms made by producers. Prudence Rice (1989) suggests that a decline in assemblage diversity correlates with a decline in social stratification. A decrease in social stratification does not necessarily imply a decrease in sociopolitical complexity in the case of Postclassic Maya society. Rather, a decrease in ceramic assemblage diversity may signal a social transformation toward more group-oriented or de-individualizing social mores, recently described by Blanton et al. (1996) as a "corporate" mode of organization.

The dual processual model of Mesoamerican political economies proposed by Blanton et al. (1996) is useful for explaining aspects of Postclassic Maya social transformations. Changes of this period are observed in different forms of architecture construction, a less pronounced social hierarchy, more open and inclusive market activities, a reduction in ceramic assemblage diversity, and the relatively equitable distribution of long-distance items among all members of society. The dual processual model distinguishes "corporate" societies, governed by more acephalous leadership, group-oriented architectural types and public spaces, and deflated intragroup social distances, from "network exclusionary" societies (Blanton et al. 1996). They suggest that decreased prestige differences among members of corporate societies are the product of consciously placed checks on quests for personal status. Archaeologically, corporate "egalitarian" codes are reflected in less individual and household differentiation based on "prestige" items. While Blanton et al. (1996) propose that the Maya rulership at the site of Chichén Itzá expressed corporate codes, these strategies remained significant beyond Chichén Itzá and are manifested in various ways throughout the Postclassic period from A.D. 1000 to 1500.

In contrast, "network exclusionary" societies are poorly integrated and they are bound by the charismatic rhetoric of political aggrandizers who compete with their cohorts for the control of prestige economies. This political strategy, which characterizes Classic period Maya kingdoms according to Blanton et al. (1996), enhanced social distances and was contingent on the maintenance of briefly enduring kingdoms that were founded primarily upon the central exchange of prestigious luxuries and the self-promotion of their leaders. According to this model, greater social differences among individuals and their families are observed in the archaeological record of these societies.

While the organization of Postclassic Maya society exhibits corporate strategies through ideals for governance such as *multepal* and the socially leveling effects of market exchange, important variation in the organization of lowland territories seems likely. As Blanton et al. (1996) observe, corporate strategies exist in dynamic tension with network strategies, and the Postclassic period reflects these dialectic codes. Hierarchical development is observed during the latter half of the Postclassic period along the east coast of the Yucatán peninsula. For example, sites such as Caye Coco constructed mound architecture and stone altars. Architecture at this site took the form of at least seven elite residences and one long structure or council house. This pattern reflects the existence of multiple factions of power and the coresidence of relatively equal elite families at this island center. At Tulum, the presence of multiple elite lineages is also indicated by the presence of multiple diving-god temples that are associated with different residential compounds (Chapter 6). This pattern is also found at Mayapan in the numerous colonnaded halls and serpent temples located in the site's monumental center (Proskouriakoff 1962a; Diane Chase 1992). Such multiple facilities suggest that power was shared or rotated at these communities as described in the documents (Roys 1957, 1962; Love 1994).

Blanton et al. (1996) observe that ambitious individuals who seek to monopolize power and prestige are present in most societies, and those social regimes that institutionalize corporate strategies have more formal mechanisms for constraining power monopolies and a cognitive code that discourages this type of behavior. The usurpations of Mayapan described in Chapter 6 reflect heavy competition among lineage factions at times in this site's history that resulted in episodic shattering of prior confederacies (Roys 1962). This site certainly represents the most centralized and hierarchical center of the Late Postclassic Maya world. Network strategies were more prevalent in the political leadership at this site despite numerous references to the desirability of forms of group rule (Barrera Vasquez and Morley 1949; Roys 1962). Throughout most regimes of Postclassic northern Yucatán, the *Books of Chilam Balam* express discontent with the abuse of power (as illustrated by examples in Table 6.8). Such literatures of resistance reflect codes held by society and espoused by competitors of existing regimes that provided a nemesis to the centralization of power in northwest Yucatán. According to Blanton (1998: 146), such societies restrict the exercise of power and reduce power monopolization through the dissemination of cognitive codes that are enacted in daily practice. Blanton suggests that democratic principles are not unique to Western civilizations, and that they may in fact have been initiated many times among preindustrial non-Western societies (1998: 147). In the more remote coastal and rural provinces such as Chetumal, power plays of local centers had far less devastating effects on the political and economic affairs of their supporting communities. Sites in northern Belize, including Laguna de On, show evidence of long-term stability (Pendergast 1985; Graham 1987; Chase and Chase 1988), despite a shift in power organization observed during the thirteenth century that is implied by a change in the location of local political centers, as argued in Chapter 2.

Postclassic social transformations are thus manifested in a variety of ways across the lowland landscape (Freidel 1986). The dual-processual model is useful for understanding the organization of Postclassic society, as it identifies important ideals of social leveling that were embraced during this period as well as contradictory forces of hierarchical development observed at some centers at this time. Consideration of the interplay of corporate and network strategies during the Postclassic Maya period builds upon previous models applied to this society that have advanced understanding of the evolutionary directions of maturing states (Webb 1964; Rathje 1975). Blanton (1998: 147) notes that corporate societies espouse an "egalitarian" cognitive code that can form in response to prior tyrannical regimes. The development of Postclassic Maya society after the collapse of Classic period kingdoms could certainly be characterized as an aftermath of tyranny. Although ideals of equality were represented in institutions such as *multepal*, and institutions such as open market exchange may have helped to decrease social distances, this does not mean that rampant inequalities were not present in such societies. For example, the institution of slavery is associated with the Cocom regime of Mayapan (Tozzer 1941: 35), and major Postclassic centers exhibit a greater degree of interhousehold status differentiation than do rural sites such as Laguna de On.

Blanton (1998) disengages the terms "state" and "centralization" that have been largely coterminous in linear models of evolution up to this point (with notable exceptions such as De Montmollin 1989, Carmack 1981, and Fox 1987), and he suggests that large, populous state societies often adopt a more decentralized configuration and can be composed of numerous "semi-autonomous subsystems" (Blanton 1998: 146). This term accurately describes the organization of the Late Postclassic Maya world, in which distant provinces were not strictly beholden to the northern center of Mayapan, though they participated heavily in its ideological realm and were connected to the same economic network as this site. Such territories were largely self-governed, but were also well-integrated with each other and with Mayapan through economic exchange and calendrical ritual celebrations.

A similar form of power organization is defined by Mann as extensive and diffused (1986: 7–10, Figure 1.1). Extensive power "refers to the ability to organize large numbers of people over far-flung territories in order to engage in minimally stable cooperation" (Mann 1986: 7). Mann defines diffused power networks as phenomena that "spread in a more spontaneous, unconscious, decentered way through a population, resulting in similar social practices that embody power relations but are not explicitly commanded" (1986: 8). This form of power is similar to the cognitive codes that are disseminated by corporate strategies described by Blanton and colleagues (Blanton et al. 1996; Blanton 1998). Well-developed systems of market exchange are identified by Mann as a circumstance that encourages the operation of extensive and diffused power networks, as it is through market interaction that members of society are integrated with one another. Extensive and diffused power networks are contrasted by Mann with alternative forms of "authoritative" or "intensive" power that are also present in complex societies (1986: 7, Figure 1.1). Markets are "enabling facilities," as are the development of class or national identities, for the universalizing tendencies of these forms of power across extensive geographic territories (Mann 1986: 10). Mann describes lateral networks of local semiautonomy among complex societies that are similar to those identified by Blanton and colleagues in the corporate model, and this type of organization is observed in the Late Postclassic Lowland Maya political landscape.

Blanton's "corporate" characteristics recall aspects of Webb's (1964) progressive model and Rathje and Sabloff's (Rathje 1975; Sabloff and Rathje 1975) mercantile model for the organization of Late Postclassic Maya society. The trends described in this book for the economy and organization of Laguna de On and the Postclassic Maya world in which it was nestled suggest that Webb, Rathje, and Sabloff astutely identified mature Maya social developments that were founded on principles of inclusiveness, prosperity, upward mobility, decentralized and weak political authority, control of labor and the distribution of local products by the producers themselves, semiautonomy, and mercantile profit. This view differs profoundly from lingering views of Postclassic Maya society as the impoverished or devolved remnants of a civilization's collapse. Original models of the Maya collapse were focused mainly on a decline in complexity that was measured by the breakdown of the following institutions: centralized authority, architectural construction, tomb burials, population levels, the erection of stela monuments, and the use of calendrical and writing systems (Tainter 1988: 166–178; Culbert 1974, 1988; Willey and Shimkin 1973). Only the first three institutions on this list actually demonstrate a tenable decline during the Maya southern lowlands collapse. Postclassic settlements were quite numerous in some regions (Don Rice 1986; Culbert 1988: 87–88), stela erection returned with the rise of Mayapan to power (Chapter 6), and the rich Postclassic Maya codex tradition indicates that writing and astronomy were present until the arrival of the Spanish. The "Maya" collapse, then, was primarily political and was most intensively felt by kingdoms of the Peten core of the southern lowlands. Other areas such as the Peten Lakes, Belize, and the northern lowlands show evidence of timely cultural transformation and reorganization (Erasmus 1965; Diane Chase 1982, 1986; Arlen Chase 1986; Chase and Chase 1988; Freidel 1986; Graham 1985; Pendergast 1985, 1986; Don Rice 1986; Rice and Rice 1985; Chase and Rice 1985).

Although this volume has recorded the affluence and development of one small community in northern Belize, more work is needed to fully understand the societal transformations of the Postclassic period and the variation among different territories that is implied by documentary evidence (Roys 1957; Marcus 1993; Okoshi 1992; Quezada 1993; Alexander 1999; Kepecs and Alexander 1999; Williams-Beck 1999). Comparative data sets from households of all Maya periods are needed, as well as from other Postclassic communities of different sizes and geographic locations that will enable a more detailed examination of the effects of changes in regional political organization on the lives of society's members. Although Rathje and Sabloff suggest that the rise of mercantile society resulted in a more horizontal distribution of social affluence, this trend must be measured through comparative household and community analysis so that we can document qualitative differences in social and economic changes from the Classic to Postclassic periods. The analysis of Laguna de On's domestic zones in this volume represents an initial effort in this direction, and comparisons over time and space will render these results more meaningful.

A VIEW FROM THE LAGOON

The perspective offered from Laguna de On provides new information regarding the economic affluence and activities of a rural community during the Late Postclassic period. This small island settlement was integrated into a thriving, mercantile economy that was fueled by well-established regional and international trade networks. From the quiet, jade green waters of Laguna de On, this community rode the waves of distant and local political undulations with a minimum of detriment to itself. This settlement was continuously occupied from the eleventh through fifteenth centuries, with no evidence of clear disruptions or discontinuities. This lengthy occupation attests to the long-term stability of this Postclassic community, and the adaptive success of the relatively decentralized political structures that replaced the more pronounced hierarchies of the earlier Classic period in this region. During these four centuries, in which basic tenets of economic organization were enduring, a trend of social, political, and religious intensification appears linked to increased coastal trade and elite interaction within the Chetumal province.

Preliminary regional patterns assessed in this volume suggest that the southern coastal realm became more hierarchical and integrated over time through greater participation in pan-lowland elite ritual and display, the growth of coastal trade, and a revival of institutions celebrating local lineage-based power and other symbolic links to the past. Local elites organized themselves into integrative assemblies that fostered economic growth and prosperity in even the most remote rural corners of the lowlands. Participation in assembly rule crosscut lineage divisions in society and provided a means for resolving factional competition that was highly effective for achieving economic stability in the Chetumal province. The Late Postclassic florescence is highly conspicuous at the political centers of Mayapan and the east coast, and in more subtle ways it is also reflected at the small island and shore settlement at the headwaters of Freshwater Creek that has been the primary focus of this book. The rural settlement of Laguna de On is thus a microcosm that reflects Postclassic Maya society in the realm of Nachan Kan, regional lord of the thriving southern territory of Chetumal at the time of Spanish contact.

Appendix:
A Comparison of Hocaba and Tases Ceramic Complexes at Mayapan

Ware	Type and Rim	# Hocaba Complex	% Chen Mul	# Tases Complex	% Chen Mul
MAYAPAN UNSLIPPED					
	Chen Mul–Modeled (all forms)	0	0%	128,809	100%

Ware	Type and Rim	# Hocaba Complex	% Unslipped	# Tases Complex	% Unslipped
MAYAPAN UNSLIPPED					
	Acansip Painted bowl or cup	0	0%	34	0%
	Acansip Painted, Chenkeken Incised jar	0	0%	8	0%
	Acansip/Thul Composite cup	0	0%	11	0%
	Cehac Painted tripod cup	1	0%	26	0%
	Cehac-Hunacti Composite tripod jar, pedestal, censer	247	5%	2,373	6%
	Chenkeken Incised basin	0	0%	15	0%
	Chenkeken Incised grater bowl	2	0%	22	0%
	Chenkeken Incised ladle	0	0%	1	0%
	Chenkeken Incised tripod bowl	0	0%	8	0%
	Chenkeken/Acansip Composite bowl	0	0%	25	0%
	Hoal-Modeled all forms	4	0%	3	0%
	Hoal-Modeled effigy censers	562	12%	3	0%
	Huhi Impressed pedestal jar or censer	0	0%	102	0%
	Huhi Impressed restr. bowls	0	0%	3	0%
	Huhi Impressed tripod bowls	0	0%	78	0%
	Kanasin Red Unslipped Jar	2	0%	299	1%
	Navula Unslipped flat-base basin	0	0%	105	0%

Continued on next page

Ware	Type and Rim	# Hocaba Complex	% Unslipped	# Tases Complex	% Unslipped
	Navula Unslipped flat-base bolster-rim dish	55	1%		
	Navula Unslipped flat-base flaring-side bowl	0	0%	180	0%
	Navula Unslipped flat-base lug handle	4	0%		
	Navula Unslipped jars	218	4%	6,835	18%
	Navula Unslipped ladle	110	2%	2,095	6%
	Navula Unslipped restricted bowls	8	0%	269	1%
	Navula Unslipped small paintpot bowls	1	0%		
	Panaba Unslipped (other)	0	0%	64	0%
	Panaba Unslipped cup	0	0%	333	1%
	Panaba Unslipped jar	0	0%	462	1%
	Panaba Unslipped thick bowl	0	0%	1	0%
	Panaba Unslipped tripod bowl	0	0%	307	1%
	Pedestal vases (Panaba Unslipped, Thul Appliqué, Cehac-Hunacti Composite, and Acansip Painted)	0	0%	214	1%
	Thul Appliqué jar	0	0%	36	0%
	Thul Appliqué tripod bowls	0	0%	49	0%
	Yacman Striated basins	51	1%	104	0%
	Yacman Striated deep-restricted bowls	1	0%	17	0%
	Yacman Striated jars	3,613	74%	23,024	62%
	Total	4,879		37,072	
MAYAPAN REDWARE					
	Chapab-Modeled effigy vessel, cups, figurines	0	0%	72	0%
	Chapab-Modeled jar and effigy	4	0%	51	0%
	Dzitxil Openwork cluster pedestal bowls	0	0%	20	0%
	Dzonot Appliqué jar	1	0%	2	0%
	Mama Red bolster-rim and other basins	5	0%	849	1%
	Mama Red cups, min jars, cylindrical vases	26	0%	327	0%
	Mama Red high- and low-neck jars	11,066	83%	48,264	63%
	Mama Red restricted bowls, tripod, cuspidor, deep	155	1%	1202	2%
	Mama Red tripod Black on Red unslipped ext.	0	0%	2	0%
	Mama Red tripod flaring- and round-sided dishes	1,256	9%	13,346	17%
	Mama Red unslipped ext. tripod flaring-side dish	0	0%	5,357	7%
	Panabchen cluster pedestal bowls and pedestal plate	0	0%	79	0%

Continued on next page

Ware	Type and Rim	# Hocaba Complex	% Unslipped	# Tases Complex	% Unslipped
	Panabchen hemisph. bowls			32	0%
	Panabchen Red parenth.-rim jar			717	1%
	Papacal Incised drums	7	0%	122	0%
	Papacal Incised tripod flaring-side dish	179	1%	1,124	1%
	Papacal Incised tripod grater and other	165	1%	572	1%
	Papacal Incised jar	510	4%	4,304	6%
	Pustunich and Yobain incised/relief bowls, vase			5	0%
	Pustunich parenth.-rim jar and mini-vessel			5	0%
	Tzitz tripod jar			629	1%
	Total	13,374		77,081	

Ware	Type and Rim	# Hocaba Complex	% Black-ware	# Tases Complex	% Black-ware
MAYAPAN BLACKWARE					
	Pacha Incised jar and dish	0	0%	2	0%
	Sacmuyna-Modeled figurine	0	0%	1	0%
	Sacmuyna-Modeled jar	0	0%	4	1%
	Sulche Black cylindrical vase	0	0%	1	0%
	Sulche Black hemisph. or restr. bowl	5	12%	5	1%
	Sulche Black tripod dishes	0	0%	47	6%
	Sulche Black water jar	36	88%	737	92%
	Total	41		797	

Ware	Type and Rim	# Hocaba Complex	% Peto	# Tases Complex	% Peto
PETO CREAMWARE					
	Kukula Cream bowls	0	0%	13	1%
	Kukula Cream jars	146	6%	71	6%
	Kukula Cream tripod dishes and vase	44	2%	11	1%
	Mataya-Modeled jar	1	0%		
	Xcanchakan Black/Cream jars	2,128	85%	1,018	83%
	Xcanchakan Black/Cream restr. and tripod bowls	67	3%	68	6%
	Xcanchakan Black/Cream tripod dishes and basins	121	5%	39	3%
	Total	2,507		1,220	
FINE ORANGE MATILLAS					
	Chilapa Gouged-Incised jar	0	0%	1	0%
	Chilapa Gouged-Incised restr., ring-base, hemis. bowl	0	0%	41	5%
	Chilapa Gouged-Incised tripod dish	3	4%	11	1%

Continued on next page

Ware	Type and Rim	# Hocaba Complex	% Peto	# Tases Complex	% Peto
	Grijalva Incised Polychrome dish	0	0%	31	4%
	Matillas Orange jar	12	15%	190	22%
	Matillas Orange restr., ring-base, and hemis. bowl	1	1%	32	4%
	Matillas Orange tripod dish	47	58%	208	25%
	Nacajuca Black/Orange restr. bowl	1	1%	1	0%
	Nacajuca Black/Orange tripod dish	9	11%		
	Salto Composite restr., ring-base, and hemis. bowl	0	0%	48	6%
	Salto Composite tripod dish	1	1%	187	22%
	Villahermosa Incised jar	2	2%		
	Villahermosa Incised restr. and ring-base bowl	0	0%	15	2%
	Villahermosa Incised tripod dish	5	6%	83	10%
	Total	81		848	
SAN JOAQUIN BUFF					
	Kimbila Incised jars and bowls	0	0%	9	100%
	Pele Polychrome jars	0	0%	100	100%
	Pele Polychrome tripod dishes	0	0%	79	100%
	Polbox Buff	0	0%	325	100%
	Polbox Buff tripod dishes	0	0%	6	100%
	Techoh Red-on-buff jars	0	0%	1,222	100%
	Techoh Red-on-buff potstands, basins, vases, covers	0	0%	4	100%
	Techoh Red-on-buff tripod dishes and various bowls	0	0%	639	100%
	Total	0			
TELCHAQUILLO BRICKWARE					
	Moyos Red candle flame shields	0	0%	263	100%
	Cozil Incised candle flame shields	0	0%	33	100%
	Uayma-Modeled effigy censers and figurines	0	0%	10	100%
	Total	0			
MAYAPAN COARSEWARE					
	Kanlum Plano-relief jars	0	0%	2	100%
TULUM REDWARE					
	Palmul Incised hemis. or restr. bowls	0	0%	3	100%
	Palmul Incised jars and tripod dishes	0	0%	9	100%
	Payil Red basin	0	0%	1	100%
	Payil Red jars and tripod dishes	0	0%	11	100%
	Total	0			

Source: from Robert E. Smith 1971: 193–245.

References

Adams, Richard E. W.
  1953 "Some Small Ceremonial Structures of Mayapan." *Current Report 8*, Carnegie Institute of Washington, Cambridge, MA.

Adams, Richard E. W., and Aubrey Trik
  1961 *Temple I (Str. 5-1): Post Constructional Activities.* University Museum Monographs 7. Philadelphia: University of Pennsylvania.

Aguilera, Miguel
  1998 "Domestic Feature Investigations at Subop 17, Laguna de On Island." In *The Belize Postclassic Project 1997: Laguna de On, Progresso Lagoon, and Laguna Seca*, edited by Marilyn A. Masson and Robert Rosenswig, pp. 11–20. Albany: Institute of Mesoamerican Studies Occasional Publication No. 2, University at Albany–SUNY.

Alexander, Rani T.
  1999 "Site Structure at Isla Civlituk, Campeche, Mexico: Political Economy on the Frontier." Paper circulated and presented at the Society for American Archaeology in a working group session entitled "Postclassic and Early Colonial Period Political Geography in the Maya Lowlands: Integrating Archaeology and Ethnohistory," organized by Rani Alexander, March 27, 1999, Chicago.

Andreson, J. M.
  1983 "Chert Artifacts," in *Archaeological Excavating in Northern Belize*, edited by Raymond V. Sidrys, pp. 277–293. Monograph XVII. Los Angeles: Institute of Archaeology, University of California.

Andrews, E. Wyllys IV
  1943 *The Archaeology of Southwestern Campeche.* Contributions to American Anthropology and History 8(40). Carnegie Institute of Washington, Publication 546. Washington, DC.

Andrews, Anthony P.

1977   "Reconocimiento arqueologico de la costa norte del Estado de Campeche." *Boletin de la Escuela de Ciencias Antropologicas de la Universidad de Yucatán* 4(24): 64–77.

1984   "The Political Geography of the 16th-Century Yucatán Maya: Comments and Revisions." *Journal of Anthropological Research* 40: 589–596.

1990   "The Fall of Chichén Itzá: A Preliminary Hypothesis." *Latin American Antiquity* 1: 258–267.

1993   "Late Postclassic Lowland Maya Archaeology." *Journal of World Prehistory* 7: 35–69.

Andrews, Anthony P., and Fernando Robles Castellanos, editors

1986   *Excavaciones arqueológicos en El Meco, Quintana Roo, 1977.* Mexico, D.F.: Colecciún Científica, Instituto Nacional de Antropología e Historia.

Andrews, Anthony P., and Gabriela Vail

1990   "Cronologia de sitios prehispanicos costeros de la peninsula de Yucatán y Belice." *Boletin de la Escuela de Ciencias Antropologicas de la Universidad de Yucatán* 18(104–105): 37–66.

Andrews, Anthony P., Frank Asaro, Helen V. Michel, Fred H. Stross, and Pura Cervera Rivero

1989   "The Obsidian Trade at Isla Cerritos, Yucatán, Mexico." *Journal of Field Archaeology* 16(4): 355–363.

Andrews, Anthony P., Tomas Gallareta N., Fernando Robles C., Rafael Cobos P., and Pura Cervera R.

1988   "Isla Cerritos: An Itzá Trading Port on the North Coast of Yucatán, Mexico." *National Geographic Research* 4: 196–207.

Ball, Joseph W.

1977   *The Archaeological Ceramics of Becan, Campeche, Mexico.* Middle American Research Institute Publication 43. New Orleans: Tulane University.

1982   "Appendix I: The Tancah Ceramic Situation: Cultural and Historical Insights from an Alternative Material Class," in *On the Edge of the Sea: Mural Painting at Tancah-Tulum, Quintana Roo, Mexico*, by Arthur Miller, pp. 105–111. Washington, DC: Dumbarton Oaks.

1985   "The Postclassic That Wasn't: The Thirteenth-Through-Seventeenth Century Archaeology of Central Eastern Campeche, Mexico," in *The Lowland Maya Postclassic*, edited by A. F. Chase and P. M. Rice, pp. 273–284. Austin: University of Texas Press.

1993   "Pottery, Potters, Palaces, and Polities: Some Socioeconomic and Political Implications of Late Classic Maya Ceramic Industries," in *Lowland Maya Civilization in the Eighth Century* A.D., edited by J. A. Sabloff and J. S. Henderson, pp. 243–272. Washington, DC: Dumbarton Oaks.

Ball, Joseph W., and Jennifer T. Taschek

1989   "Teotihuacán's Role and the Rise and Fall of the Itzá: Realignments and Role Changes in the Terminal Classic Maya Lowlands," in *Mesoamerica After the Decline of Teotihuacán* A.D. *700–900*, edited by Richard A. Diehl and Janet Catherine Berlo, pp. 187–200. Washington, DC: Dumbarton Oaks.

Barnhart, Edward

1998a   "Subop 20: A Linear Depression Feature at the North End of Laguna de On Island," in *The Belize Postclassic Project 1997: Laguna de On, Progresso Lagoon, Laguna Seca*, edited by Marilyn A. Masson and Robert Rosenswig, pp. 71–80. Albany: Institute of Mesoamerican Studies Occasional Publication No. 2, University at Albany–SUNY.

1998b   "The Map of Caye Coco," in *The Belize Postclassic Project 1997: Laguna de On, Progresso Lagoon, Laguna Seca*, edited by Marilyn A. Masson and Robert Rosenswig, pp. 107–111. Albany: Institute of Mesoamerican Studies Occasional Publication No. 2, University at Albany–SUNY.

Barnhart, Edward, and Sarah Howard

1997   "Testing Explorations at Laguna de On Island: Landscape Modification, a Burial Area, and Courtyard Walls," in *The Belize Postclassic Project: Laguna de On Island Excavations 1996*, edited by Marilyn A. Masson and Robert Rosenswig, pp. 43–60. Albany: Institute of Mesoamerican Studies Occasional Publication No. 1, University at Albany–SUNY.

Barrera Rubio, Alfredo

1977   "Exploraciones arqueologicas en Tulum, Quintana Roo." *Boletin de la Escuela de Ciencias Antropologicas de la Universidad de Yucatán* 4(24) (Merida): 23–63.

Barrera Vasquez, Alfredo, and Sylvanus G. Morley

1949   *The Maya Chronicles*. Carnegie Institute of Washington Publication 585, Contribution 48. Washington, DC.

Becker, Marshall J.

1973   "Archaeological Evidence for Occupational Specialization Among the Classic Period Maya of Tikal, Guatemala." *American Antiquity* 38: 396–406.

Bey, George J. III, Craig A. Hanson, and William M. Ringle

1997   "Classic to Postclassic at Ek Balam, Yucatán: Architectural and Ceramic Evidence for Defining the Transition." *Latin American Antiquity* 8(3): 237–254.

Binford, Lewis R., Sally R. Binford, Robert Whallon, and Michael A. Hardin

1970   *Archaeology at Hatchery West*. Washington, DC: Memoirs of the Society for American Archaeology No. 24.

Blake, Michael

1985   "Canajaste: An Evolving Postclassic Maya State." Ph.D. dissertation, University of Michigan.

Blanton, Richard E.

1998   "Beyond Centralization: Toward a Theory of Egalitarian Behavior in Archaic States," in *Archaic States*, edited by Gary M. Feinman and Joyce Marcus, pp. 135–172. Santa Fe: School of American Research Press.

Blanton, Richard E., and Gary M. Feinman

1984   "The Mesoamerican World System." *American Anthropologist* 86: 673–682.

Blanton, Richard E., Stephen A. Kowalewski, Gary M. Feinman, and Laura M. Finsten

1993   *Ancient Mesoamerica: A Comparison of Change in Three Regions*. Cambridge: Cambridge University Press.

Blanton, Richard E., Gary M. Feinman, Stephen A. Kowalewski, and Peter N. Peregrine

1996   "A Dual-Processual Theory for the Evolution of Mesoamerican Civilization." *Current Anthropology* 37(1): 1–14.

Brainerd, George W.

1958   *The Archaeological Ceramics of Yucatán*. Anthropological Records, vol. 19. Berkeley: University of California Press.

Braswell, Geoffrey E.

1992   "Obsidian-Hydration Dating, the Coner Phase, and Revisionist Chronology at Copan, Honduras." *Latin American Antiquity* 3: 130–147.

Brenner, Mark

1987   Letter sent to Mary Deland Pohl in 1987, copy on file in author's office.

Bricker, Victoria Reifler

1981   *Indian Christ, Indian King: The Historical Substrate of Maya Myth and Ritual*. Austin: University of Texas Press.

Bullard, William R. Jr.

1970   "Topoxte: A Postclassic Maya Site in Peten, Guatemala," in *Monographs and Papers in Maya Archaeology*, edited by William R. Bullard, pp. 245–308. Cambridge, MA: Papers of the Peabody Museum of Archaeology and Ethnology, vol. 61, Harvard University Press.

1973   "Postclassic Culture in Central Peten and Adjacent British Honduras," in *The Classic Maya Collapse*, edited by T. Patrick Culbert, pp. 225–242. Albuquerque: University of New Mexico Press.

Carmack, Robert

1977   "Ethnohistory of the Central Quiche: The Community of Utatlan," in *Archaeology and Ethnohistory of the Central Quiche*, edited by Dwight

T. Wallace and Robert M. Carmack, pp. 1–19. Albany: Institute for Mesoamerican Studies, University at Albany–SUNY.

1981   *The Quiche Mayas of Utatlan.* Norman: University of Oklahoma Press.

1996   "Mesoamerica at Spanish Contact," in *The Legacy of Mesoamerica: History and Culture of a Native American Civilization*, edited by Robert M. Carmack, Janine Gasco, and Gary H. Gossen, pp. 80–121. Englewood Cliffs, NJ: Prentice-Hall.

Caso, Alfonso

1928   *Las estelas zapotecas.* Mexico, D.F.: Secretaria de Educacion Publica, Talleres Graficos de la Nacion.

Chase, Arlen F.

1983   "A Contextual Consideration of the Tayasal-Paxcaman Zone, El Peten, Guatemala." Ph.D. dissertation, Department of Anthropology, University of Pennsylvania. Ann Arbor, MI: University Microfilms.

1985   "Postclassic Peten Interaction Spheres: The View from Tayasal," in *The Lowland Maya Postclassic*, edited by A. F. Chase and P. M. Rice, pp. 184–205. Austin: University of Texas Press.

1986   "Time Depth or Vacuum: The 11.3.0.0.0 Correlation and the Lowland Maya Postclassic," in *Late Lowland Maya Civilization: Classic to Postclassic*, edited by J. A. Sabloff and E. W. Andrews V, pp. 99–140. Albuquerque: University of New Mexico Press.

Chase, Arlen F., and Prudence M. Rice, editors

1985   *The Lowland Maya Postclassic.* Austin: University of Texas Press.

Chase, Arlen F., and Diane Z. Chase

1985   "Postclassic Temporal and Spatial Frames for the Maya: A Background," in *The Lowland Maya Postclassic*, edited by A. F. Chase and P. M. Rice, pp. 9–23. Austin: University of Texas Press.

1996   "More Kin Than King: Centralized Political Organization Among the Late Classic Maya." *Current Anthropology* 37(5): 803–810.

Chase, Diane Z.

1982   "Spatial and Temporal Variability in Postclassic Northern Belize." Ph.D. dissertation, Department of Anthropology, University of Pennsylvania. Ann Arbor, MI: University Microfilms.

1984   "The Late Postclassic Pottery of Santa Rita Corozal, Belize: The Xabalxab Ceramic Complex." *Ceramica de Cultura Maya* 13: 18–26.

1985   "Ganned but Not Forgotten: Late Postclassic Archaeology and Ritual at Santa Rita Corozal, Belize," in *The Lowland Maya Postclassic*, edited by A. F. Chase and P. M. Rice, pp. 104–125. Austin: University of Texas Press.

1986   "Social and Political Organization in the Land of Milk and Honey: Correlating the Archaeology and Ethnohistory of the Postclassic Lowland Maya," in *Late Lowland Maya Civilization: Classic to Postclassic*, edited by J. A. Sabloff and E. W. Andrews V, pp. 347–378. Albuquerque: University of New Mexico Press.

1988   "Caches and Censerwares: Meaning from Maya Pottery," in *A Pot for All Reasons: Ceramic Ecology Revisited*, edited by Charles C. Kolb and Louana M. Lackey, pp. 81–104. Philadephia: Special Publication of Ceramica de Cultura Maya et al., Laboratory of Anthropology, Temple University.

1990   "The Invisible Maya: Population History and Archaeology at Santa Rita Corozal," in *Precolumbian Population History in the Maya Lowlands*, edited by T. Patrick Culbert and Don S. Rice, pp. 190–214. Albuquerque: University of New Mexico Press.

1992   "Postclassic Maya Elites: Ethnohistory and Archaeology," in *Mesoamerican Elites: An Archaeological Assessment*, edited by Diane Z. Chase and Arlen F. Chase, pp.118–134. Norman: University of Oklahoma Press.

Chase, Diane Z., and Arlen F. Chase

1982   "Yucatec Influence in Terminal Classic Northern Belize." *American Antiquity* 47: 596–614.

1988   *A Postclassic Perspective: Excavations at the Maya Site of Santa Rita Corozal, Belize.* San Francisco: Precolumbian Art Research Institute, Monograph 4.

Childe, V. Gordon

1959   "The Birth of Civilization," in *Readings in Anthropology*, edited by Morton H. Fried, pp. 412–421. New York: Thomas Y. Crowell Co.

1960   *What Happened in History.* Harmondsworth, Middlesex: Penguin Books, Ltd.

Clark, John E.

1987   "Politics, Prismatic Blades, and Mesoamerican Civilization," in *The Organization of Core Technology*, edited by J. K. Johnson and C. A. Morrow, pp. 259–284. Boulder, CO: Westview Press.

Clark, John E., and Michael Blake

1994   "The Power of Prestige: Competitive Generosity and the Emergence of Rank Societies in Lowland Mesoamerica," in *Factional Competition and Political Development in the New World*, edited by Elizabeth M. Brumfiel and John W. Fox, pp. 17–30. New York: Cambridge University Press.

Clark, John E., and Dennis Gosser

1993   "Reinventing America's First Pottery." Paper presented at the 58th Annual Meeting of the Society for American Archaeology, St. Louis. Manuscript in possession of the author.

Coe, Michael D.

1965   "A Model of Ancient Community Structure in the Maya Lowlands." *Southwestern Journal of Anthropology* 21: 97–114.

1973   *The Maya Scribe and His World*. New York: The Grolier Club.

1989   "The Hero Twins: Myth and Image," in *The Vase Book: A Corpus of Rollout Photographs of Maya Vases*, vol. 1, by Justin Kerr, pp. 161–184. New York: Kerr and Associates.

Coggins, Clemency C.

1979   "A New Order and the Role of the Calendar: Some Characteristics of the Middle Classic Period at Tikal," in *Maya Archaeology and Ethnohistory*, edited by N. Hammond and G. Willey, pp. 38–50. Austin: University of Texas Press.

1983   "An Instrument of Expansion: Monte Alban, Teotihuacán, and Tikal," in *Highland-Lowland Interaction in Mesoamerica: Interdisciplinary Approaches*, edited by Arthur G. Miller, pp. 49–68. Washington, DC: Dumbarton Oaks Research Library and Collection.

1988   "The Manikin Scepter: Emblem of Lineage." *Estudios de Cultura Maya* 17: 123–158.

Collins, Michael B.

1994   "Introduction to a Replication Technology for Andice/Bell Points," in *Archaic and Late Prehistoric Human Ecology in the Middle Onion Creek Valley, Hays County, Texas*, edited by Robert A. Ricklis and Michael B. Collins, pp. 629–651. Austin: Studies in Archaeology 19, Texas Archeological Research Laboratory, University of Texas.

Connor, Judith G.

1983   "The Ceramics of Cozumel, Quintana Roo, Mexico." Ph.D. dissertation, Department of Anthropology, University of Arizona. Ann Arbor, MI: University Microfilms.

Costin, Cathy L.

1991   "Craft Specialization: Issues in Defining, Documenting, and Explaining the Organization of Production," in *Archaeological Method and Theory*, edited by M. B. Schiffer, pp. 1–56. Tucson: University of Arizona Press.

Cowgill, George L.

1963   "Postclassic Period Culture in the Vicinity of Flores, Peten, Guatemala." Ph.D. dissertation, Harvard University.

1988   "Onward and Upward with Collapse," in *The Collapse of Ancient States and Civilizations*, edited by Norman Yoffee and George Cowgill, pp. 244–276. Tucson: University of Arizona Press.

Culbert, T. Patrick

1974   *The Lost Civilization: The Story of the Classic Maya*. New York: Harper and Row.

1988   "The Collapse of Classic Maya Civilization," in *The Collapse of Ancient States and Civilizations*, edited by Norman Yoffee and George Cowgill, pp. 69–101. Tucson: University of Arizona Press.

Dahlin, Bruce Harrison

1976   "An Anthropologist Looks at the Pyramids: A Late Classic Revitalization Movement at Tikal, Guatemala." Ph.D. dissertation, Temple University.

De Montmollin, Olivier

1989   *The Archaeology of Political Structure*. Cambridge: Cambridge University Press.

Deal, Michael

1988a   "An Ethnoarchaeological Approach to the Identification of Maya Domestic Pottery Production," in *Ceramic Ecology Revisited: The Technology and Socioeconomics of Pottery*, edited by Charles C. Kolb and Louana M. Lackey, pp. 111–142. Philadephia: Special Publication of Ceramica de Cultura Maya et al., Laboratory of Anthropology, Temple University.

1988b   "Recognition of Ritual Pottery in Residential Units: An Ethnoarchaeological Model of the Maya Family Altar Tradition," in *Ethnoarchaeology Among the Highland Maya of Chiapas*, edited by Thomas A. Lee Jr. and Brian Hayden, pp. 61–89. Provo, UT: Papers of the New World Archaeological Foundation No. 56.

Deane, Anne

1999   "Experiments in Ceramic Technology," in *The Belize Postclassic Project 1998: Investigations at Progresso Lagoon*, edited by Marilyn A. Masson and Robert Rosenswig, pp. 169–171. Albany: Institute of Mesoamerican Studies Occasional Publication No. 3, University at Albany–SUNY.

Demarest, Arthur A.

1992   "Ideology in Ancient Maya Cultural Evolution: The Dynamics of Galactic Polities," in *Ideology and Pre-Columbian Civilizations*, edited by Arthur A. Demarest and Geoffrey W. Conrad, pp. 135–158. Santa Fe: School of American Research Press.

1996   "Closing Comment." *Current Anthropology* 37(5): 821–830.

1997   "The Vanderbilt Petexbatun Regional Archaeological Project 1989–1994: Overview, History, and Major Results of a Multi-Disciplinary Study of the Classic Maya Collapse." *Ancient Mesoamerica* 8(2): 209–227.

Dreiss, Meredith L.

1994   "The Shell Artifacts of Colha: The 1983 Season," in *Continuing Archaeology at Colha, Belize*, edited by Thomas R. Hester, Harry J. Shafer, and Jack D. Eaton, pp. 177–200. Austin: Studies in Archaeology 16, Texas Archeological Research Laboratory, University of Texas.

Dreiss, Meredith L., and David O. Brown

1989   "Obsidian Exchange Patterns in Belize," in *Prehistoric Maya Economies*, edited by P. A. McAnany and B. L. Isaac, pp. 57–90. Greenwich, CT: Research in Economic Anthropology Supplement 4, JAI Press.

Dresden Codex

1880   *Die Maya-Handschrift der Königiehen Bibliothek zu Dresden*, edited by E. Förstemann. Liepzig: Roder, 2d edition, 1892. Reprinted as *Codex Dresdensis: Die Maya-Handschrift in der Sächsischen Landesbibliothek Dresden*. Foreword by E. Lips. Berlin: Akademie-Verlag, 1962.

Dunham, Peter S.

1990   "Coming Apart at the Seams: The Classic Development and the Demise of Maya Civilization, A Segmentary View from Xnaheb, Belize." Ph.D. dissertation, State University of New York, Albany.

Eaton, Jack D.

1974   "Shell Celts from Coastal Yucatán, Mexico." *Bulletin of the Texas Archaeological Society* 45: 197–208.

1980   "Architecture and Settlement at Colha," in *The Colha Project, Second Season, 1980 Interim Report*, edited by T. R. Hester, J. D. Eaton, and H. J. Shafer, pp. 41–50. San Antonio: Center for Archaeological Research, the University of Texas at San Antonio and Centro Studi e Ricerche Ligabue, Venice.

1982   "Colha: An Overview of Architecture and Settlement," in *Archaeology at Colha, Belize: The 1981 Interim Report*, edited by T. R. Hester, H. J. Shafer, and J. D. Eaton, pp. 11–20. San Antonio: Center for Archaeological Research, the University of Texas at San Antonio and Centro Studi e Ricerche Ligabue, Venice.

1991   "Tools of Ancient Maya Builders," in *Maya Stone Tools: Selected Papers from the Second Maya Lithic Conference*, edited by T. R. Hester and H. J. Shafer, pp. 219–228. Madison, WI: Monographs in World Archaeology No. 1, Prehistory Press.

Eaton, Jack D., Thomas R. Hester, and Fred Valdez Jr.

1994   "Notes on Eccentric Lithics from Colha and Northern Belize," in *Continuing Archaeology at Colha, Belize*, edited by Thomas R. Hester, Harry J. Shafer, and Jack D. Eaton, pp. 257–266. Austin: Studies in Archaeology 16, Texas Archeological Research Laboratory, University of Texas.

Eisenstadt, Shmuel N.

1988   "Beyond Collapse," in *The Collapse of Ancient States and Civilizations*, edited by Norman Yoffee and George Cowgill, pp. 236–243. Tucson: University of Arizona Press.

Erasmus, Charles J.

1968   "Thoughts on Upward Collapse: An Essay on Explanation in Archaeology." *Southwestern Journal of Anthropology* 24: 170–194.

Escalona Ramos, A.

1946   "Algunas ruinas prehispanicas en Quintana Roo." *Boletin de la Sociedad Mexicana de Geografia y Estadistica* 61(3): 513–628.

Fancourt, C.

1854   *The History of Yucatán from Its Discover to the Close of the Seventeenth Century.* London: John Murray, Albemarle Street.

Flannery, Kent V.

1976   "Evolution of Complex Settlement Systems," in *The Early Mesoamerican Village*, edited by K. V. Flannery, pp. 162–173. New York: Academic Press.

Flenniken, J. J., and A. W. Raymond

1986   "Morphological Projectile Point Typology: Replication, Experimentation, and Technological Analysis." *American Antiquity* 51: 603–614.

Fox, John W.

1987   *Late Postclassic State Formation.* Cambridge: Cambridge University Press.

Fox, John W., Garrett W. Cook, Arlen F. Chase, and Diane Z. Chase

1996   "Questions of Political and Economic Integration: Segmentary Versus Centralized States Among the Ancient Maya." *Current Anthropology* 37(5): 795–801.

Freidel, David A.

1981   "The Political Economics of Residential Dispersion Among the Lowland Maya," in *Lowland Maya Settlement Patterns*, edited by Wendy Ashmore, pp. 371–382. Albuquerque: University of New Mexico Press.

1983a   "Political Systems in Lowland Yucatán: Dynamics and Structure in Maya Settlement," in *Prehistoric Settlement Patterns: Essays in Honor of Gordon R. Willey*, edited by Evon Z. Vogt and Richard M. Levanthal, pp. 375–386. Albuquerque and Cambridge, MA: University of New Mexico Press/ Peabody Museum, Harvard University Press.

1983b   "Lowland Maya Political Economy: Historical and Archaeological Perspectives in Light of Intensive Agriculture," in *Spaniards and Indians in Southeastern Mesoamerica: Essays on the History of Ethnic Relations*, edited by Robert Wasserstrom and Murdo J. Macleod, pp. 40–63. Lincoln: University of Nebraska Press.

1985   "New Light on a Dark Age: A Summary of Major Themes," in *The Lowland Maya Postclassic*, edited by A. F. Chase and P. M. Rice, pp. 285–310. Austin: University of Texas Press.

1986 "Terminal Classic Lowland Maya: Successes, Failures, and Aftermaths," in *Late Lowland Maya Civilization: Classic to Postclassic*, edited by J. A. Sabloff and E. W. Andrews V, pp. 409–430. Albuquerque: University of New Mexico Press.

Freidel, David A., and Jeremy A. Sabloff

1984 *Cozumel: Late Maya Settlement Patterns*. New York: Academic Press.

Freidel, David A., Linda Schele, and Joy Parker

1993 *The Maya Cosmos: Three Thousand Years on the Shaman's Path*. New York: William Morrow and Co.

Fry, Robert E.

1985 "Revitalization Movements Among the Postclassic Lowland Maya," in *The Lowland Maya Postclassic*, edited by A. F. Chase and P. M. Rice, pp. 126–150. Austin: University of Texas Press.

1990 "Disjunctive Growth in the Maya Lowlands," in *Precolumbian Population History in the Maya Lowlands*, edited by T. Patrick Culbert and Don S. Rice, pp. 285–300. Albuquerque: University of New Mexico Press.

Gann, Thomas W.

1900 *Mounds in Northern Honduras*. Nineteenth Annual Report of the Bureau of American Ethnology 1897–1898, part 2: 655–692.

1918 *The Maya Indians of Southern Yucatán and Northern British Honduras*. Washington, DC: Bureau of American Ethnology 64, Smithsonian Institution.

1926 *Ancient Cities and Modern Tribes: Exploration and Adventure in the Maya Lands*. London: Duckworth.

1928 *Maya Cities*. London and New York: self-published.

Gates, William Edmond

1978 *Yucatán Before and After the Conquest, Diego de Landa*. New York and London: Dover Publications.

Gossen, Gary H., and Richard M. Levanthal

1993 "The Topography of Ancient Maya Religious Pluralism," in *Lowland Maya Civilization in the Eighth Century A.D.*, edited by Jeremy Sabloff and John Henderson, pp. 185–218. Washington, DC: Dumbarton Oaks Research Library and Collection.

Graff, Donald H.

1997 "Dating a Section of the *Madrid Codex*: Astronomical and Iconographic Evidence," in *Papers on the Madrid Codex*, edited by Victoria R. Bricker and Gabrielle Vail, pp. 147–167. New Orleans: Middle American Research Institute Publication 64, Tulane University.

Graham, Elizabeth A.

1985 "Facets of Terminal to Postclassic Activity in the Stann Creek District, Belize," in *The Lowland Maya Postclassic*, edited by A. F.

Chase and P. M. Rice, pp.215–230. Austin: University of Texas Press.

1987   "Terminal Classic to Early Historic Period Vessel Forms from Belize," in *Maya Ceramics*, edited by Prudence Rice and Robert Sharer, pp. 73–98. Great Britain: BAR International Series 345.

1994   *The Highlands of the Lowlands: Environment and Archaeology in the Stann Creek District, Belize, Central America.* Madison, WI: Prehistory Press.

Graham, Elizabeth, and David M. Pendergast

1989   "Excavations at the Marco Gonzalez Site, Ambergris Cay, Belize, 1986." *Journal of Field Archaeology* 16: 1–16.

Graham, Elizabeth A., David M. Pendergast, and Grant D. Jones

1989   "On the Fringes of Conquest: Maya-Spanish Contact in Colonial Belize." *Science* 246: 1254–1259.

Grube, Nikolai

1992   "Classic Maya Dance: Evidence from Hieroglyphs and Iconography." *Ancient Mesoamerica* 3(2): 201–218.

Guderjan, Thomas H., and James F. Garber

1995   *Maya Maritime Trade, Settlement, and Populations on Ambergris Caye, Belize.* San Antonio: Maya Research Program and Labyrinthos.

Harrison, Peter D.

1981   "Some Aspects of Preconquest Settlement in Southern Quintana Roo, Mexico," in *Lowland Maya Settlement Patterns*, edited by Wendy Ashmore, pp. 259–286. Albuquerque: School of American Research, University of New Mexico Press.

Headrick, Annabeth

1991   "The Chicomoztoc of Chichén Itzá." M.A. thesis, Department of Art History, University of Texas at Austin.

1995   "Las Monjas and the Tradition of Founder's House." Paper presented at the XIth Texas Symposium, The Maya Meetings at Texas, March 10, Austin. Manuscript in possession of the author.

Hester, Thomas R., editor

1982   "The Maya Lithic Sequence in Northern Belize," in *Archaeology at Colha, Belize: The 1981 Interim Report*, edited by T. R. Hester, H. J. Shafer, and J. D. Eaton, pp. 39–59. San Antonio: Center for Archaeological Research, the University of Texas at San Antonio and Centro Studi e Ricerche Ligabue, Venice.

1985   "Late Classic–Early Postclassic Transitions: Archaeological Investigations at Colha, Belize." Final Performance Report to the National Endowment for the Humanities Grants RO 20534-83 and RO 20755. Center for Archaeological Research, the University of Texas at San Antonio. On file at Texas Archeological Research Laboratory, University of Texas at Austin.

Hester, Thomas R., and Harry J. Shafer

1984   "Exploitation of Chert Resources by the Ancient Maya of Northern Belize, Central America." *World Archaeology* 16: 157–173.

1991   "Lithics of the Early Postclassic at Colha, Belize," in *Maya Stone Tools: Selected Papers from the Second Maya Lithic Conference*, edited by Thomas R. Hester and Harry J. Shafer, pp. 155–162. Madison, WI: Monographs in World Archaeology No. 1, Prehistory Press.

1994   "The Ancient Maya Craft Community at Colha, Belize, and Its External Relationships," in *Archaeological Views from the Countryside: Village Communities in Early Complex Societies*, edited by G. M. Schwartz and S. E. Falconer, pp. 48–63. Washington, DC: Smithsonian Institution Press.

Hester, Thomas R., Harry J. Shafer, and Thena Berry

1991   "Technological and Comparative Analyses of the Chipped Stone Artifacts from El Pozito, Belize," in *Maya Stone Tools*, edited by Thomas Hester and Harry Shafer, pp. 67–84. Madison, WI: Monographs in World Prehistory No. 1, Prehistory Press.

Hester, Thomas R., Harry B. Iceland, Dale B. Hudler, and Harry J. Shafer

1996   "The Colha Preceramic Project: Preliminary Results from the 1993–1995 Field Season." *Mexicon* 18: 45–50.

Hicks, David

1998   *Ritual and Belief: Readings in the Anthropology of Religion*. Boston: McGraw-Hill.

Hirth, Kenneth G.

1998   "The Distributional Approach: A New Way to Identify Marketplace Exchange in the Archaeological Record." *Current Anthropology* 39: 451–476.

Houston, Stephen D.

1984   "An Example of Homophony in Maya Script." *American Antiquity* 49(4): 790–805.

1993   *Hieroglyphs and History at Dos Pilas: Dynastic Politics of the Classic Maya*. Austin: University of Texas Press.

Houston, Stephen, and David Stuart

1989   "The Way Glyph: Evidence for 'Co-essences' Among the Classic Maya." *Research Reports on Ancient Maya Writing 30*. Washington, DC: Center for Maya Research.

Jaeger, Susan E.

1988   "Appendix II: The Manos and Metates of Santa Rita Corozal," in *A Postclassic Perspective: Excavations at the Maya Site of Santa Rita Corozal, Belize*, by D. Z. Chase and A. F. Chase, pp. 99–117. San Francisco: Precolumbian Art Research Institute Monograph 4.

Johnson, Jay K.

1985 "Postclassic Maya Site Structure at Topoxte, El Peten, Guatemala," in *The Lowland Maya Postclassic*, edited by A. F. Chase and P. M. Rice, pp. 151–165. Austin: University of Texas Press.

Jones, Grant D.

1989 *Maya Resistance to Spanish Rule: Time and History on a Colonial Frontier*. Albuquerque: University of New Mexico Press.

1999 *The Conquest of the Last Maya Kingdom*. Stanford, CA: Stanford University Press.

Jones, Grant D., Don S. Rice, and Prudence M. Rice

1991 "The Location of Tayasal: A Reconsideration in Light of Peten Maya Ethnohistory and Archaeology." *American Antiquity* 45: 530–547.

Jones, Morris

1962 Map of Mayapan, in "Introduction," in *Mayapan, Yucatán, Mexico*, by Harry E. D. Pollock, Ralph L. Roys, Tatiana Proskouriakoff, and A. L. Smith. Washington, DC: Carnegie Institute of Washington Publication No. 619.

Kelly, Thomas C.

1980 "The Colha Regional Survey," in *The Colha Project, Second Season, 1980 Interim Report*, edited by T. R. Hester, J. D. Easton, and H. J. Shafer, pp. 51–69. San Antonio: Center for Archaeological Research, the University of Texas at San Antonio and Centro Studi e Ricerche Ligabue, Venice.

Kent, Kate P., and Sarah M. Nelson

1976 "Net Sinkers or Weft Weights?" *Current Anthropology* 17(1): 152.

Kepecs, Susan

1998 "Diachronic Ceramic Evidence and Its Social Implications in the Chikinchel Region, Northeast Yucatán, Mexico." *Ancient Mesoamerica* 9(1): 121–136.

Kepecs, Susan, and Rani T. Alexander

1999 "Introductory Discussion: Archaeological Correlates of Cultural Processes at the Regional, Intra-Site, and Household Scales of Analysis." Paper presented at the 64th Annual Meeting of the Society for American Archaeology, March 27, Chicago.

Kepecs, Susan, Gary M. Feinman, and Sylviane Boucher

1994 "Chichén Itzá and Its Hinterland: A World Systems Perspective." *Ancient Mesoamerica* 5: 141–158.

King, Eleanor, and Daniel Potter

1994 "Small Sites in Prehistoric Maya Socioeconomic Organization: A Perspective from Colha, Belize," in *Archaeological Views from the Countryside: Village Communities in Early Complex Societies*, edited by G. M.

Schwartz and S. E. Falconer, pp. 64–90. Washington, DC: Smithsonian Institution Press.

Klein, Richard G., and Katherine Cruz-Uribe

1984   *The Analysis of Animal Bones from Archaeological Sites.* Chicago: University of Chicago Press.

Kroeber, A. L.

1948   *Anthropology.* New York: Harcourt, Brace & Co.

Landa, Friar Diego de

1941   *Landa's Relaciones de las Cosas de Yucatán.* Translated by Alfred Tozzer. Cambridge, MA: Papers of the Peabody Museum of Archaeology and Ethnology 18, Harvard University Press.

Levanthal, Richard M.

1983   "Household Groups and Classic Maya Religion," in *Prehistoric Settlement Patterns: Essays in Honor of Gordon R. Willey,* edited by Evon Z. Vogt and Richard M. Levanthal, pp. 55–76. Albuquerque and Cambridge, MA: University of New Mexico Press/ Peabody Museum of Archaeology and Ethnology, Harvard University Press.

Levanthal, Richard M., and Kevin H. Baxter

1988   "The Use of Ceramics to Identify the Function of Copan Structures," in *Household and Community in the Mesoamerican Past,* edited by R. R. Wilk and W. Ashmore, pp. 51–71. Albuquerque: University of New Mexico Press.

Lewenstein, Susan, and Bruce Dahlin

1990   "The Albion Island Transect Survey: Coming to Terms with the Belizean Second Growth," in *Ancient Maya Wetland Agriculture: Excavations on Albion Island, Northern Belize,* edited by Mary Pohl, pp. 339–356. Boulder, CO: Westview Press.

Lincoln, Charles

1986   "The Chronology of Chichén Itzá: A Review of the Literature," in *Late Lowland Maya Civilization: Classic to Postclassic,* edited by J. A. Sabloff and E. W. Andrews V, pp. 141–198. Albuquerque: University of New Mexico Press.

Long, Richard

1919   "The Date of Maya Ruins at Santa Rita, British Honduras." *Man* 19: 59–61.

Looper, Matthew

1991   "The Dances of Classic Maya Deities Chak and Hu Nal Ye." Master's thesis, Department of Art, University of Texas at Austin.

Lothrop, Samuel K.

1924   *Tulum, An Archaeological Study of the East Coast of Yucatán.* Washington, DC: Carnegie Institute of Washington Publication 335.

Love, Bruce

1989   "Yucatec Sacred Breads Through Time," in *Word and Image in Maya Culture: Explorations in Language, Writing, and Representation*, edited by William F. Hanks and Don Rice, pp. 336–350. Salt Lake City: University of Utah Press.

1994   *The Paris Codex: Handbook for a Maya Priest*. Austin: University of Texas Press.

Luer, George

1985   "Strombus Lip Shell Tools of the Tequesta Sub-Area." *The Florida Anthropologist* 17: 215–220.

McAnany, Patricia A.

1986   "Lithic Technology and Exchange Among Westland Farmers of the Eastern Maya Lowlands." Unpublished Ph.D. dissertation, Department of Anthropology, University of New Mexico.

1989   "Stone Tool Production and Exchange in the Eastern Maya Lowlands: The Consumer Perspective from Pulltrouser Swamp, Belize." *American Antiquity* 54: 332–346.

1991   "The Structure and Dynamics of Intercommunity Exchange," in *Maya Stone Tools*, edited by T. R. Hester and H. J. Shafer, pp. 271–293. Madison, WI: Prehistory Press.

1993   "The Economics of Social Power and Wealth Among Eighth-Century Maya Households," in *Lowland Maya Civilization in the Eighth Century A.D.*, edited by J. A. Sabloff and J. S. Henderson, pp. 65–89. Washington, DC: Dumbarton Oaks.

1995   *Living with the Ancestors: Kinship and Kingship in Ancient Maya Society*. Austin: University of Texas Press.

McAnany, Patricia A., William K. Barnett, Ronnie Reese, and Marvin Rowe

n.d.   "Chalcedony Source Determination Through the Coupling of NAA with Petrographic Analysis." Manuscript in possession of the author.

McGee, R. Jon

1990   *Life, Ritual, and Religion Among the Lacandon Maya*. Belmont, CA: Wadsworth Publishing Company.

McKillop, Heather I.

1980   "Moho Cay, Belize: Preliminary Investigations of Trade, Settlement, and Marine Resource Exploitation." Master's thesis, Trent University, Peterborough, Ontario. Ann Arbor, MI: University Microfilms.

McKillop, Heather, and Paul F. Healy

1989   *Coastal Maya Trade*. Occasional Papers in Archaeology, Trent University, Peterborough, Ontario.

Madrid Codex

1869– *Manucrit Troano: études sur le sistéme graphique et la langue des Mayas*
1870 (Tro Fragment), compiled by C. E. Brasseur de Bourbourg. Paris: Imprimerie Impériale.

Malinowski, Bronislaw

1922 *Argonauts of the Western Pacific*. New York/London: Dutton/ Routledge.

Mann, Michael

1986 *The Sources of Social Power*, vol. I: *A History of Power from the Beginning to A.D. 1760*. Cambridge: Cambridge University Press.

Marcus, Joyce

1976 *Emblem and State in the Classic Maya Lowlands: An Epigraphic Approach to Territorial Organization*. Washington, DC: Dumbarton Oaks.

1982 "The Plant World of the Sixteenth and Seventeenth Century Lowland Maya," in *Maya Subsistence: Studies in Memory of Dennis E. Puleston*, edited by Kent V. Flannery, pp. 239–273. New York: Academic Press.

1983 "Topic 43: Rethinking the Zapotec Urn," in *The Cloud People: Divergent Evolution of the Zapotec and Mixtec Civilizations*, edited by K. V. Flannery and J. Marcus, pp. 144–148. New York: Academic Press.

1993 "Ancient Maya Political Organization," in *Lowland Maya Civilization in the Eighth Century A.D.*, edited by J. A. Sabloff and J. S. Henderson, pp. 111–184. Washington, DC: Dumbarton Oaks.

Marquez Morfin, Lourdes

1982 *Playa del Carmen: Una poblacion de la costa oriental en el postclasico*. Mexico, D.F.: Coleccion Cientifica, Instituto Nacional de Antropologia e Historia.

Martin, Simon, and Nikolai Grube

1995 "Maya Superstates." *Archaeology* 48(3): 41–46.

Masson, Marilyn A.

1988 "Shell Celt Morphology and Breakage Patterns: An Analogy to Lithic Research." *Florida Anthropologist* 41(3): 322–335.

1993 "Changes in Maya Community Organization from the Classic to Postclassic Periods: A View from Laguna de On, Belize." Ph.D. dissertation, University of Texas at Austin.

1995 "Understanding the Stratigraphic Context of the Maya Postclassic in Belize." *Geoarchaeology* 10(5): 389–404.

1997 "Cultural Transformations at the Maya Postclassic Community of Laguna de On, Belize." *Latin American Antiquity* 8(4): 293–316.

1998 "Introduction," in *The Belize Postclassic Project 1997: Laguna de On, Progresso Lagoon, and Laguna Seca*, edited by Marilyn A. Masson and Robert Rosenswig, pp. 1–8. Albany: Institute of Mesoamerican

Studies Occasional Publication No. 2, University at Albany–SUNY.

1999a   "Animal Resource Manipulation in Ritual and Domestic Contexts at Postclassic Maya Sites." *World Archaeology* 31: 93–120.

1999b   "Postclassic Maya Ritual at Laguna de On Island Belize." *Ancient Mesoamerica* 10: 51–68.

1999c   "The Chicanel and Payil States: Economic Centralization versus Kingship in the Late Formative and Late Postclassic Maya Lowlands." Paper presented at the Society for American Archaeology Meetings, Chicago.

n.d.a   "Exploitation of Aquatic and Terrestrial Vertebrates and Changing Community Ecologies in Northern Belize," in *Maya Zooarchaeology*, edited by Kitty Emory and Norbert Staunchly. Los Angeles: University of California Los Angeles Press, in press.

n.d.b   "Cocijo and the Ancestors: Kin-Focused Ritual and Power Among the Ancient Zapotec." Manucript in revision for publication in *Mesoamérica*.

Masson, Marilyn A., and Sarah Gonzalez

1997   "Structure III, a Stone Dock at Laguna de On Island," in *The Belize Postclassic Project: Laguna de On Island Excavations 1996*, edited by Marilyn A. Masson and Robert Rosenswig, pp. 39–42. Albany: Institute of Mesoamerican Studies Occasional Publication No. 1, University at Albany–SUNY.

Masson, Marilyn A., and Heather Orr

1998a   "The Role of Zapotec Genealogical Records in Late Precolumbian Valley of Oaxaca Political History." *Mexicon* 20: 10–15.

1998b   "The Writing on the Wall: Political Representation and Sacred Geography at Monte Alban," in *The Sowing and the Dawning: Termination and Dedication Processes in the Archaeological and Ethnographic Record of Mesoamerica*, edited by Shirley Mock, pp. 165–176. Albuquerque: University of New Mexico Press.

Masson, Marilyn A., and Shirley Boteler Mock

n.d.   "Transformations in Ceramic Economies from the Terminal Classic to Postclassic Periods at Lagoon Sites of Northern Belize," in *The Terminal Classic in the Maya Lowlands: Collapse, Transition, and Transformation*, edited by Don S. Rice, Prudence M. Rice, and Arthur A. Demarest. In press.

Masson, Marilyn A., and Robert M. Rosenswig, editors

1997   *The Belize Postclassic Project 1996: Laguna de On Excavations 1996*. Albany: Institute of Mesoamerican Studies Occasional Publication No. 1, University at Albany–SUNY.

1998a   *The Belize Postclassic Project 1997: Laguna de On, Progresso Lagoon, and Laguna Seca.* Albany: Institute of Mesoamerican Studies Occasional Publication No. 2, University at Albany–SUNY.

1998b   "Postclassic Monumental Center Discovered at Caye Coco, Belize." *Mexicon* 20(1): 4–5.

1999   *Belize Postclassic Project 1998: Investigations at Progresso Lagoon.* Albany: Institute of Mesoamerican Studies Occasional Publication No. 3, University at Albany–SUNY.

Masson, Marilyn A., and Thomas W. Stafford Jr.

1998   "The Role of Laguna de On in the Postclassic Political Hierarchy of Northern Belize." Paper presented at the Society for American Archaeology Meetings, Seattle.

Masson, Marilyn, Melissa Joy Shumake, and Evon Moan

1997   "Structure I, a C-shaped Building at Laguna de On Island," in *The Belize Postclassic Project 1996: Laguna de On Island Excavations 1996,* edited by Marilyn A. Masson and Robert Rosenswig, pp. 11–24. Albany: Institute of Mesoamerican Studies Occasional Publication No. 1, University at Albany–SUNY. Report submitted to the Department of Archaeology, Belmopan, Belize.

Matola, Sharon

1995   *The Mammals of Belize: A Handbook.* Belize City, Belize: The Belize Zoo and Tropical Education Center.

Mathews, Peter

1991   "Classic Maya Emblem Glyphs," in *Classic Maya Political History: Hieroglyphic and Archaeological Evidence,* edited T. Patrick Culbert, pp. 19–29. Cambridge: School of American Research Advanced Seminar Series, Cambridge University Press.

Mauss, Marcel

1925   *The Gift.* London: Routledge.

Michaels, George H.

1987   "A Description of Early Postclassic Lithic Technology at Colha, Belize." M.A. thesis, Department of Anthropology, Texas A&M University.

1994   "The Postclassic at Colha, Belize: A Summary Overview and Directions for Future Research," in *Continuing Archaeology at Colha, Belize,* edited by Thomas R. Hester, Harry J. Shafer, and Jack D. Eaton, pp. 129–136. Austin: Studies in Archaeology 16, Texas Archeological Research Laboratory, University of Texas.

Michaels, George H., and Harry J. Shafer

1994   "Excavations at Operation 2037 and 2040," in *Continuing Archaeology at Colha, Belize,* edited by Thomas R. Hester, Harry J. Shafer, and Jack D. Eaton, pp. 117–129. Austin: Studies in Archaeology 16, Texas Archeological Research Laboratory, University of Texas.

Miksicek, Charles H.

1990 "Early Wetland Agriculture in the Maya Lowlands: Clues from Preserved Plant Remains," in *Ancient Maya Wetland Agriculture: Excavations on Albion Island, Northern Belize*, edited by Mary Pohl, pp. 295–312. Boulder, CO: Westview Press.

Milbrath, Susan

1999 *Star Gods of the Maya: Astronomy in Art, Folklore, and Calendars*. Austin: University of Texas Press.

n.d. "The Planet of Kings: Jupiter in Maya Cosmology," in *Cosmos and History: A Mesoamerican Legacy*, edited by Andrea Stone. Tuscaloosa: University of Alabama Press, in press.

Miller, Arthur G.

1974 "The Iconography of the Painting in the Temple of the Diving God, Tulum, Quintana Roo, Mexico: The Twisted Cords," in *Mesoamerican Archaeology: New Approaches*, edited by Norman Hammond, pp. 167–186. Austin: University of Texas Press.

1982 *On the Edge of the Sea: Mural Painting at Tancah-Tulum, Quintana Roo, Mexico*. Washington, DC: Dumbarton Oaks.

Miller, Arthur G., and Nancy M. Farriss

1979 "Religious Syncretism in Colonial Yucatán: The Archaeological and Ethnohistorical Evidence from Tancah, Quintana Roo," in *Maya Archaeology and Ethnohistory*, edited by Norman Hammond and Gordon R. Willey, pp. 223–240. Austin: University of Texas Press.

Mock, Shirley Boteler

1994 "Yucatecan Presence in Northern Belize Postclassic Ceramics at Colha," in *Continuing Archaeology at Colha, Belize*, edited by Thomas R. Hester, Harry J. Shafer, and Jack D. Eaton, pp. 9–16. Austin: Studies in Archaeology 16, Texas Archeological Research Laboratory, University of Texas.

1997 "Preliminary Ceramic Analysis: Laguna de On 1996 Season," in *The Belize Postclassic Project: Laguna de On Island Excavations 1996*, edited by Marilyn A. Masson and Robert Rosenswig, pp. 61–68. Albany: Institute of Mesoamerican Studies Occasional Publication No. 1, University at Albany–SUNY. Report submitted to the Department of Archaeology, Belmopan, Belize.

1998 "Ceramics from Laguna de On, 1996 and 1997," in *The Belize Postclassic Project 1997: Laguna de On, Progresso Lagoon, and Laguna Seca*, edited by Marilyn A. Masson and Robert Rosenswig, pp. 192–202. Albany: Institute of Mesoamerican Studies Occasional Publication No. 2, University at Albany–SUNY.

Mooney, James

1892– *The Ghost Dance Religion and Wounded Knee*. Part 2, Fourteenth

1893   Annual Report 1892–1893, Bureau of Ethnology. Washington, DC: Government Printing Office.)

Morley, Sylvanus G.

1920   *The Inscriptions at Copan.* Washington, DC: Carnegie Institute of Washington Publication 219.

Morley, Sylvanus G., George Brainerd, and Robert J. Sharer

1983   *The Ancient Maya.* Stanford, CA: Stanford University Press.

Morton, June D.

1988   "Appendix IV: Preliminary Report on the Faunal Remains," in *A Postclassic Perspective: Excavations at the Maya Site of Santa Rita Corozal, Belize,* by Diane Z. Chase and Arlen F. Chase, pp. 118–122. San Francisco: Precolumbian Art Research Institute Monograph 4.

Mullen, Alex

1999   "Investigations at Caye Muerto, Progresso Lagoon," in *The Belize Postclassic Project 1998: Investigations at Progresso Lagoon,* edited by Marilyn A. Masson and Robert Rosenswig, pp. 73–82. Albany: Institute of Mesoamerican Studies Occasional Publication No. 3, University at Albany–SUNY.

Murray, Elizabeth

1998   "Spindle Whorls from Laguna de On," in *The Belize Postclassic Project 1997: Laguna de On, Progresso Lagoon, and Laguna Seca,* edited by Marilyn A. Masson and Robert Rosenswig, pp. 157–162. Albany: Institute of Mesoamerican Studies Occasional Publication No. 2, University at Albany–SUNY.

Nash, Michael A.

1980   "An Analysis of a Debitage Collection from Colha, Belize," in *The Colha Project: Second Season, 1980 Interim Report,* edited by Thomas R. Hester, Jack D. Eaton, and Harry J. Shafer, pp. 333–352. San Antonio: Center for Archaeological Research, University of Texas at San Antonio and Centro Studi e Ricerche Ligabue, Venice.

Nassaney, Michael

1996   "The Role of Chipped Stone in the Political Economy of Social Ranking," in *Stone Tools: Theoretical Insights into Human Prehistory,* edited by G. H. Odell, pp. 181–224. New York: Plenum Press.

Navarrete, Carlos, Maria Jose Con Uribe, and Alejandro Martinez Muriel

1979   *Observaciones arqueologicas en Coba, Quintana Roo.* Mexico, D.F.: Universidad Nacional Autonoma de Mexico.

Okoshi Harada, Tsubasa

1992   "Los canules: Analisis etnohistorico del Codice de Calkini." Doctoral thesis, Universidad Nacional Autonoma de Mexico, Mexico, D.F.

Oland, Maxine

    1998   "Lithic Raw Material Sources at the Southern End of the Freshwater Creek Drainage," in *The Belize Postclassic Project 1997: Laguna de On, Progresso Lagoon, and Laguna Seca*, edited by Marilyn A. Masson and Robert Rosenswig, pp. 163–176. Albany: Institute of Mesoamerican Studies Occasional Publication No. 2, University at Albany–SUNY.

    1999   "Lithic Raw Material Sources at the Southern End of the Freshwater Creek Drainage: A View from Laguna de On, Belize." *Lithic Technology* 24(2): 91–110.

Olsen, Stanley

    1982   *An Osteology of Some Maya Mammals.* Cambridge, MA: Peabody Museum of Archaeology and Ethnology, vol. 73, Harvard University Press.

Oviedo y Valdes, Gonzalo Fernando de

    1851– *Historia general y natural de las indias.* Biblioteca de autores españoles
    1855   desde la formacion del lenguaje hasta nuestros dias. Madrid: Real Academia de la Historia.

Pendergast, David M.

    1977   "Royal Ontario Museum Excavation: Finds at Lamanai, Belize." *Archaeology* 30: 129–131.

    1981   "Lamanai, Belize: Summary of Excavation Results, 1974–1980." *Journal of Field Archaeology* 8(1): 29–53.

    1982   *Excavations at Altun Ha, Belize 1964–1970.* Toronto: Archaeological Monographs of the Royal Ontario Museum, The Alger Press.

    1985   "Lamanai, Belize: An Updated View," in *The Lowland Maya Postclassic*, edited by A. F. Chase and P. M. Rice, pp. 91–103. Austin: University of Texas Press.

    1986   "Stability Through Change: Lamanai, Belize, from the Ninth to the Seventeenth Century," in *Late Lowland Maya Civilization: Classic to Postclassic*, edited by J. A. Sabloff and E. W. Andrews V, pp. 223–250. Albuquerque: University of New Mexico Press.

Pendergast, David M., Grand D. Jones, and Elizabeth Graham

    1993   "Locating Maya Lowland Spanish Colonial Towns: A Case Study from Belize." *Latin American Antiquity* 4(1): 59–73.

Pina Chan, R.

    1978   "Commerce in the Yucatec Peninsula: The Conquest and Colonial Period," in *Mesoamerican Communication Routes and Culture Contacts*, edited by T. A. Lee and C. Navarrete, pp. 37–48. Papers of the New World Archaeological Foundation 40. Provo, UT: Brigham Young University.

Pohl, John M. D.

    1994   *The Politics of Symbolism in the Mixtec Codices.* Nashville: Vanderbilt University Publications in Anthropology No. 46.

Pohl, Mary Deland, Paul R. Bloom, and Kevin O. Pope

1990   "Interpretation of Wetland Farming in Northern Belize: Excavations at San Antonio Rio Hondo," in *Ancient Maya Wetland Agriculture: Excavations on Albion Island, Northern Belize*, edited by Mary Pohl, pp. 187–254. Boulder, CO: Westview Press.

Pollock, Harry E. D.

1962   "Introduction," in *Mayapan, Yucatán, Mexico*, by Harry E. D. Pollock, Ralph L. Roys, Tatiana Proskouriakoff, and A. L. Smith, pp. 1–24. Washington, DC: Carnegie Institute of Washington Publication No. 619.

Pollock, Harry E. D., Ralph L. Roys, Tatiana Proskouriakoff, and A. L. Smith, editors

1962   *Mayapan, Yucatán, Mexico*. Washington, DC: Carnegie Institute of Washington Publication No. 619.

Potter, Daniel R., and Eleanor M. King

1995   "A Heterarchical Approach to Lowland Maya Socioeconomies," in *Heterarchy and the Analysis of Complex Societies*, edited by R. M. Ehrenreich, C. L. Crumley, and J. E. Levy, pp. 17–32. Arlington, VA: Archaeological Papers of the American Anthropological Association No. 6.

Proskouriakoff, Tatiana

1955   "The Death of a Civilization." *Scientific American* 192: 82–88.

1962a   "Civic and Religious Structures of Mayapan," in *Mayapan, Yucatán, Mexico*, edited by Harry E. D. Pollock, Ralph L. Roys, Tatiana Proskouriakoff, and A. L. Smith, pp. 87–164. Washington, DC: Carnegie Institute of Washington Publication No. 619.

1962b   "The Artifacts of Mayapan," in *Mayapan Yucatán, Mexico*, edited by Harry E. D. Pollock, Ralph L. Roys, Tatiana Proskouriakoff, and A. L. Smith, pp. 321–531. Washington, DC: Carnegie Institute of Washington Publication No. 619.

1963   *An Album of Maya Architecture*. Norman: University of Oklahoma Press.

Proskouriakoff, Tatiana, and C. R. Temple

1955   "Excavations in a Large Residence at Mayapan," in *Carnegie Institute of Washington Year Book 54*, pp. 271–273. Washington, DC: Carnegie Institute.

Pyburn, K. Anne

1989   *Prehistoric Maya Settlement at Nohmul, Belize*. Oxford: B.A.R. International Series 509.

Quezada, Sergio

1993   *Pueblos y caciques yucatecos 1550–1580*. Mexico, D.F.: El Colegio de Mexico.

Quinones, Eduardo Toro

1980   "Estudio de la ceramica arqueologica de San Gervasio," in *Informe anual del Proyecto Arqueologico Cozumel: Temporada 1980*, edited by Fernando Robles, pp. 67–82. Mexico, D.F.: Centro Regional de Yucatán, Instituto Nacional de Antropologia e Historia.

Quirarte, Jacinto

1982   "The Santa Rita Murals: A Review," in *Aspects of Mixteca-Puebla Style and Mixtec and Central Mexican Culture in Southern Mesoamerica*, edited by D. Stone, pp. 43–57. Middle American Research Institute Occasional Paper No. 4. New Orleans: Tulane University Press.

Rands, Robert L., and Ronald L. Bishop

1980   "Resource Procurement Zones and Patterns of Ceramic Exchange in the Palenque Region, Mexico," in *Models and Methods in Regional Exchange*, edited by Robert E. Fry, pp. 19–46. Washington, DC: SAA Papers No. 1, Society for American Archaeology.

Rathje, William L.

1975   "The Last Tango in Mayapan: A Tentative Trajectory of Production-Distribution Systems," in *Ancient Civilization and Trade*, edited by J. A. Sabloff and C. C. Lamberg-Karlovsky, pp. 409–448. Albuquerque: University of New Mexico Press.

1983   "To the Salt of the Earth: Some Comments on Household Archaeology Among the Maya," in *Prehistoric Settlement Patterns: Essays in Honor of Gordon R. Willey*, edited by Evon Vogt and Richard Levanthal, pp. 23–34. Albuquerque and Cambridge, MA: University of New Mexico Press/Peabody Museum of Archaeology and Ethnology, Harvard University.

Rathje, William L., D. A. Gregory, and F. M. Wiseman

1978   "Trade Models and Archaeological Problems: Classic Maya Examples," in *Mesoamerican Communication Routes and Culture Contacts*, edited by T. A. Lee and C. Navarrete, pp. 147–175. Provo, UT: Papers of the New World Archaeological Foundation 40, Brigham Young University.

Reents-Budet, Dorie

1994   *Painting the Maya Universe: Royal Ceramics of the Classic Period*. Durham, NC: Duke University Press.

Renfrew, Colin

1975   "Trade as Action at a Distance: Questions of Integration and Communication," in *Ancient Civilization and Trade*, edited by Jeremy A. Sabloff and C. C. Lamberg-Karlovsky, pp. 3–59. Albuquerque: University of New Mexico Press.

1986   "Introduction: Peer Polity Interaction and Sociopolitical Change," in *Peer Polity Interaction and Sociopolitical Change*, edited by Colin Renfrew and John Cherry, pp. 1–18. Cambridge: Cambridge University Press.

Renfrew, Colin, and Paul Bahn

1991 *Archaeology: Theories, Methods, and Practice*. London: Thames and Hudson.

Rice, Don S.

1974 *Archaeology of Northern British Honduras*. Katunob, Occasional Publications in Mesoamerica No. 6. Greeley: University of Northern Colorado.

1986 "The Peten Postclassic: A Settlement Perspective," in *Late Lowland Maya Civilization: Classic to Postclassic*, edited by J. A. Sabloff and E. W. Andrews V, pp. 301–346. Albuquerque: University of New Mexico Press.

1988 "Classic to Postclassic Maya Household Transitions in the Central Peten, Guatemala," in *Household and Community in the Mesoamerican Past*, edited by Richard R. Wilk and Wendy Ashmore, pp. 227–248. Albuquerque: University of New Mexico Press.

Rice, Don S., and T. Patrick Culbert

1990 "Historical Contexts for Population Reconstruction in the Maya Lowlands," in *Precolumbian Population History in the Maya Lowlands*, edited by T. Patrick Culbert and Don S. Rice, pp. 1–36. Albuquerque: University of New Mexico Press.

Rice, Don S., Prudence M. Rice, and Timothy Pugh

1998 "Settlement Continuity and Change in the Central Peten Lakes Region: The Case of Zacpeten," in *Anatomia de una civilizacion: Aproximaciones interdisciplinarias a la cultura maya*, edited by Andres Ciudad Ruiz, Yolanda Fernandez Marquinez, Jose Miguel Garcia Campiloo, Josefa Iglesias Ponce de Leon, Alofonso Lacadena Garcia-Gallo, and Luis T. Sanz Castro, pp. 207–252. Madrid: Publicaciones de la S.E.E.M. No. 4, Sociedad Espanola de Estudios Mayas.

Rice, Prudence M.

1980 "Peten Postclassic Pottery Production and Exchange: A View from Macanche," in *Models and Methods in Regional Exchange*, edited by R. E. Fry, pp. 67–82. Washington, DC: SAA Papers No. 1, Society for American Archaeology.

1986 "The Peten Postclassic: Perspectives from the Central Peten Lakes," in *Late Lowland Maya Civilization: Classic to Postclassic*, edited by J. A. Sabloff and E. W. Andrews V, pp. 251–299. Albuquerque: University of New Mexico Press.

1987a *Macanche Island, El Peten, Guatemala: Excavations, Pottery, and Artifacts*. Gainesville: University of Florida Press.

1987b "Economic Change in the Lowland Maya Late Classic Period," in *Specialization, Exchange, and Complex Societies*, edited by E. M. Brumfiel and T. K. Earle, pp. 76–85. Cambridge: Cambridge University Press.

1989   "Reptiles and Rulership: A Stylistic Analysis of Peten Postclassic Pottery," in *Word and Image in Maya Culture*, edited by William F. Hanks and Don S. Rice, pp. 306–318. Salt Lake City: University of Utah Press.

Rice, Prudence M., and Don S. Rice

1985   "Topoxte, Macanche, and the Central Peten Postclassic," in *The Lowland Maya Postclassic*, edited by A. F. Chase and P. M. Rice, pp. 166–183. Austin: University of Texas Press.

Ringle, William M., Tomas Gallareta Negron, and George J. Bey III

1998   "The Return of Quetzalcoatl: Evidence for the Spread of a World Religion during the Epiclassic Period." *Ancient Mesoamerica* 9: 183–232.

Robertson, Donald

1970   "The Tulum Murals: The International Style of the Late Post-Classic." *Thirty-eighth International Congress of Americanists* 2 (Stuttgart): 77–88.

Robles, Fernando

1986a   "Informe anual del Proyecto Arqueologico Cozumel: Temporada 1980." Centro Regional de Yucatán, 2 Cuaderno de Trabajo. Mexico, D.F.: Instituto Nacional de Antropología e Historia.

1986b   "Informe anual del Proyecto Arqueologico Cozumel: Temporada 1981." Centro Regional de Yucatán, 3 Cuaderno de Trabajo. Mexico, D.F.: Instituto Nacional de Antropología e Historia.

1986c   "Cronologia ceramica de El Meco," in *Excavaciones arqueologicas en El Meco, Quintana Roo, 1977*, edited by Antonio P. Andrews and Fernando Robles Castellanos, pp. 77–130. Mexico, D.F.: Colección Científica, Instituto Nacional de Antropología e Historia.

Robles C., Fernando, and Anthony P. Andrews

1986   "A Review and Synthesis of Recent Postclassic Archaeology in Northern Yucatán," in *Late Lowland Maya Civilization: Classic to Postclassic*, edited by J. A. Sabloff and E. W. Andrews V, pp. 53–98. Albuquerque: University of New Mexico Press.

Roemer, Erwin Jr.

1984   "A Late Classic Maya Lithic Workshop at Colha, Belize." Master's thesis, Department of Anthropology, Texas A&M University.

Rosenswig, Robert M.

1998   "Burying the Dead at Laguna de On: A Summary of Mortuary Remains from the 1991, 1996, and 1997 Field Seasons," in *The Belize Postclassic Project: Laguna de On, Progresso Lagoon, and Laguna Seca 1997*, edited by Marilyn A. Masson and Robert Rosenswig, pp. 149–156. Albany: Institute of Mesoamerican Studies, Occasional Publication No. 2, University of Albany–SUNY.

Rosenswig, Robert, and Joy Becker

1997   "Structure II: A Rubble Platform Shrine at Laguna de On Island," in *The Belize Postclassic Project: Laguna de On Island Excavations 1996*, edited by Marilyn A. Masson and Robert Rosenswig, pp. 29–38. Albany: Institute of Mesoamerican Studies Occasional Publication No. 1, University at Albany–SUNY. Report submitted to the Department of Archaeology, Belmopan, Belize.

Rosenswig, Robert M., and Thomas W. Stafford Jr.

1999   "Archaic Component Beneath a Postclassic Terrace at Subop 19, Laguna de On Island," in *The Belize Postclassic Project 1997: Laguna de On, Progresso Lagoon, and Laguna Seca*, edited by Marilyn A. Masson and Robert Rosenswig, pp. 81–89. Albany: Institute of Mesoamerican Studies Occasional Publication No. 2, University at Albany–SUNY.

Roys, Lawrence

1934   *The Engineering Knowledge of the Maya*. Contributions to American Archaeology No. 6. Washington, DC: Carnegie Institute of Washington.

Roys, Ralph L.

1933   *The Book of the Chilam Balam of Chumayel*. Washington, DC: Carnegie Institute of Washington Publication 438.

1957   *The Political Geography of the Yucatán Maya*. Washington, DC: Carnegie Institute of Washington Publication 613.

1962   "Literary Sources for the History of Mayapan," in *Mayapan, Yucatán, Mexico*, edited by Harry E.D. Pollock, Ralph L. Roys, Tatiana Proskouriakoff, and A. L. Smith, pp. 25–86. Washington, DC: Carnegie Institute of Washington Publication No. 619.

Sabloff, Jeremy A., and William L. Rathje

1975   "The Rise of a Maya Merchant Class." *Scientific American* 233: 72–82.

Sabloff, Jeremy A., and E. Wyllys Andrews V

1986   *Late Lowland Maya Civilization: Classic to Postclassic*. Albuquerque: University of New Mexico Press.

Sabloff, Jeremy A., William L. Rathje, David A. Freidel, Judith G. Connor, and Paula W. Sabloff

1974   "Trade and Power in Postclassic Yucatán: Initial Observations," in *Mesoamerican Archaeology, New Approaches*, edited by Norman Hammond, pp. 397–416. Austin: University of Texas Press.

Sahlins, Marshall D.

1961   "The Segmentary Lineage: An Organization of Predatory Expansion." *American Anthropologist* 63(2): 332–345. Reprinted in *Comparative Political Systems*, edited by Ronald Cohen and John Middleton, pp. 89–120. New York: The Natural History Press.

Sanders, William T.
1960   *Prehistoric Ceramics and Settlement Patterns in Quintana Roo, Mexico.* Contributions to American Anthropology and History 12(60). Washington, DC: Carnegie Institute of Washington Publication 606.

Sanders, William T., and Barbara J. Price
1968   *Mesoamerica: The Evolution of a Civilization.* New York: Random House.

Scarborough, Vernon L., Robert P. Connolly, and Steven P. Ross
1994   "The Prehispanic Maya Reservoir System at Kinal, Peten, Guatemala." *Ancient Mesoamerica* 5(1): 97–106.

Schele, Linda
1976   "Accession Iconography of Chan-Bahlum in the Group of the Cross at Palenque," in *The Art, Iconography, and Dynastic History of Palenque,* part 3, edited by Merle Greene Robertson, pp. 9–34. Pebble Beach, CA: Robert Louis Stevenson School.

1982   *Maya Glyphs: The Verbs.* Austin: University of Texas Press.

1989   *Notebook for the XIVth Maya Hieroglyphic Workshop at Texas.* Austin: University of Texas Press.

Schele, Linda, and Mary Ellen Miller
1986   *The Blood of Kings: Dynasty and Ritual in Maya Art.* Fort Worth: Kimbell Art Museum.

Schele, Linda, and David A. Freidel
1990   *A Forest of Kings.* New York: William Morrow & Co.

Schele, Linda, and Nikolai Grube
1997   "Notebook for the XXIst Maya Hieroglyphic Workshop." Maya Meetings of Texas, University of Texas at Austin.

Schele, Linda, and Julia Kappelman
1998   "What the Heck is Coatepec?" Paper presented at the XIV Texas Symposium, The Maya Meetings at Texas, March 10, Austin.

Schele, Linda, and Peter Matthews
1998   *The Code of Kings: The Language of Seven Sacred Maya Temples and Tombs.* New York: Scribner.

Schele, Linda, Nikolai Grube, and Erik Boot
1995   *Some Suggestions on the Katun Prophecies in the Books of the Chilam Balam in Light of Classic Period History.* Texas Notes on PreColumbian Art, Writing and Culture No. 72. Austin: University of Texas Press.

Schellhas, Paul
1904   "Representations of Deities in the Maya Manuscripts." *Papers of the Peabody Museum of American Archaeology and Ethnology* 4(1). Cambridge, MA: Harvard University Press.

Scholes, Frances V., and Ralph L. Roys

1938   "Fray Diego de Landa and the Problem of Idolatry in Yucatán," in *Cooperation in Research*, pp. 585–620. Washington, DC: Carnegie Institute of Washington Publication 501.

1948   *The Maya Chontal Indians of Acalan-Tixchel: A Contribution to the History and Ethnography of the Yucatán Peninsula.* Washington, DC: Carnegie Institute of Washington Publication 560.

Schuyler, Robert L.

1980   *Archaeological Perspectives on Ethnicity in America: Afro-American and Asian American Culture History.* Farmingdale, NY: Baywood Publishing Company, Inc.

Scott, Robert F. IV

1981   "Further Comments on Faunal Analysis and Ancient Subsistence Activities at Colha," in *The Colha Project, Second Season, 1980 Interim Report*, edited by T. R. Hester, J. D. Eaton, and H. J. Shafer, pp. 281–288. San Antonio: Center for Archaeological Research, University of Texas at San Antonio and Centro Studi e Ricerche Ligabue, Venice.

1982   "Notes on Continuing Faunal Analysis for the Site of Colha, Belize: Data from the Early Postclassic," in *Archaeology at Colha, Belize: The 1981 Interim Report*, edited by Thomas R. Hester, Harry J. Shafer, and Jack D. Eaton, pp. 203–207. San Antonio: Center for Archaeological Research, University of Texas at San Antonio and Centro Studi e Ricerche Ligabue, Venice.

Service, Elman R.

1962   *Primitive Social Organization: An Evolutionary Perspective.* New York: Random House.

Shafer, Harry J.

1979   "A Technological Study of Two Maya Lithic Workshops at Colha, Belize," in *The Colha Project, 1979: A Collection of Interim Papers*, edited by T. R. Hester, pp. 28–78. San Antonio: Center for Archaeological Research, University of Texas at San Antonio.

1982   "Maya Lithic Craft Specialization in Northern Belize," in *Archaeology at Colha, Belize: The 1981 Interim Report*, edited by Thomas R. Hester, Harry J. Shafer, and Jack D. Eaton, pp. 31–38. San Antonio: Center for Archaeological Research, University of Texas at San Antonio and Centro Studi e Ricerche Ligabue, Venice.

Shafer, Harry J., and Thomas R. Hester

1983   "Ancient Maya Chert Workshops in Northern Belize, Central America." *American Antiquity* 48(3): 519–543.

1988   "Appendix III: Preliminary Analysis of Postclassic Lithics," in *A Postclassic Perspective: Excavations at the Maya Site of Santa Rita Corozal,*

Belize, by Diane Z. Chase and Arlen F. Chase, pp. 111–117. San Francisco: Precolumbian Art Research Institute Monograph 4.

Shaw, Leslie C.

1990   "The Articulation of Social Inequality and Faunal Resource Use in the Preclassic Community of Colha, Northern Belize." Ph.D. dissertation, University of Massachusetts at Amherst.

Shaw, Leslie C., and Patricia H. Mangan

1994   "Faunal Analysis of an Early Postclassic Midden. Operation 2032, Colha, Belize," in *Continuing Archaeology at Colha, Belize,* edited by Thomas R. Hester, Harry J. Shafer, and Jack D. Eaton, pp. 69–78. Austin: Studies in Archaeology 16, Texas Archeological Research Laboratory, University of Texas.

Sheets, Payson D.

1991   "Flakes Lithics from the Cenote of Sacrifice, Chichén Itzá, Yucatán," in *Maya Stone Tools,* edited by T. R. Hester and H. J. Shafer, pp. 163–188. Madison, WI: Prehistory Press.

Sheldon, Stephanie M.

1998   "Excavations at Subop 5: Testing for Cemetery Boundaries and Landscape Modification at Laguna de On Island," in *The Belize Postclassic Project 1997: Laguna de On, Progresso Lagoon, and Laguna Seca,* edited by Marilyn A. Masson and Robert Rosenswig, pp. 25–38. Albany: Institute of Mesoamerican Studies Occasional Publication No. 2, University at Albany–SUNY.

Shepard, Anna O.

1957   *Ceramics for the Archaeologist.* Washington, DC: Carnegie Institute of Washington Publication 609.

Sidrys, Raymond V.

1976   "Mesoamerica: An Archaeological Analysis of a Low-Energy Civilization." Ph.D. dissertation, University of California, Los Angeles.

1983   *Archaeological Excavations in Northern Belize, Central America.* Monograph XVII. Los Angeles: Institute of Archaeology, University of California, Los Angeles.

Sierra Sosa, Thelma Noemi

1994   "Contribucion al Estudio de Los Asentamientos de San Gervasio, Isla de Cozumel." Mexico, D.F.: Instituto Nacional de Antropologia e Historia, Coleccion Cientifica.

Silva Rhoads, Carlos, and Concepcion Maria del Carmen Hernandez

1991   "Estudios de patron de asentamiento en Playa del Carmen, Quintana Roo." Mexico, D.F.: Serie Arqueologica, Instituto Nacional de Antropologia e Historia, Coleccion Cientifica.

Simmons, Scott

1995   "Maya Resistance, Maya Resolve: The Tools of Autonomy from Tipu, Belize." *Ancient Mesoamerica* 6: 135–146.

Simon, Herbert

1965   "The Architecture of Complexity." *Yearbook for the Society of General Systems Research* 10: 63–76.

Smith, A. Ledyard

1962   "Residential and Associated Structures at Mayapan," in *Mayapan, Yucatán, Mexico*, edited by Harry E. D. Pollock, Ralph L. Roys, Tatiana Proskouriakoff, and A. L. Smith, pp. 165–320. Washington, DC: Carnegie Institute of Washington Publication No. 619.

Smith, Bruce D.

1978   *Mississippian Settlement Patterns*. New York: Academic Press.

Smith, Michael E.

1999   "Comment on Hirth's 'The Distributional Approach'." *Current Anthropology* 40: 528–529.

Smith, Michael E., and Cynthia Heath-Smith

1980   "Waves of Influence in Postclassic Mesoamerica? A Critique of the Mixteca-Puebla Concept." *Anthropology* 4: 15–20.

Smith, Michael E., and Frances Berdan

2000   "The Postclassic Mesoamerican World System." *Current Anthropology* 41: 283–286.

Smith, Robert E.

1971   *The Pottery of Mayapan*. Cambridge, MA: Papers of the Peabody Museum of Archaeology and Ethnology 66, Harvard University Press.

Smith, Robert E., and James C. Gifford

1965   "Pottery of the Maya Lowlands," in *Handbook of Middle American Indians*, vol. 2: *Archaeology of Southern Mesoamerica Part 1*, edited by Gordon R. Willey, pp. 498–534. Austin: University of Texas Press.

Stafford, Thomas W. Jr.

1998   "Appendix A: Radiocarbon Dates from the 1996 Season," in *The Belize Postclassic Project 1997: Laguna de On, Progresso Lagoon, and Laguna Seca*, edited by Marilyn A. Masson and Robert Rosenswig, p. 183. Albany: Institute of Mesoamerican Studies Occasional Publication No. 2, University at Albany–SUNY.

Stark, Barbara

1984   "Archaeological Identifications of Pottery Production Locations: Ethnoarchaeological and Archaeological Data in Mesoamerica," in *Decoding Prehistoric Ceramics*, edited by Ben. A. Nelson, pp. 158–194. Carbondale: Southern Illinois University Press.

Steponaitis, Vincas P.

1983   *Ceramics, Chronology, and Community Patterns: An Archaeological Study at Moundville.* New York: Academic Press.

Steward, Julian H., editor

1955   *Irrigation Civilizations: A Comparative Survey.* Washington, DC: Pan-American Union.

Suhler, Charles, and David A. Freidel

1998   "Life and Death in a Maya War Zone." *Archeology* 51: 28–34.

Tainter, Joseph

1988   *The Collapse of Complex Societies.* Cambridge: Cambridge University Press.

Taube, Karl A.

1988   "The Ancient Maya Yucatec New Year Festival: The Liminal Period in Maya Ritual and Cosmology." Ph.D. dissertation, Department of Anthropology, Yale University.

1992   *The Major Gods of Yucatán.* Studies in Pre-Columbian Art and Archaeology No. 32. Washington, DC: Dumbarton Oaks.

Taylor, A. J.

1980   "Excavations at Op2010: An Early Postclassic Midden," in *The Colha Project, Second Season, 1980 Interim Report,* edited by T. R. Hester, J. D. Eaton, and H. J. Shafer, pp. 133–144. San Antonio: Center for Archaeological Research, University of Texas at San Antonio and Centro Studi e Ricerche Ligabue, Venice.

Thompson, J. Eric S.

1939   *Excavations at San Jose, British Honduras.* Washington, DC: Carnegie Institute of Washington Publication 506.

1942   *Late Ceramic Horizons at Benque Viejo, British Honduras.* Contributions to Anthropology and History 35. Washington, DC: Carnegie Institution of Washington Publication 528.

1954   "A Presumed Residence of the Nobility at Mayapan." *Current Reports* 19, Carnegie Institute of Washington, Department of Archaeology, Cambridge, MA.

1957   "Deities Portrayed on Censers at Mayapan." *Current Reports* 40, Carnegie Institute of Washington, Department of Archaeology, Washington, DC.

1965   "Archaeological Synthesis of the Southern Maya Lowlands," in *Handbook of Middle American Indians,* vol. 2: *Archaeology of Southern Mesoamerica Part 1,* edited by Gordon R. Willey, pp. 331–337. Austin: University of Texas Press.

1970   *Maya History and Religion.* Norman: University of Oklahoma Press.

1977   "A Proposal for Constituting a Maya Subgroup, Cultural and Linguistic, in the Peten and Adjacent Regions," in *Anthropology and History of Yucatán*, edited by Grant D. Jones, pp. 3–42. Austin: University of Texas Press.

Tourtellot, Gair, Jeremy A. Sabloff, and Kelli Carmean

1992 "Will the Real Elites Please Stand Up? An Archaeological Assessment of Maya Elite Behavior in the Terminal Classic Period," in *Mesoamerican Elites: An Archaeological Assessment*, edited by Diane Z. Chase and Arlen F. Chase, pp. 80–98. Norman: University of Oklahoma Press.

Tozzer, Alfred M.

1941 "Notes." *Landa's Relaciones de las Cosas de Yucatán*, translated by Alfred Tozzer. Cambridge, MA: Papers of the Peabody Museum of Archaeology and Ethnology 18, Harvard University Press.

Turner, Billie Lee III, and Peter D. Harrison

1983 *Pulltrouser Swamp: Ancient Maya Habitat, Agriculture, and Settlement in Northern Belize*. Austin: University of Texas Press.

Turner, Victor

1974 *Dramas, Fields, and Metaphors*. Ithaca, NY: Cornell University Press.

Urcid, Javier

1991a "A Zapotec Slab in the Friedenberg Collection." Manuscript on file at Dumbarton Oaks, Washington, DC.

1991b "Stela NP-9 and PH-1 of Monte Alban, Oaxaca." Manuscript on file at Dumbarton Oaks, Washington, DC.

Vail, Gabriel

1988 *The Archaeology of Coastal Belize*. London: British Archaeological Reports, International Series 463.

Valdez, Fred Jr.

1987 "The Ceramics of Colha, Northern Belize." Ph.D. dissertation, Department of Anthropology, Harvard University.

1993a "Appendix I: Ceramic Types from Laguna de On Shore," in "Changes in Maya Community Organization from the Classic to Postclassic Periods: A View from Laguna de On, Belize," by Marilyn A. Masson, p. 280. Ph.D. dissertation, Department of Anthropology, University of Texas at Austin.

1993b "Appendix X: Obsidian Artifacts from Laguna de On Island," in "Changes in Maya Community Organization from the Classic to Postclassic Periods: A View from Laguna de On, Belize," by Marilyn A. Masson, pp. 354–361. Ph.D. dissertation, Department of Anthropology, University of Texas at Austin.

1994 "The Colha Ceramic Complexes," in *Continuing Archaeology at Colha, Belize*, edited by Thomas R. Hester, Harry J. Shafer, and Jack D. Eaton, pp. 9–16. Austin: Studies in Archaeology 16, Texas Archeological Research Laboratory, University of Texas.

Valdez, Fred Jr., and Shirley B. Mock

1985   "Early Postclassic Settlements at Colha, Belize: Problems in Ceramic Typology and Chronology," in "Final Performance Report to the National Endowment for the Humanities Grants RO 20534-83 and RI 20755," edited by Thomas R. Hester, pp. 45–69. Center for Archaeological Research, the University of Texas at San Antonio.

Valdez, Fred Jr., Marilyn A. Masson, and Lenore Santone

1992   "Report from the 1991 Field Season at Laguna de On." Report on file, Department of Archaeology, Belmopan, Belize.

Villaguitierre Soto-Mayor, Juan de

1983   *History of the Conquest of the Province of the Itzá*. 1983 English translation of 1701 document by Brother Robert D. Wood, S.M., edited with notes by Frank E. Comparato. Culver City, CA: Labyrinthos.

Vogt, Evon Z.

1976   *Tortillas for the Gods: A Symbolic Analysis of Zinacanteco Rituals*. Cambridge, MA: Harvard University Press.

Voorhies, Barbara

1982   "An Ecological Model of the Early Maya of the Central Lowlands," in *Maya Subsistence: Studies in Memory of Dennis E. Puleston*, edited by Kent V. Flannery, pp. 65–95. New York: Academic Press.

Voorhies, Barbara, and Janine Gasco

n.d.   "Postclassic Archaeology of the Soconusco." Manuscript accepted for publication by the Institute of Mesoamerican Studies, University at Albany–SUNY (in press).

Waid, Alice, and Marilyn A. Masson

1998   "Laguna de On Shore Reconnaissance and Testing," in *The Belize Postclassic Project 1997: Laguna de On, Progresso Lagoon, and Laguna Seca*, edited by Marilyn A. Masson and Robert Rosenswig, pp. 93–106. Albany: Institute of Mesoamerican Studies Occasional Publication No. 2, University at Albany–SUNY.

Walker, Debra

1990   "Cerros Revisited: Ceramic Indicators of Terminal Classic and Postclassic Settlement and Pilgrimage in Northern Belize." Ph.D. dissertation, Southern Methodist University.

Wallace, Anthony F. C.

1956   "Revitalization Movements: Some Theoretical Considerations for Their Comparative Study." *American Anthropologist* 58: 264–281.

Wallace, Dwight T.

1977   "An Intra-Site Locational Analysis of Utatlan: The Structure of an Urban Site," in *Archaeology and Ethnohistory of the Central Quiche*, edited by Dwight T. Wallace and Robert M. Carmack, pp. 20–54.

Albany: Institute for Mesoamerican Studies, University at Albany–SUNY.

Webb, Malcolm C.

1964   "The Post-Classic Decline of the Peten Maya: An Interpretation in Light of a General Theory of State Society." Ph.D. dissertation, University of Michigan. Ann Arbor: University Microfilms.

Webster, David L.

1977   "Warfare and the Evolution of Maya Civilization," in *The Origins of Maya Civilization*, edited by R.E.W. Adams, pp. 335–371. Albuquerque: University of New Mexico Press.

Webster, David L., and Ann Corrine Freter

1990   "The Demography of Late Classic Copan," in *Precolumbian Population History in the Maya Lowlands*, edited by T. Patrick Culbert and Don S. Rice, pp. 37–62. Albuquerque: University of New Mexico Press.

West, Georgia

1998a   "Domestic Feature Investigations at Subops 15 & 16, Laguna de On Island," in *The Belize Postclassic Project 1997: Laguna de On, Progresso Lagoon, and Laguna Seca*, edited by Marilyn A. Masson and Robert Rosenswig, pp. 43–54. Albany: Institute of Mesoamerican Studies Occasional Publication No. 2, University at Albany–SUNY.

1998b   "The Search for Uatibal: Survey at Laguna Seca," in *The Belize Postclassic Project 1997: Laguna de On, Progresso Lagoon, and Laguna Seca*, edited by Marilyn A. Masson and Robert Rosenswig, pp. 137–148. Albany: Institute of Mesoamerican Studies Occasional Publication No. 2, University at Albany–SUNY.

Wharton, Jennifer

1997   "A Preliminary Analysis of Faunal Remains at the Postclassic Site of Laguna de On Island, Belize," in *The Belize Postclassic Project: Laguna de On Island Excavations 1996*, edited by Marilyn A. Masson and Robert Rosenswig, pp. 69–76. Albany: Institute for Mesoamerican Studies Occasional Publications No. 1, University at Albany–SUNY.

1998   "Domestic Feature Investigations at Subop 7, Laguna de On Island," in *The Belize Postclassic Project 1997: Laguna de On, Progresso Lagoon, and Laguna Seca*, edited by Marilyn A. Masson and Robert Rosenswig, pp. 67–70. Albany: Institute of Mesoamerican Studies Occasional Publication No. 2, University at Albany–SUNY.

n.d.   "Postclassic Maya Fauna from the 1996 Season at Laguna de On." (title subject to change) Master's thesis in preparation, University at Albany–SUNY.

Wharton, Jennifer, and Norbert Stanchly

1998   "Postclassic Maya Ritual and Staple Faunas of Laguna de On." Paper presented at the Society for American Archaeology Meetings, Seattle.

White, Leslie

1959   *The Evolution of Culture.* New York: McGraw-Hill Book Co.

Willey, Gordon R.

1953   *Prehistoric Settlement Patterns in the Viru Valley, Northern Peru.* Bureau of American Ethnology Bulletin No. 155. Washington, DC: Smithsonian Institution.

1986   "The Postclassic of the Maya Lowlands: A Preliminary Overview," in *Late Lowland Maya Civilization: Classic to Postclassic,* edited by J. A. Sabloff and E. W. Andrews V, pp. 17–52. Albuquerque: University of New Mexico Press.

Willey, Gordon R., and Demitri B. Shimkin

1973   "The Maya Collapse: A Summary View," in *The Classic Maya Collapse,* edited by T. Patrick Culbert, pp. 457–501. Albuquerque: University of New Mexico Press.

Willey, Gordon R., W. R. Bullard, J. Glass, and J. Gifford

1965   *Prehistoric Maya Settlements in the Belize Valley.* Cambridge, MA: Papers of the Peabody Museum of American Archaeology and Ethnology vol. 54, Harvard University Press.

Williams-Beck, Lorraine

1999   "Site and Community Organization in an Expanding Political Frontier: The Calkini Jurisdiction on the Ah Canul Province, Campeche, Mexico." Paper presented at the 64th Annual Meeting of the Society for American Archaeology, March 27, Chicago.

Wright, A.C.S., D. Romney, R. Arbuckle, and V. Vial

1959   *Land in British Honduras: Report of the British Honduras Land Use Survey Team.* London: Colonial Research Publications 24.

Yoffee, Norman

1988   "Orienting Collapse," in *The Collapse of Ancient States and Civilizations,* edited by Norman Yoffee and George Cowgill, pp. 1–19. Tucson: University of Arizona Press.

Index

www.ingramcontent.com/pod-product-compliance
Lightning Source LLC
Chambersburg PA
CBHW052009030426
42334CB00029BA/3147